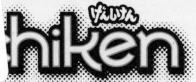

げんしけん
hiken
SECOND SEASON

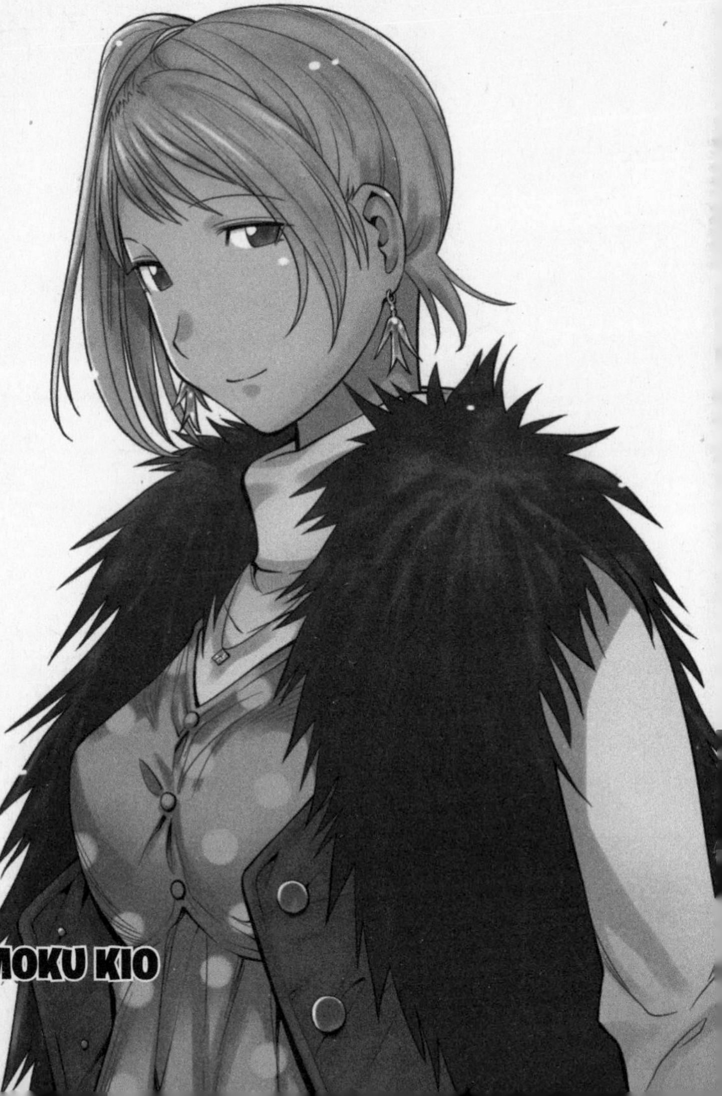

SHIMOKU KIO

genshiken
げんしけん
SECOND SEASON
Vol. 5
CONTENTS

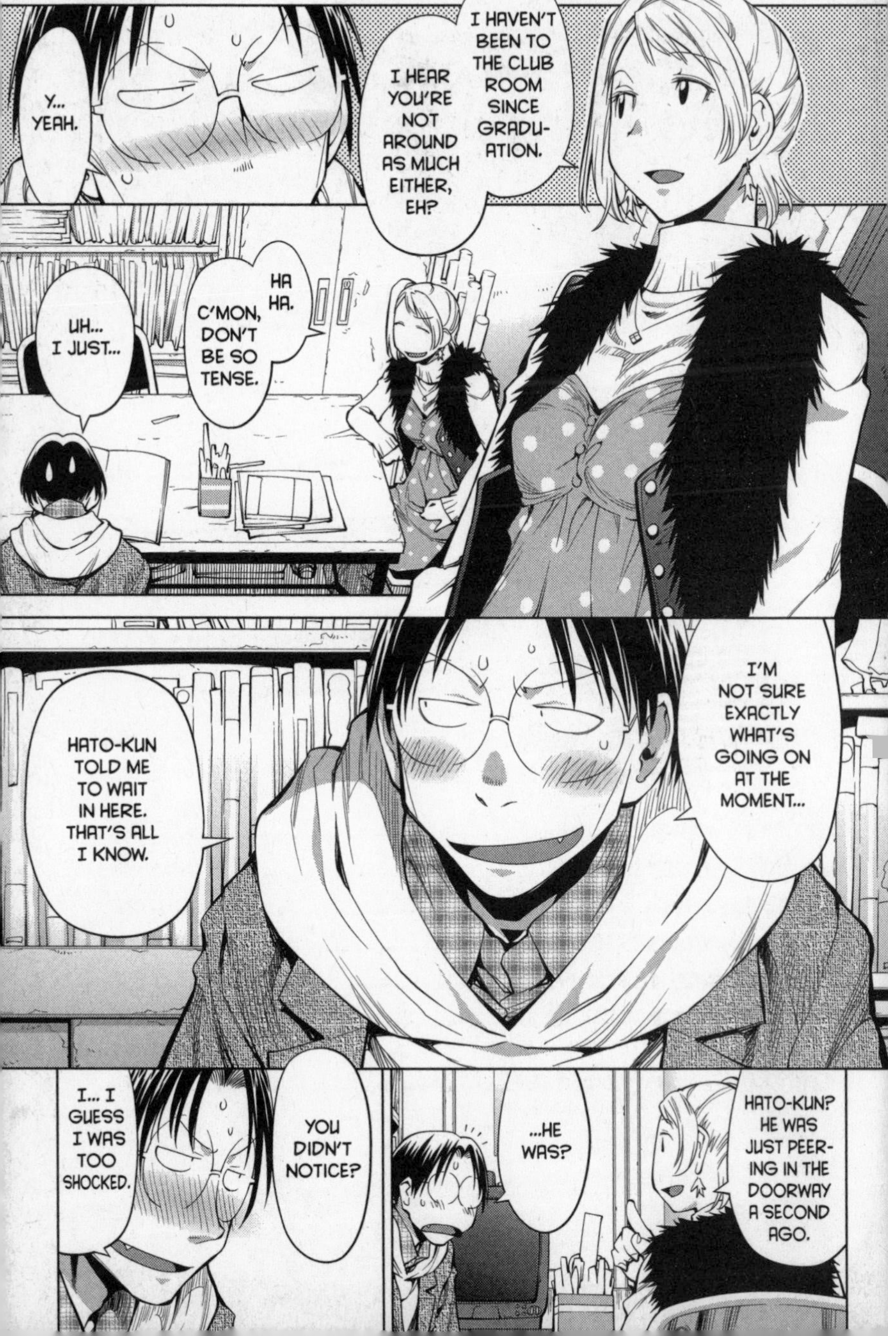
I HAVEN'T BEEN TO THE CLUB ROOM SINCE GRADUATION.
I HEAR YOU'RE NOT AROUND AS MUCH EITHER, EH?
Y... YEAH.
HA HA.
C'MON, DON'T BE SO TENSE.
UH... I JUST...
I'M NOT SURE EXACTLY WHAT'S GOING ON AT THE MOMENT...
HATO-KUN TOLD ME TO WAIT IN HERE. THAT'S ALL I KNOW.
HATO-KUN? HE WAS JUST PEERING IN THE DOORWAY A SECOND AGO.
...HE WAS?
YOU DIDN'T NOTICE?
I... I GUESS I WAS TOO SHOCKED.

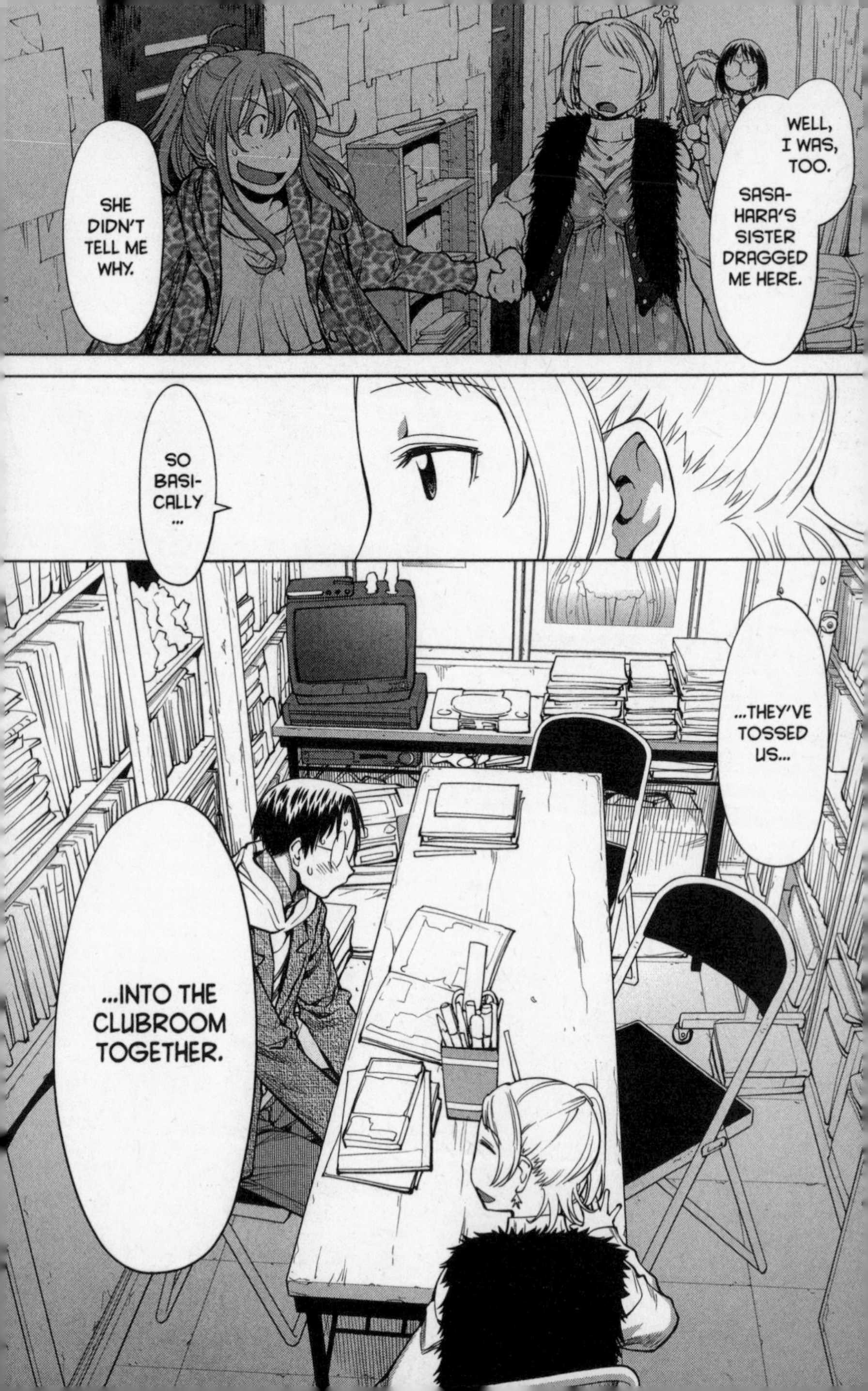
WELL, I WAS, TOO. SASAHARA'S SISTER DRAGGED ME HERE.
SHE DIDN'T TELL ME WHY.
SO BASICALLY ...
...THEY'VE TOSSED US...
...INTO THE CLUBROOM TOGETHER.

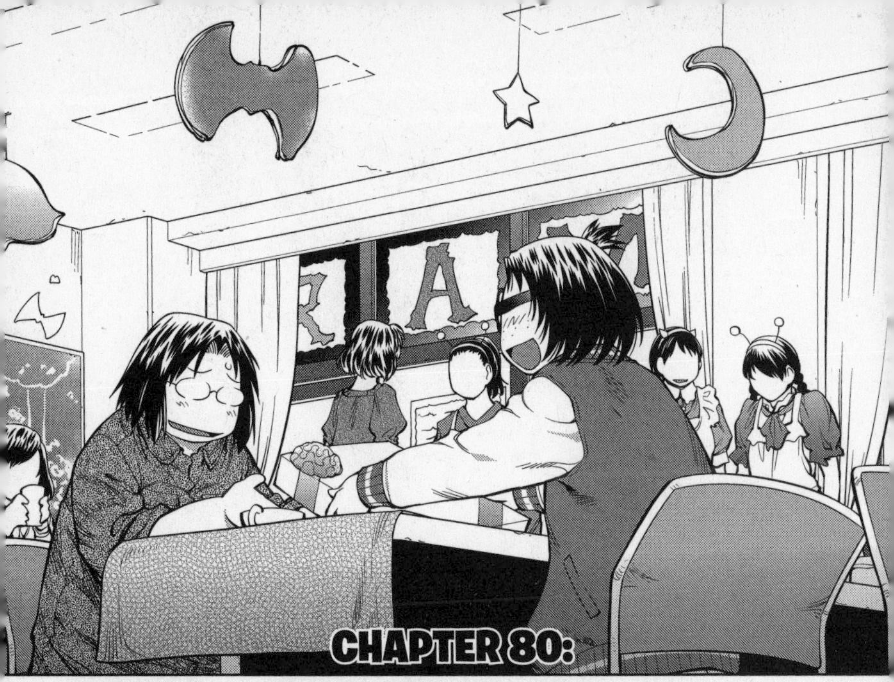

CHAPTER 80:
IT WAS A GOOD FINALE (CONFESSION II)

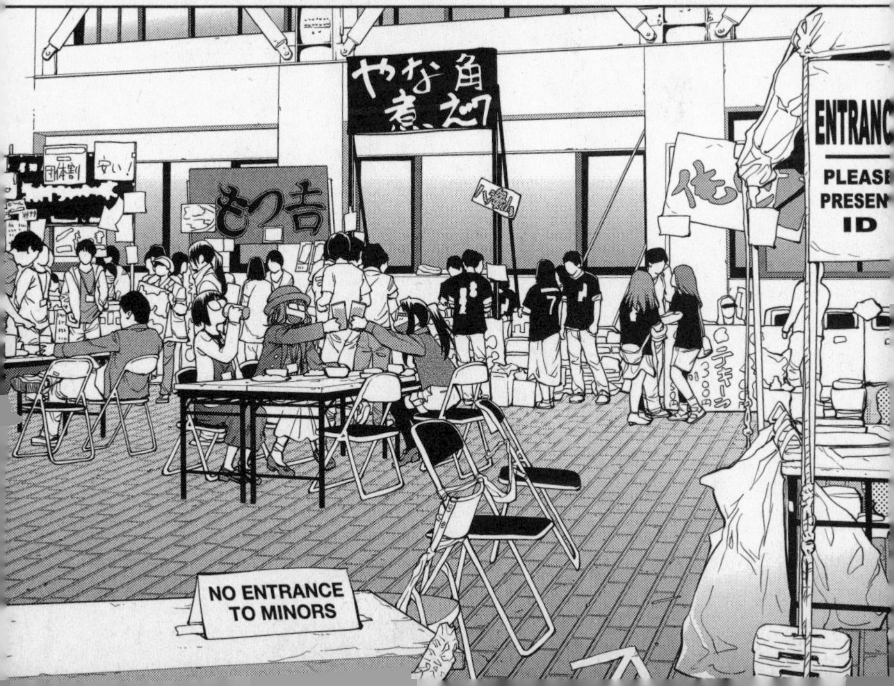
ENTRANC
PLEASE PRESEN ID
NO ENTRANCE TO MINORS

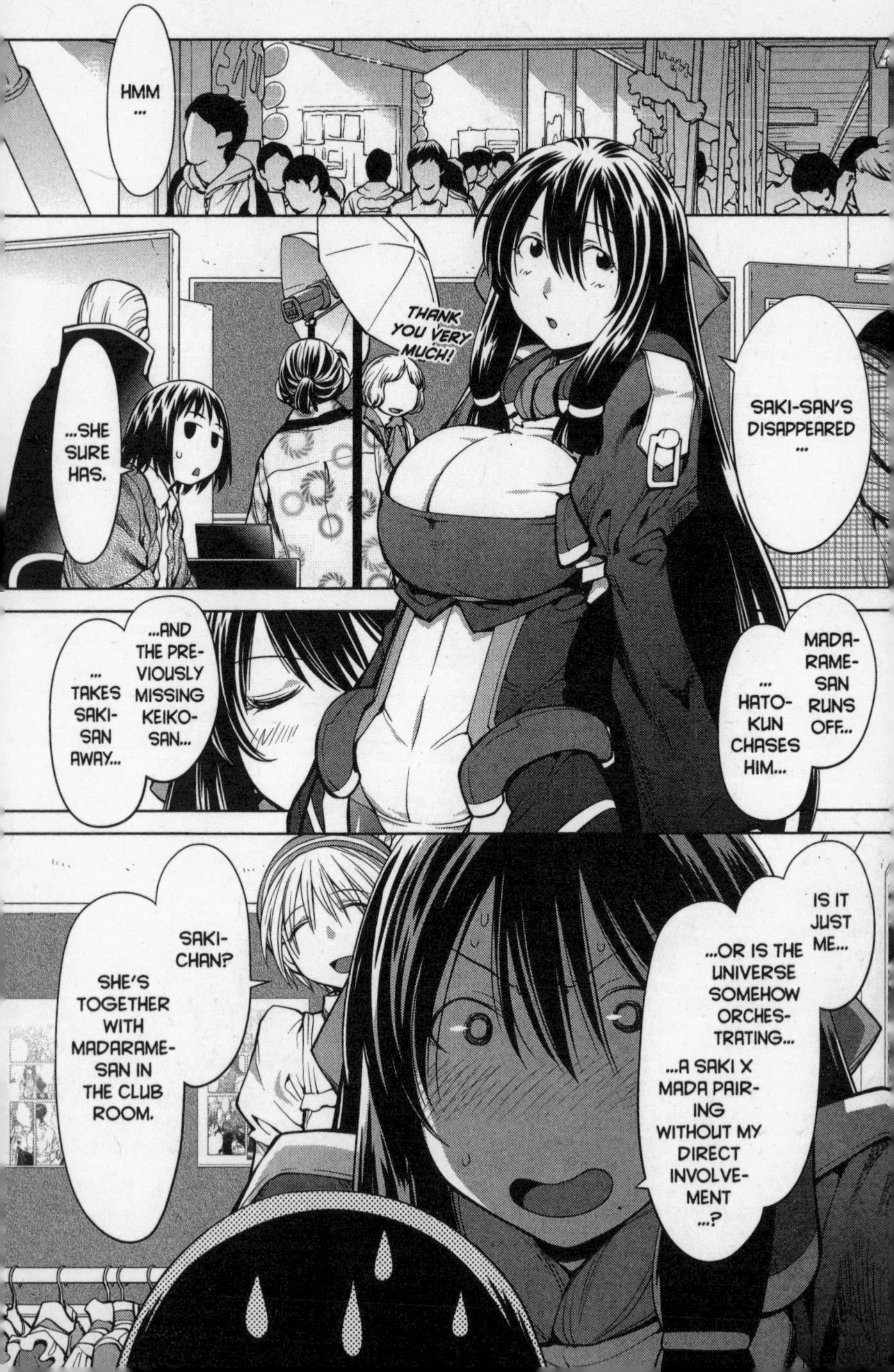
HMM...
SAKI-SAN'S DISAPPEARED...
THANK YOU VERY MUCH!
...SHE SURE HAS.
MADA-RAME-SAN RUNS OFF...
... HATO-KUN CHASES HIM...
...AND THE PRE-VIOUSLY MISSING KEIKO-SAN...
... TAKES SAKI-SAN AWAY...
IS IT JUST ME...
...OR IS THE UNIVERSE SOMEHOW ORCHES-TRATING...
...A SAKI X MADA PAIR-ING WITHOUT MY DIRECT INVOLVE-MENT...?
SAKI-CHAN?
SHE'S TOGETHER WITH MADARAME-SAN IN THE CLUB ROOM.

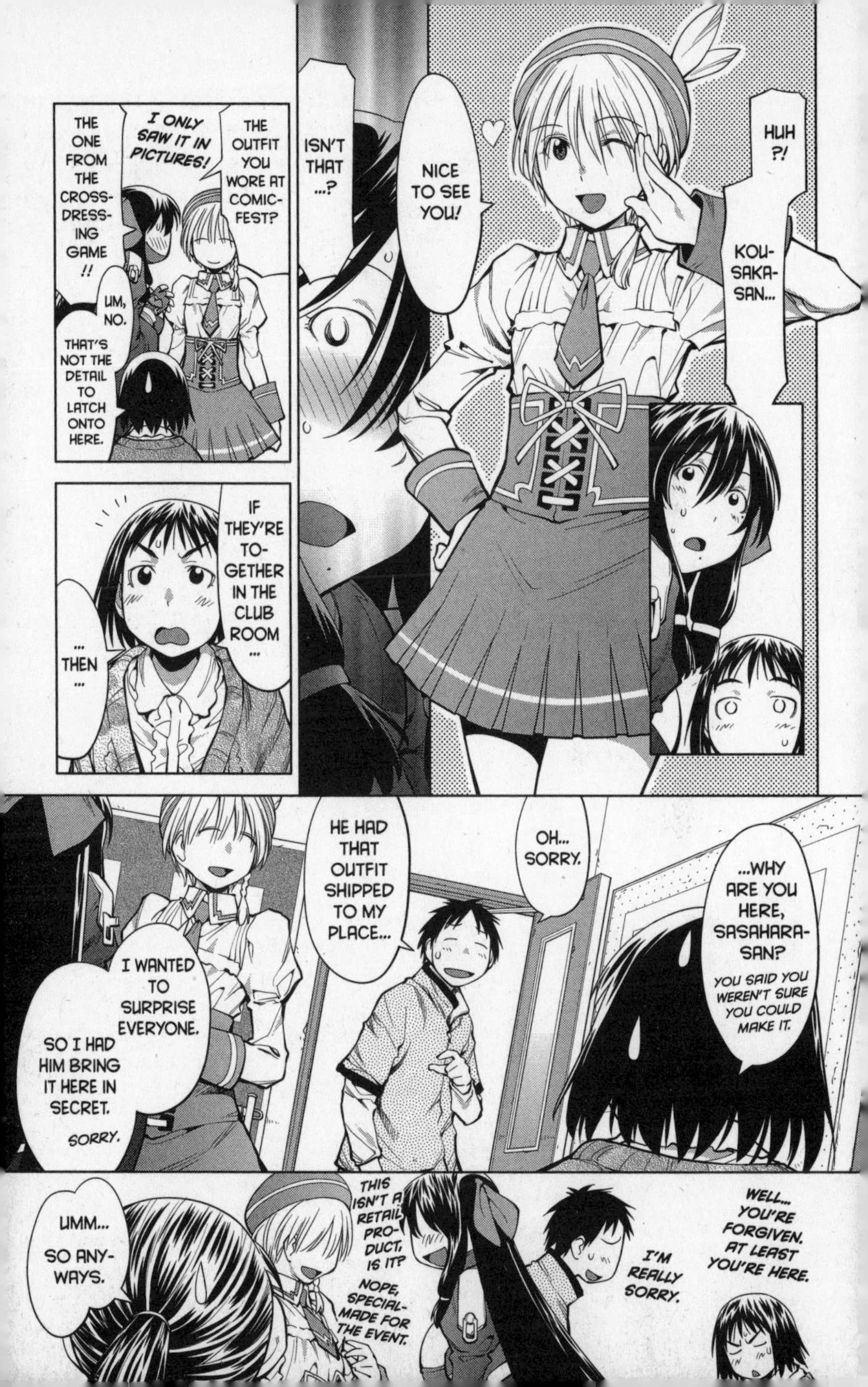
HUH?!
KOU-SAKA-SAN...
NICE TO SEE YOU!
ISN'T THAT ...?
THE OUTFIT YOU WORE AT COMIC-FEST?
I ONLY SAW IT IN PICTURES!
THE ONE FROM THE CROSS-DRESSING GAME!!
UM, NO.
THAT'S NOT THE DETAIL TO LATCH ONTO HERE.
IF THEY'RE TO-GETHER IN THE CLUB ROOM...
...THEN...
...WHY ARE YOU HERE, SASAHARA-SAN?
YOU SAID YOU WEREN'T SURE YOU COULD MAKE IT.
OH... SORRY.
HE HAD THAT OUTFIT SHIPPED TO MY PLACE...
I WANTED TO SURPRISE EVERYONE.
SO I HAD HIM BRING IT HERE IN SECRET.
SORRY.
WELL... YOU'RE FORGIVEN. AT LEAST YOU'RE HERE.
I'M REALLY SORRY.
THIS ISN'T A RETAIL PRODUCT, IS IT?
NOPE, SPECIAL-MADE FOR THE EVENT.
UMM...
SO ANY-WAYS.

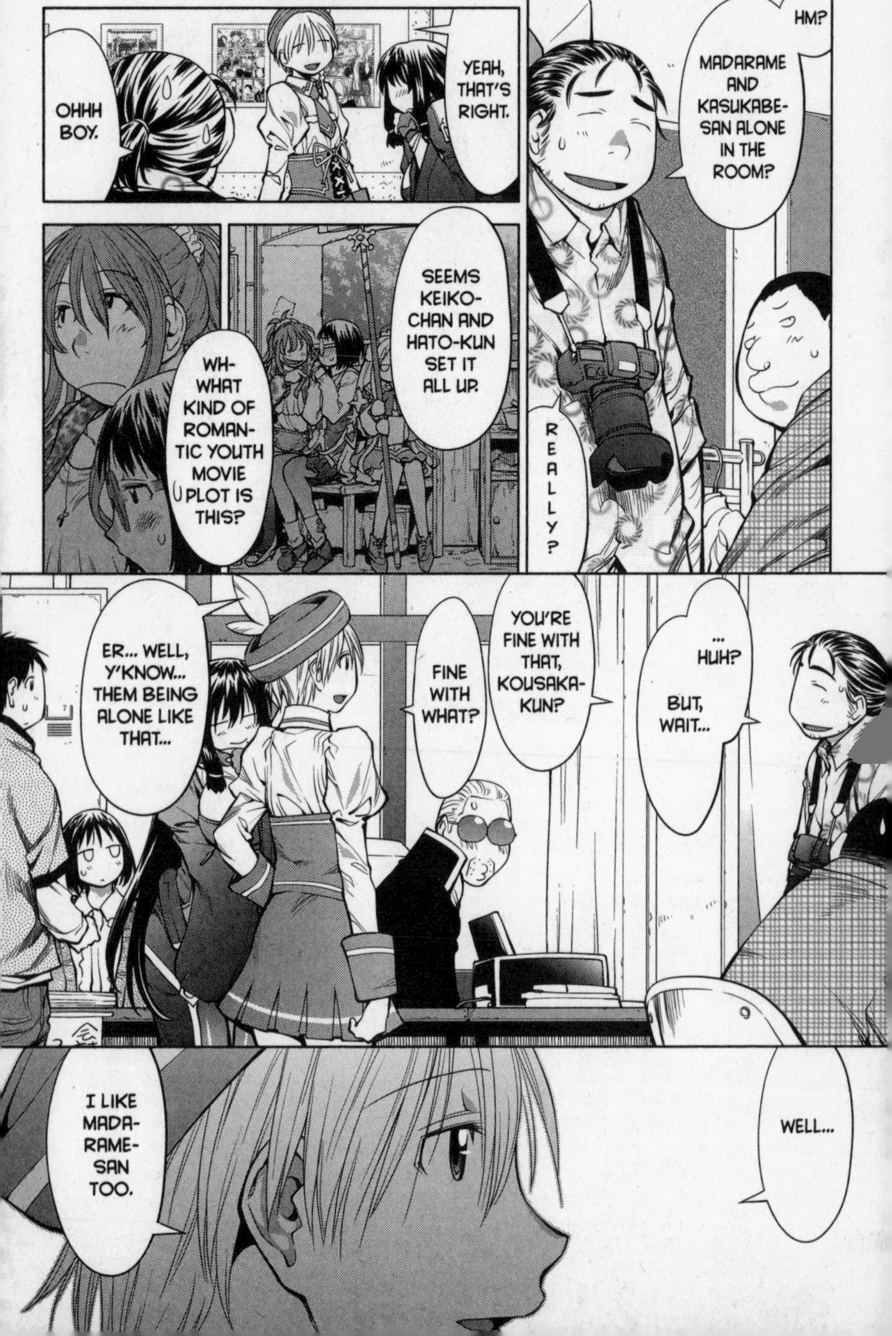
HM?
MADARAME AND KASUKABE-SAN ALONE IN THE ROOM?
REALLY?
YEAH, THAT'S RIGHT.
OHHH BOY.
SEEMS KEIKO-CHAN AND HATO-KUN SET IT ALL UP.
WH-WHAT KIND OF ROMANTIC YOUTH MOVIE PLOT IS THIS?
... HUH?
BUT, WAIT...
YOU'RE FINE WITH THAT, KOUSAKA-KUN?
FINE WITH WHAT?
ER... WELL, Y'KNOW... THEM BEING ALONE LIKE THAT...
WELL...
I LIKE MADARAME-SAN TOO.

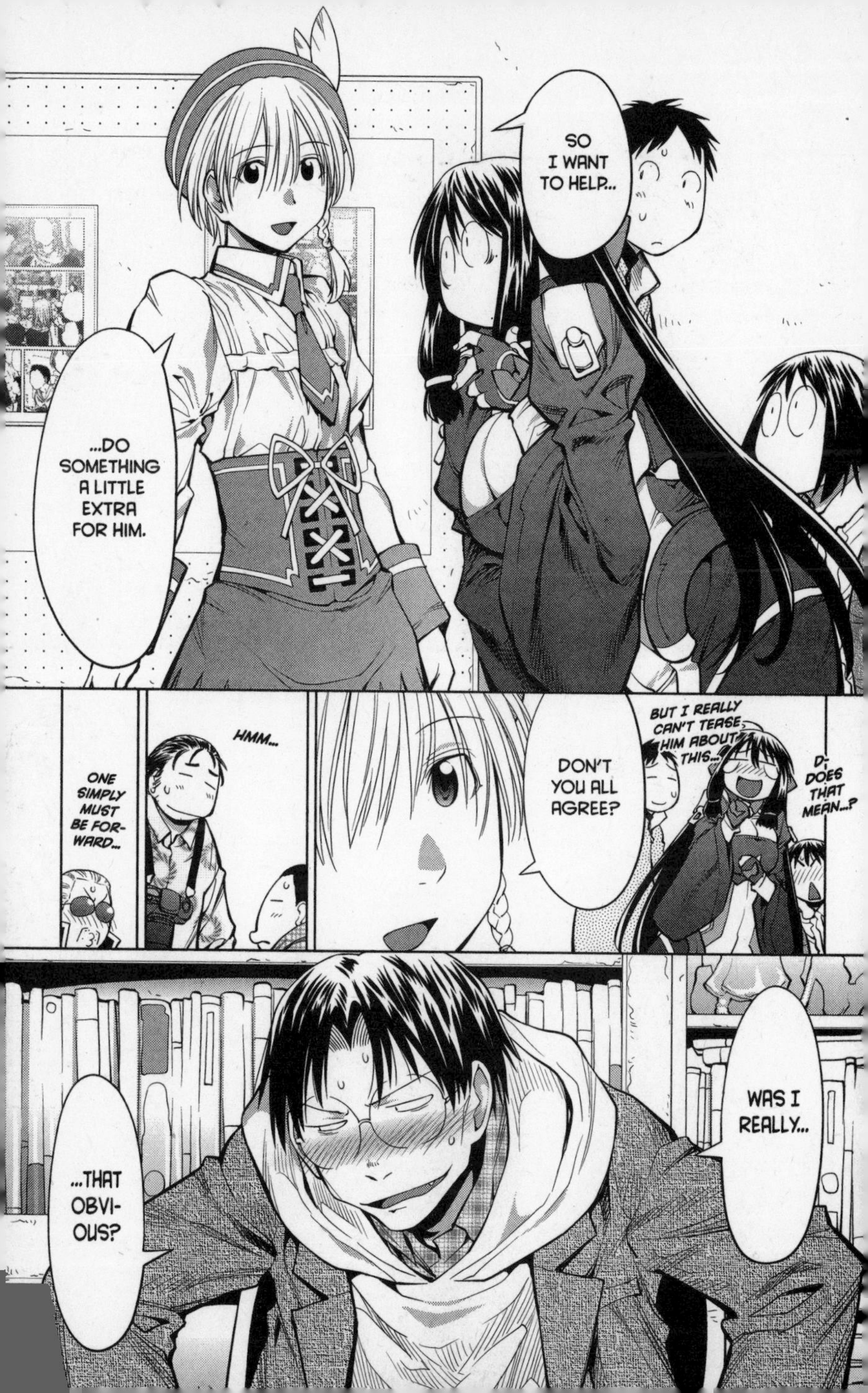
SO I WANT TO HELP...
...DO SOMETHING A LITTLE EXTRA FOR HIM.
D-DOES THAT MEAN...?
BUT I REALLY CAN'T TEASE HIM ABOUT THIS...
DON'T YOU ALL AGREE?
HMM...
ONE SIMPLY MUST BE FORWARD...
WAS I REALLY...
...THAT OBVIOUS?

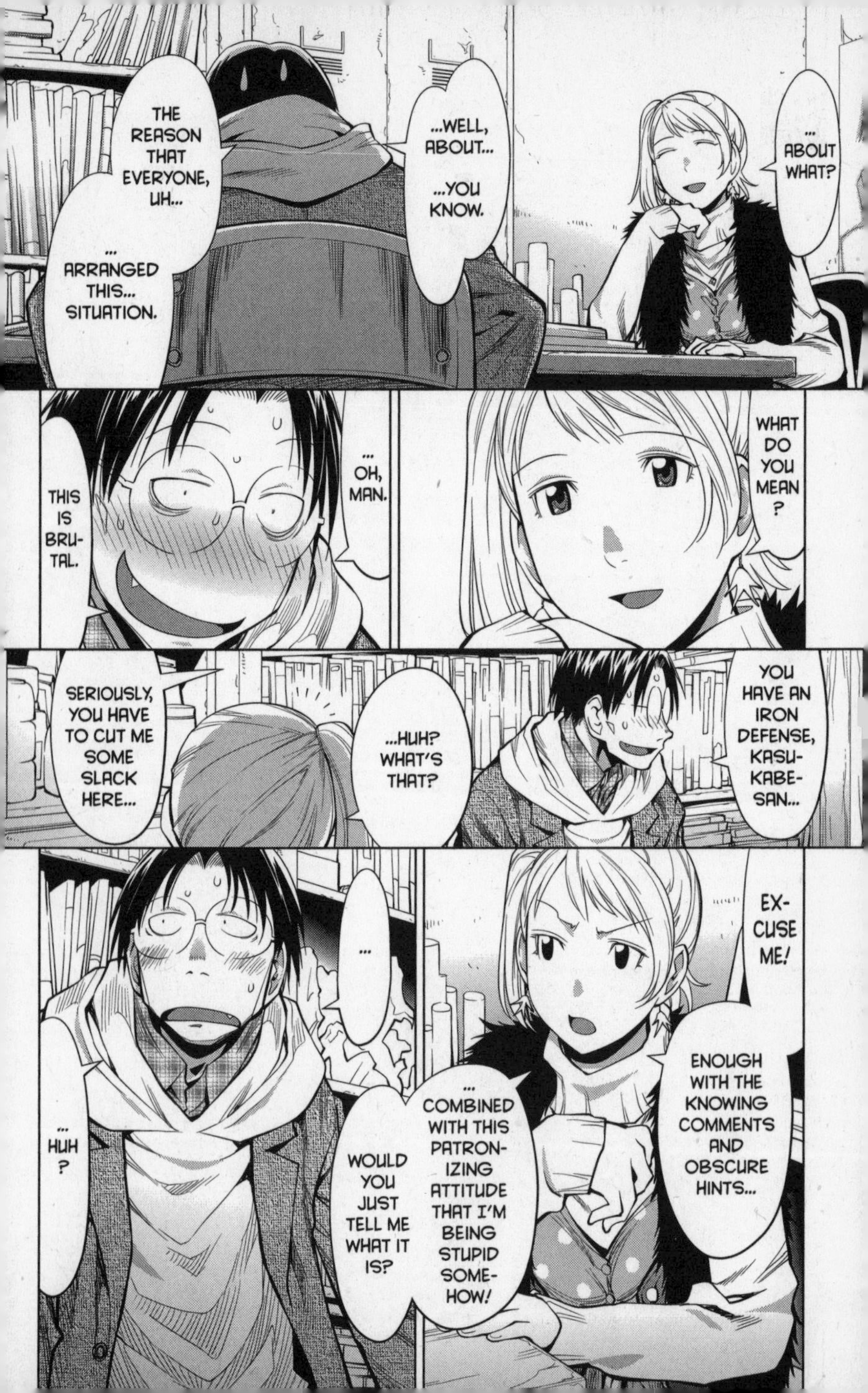
... ABOUT WHAT?
...WELL, ABOUT... ...YOU KNOW.
THE REASON THAT EVERYONE, UH...
... ARRANGED THIS... SITUATION.
WHAT DO YOU MEAN?
... OH, MAN.
THIS IS BRUTAL.
YOU HAVE AN IRON DEFENSE, KASUKABE-SAN...
...HUH? WHAT'S THAT?
SERIOUSLY, YOU HAVE TO CUT ME SOME SLACK HERE...
EXCUSE ME!
ENOUGH WITH THE KNOWING COMMENTS AND OBSCURE HINTS...
... COMBINED WITH THIS PATRONIZING ATTITUDE THAT I'M BEING STUPID SOMEHOW!
WOULD YOU JUST TELL ME WHAT IT IS?
...
... HUH?

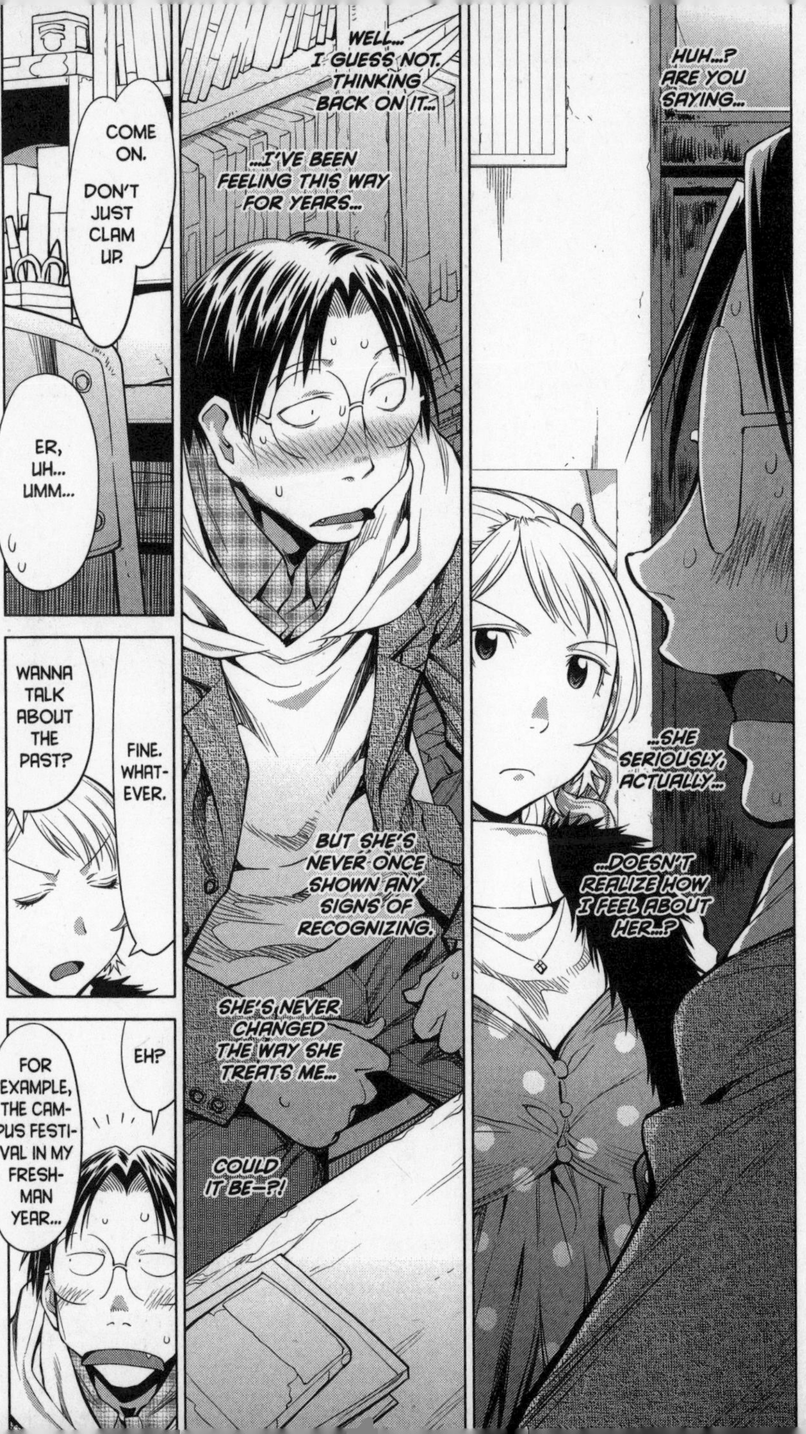
HUH...? ARE YOU SAYING...
...SHE SERIOUSLY, ACTUALLY...
...DOESN'T REALIZE HOW I FEEL ABOUT HER...?
WELL... I GUESS NOT. THINKING BACK ON IT...
...I'VE BEEN FEELING THIS WAY FOR YEARS...
BUT SHE'S NEVER ONCE SHOWN ANY SIGNS OF RECOGNIZING.
SHE'S NEVER CHANGED THE WAY SHE TREATS ME...
COULD IT BE—?!
COME ON. DON'T JUST CLAM UP.
ER, UH... UMM...
FINE. WHATEVER.
WANNA TALK ABOUT THE PAST?
EH?
FOR EXAMPLE, THE CAMPUS FESTIVAL IN MY FRESHMAN YEAR...

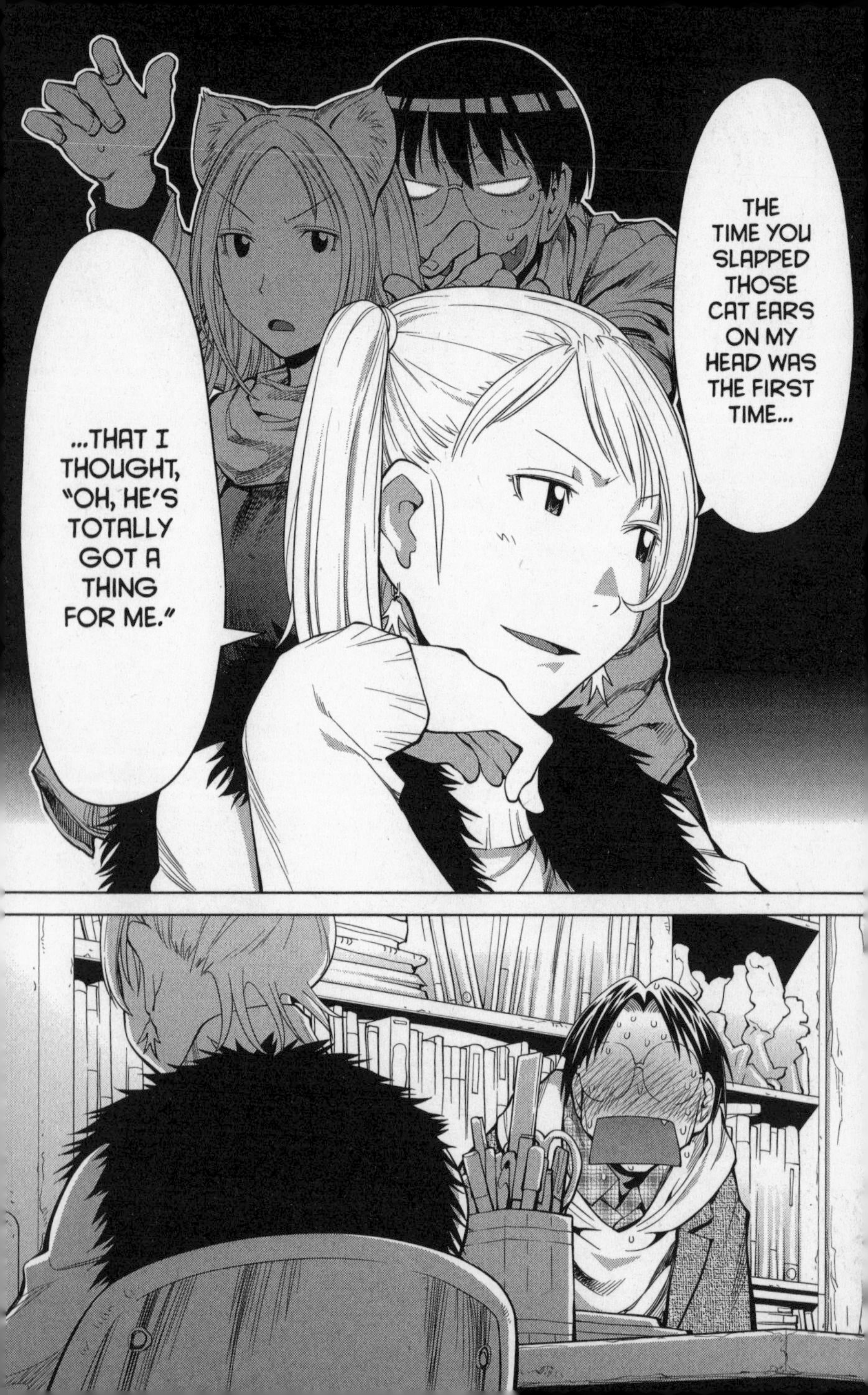
THE TIME YOU SLAPPED THOSE CAT EARS ON MY HEAD WAS THE FIRST TIME...
...THAT I THOUGHT, "OH, HE'S TOTALLY GOT A THING FOR ME."

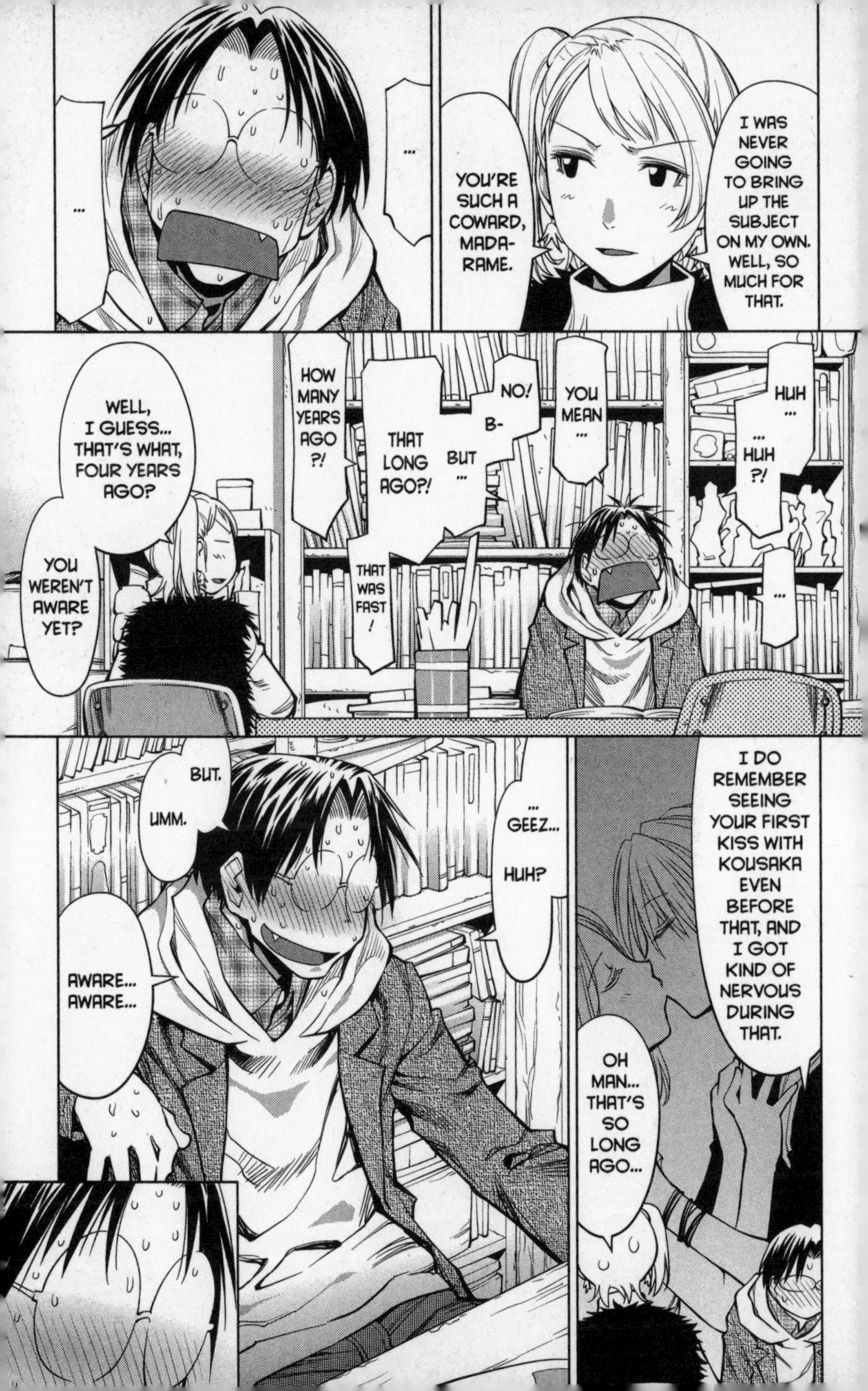
I WAS NEVER GOING TO BRING UP THE SUBJECT ON MY OWN. WELL, SO MUCH FOR THAT.
YOU'RE SUCH A COWARD, MADA-RAME.
...
...
HUH...
...HUH?!
...
YOU MEAN...
NO!
B-
BUT...
THAT LONG AGO?!
HOW MANY YEARS AGO?!
THAT WAS FAST!
WELL, I GUESS... THAT'S WHAT, FOUR YEARS AGO?
YOU WEREN'T AWARE YET?
I DO REMEMBER SEEING YOUR FIRST KISS WITH KOUSAKA EVEN BEFORE THAT, AND I GOT KIND OF NERVOUS DURING THAT.
OH MAN... THAT'S SO LONG AGO...
...GEEZ...
HUH?
BUT.
UMM.
AWARE... AWARE...

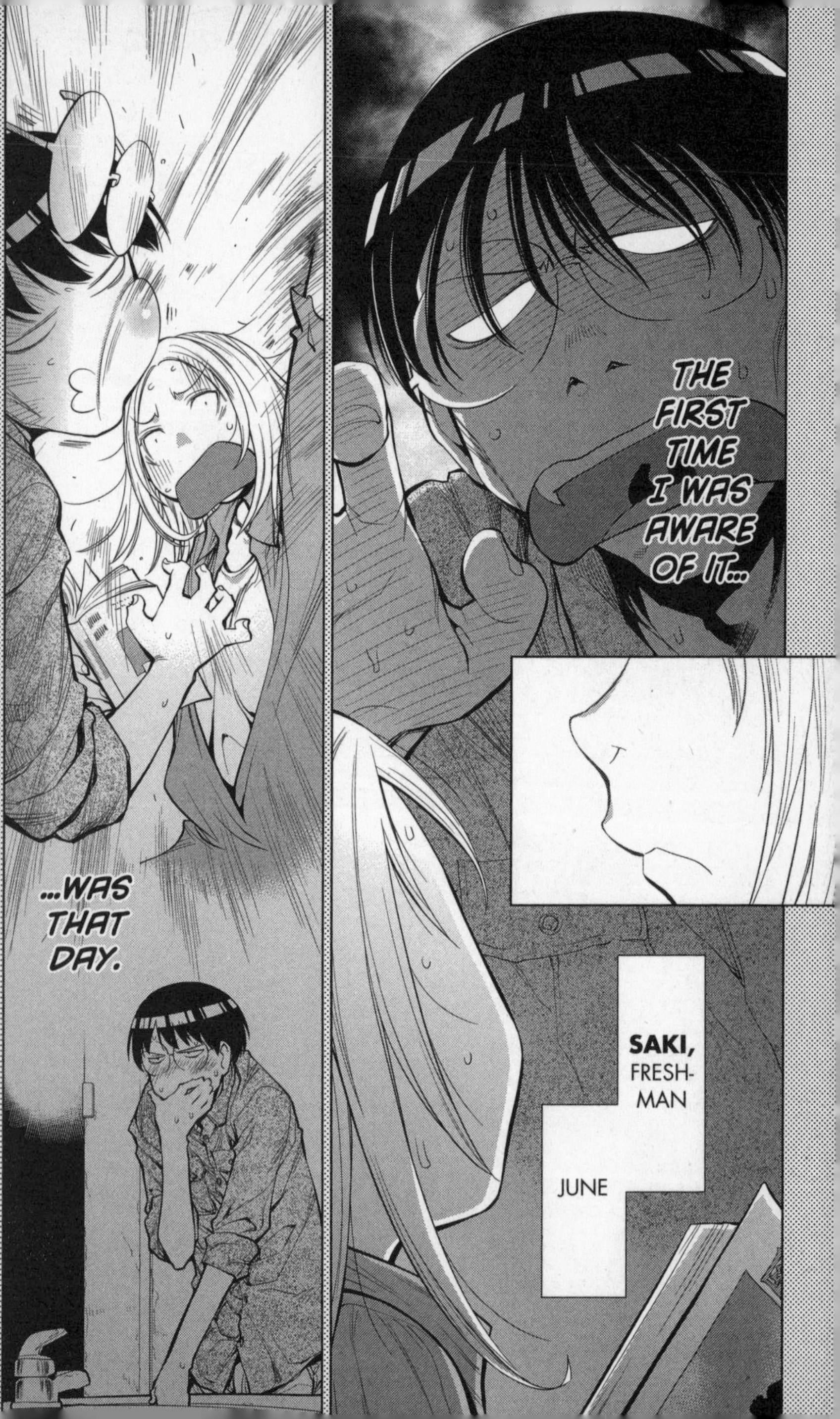
THE FIRST TIME I WAS AWARE OF IT...
SAKI, FRESHMAN
JUNE
...WAS THAT DAY.

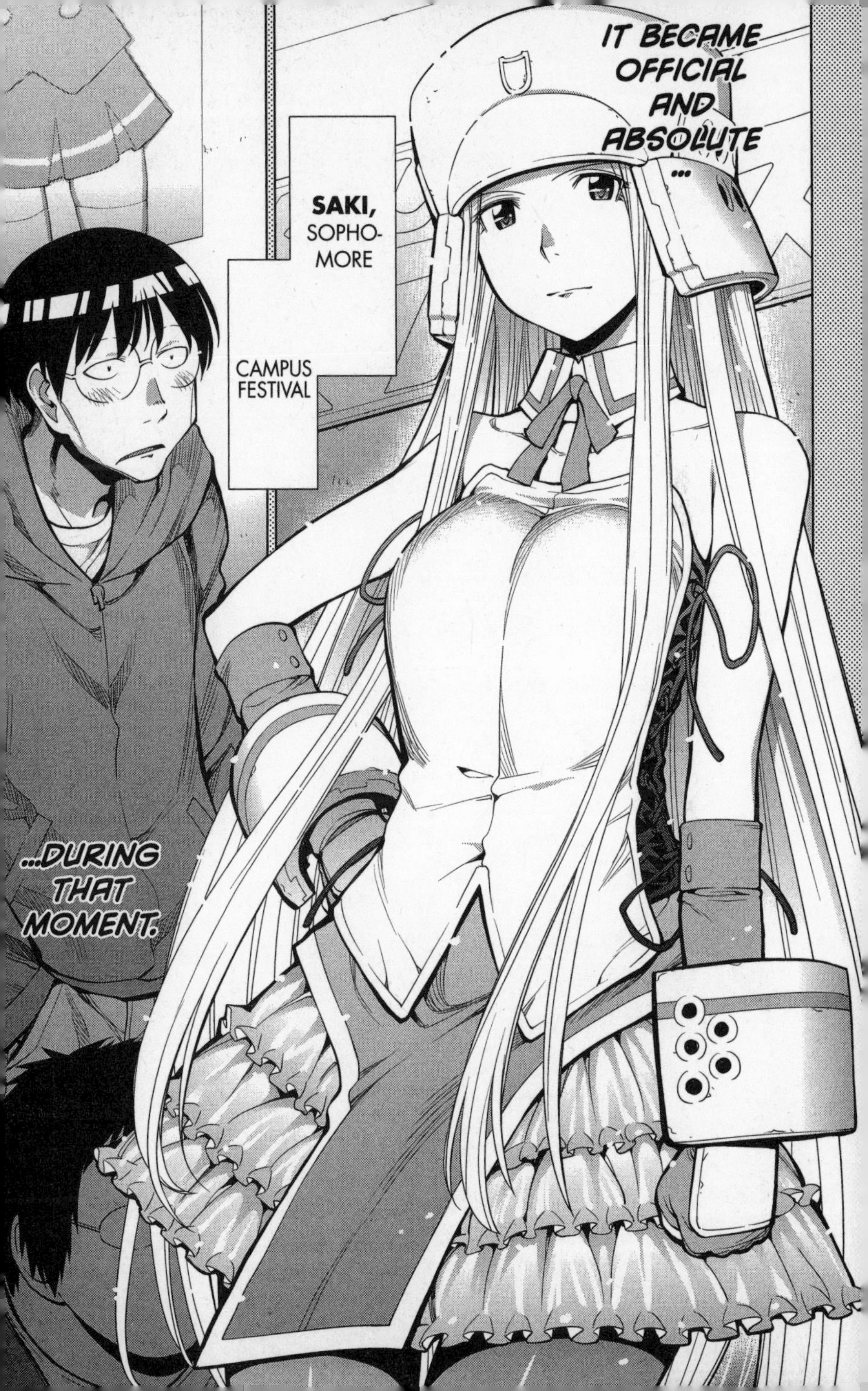
IT BECAME OFFICIAL AND ABSOLUTE ...
SAKI, SOPHOMORE
CAMPUS FESTIVAL
...DURING THAT MOMENT.

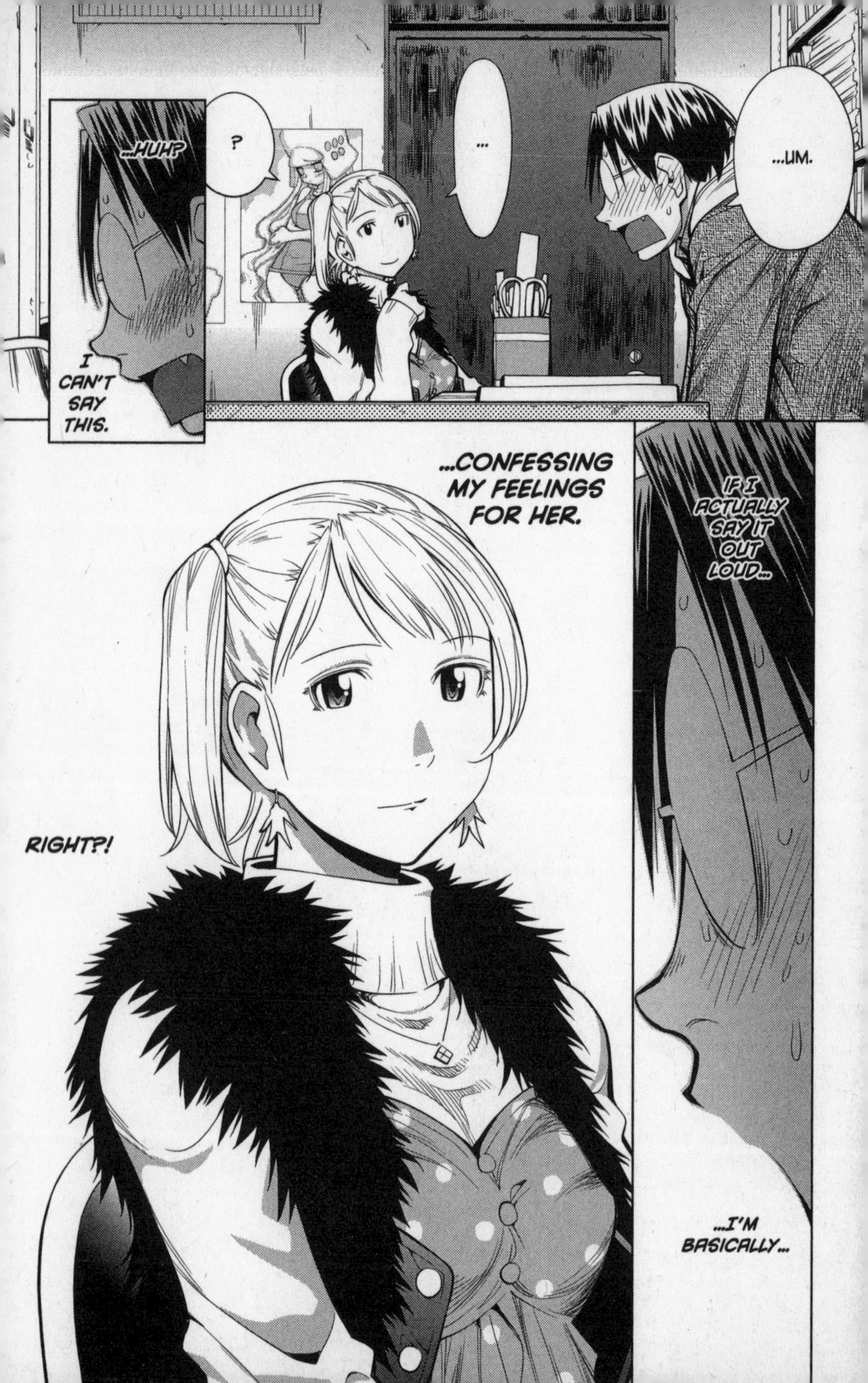
...UM.
...
?
...HUH?
I CAN'T SAY THIS.
IF I ACTUALLY SAY IT OUT LOUD...
...I'M BASICALLY...
...CONFESSING MY FEELINGS FOR HER.
RIGHT?!

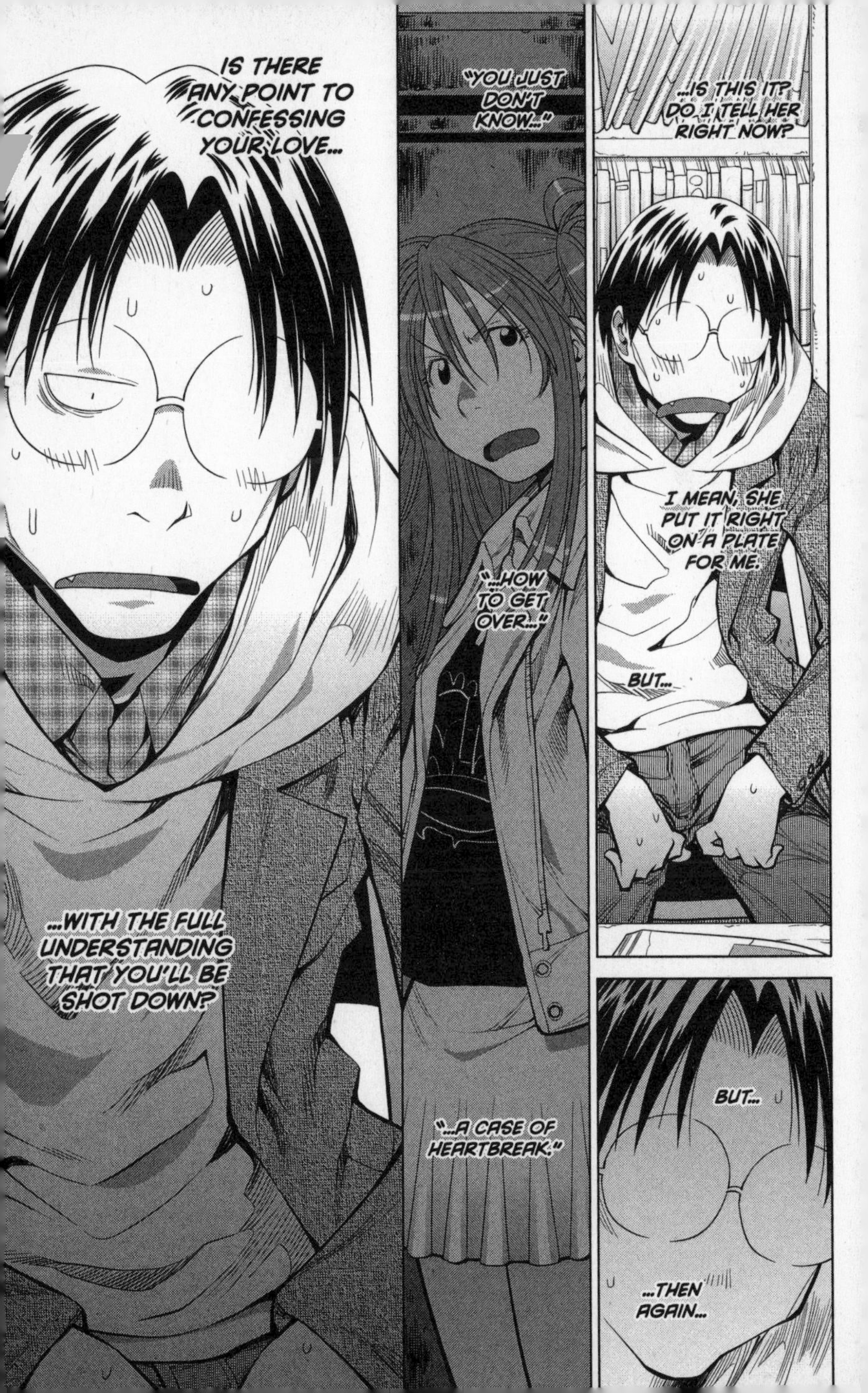
...IS THIS IT? DO I TELL HER RIGHT NOW?
I MEAN, SHE PUT IT RIGHT ON A PLATE FOR ME.
BUT...
BUT...
...THEN AGAIN...
"YOU JUST DON'T KNOW..."
"...HOW TO GET OVER..."
"...A CASE OF HEARTBREAK."
IS THERE ANY POINT TO CONFESSING YOUR LOVE...
...WITH THE FULL UNDERSTANDING THAT YOU'LL BE SHOT DOWN?

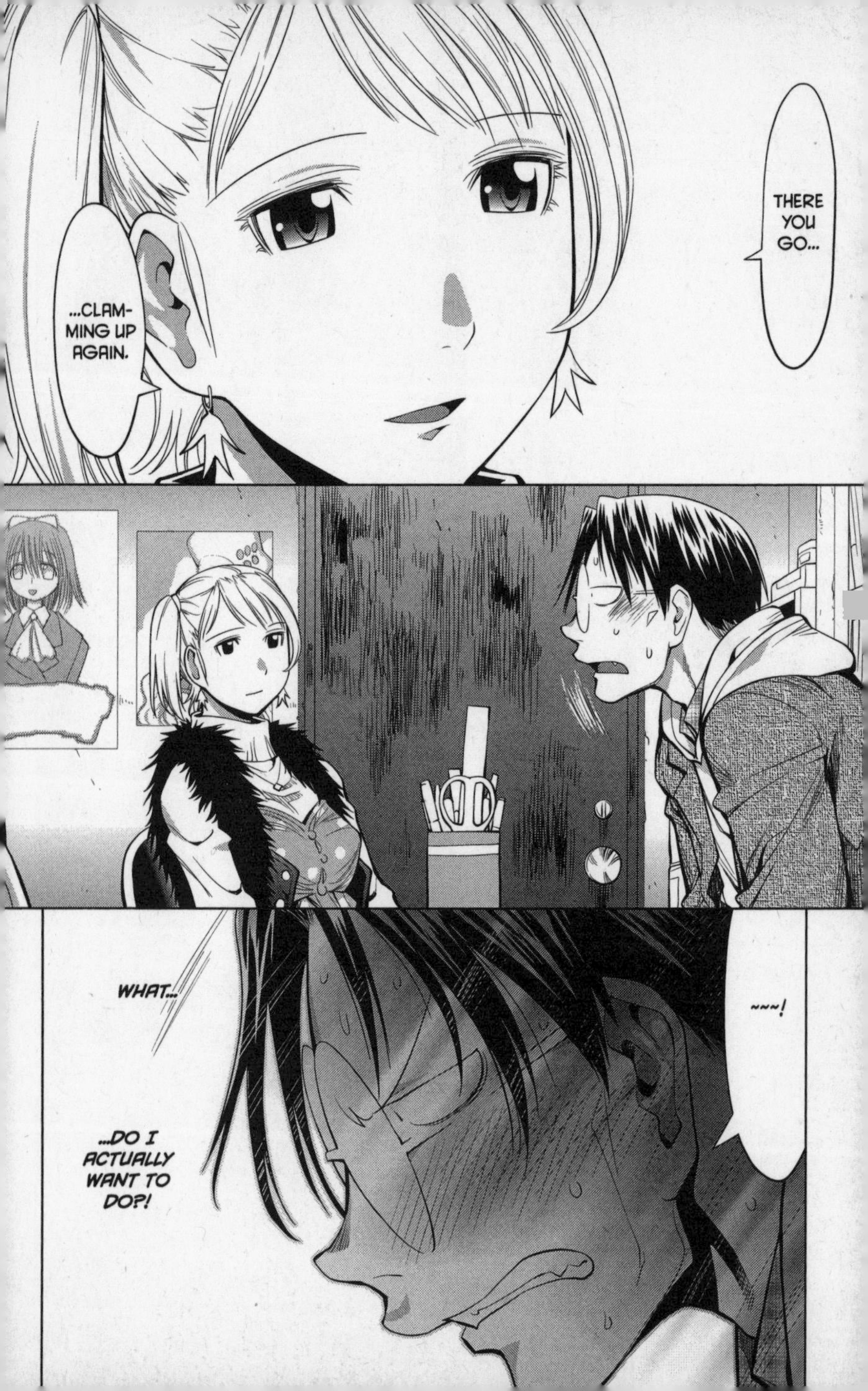
THERE YOU GO...
...CLAMMING UP AGAIN.
~~~!
WHAT...
...DO I ACTUALLY WANT TO DO?!
~~~

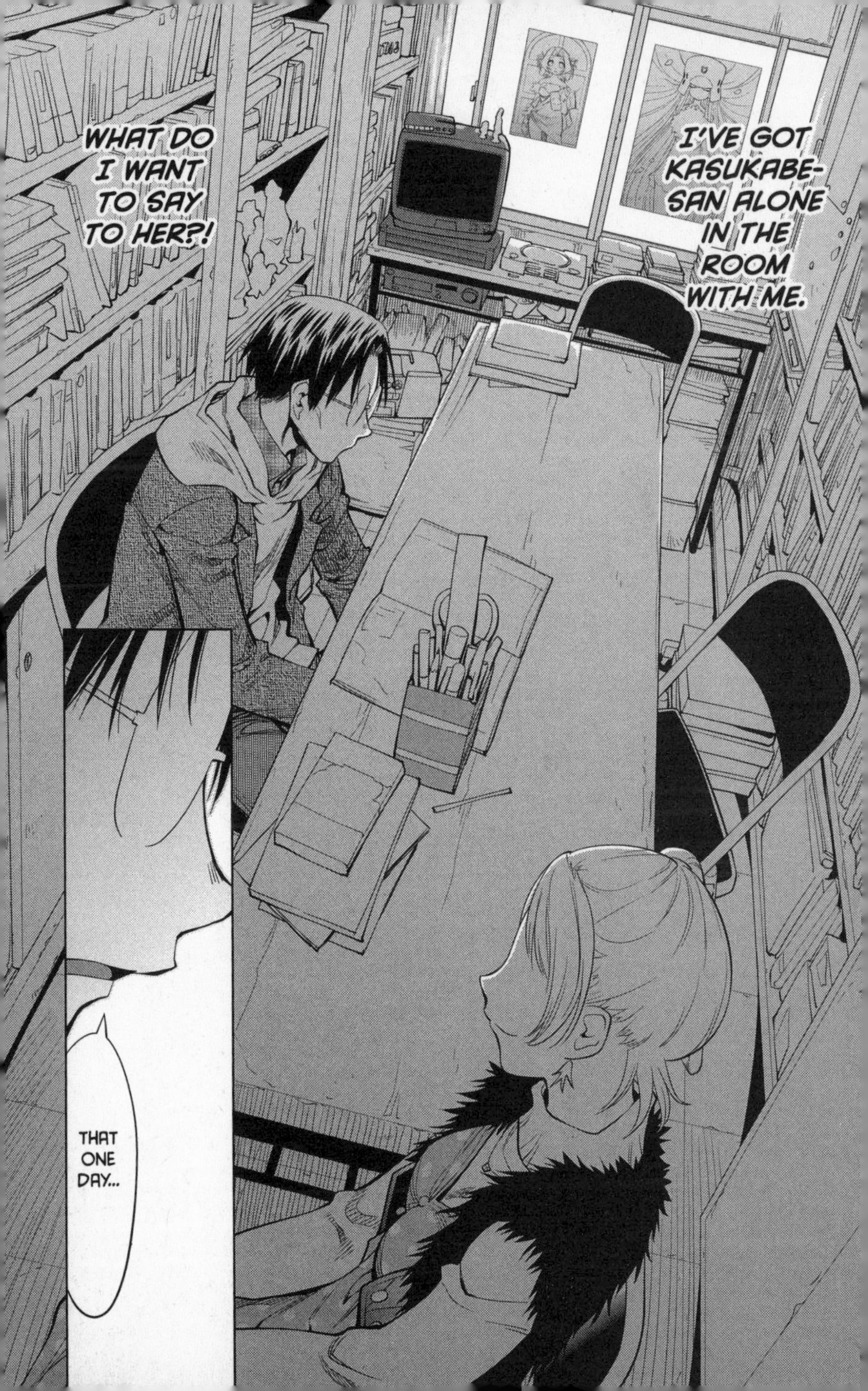
I'VE GOT KASUKABE-SAN ALONE IN THE ROOM WITH ME.
WHAT DO I WANT TO SAY TO HER?!
THAT ONE DAY...

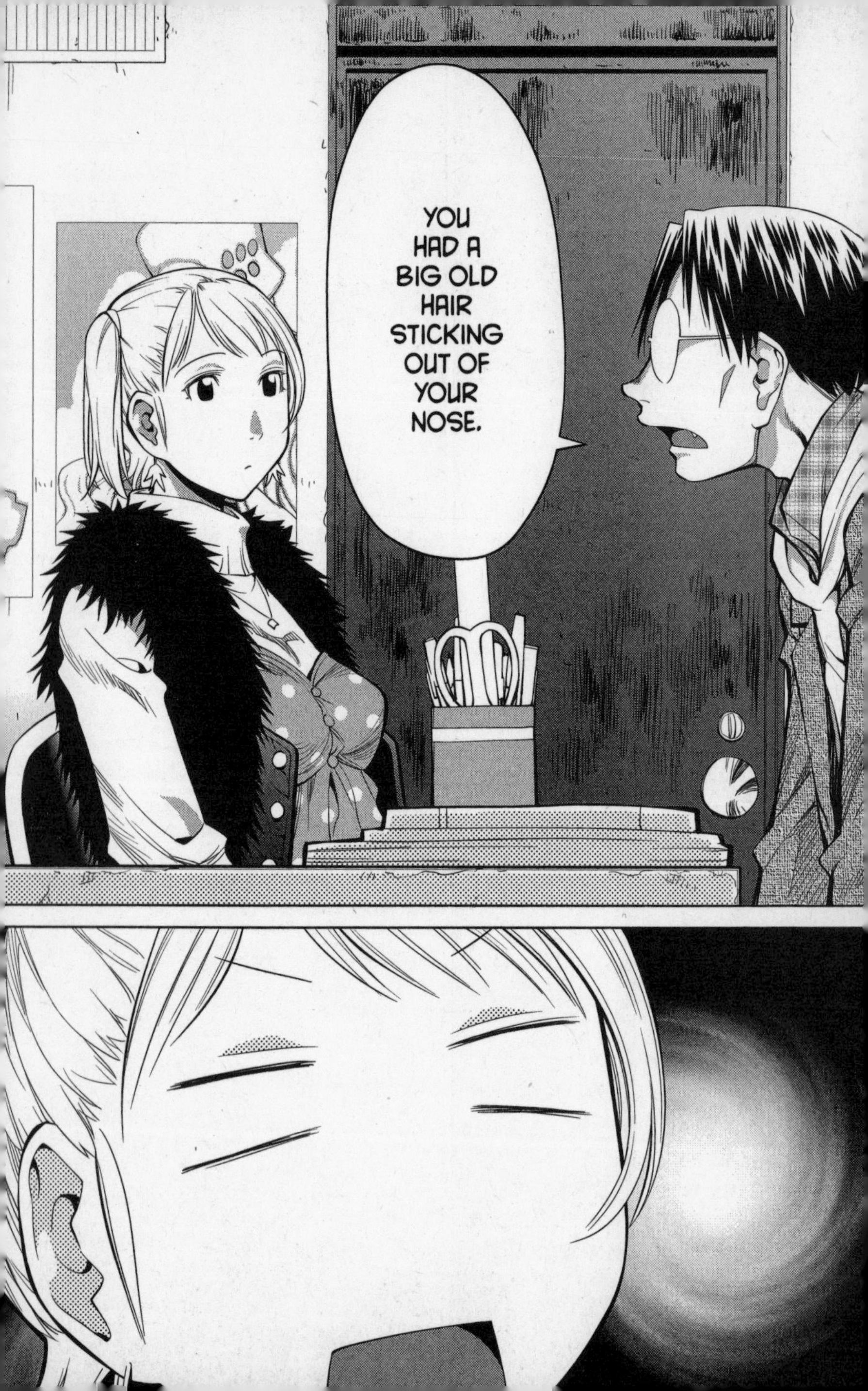
YOU HAD A BIG OLD HAIR STICKING OUT OF YOUR NOSE.

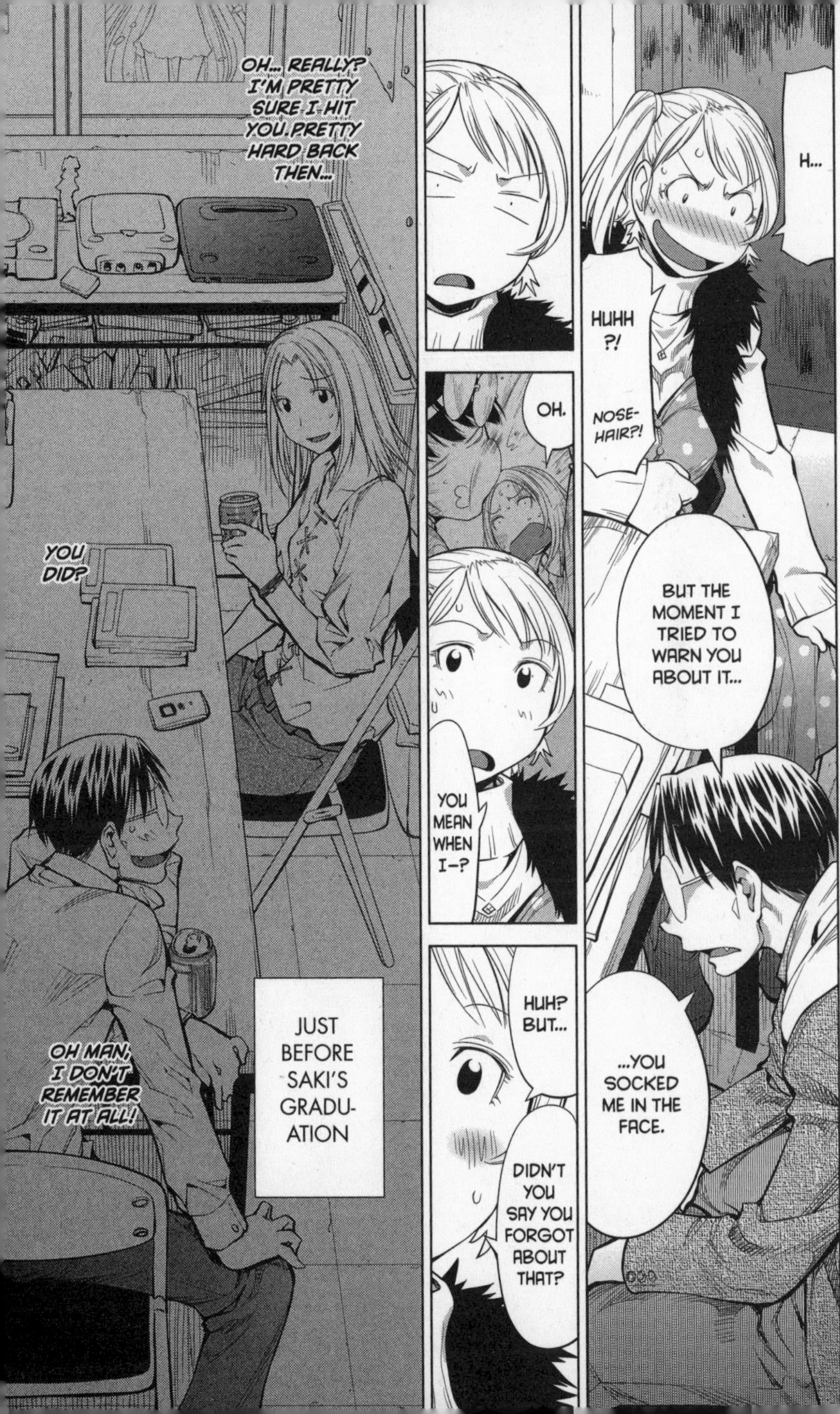
H...
HUHH ?!
NOSE-HAIR?!
BUT THE MOMENT I TRIED TO WARN YOU ABOUT IT...
...YOU SOCKED ME IN THE FACE.
OH.
YOU MEAN WHEN I–?
HUH? BUT...
DIDN'T YOU SAY YOU FORGOT ABOUT THAT?
OH... REALLY? I'M PRETTY SURE I HIT YOU PRETTY HARD BACK THEN...
YOU DID?
JUST BEFORE SAKI'S GRADUATION
OH MAN, I DON'T REMEMBER IT AT ALL!

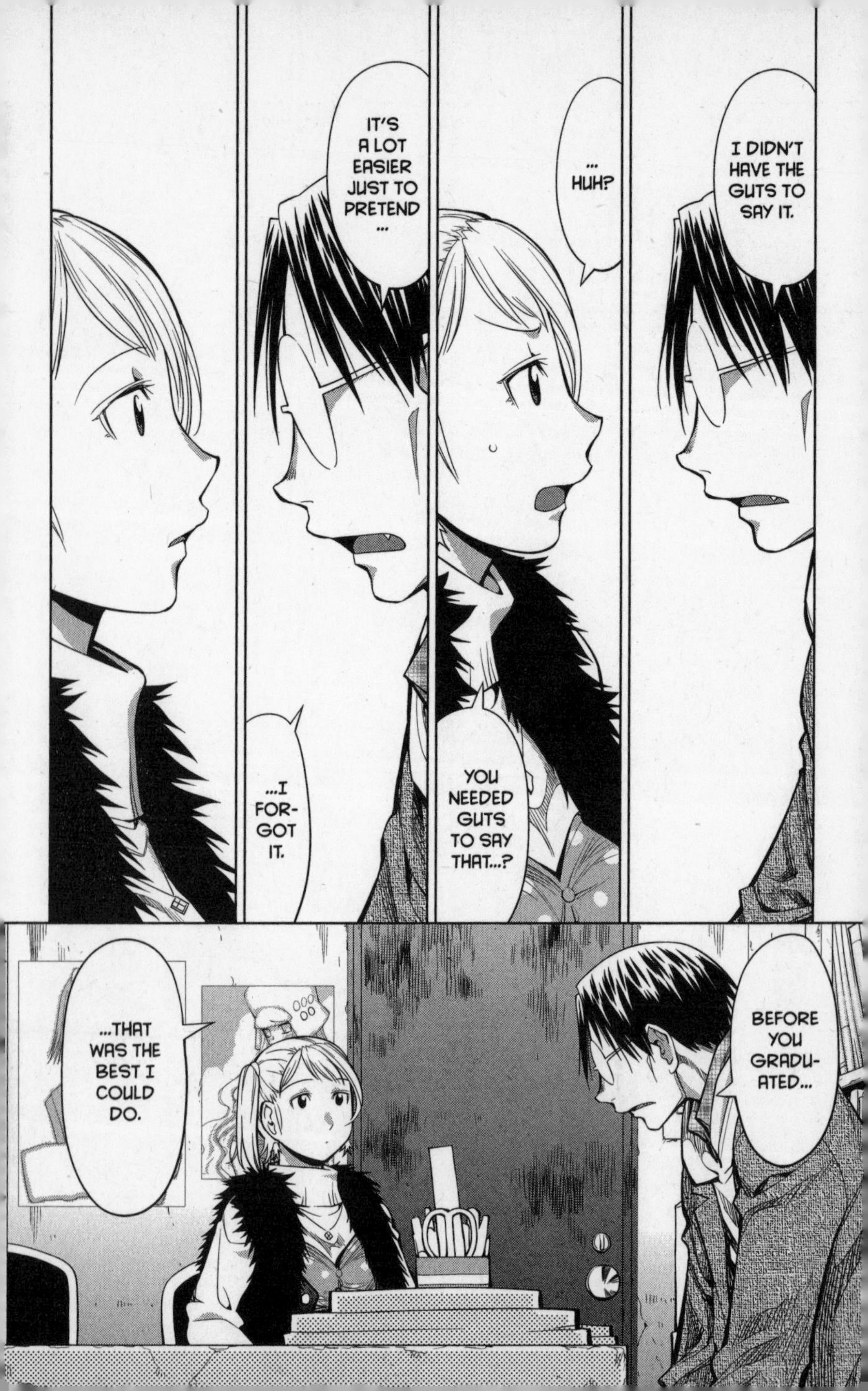
I DIDN'T HAVE THE GUTS TO SAY IT.
... HUH?
YOU NEEDED GUTS TO SAY THAT...?
IT'S A LOT EASIER JUST TO PRETEND ...
...I FOR-GOT IT.
BEFORE YOU GRADU-ATED...
...THAT WAS THE BEST I COULD DO.

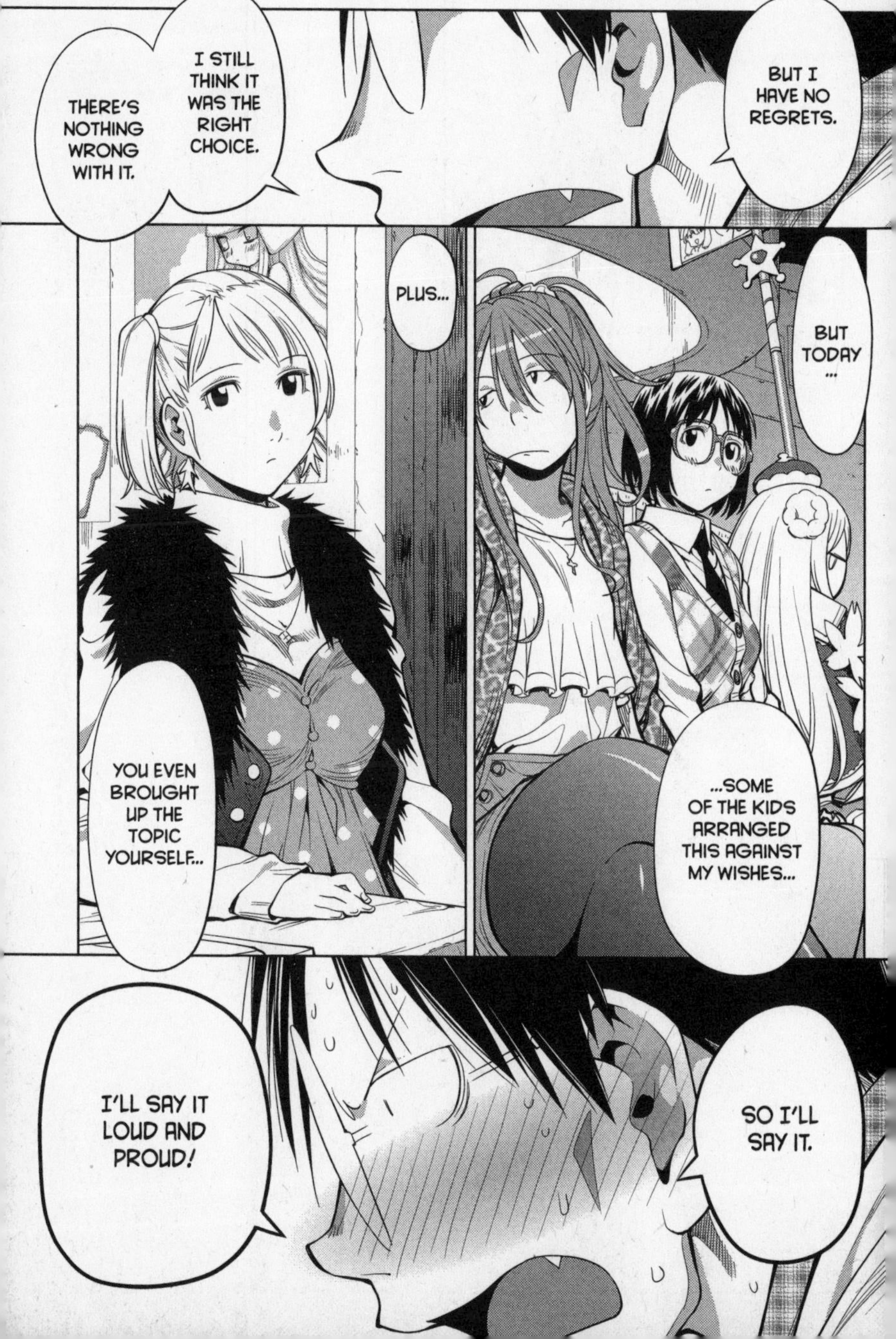
BUT I HAVE NO REGRETS.
I STILL THINK IT WAS THE RIGHT CHOICE.
THERE'S NOTHING WRONG WITH IT.
BUT TODAY ...
...SOME OF THE KIDS ARRANGED THIS AGAINST MY WISHES...
PLUS...
YOU EVEN BROUGHT UP THE TOPIC YOURSELF...
SO I'LL SAY IT.
I'LL SAY IT LOUD AND PROUD!

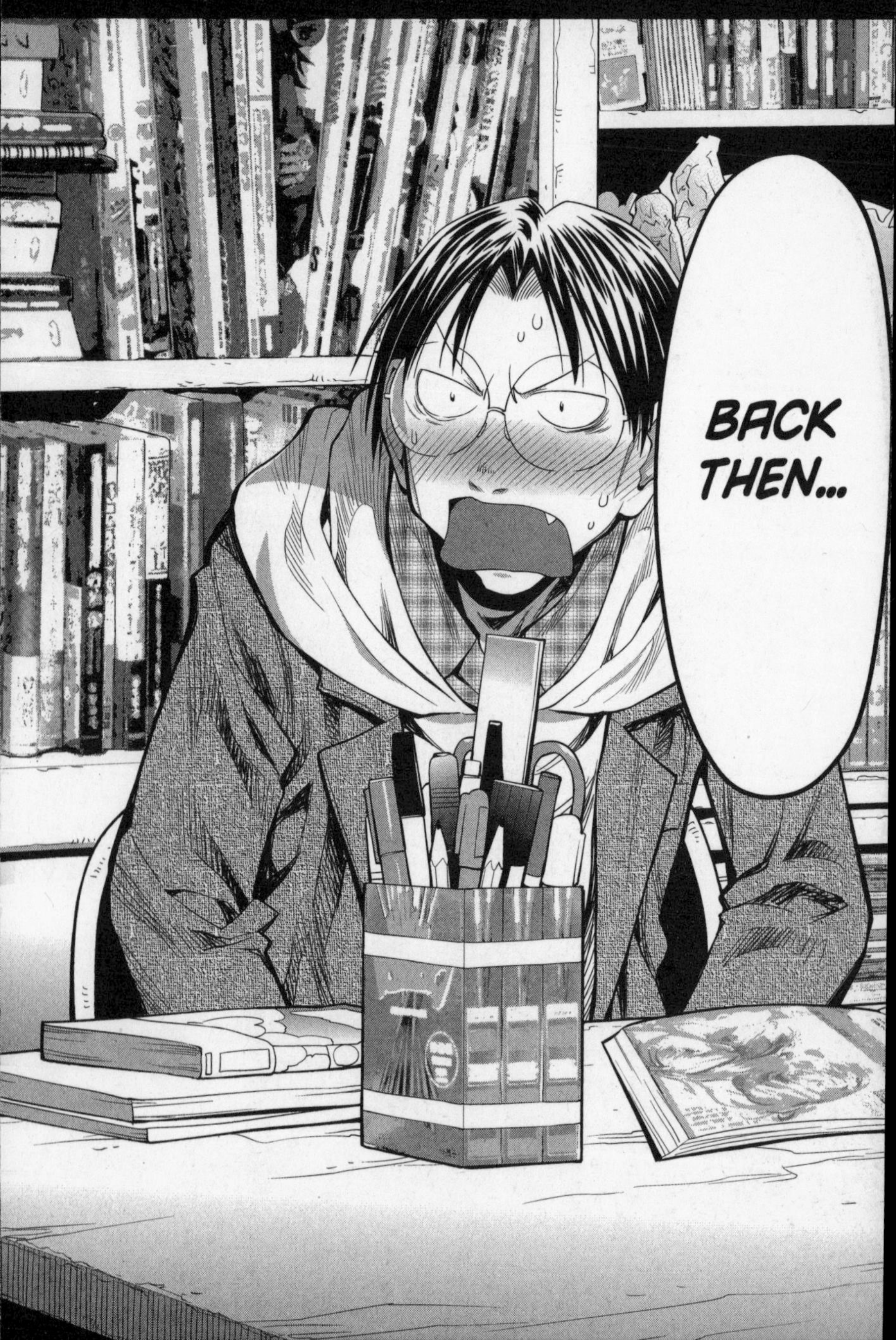
BACK THEN...

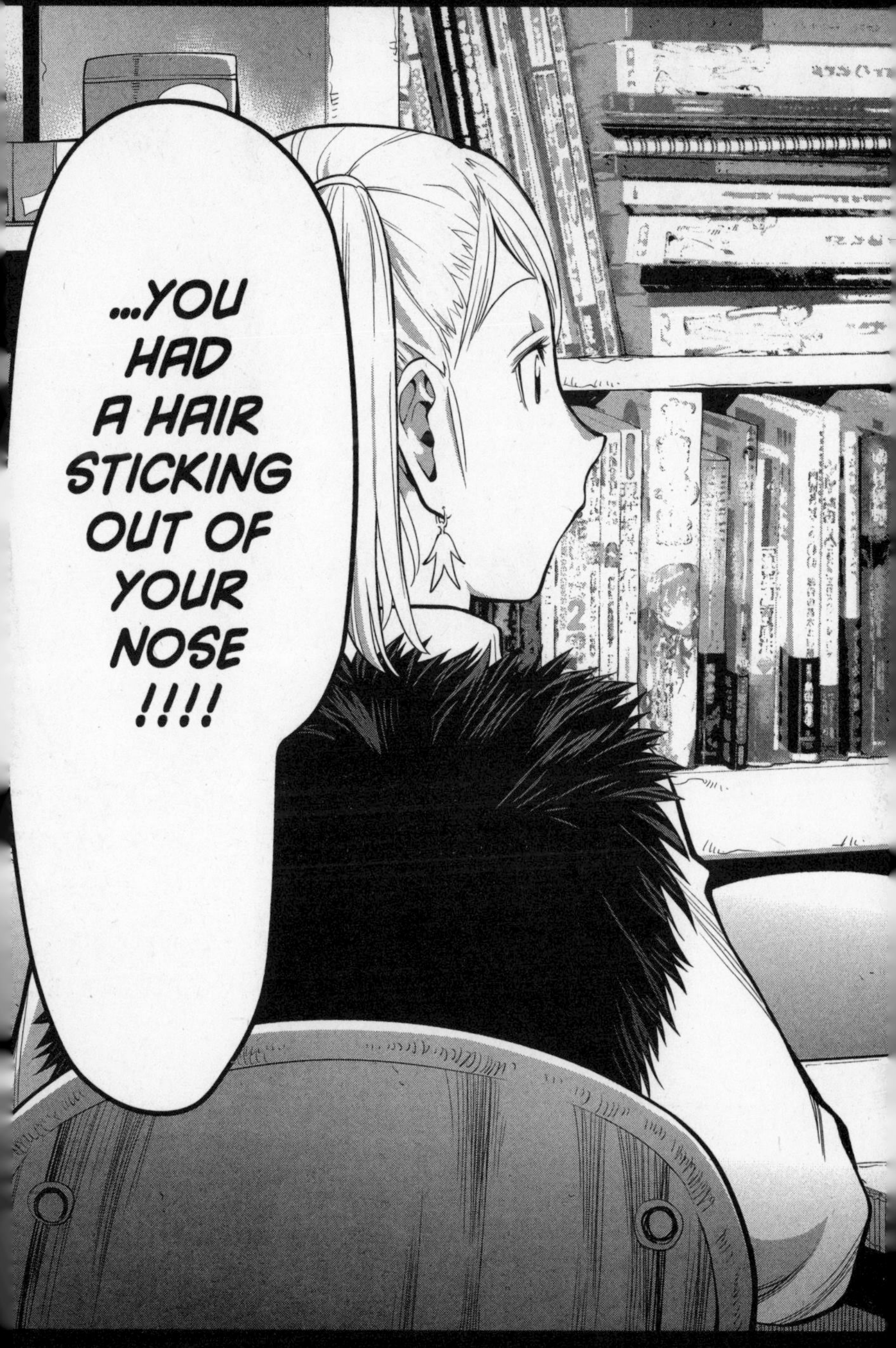
...YOU HAD A HAIR STICKING OUT OF YOUR NOSE !!!!

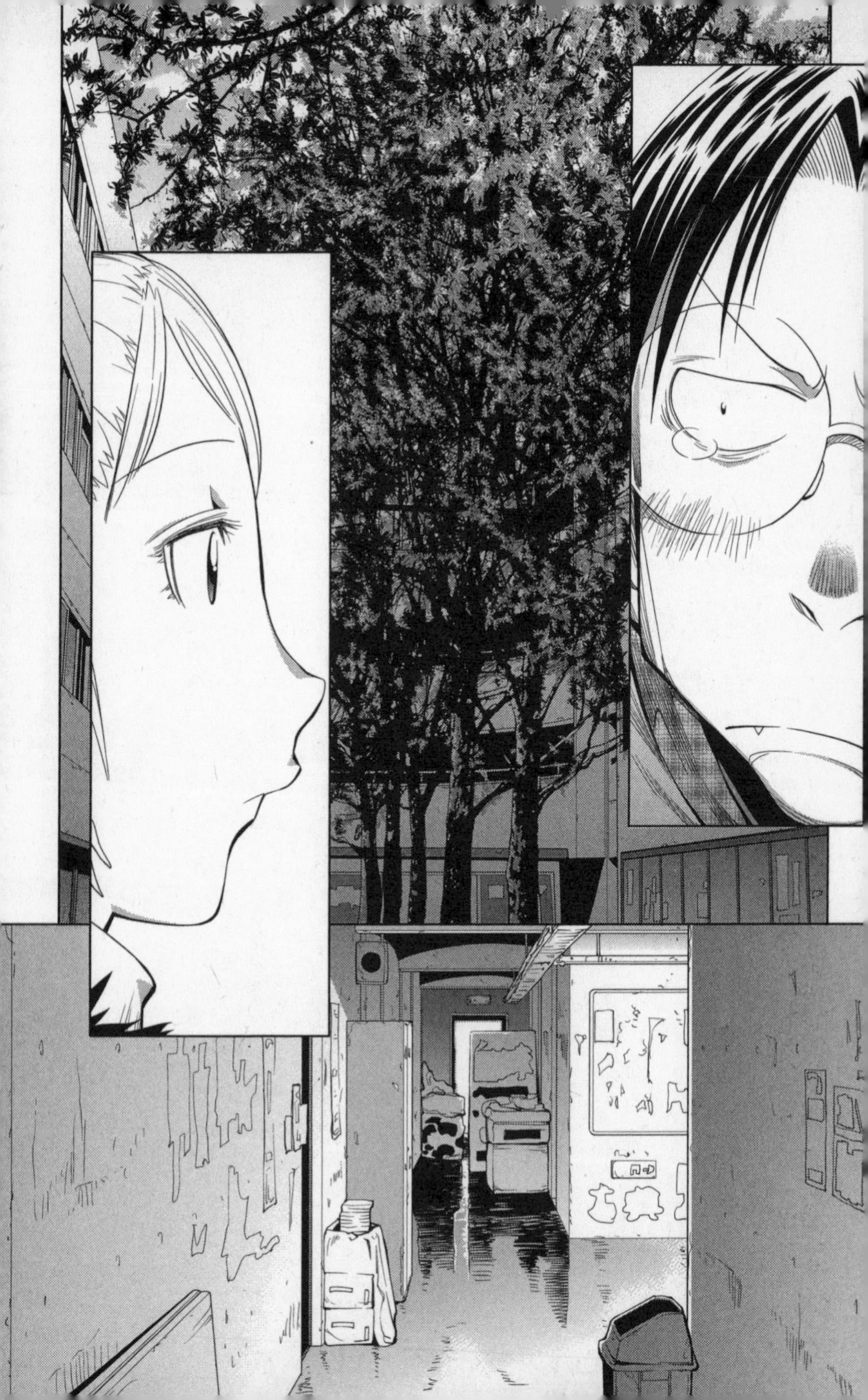

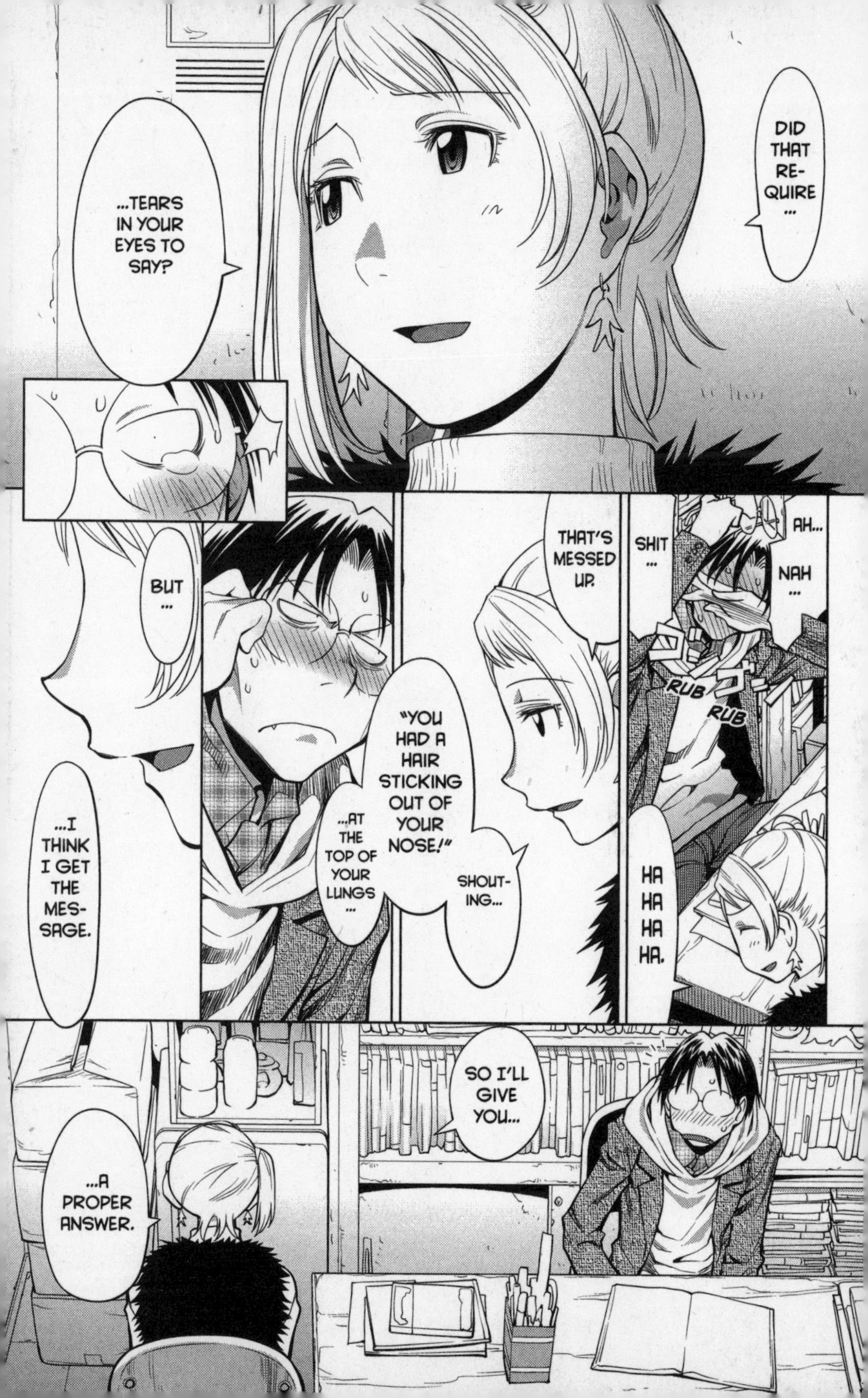
DID THAT RE-QUIRE...
...TEARS IN YOUR EYES TO SAY?
AH... NAH...
SHIT...
RUB RUB
HA HA HA HA.
THAT'S MESSED UP.
SHOUT-ING...
"YOU HAD A HAIR STICKING OUT OF YOUR NOSE!"
...AT THE TOP OF YOUR LUNGS...
BUT...
...I THINK I GET THE MES-SAGE.
SO I'LL GIVE YOU...
...A PROPER ANSWER.

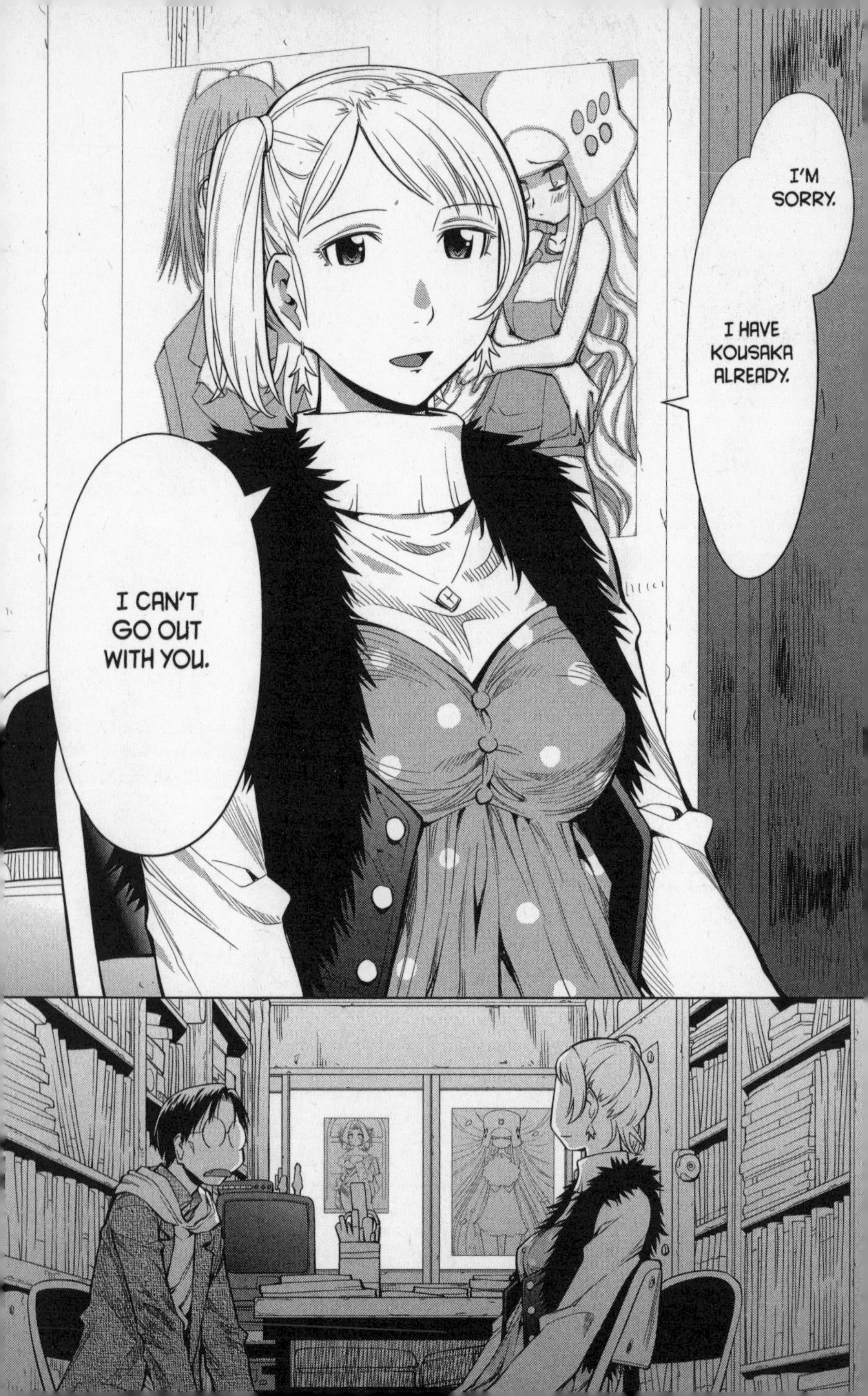
I'M SORRY.
I HAVE KOUSAKA ALREADY.
I CAN'T GO OUT WITH YOU.

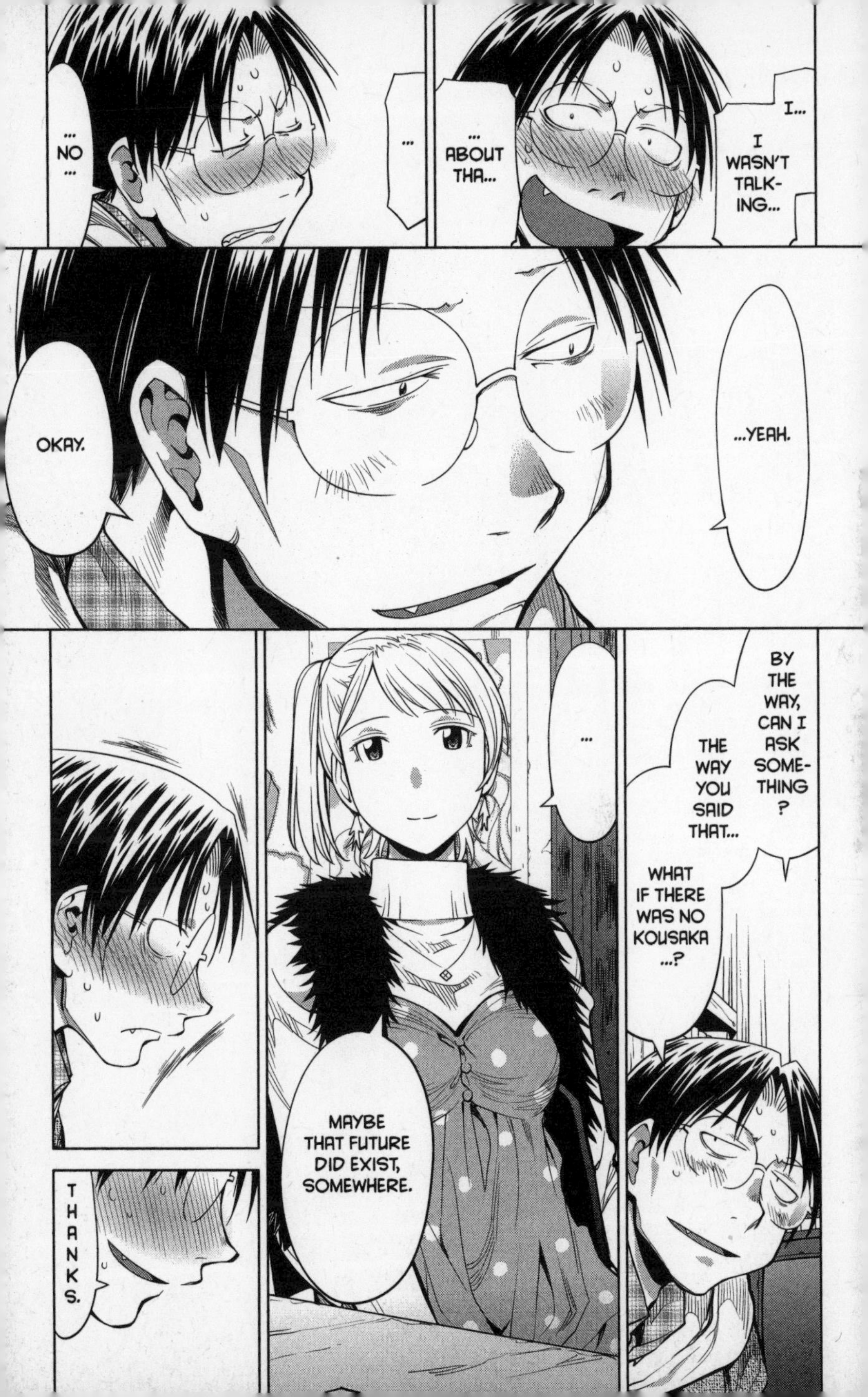
I...
I WASN'T TALKING...
... ABOUT THA...
...
... NO ...
...YEAH.
OKAY.
BY THE WAY, CAN I ASK SOMETHING?
THE WAY YOU SAID THAT...
WHAT IF THERE WAS NO KOUSAKA ...?
...
MAYBE THAT FUTURE DID EXIST, SOMEWHERE.
THANKS.

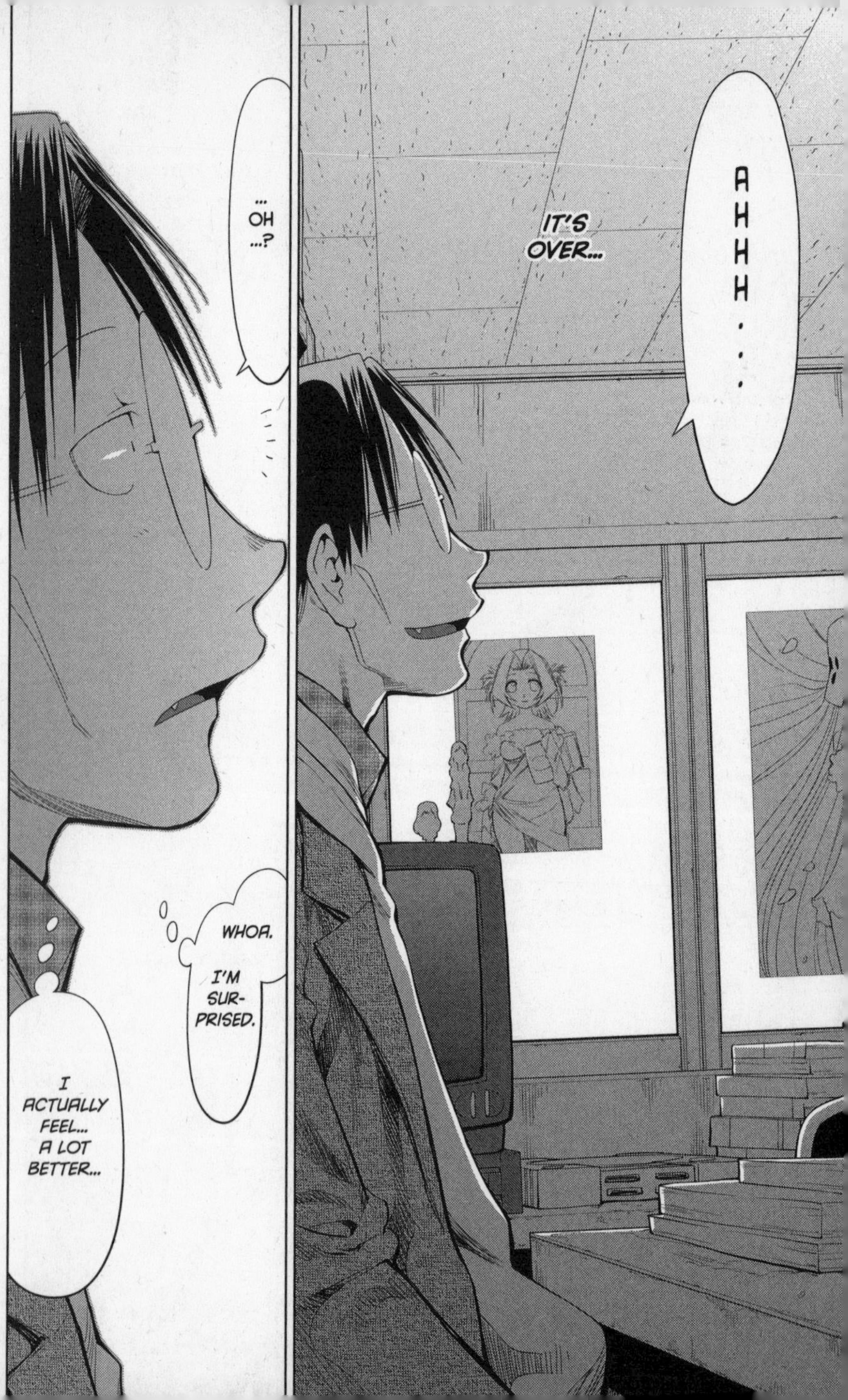
AHHH...
IT'S OVER...
...OH...?
WHOA.
I'M SURPRISED.
I ACTUALLY FEEL... A LOT BETTER...

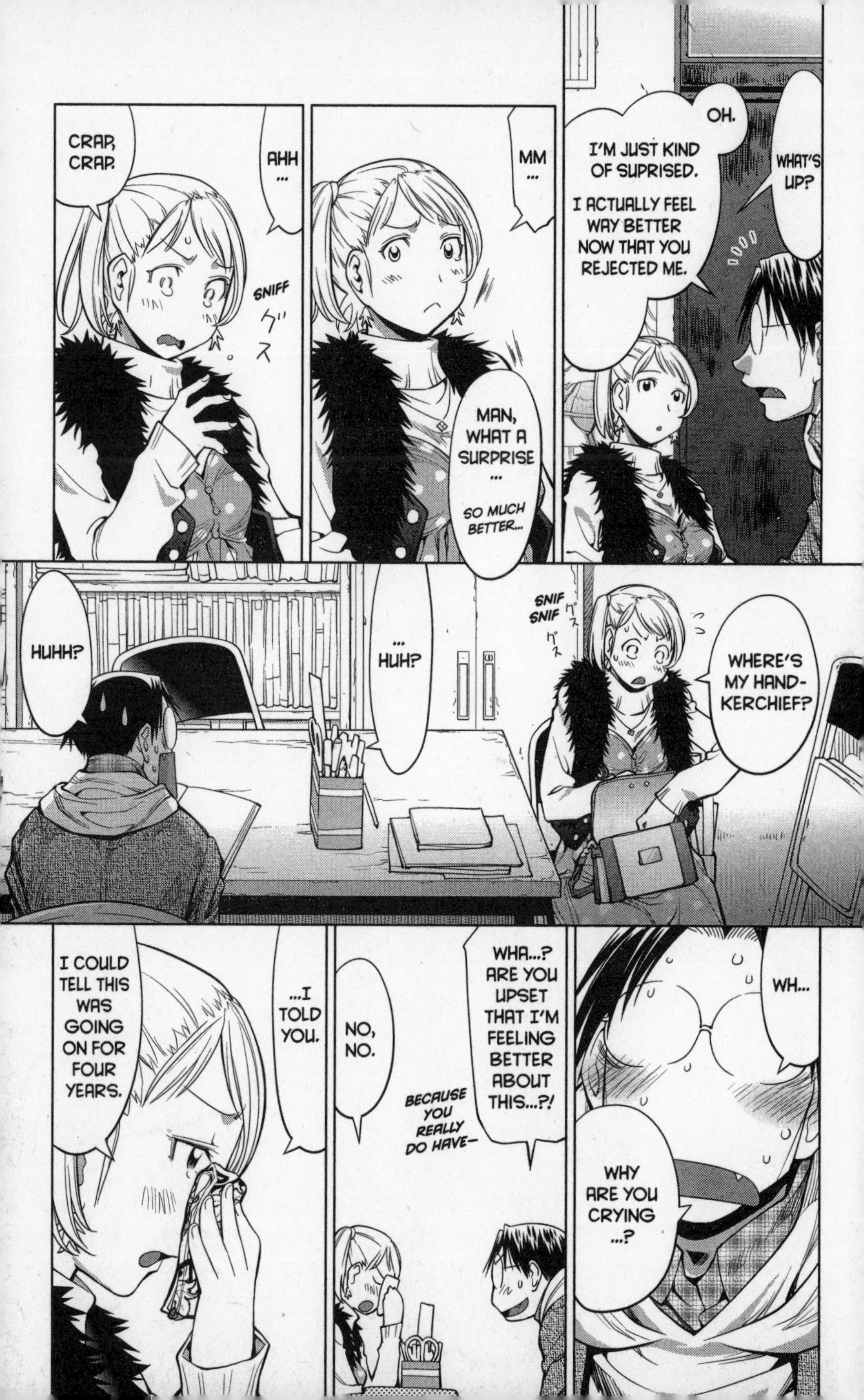
WHAT'S UP?
OH.
I'M JUST KIND OF SUPRISED.
I ACTUALLY FEEL WAY BETTER NOW THAT YOU REJECTED ME.
MM ...
MAN, WHAT A SURPRISE ...
SO MUCH BETTER...
AHH ...
CRAP, CRAP.
SNIFF
グス
WHERE'S MY HAND-KERCHIEF?
SNIF SNIF
グス グス
... HUH?
HUHH?
WH...
WHY ARE YOU CRYING ...?
WHA...? ARE YOU UPSET THAT I'M FEELING BETTER ABOUT THIS...?!
BECAUSE YOU REALLY DO HAVE-
NO, NO.
...I TOLD YOU.
I COULD TELL THIS WAS GOING ON FOR FOUR YEARS.

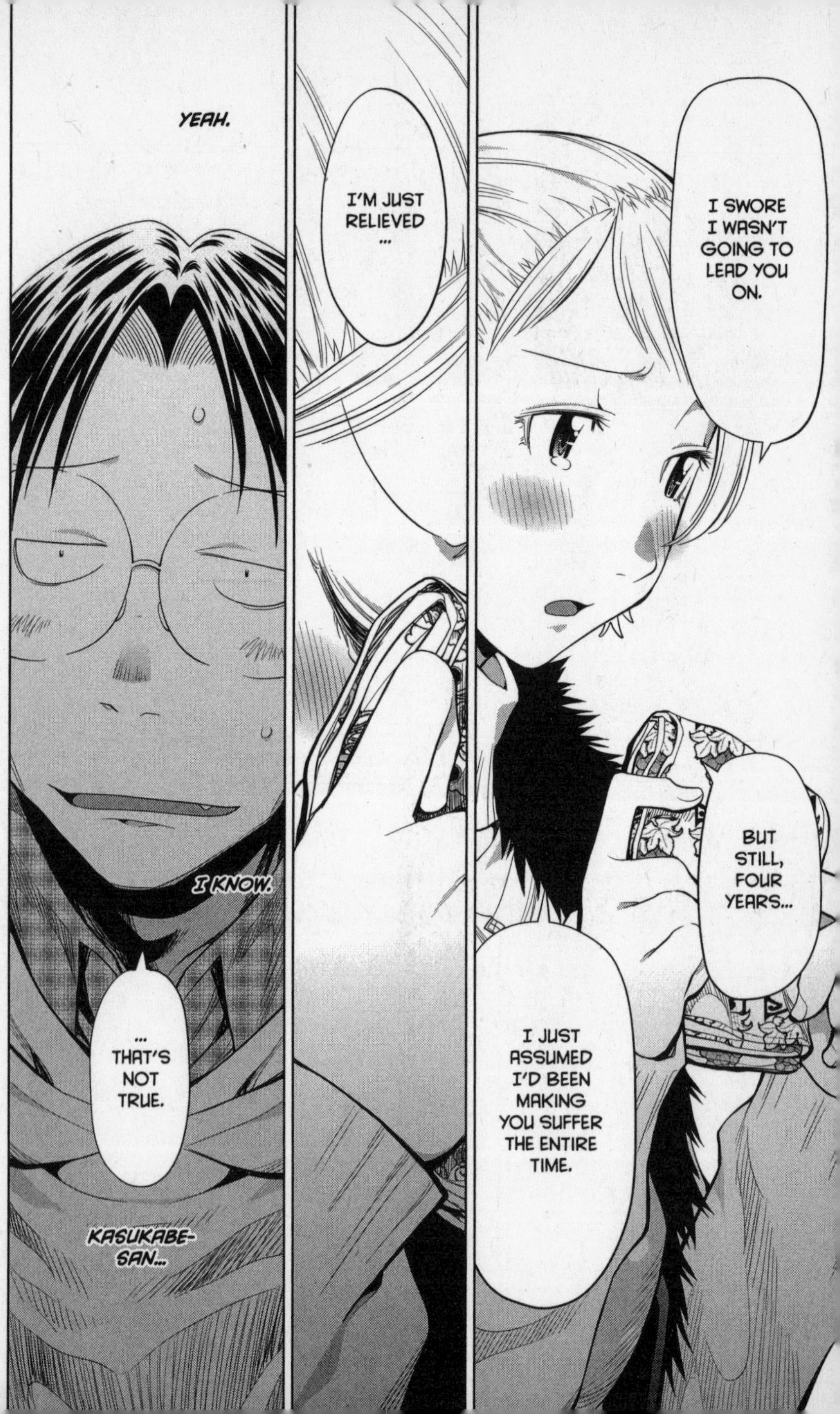
I SWORE I WASN'T GOING TO LEAD YOU ON.
BUT STILL, FOUR YEARS...
I JUST ASSUMED I'D BEEN MAKING YOU SUFFER THE ENTIRE TIME.
I'M JUST RELIEVED ...
YEAH.
I KNOW.
... THAT'S NOT TRUE.
KASUKABE-SAN...

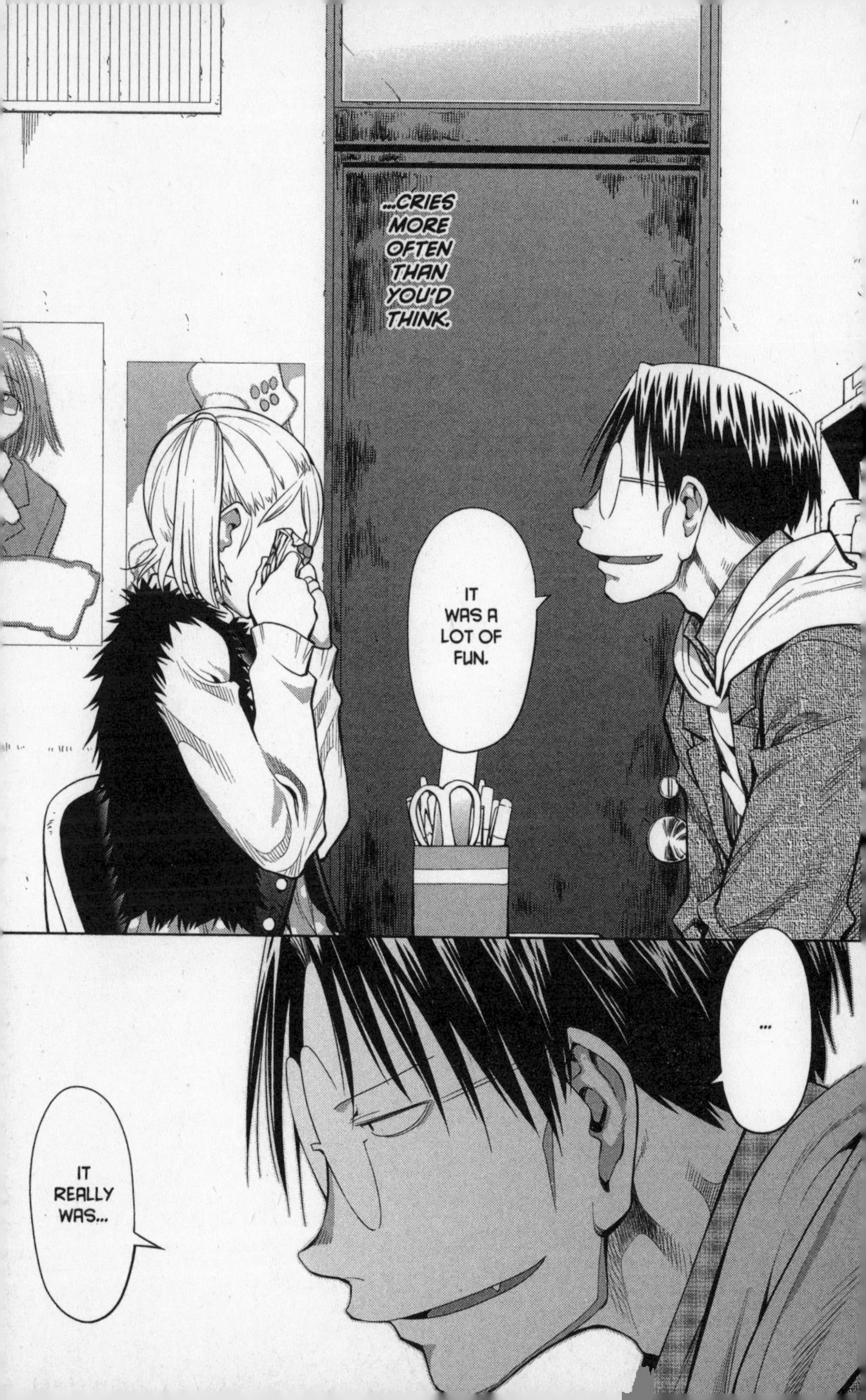
...CRIES MORE OFTEN THAN YOU'D THINK.
IT WAS A LOT OF FUN.
...
IT REALLY WAS...

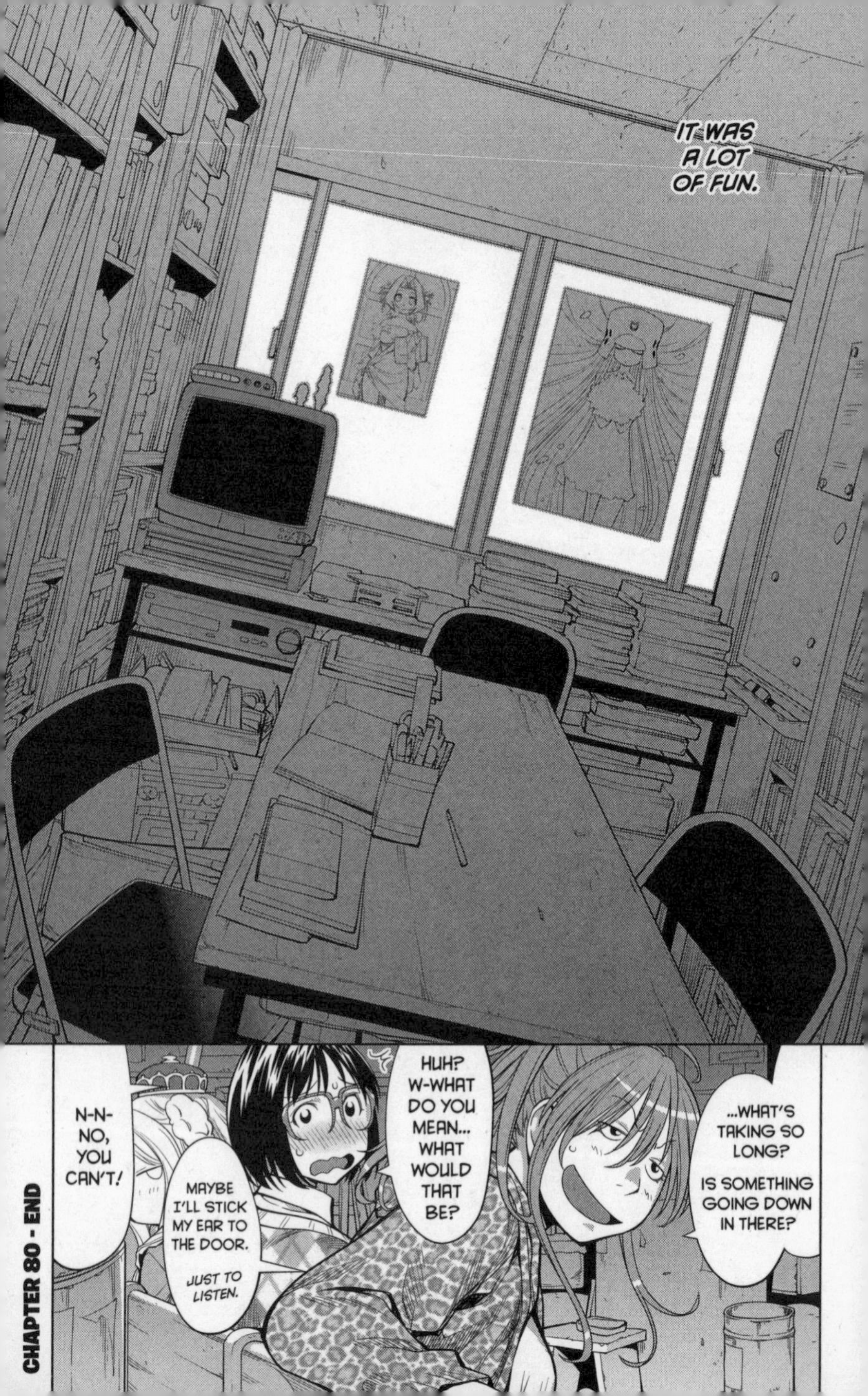
IT WAS A LOT OF FUN.
...WHAT'S TAKING SO LONG?
IS SOMETHING GOING DOWN IN THERE?
HUH? W-WHAT DO YOU MEAN... WHAT WOULD THAT BE?
MAYBE I'LL STICK MY EAR TO THE DOOR.
JUST TO LISTEN.
N-N-NO, YOU CAN'T!

CHAPTER 80 - END

BACK ON YOUR FEET

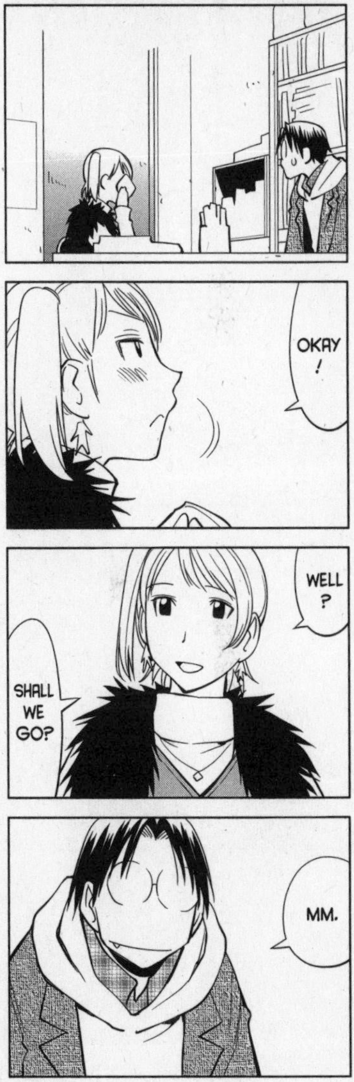
OKAY!
WELL?
SHALL WE GO?
MM.

UP ON YOUR FEET

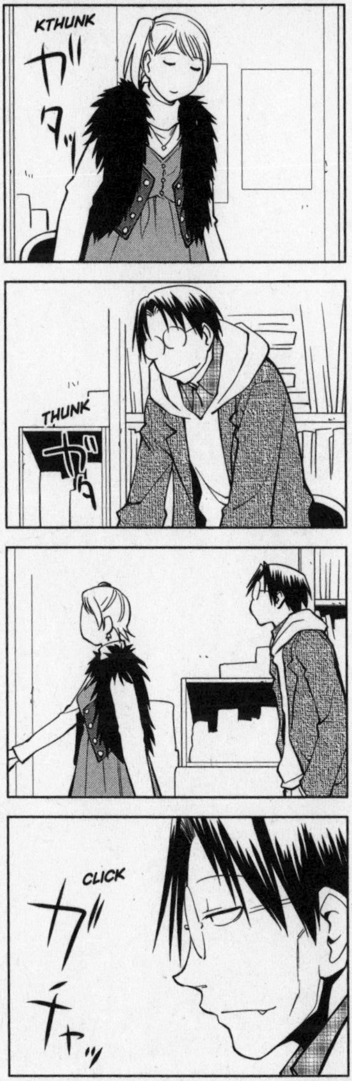
KTHUNK
THUNK
CLICK

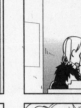

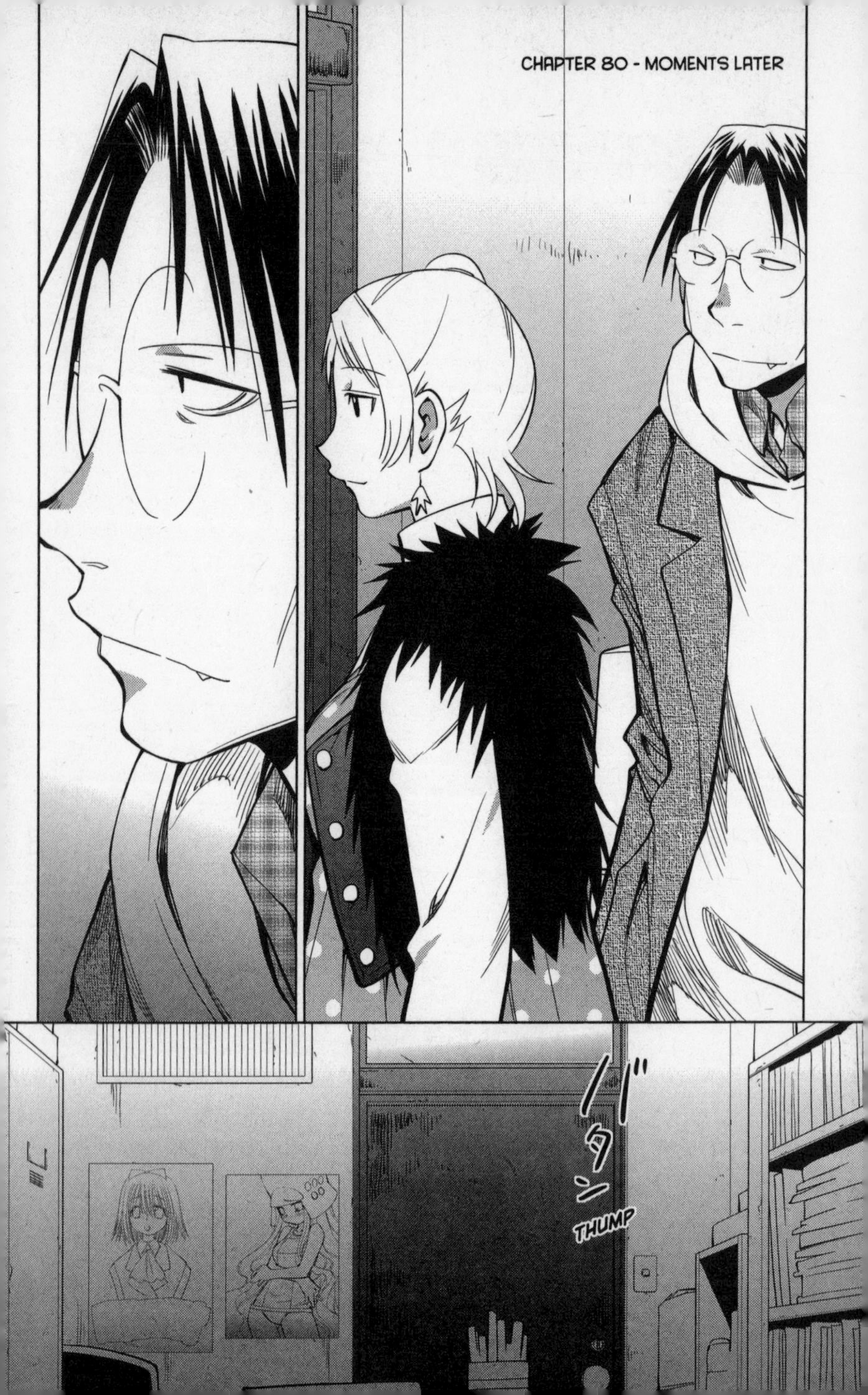
CHAPTER 80 - MOMENTS LATER
バタン
THUMP

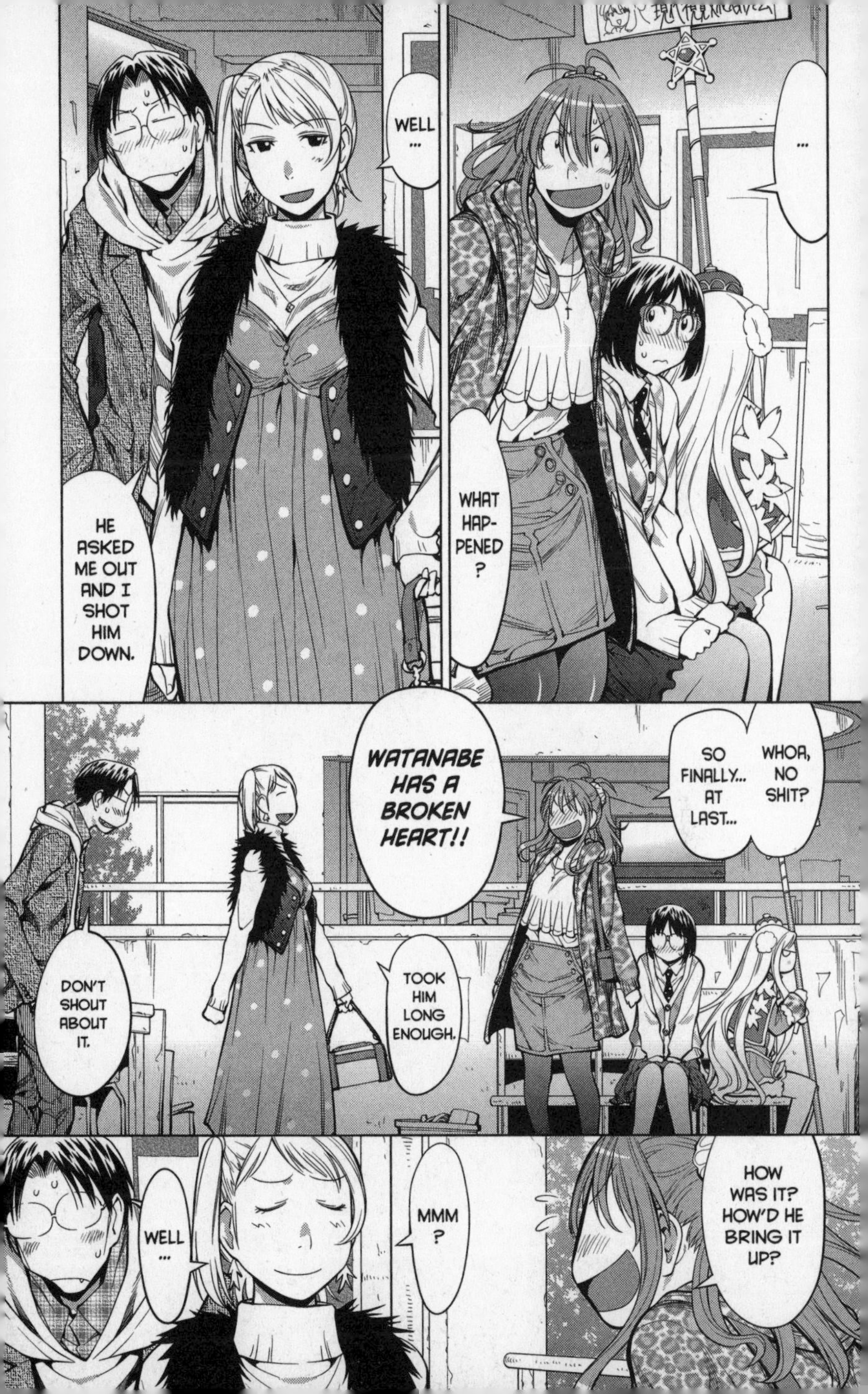
...
WHAT HAPPENED?
WELL ...
HE ASKED ME OUT AND I SHOT HIM DOWN.
WHOA, NO SHIT?
SO FINALLY... AT LAST...
WATANABE HAS A BROKEN HEART!!
TOOK HIM LONG ENOUGH.
DON'T SHOUT ABOUT IT.
HOW WAS IT? HOW'D HE BRING IT UP?
MMM ?
WELL ...

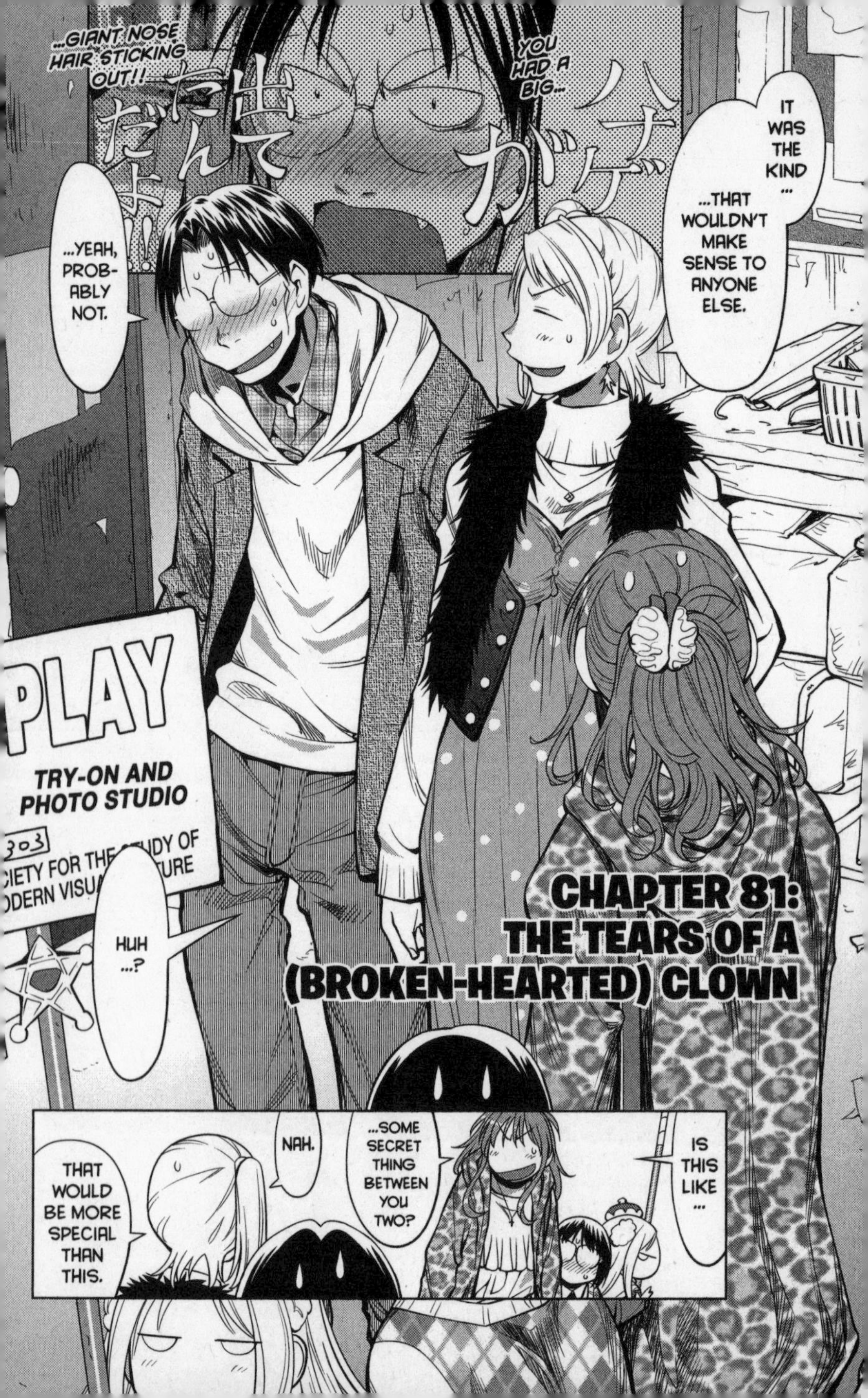
YOU HAD A BIG...
...GIANT NOSE HAIR STICKING OUT!!
IT WAS THE KIND ...
...THAT WOULDN'T MAKE SENSE TO ANYONE ELSE.
...YEAH, PROBABLY NOT.
PLAY
TRY-ON AND PHOTO STUDIO
303
CIETY FOR THE STUDY OF
DERN VISUA TURE
CHAPTER 81: THE TEARS OF A (BROKEN-HEARTED) CLOWN
HUH ...?
IS THIS LIKE ...
...SOME SECRET THING BETWEEN YOU TWO?
NAH.
THAT WOULD BE MORE SPECIAL THAN THIS.

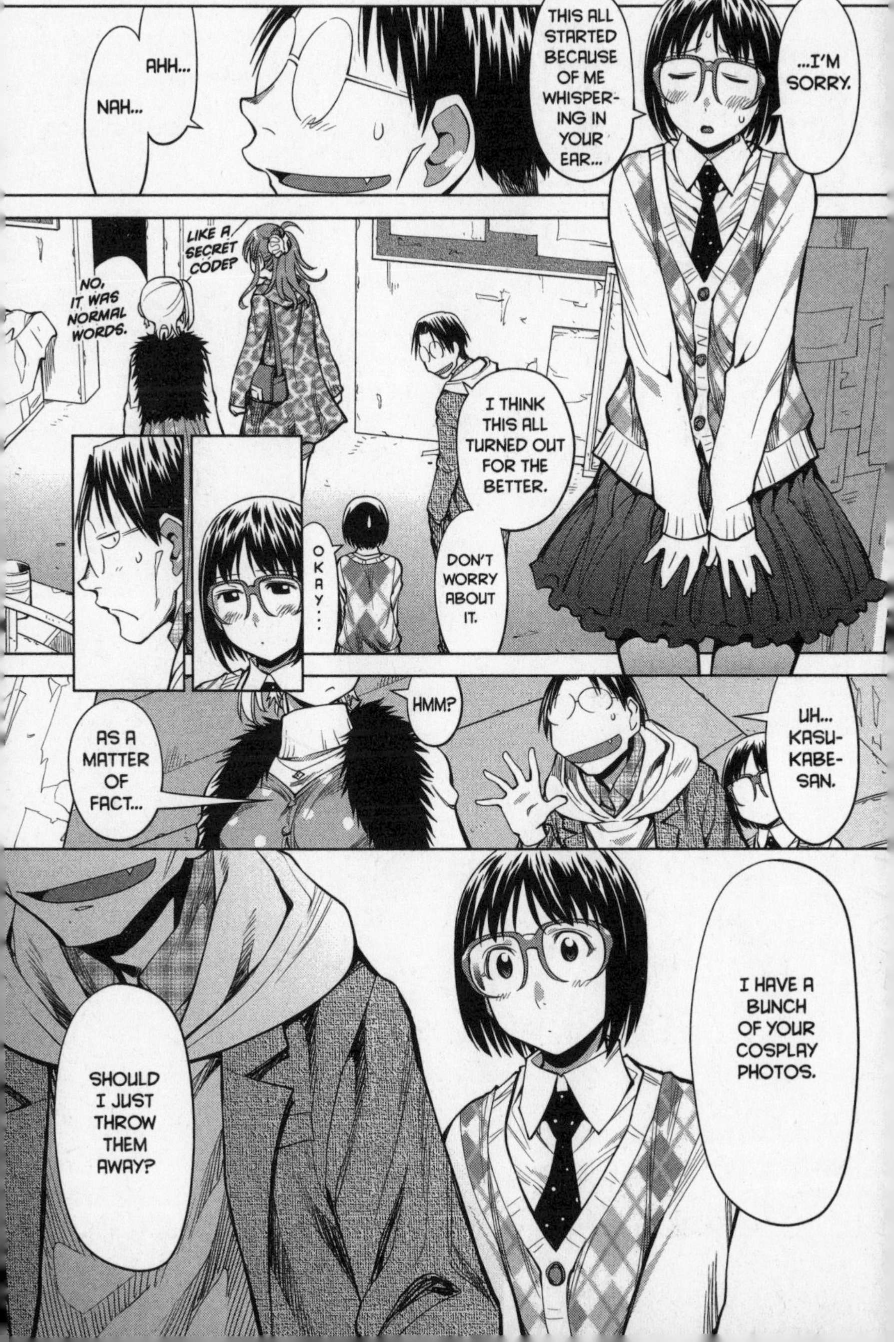
...I'M SORRY.
THIS ALL STARTED BECAUSE OF ME WHISPERING IN YOUR EAR...
AHH... NAH...
I THINK THIS ALL TURNED OUT FOR THE BETTER.
DON'T WORRY ABOUT IT.
OKAY...
LIKE A SECRET CODE?
NO, IT WAS NORMAL WORDS.
UH... KASUKABE-SAN.
HMM?
AS A MATTER OF FACT...
I HAVE A BUNCH OF YOUR COSPLAY PHOTOS.
SHOULD I JUST THROW THEM AWAY?

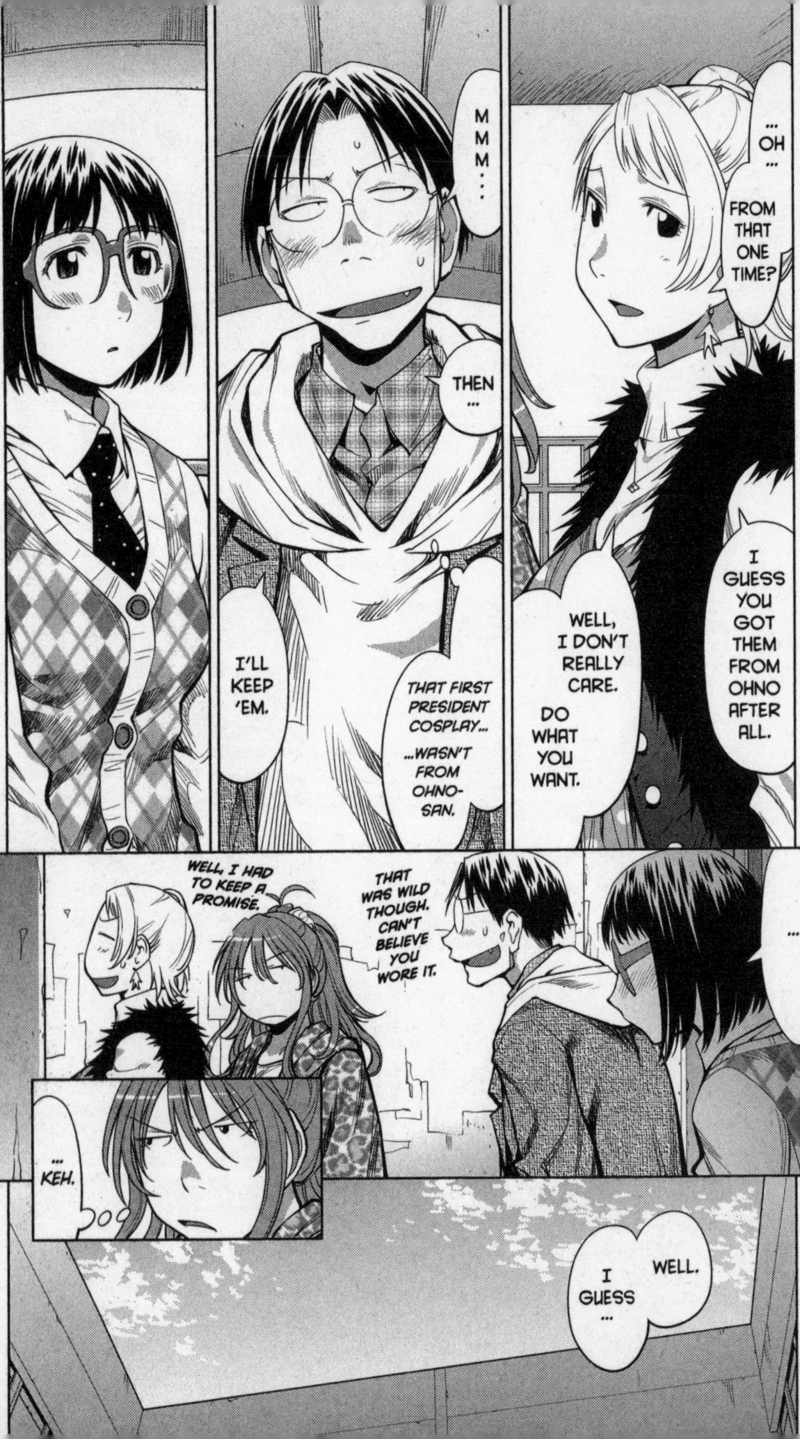
...OH...
FROM THAT ONE TIME?
I GUESS YOU GOT THEM FROM OHNO AFTER ALL.
WELL, I DON'T REALLY CARE.
DO WHAT YOU WANT.
MMM...
THEN...
THAT FIRST PRESIDENT COSPLAY...
...WASN'T FROM OHNO-SAN.
I'LL KEEP 'EM.
...
THAT WAS WILD THOUGH. CAN'T BELIEVE YOU WORE IT.
WELL, I HAD TO KEEP A PROMISE.
...KEH.
WELL.
I GUESS...

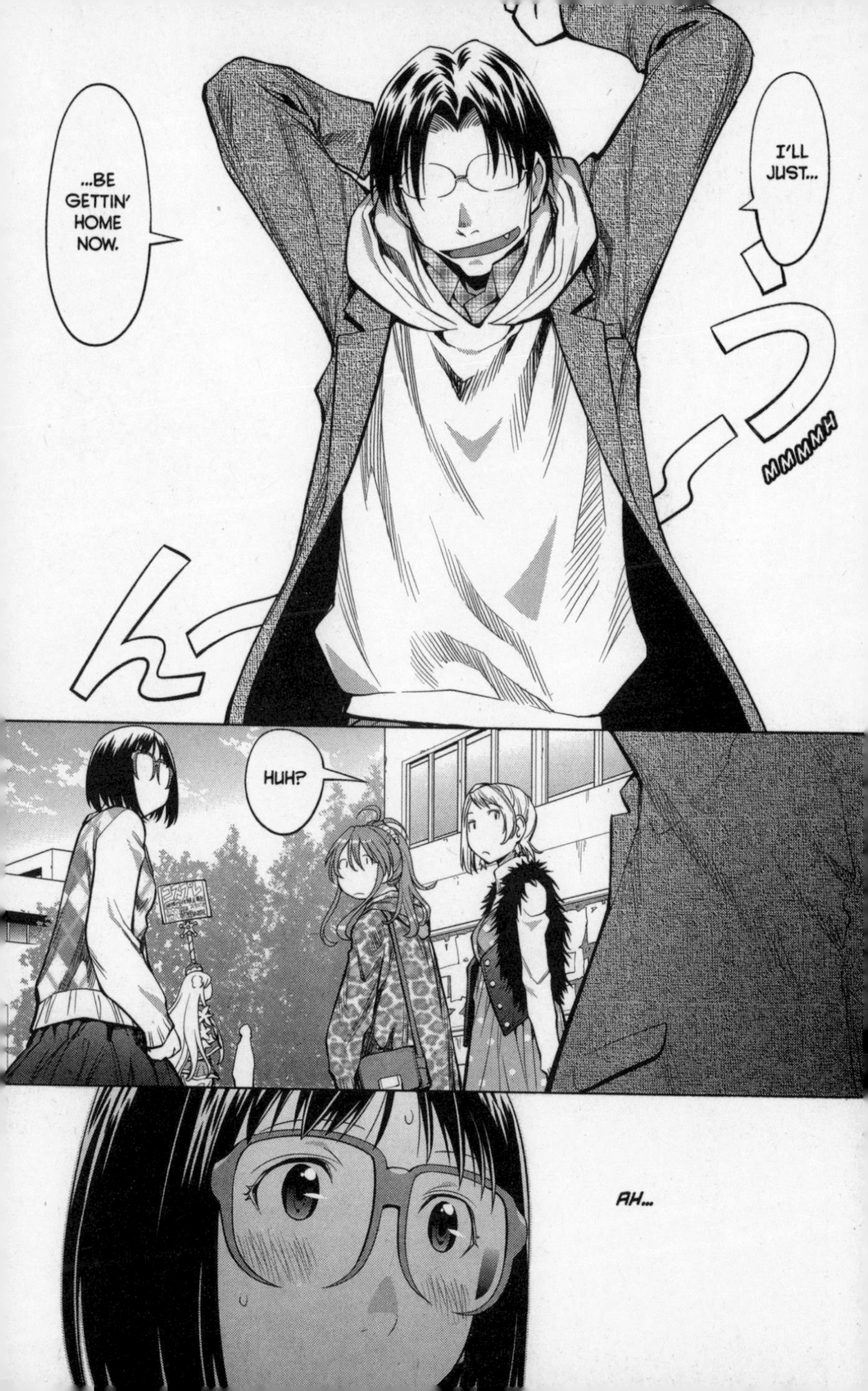
I'LL JUST...
...BE GETTIN' HOME NOW.
MMMMH
HUH?
AH...

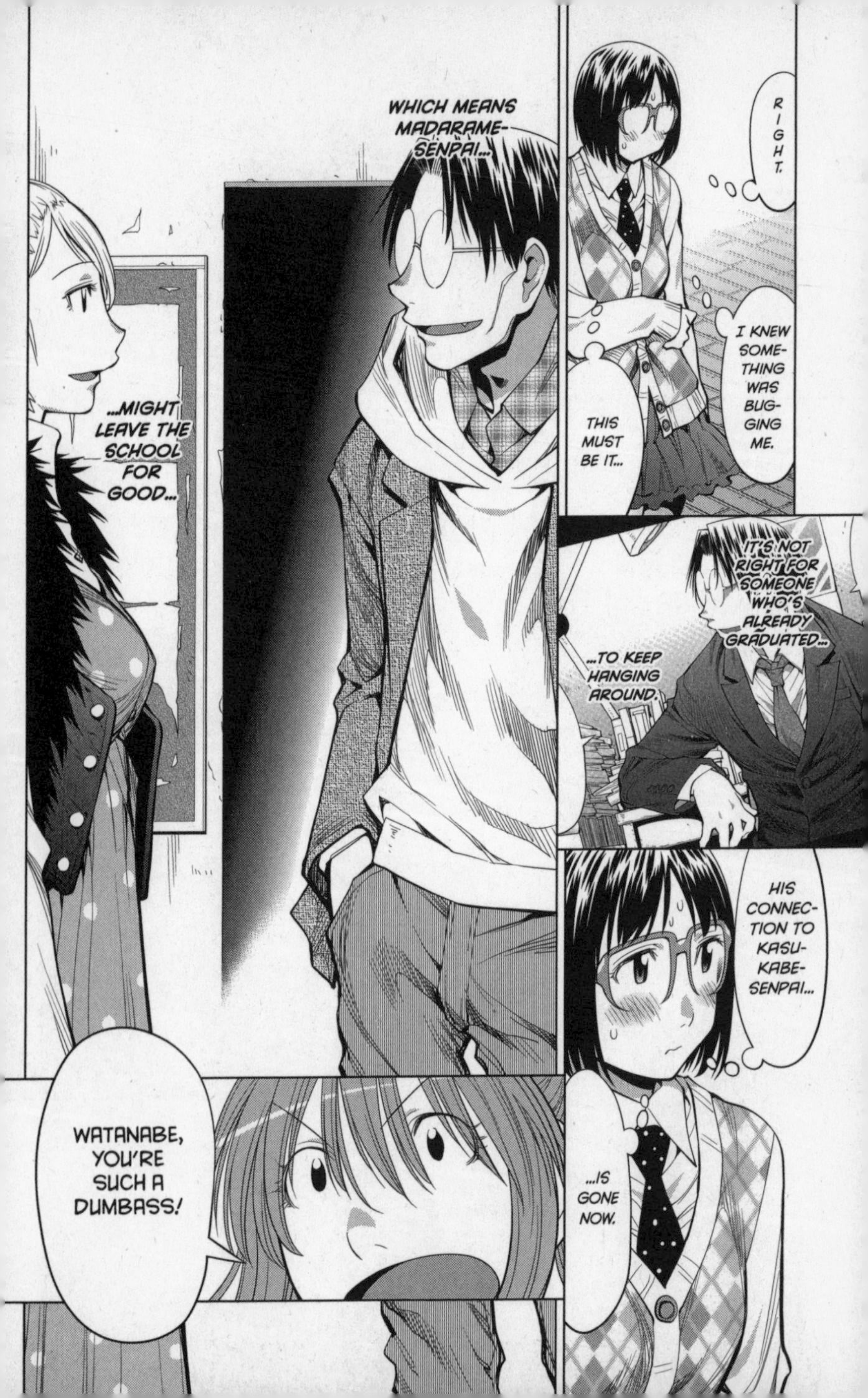
RIGHT.
I KNEW SOMETHING WAS BUGGING ME.
THIS MUST BE IT...
IT'S NOT RIGHT FOR SOMEONE WHO'S ALREADY GRADUATED...
...TO KEEP HANGING AROUND.
HIS CONNECTION TO KASUKABE-SENPAI...
...IS GONE NOW.
WHICH MEANS MADARAME-SENPAI...
...MIGHT LEAVE THE SCHOOL FOR GOOD...
WATANABE, YOU'RE SUCH A DUMBASS!

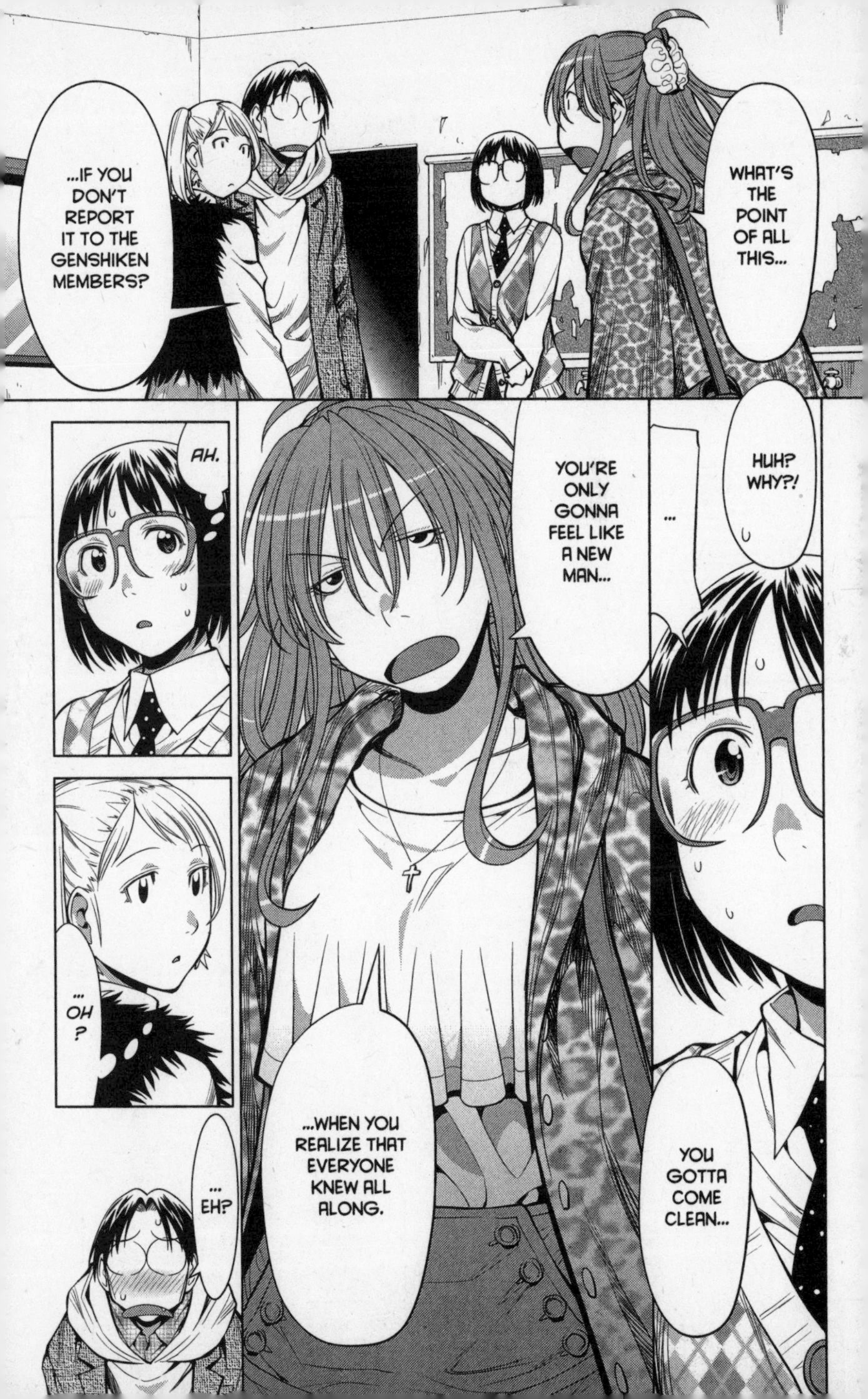
WHAT'S THE POINT OF ALL THIS...
...IF YOU DON'T REPORT IT TO THE GENSHIKEN MEMBERS?
HUH? WHY?!
...
YOU GOTTA COME CLEAN...
YOU'RE ONLY GONNA FEEL LIKE A NEW MAN...
...WHEN YOU REALIZE THAT EVERYONE KNEW ALL ALONG.
AH.
...OH?
...EH?

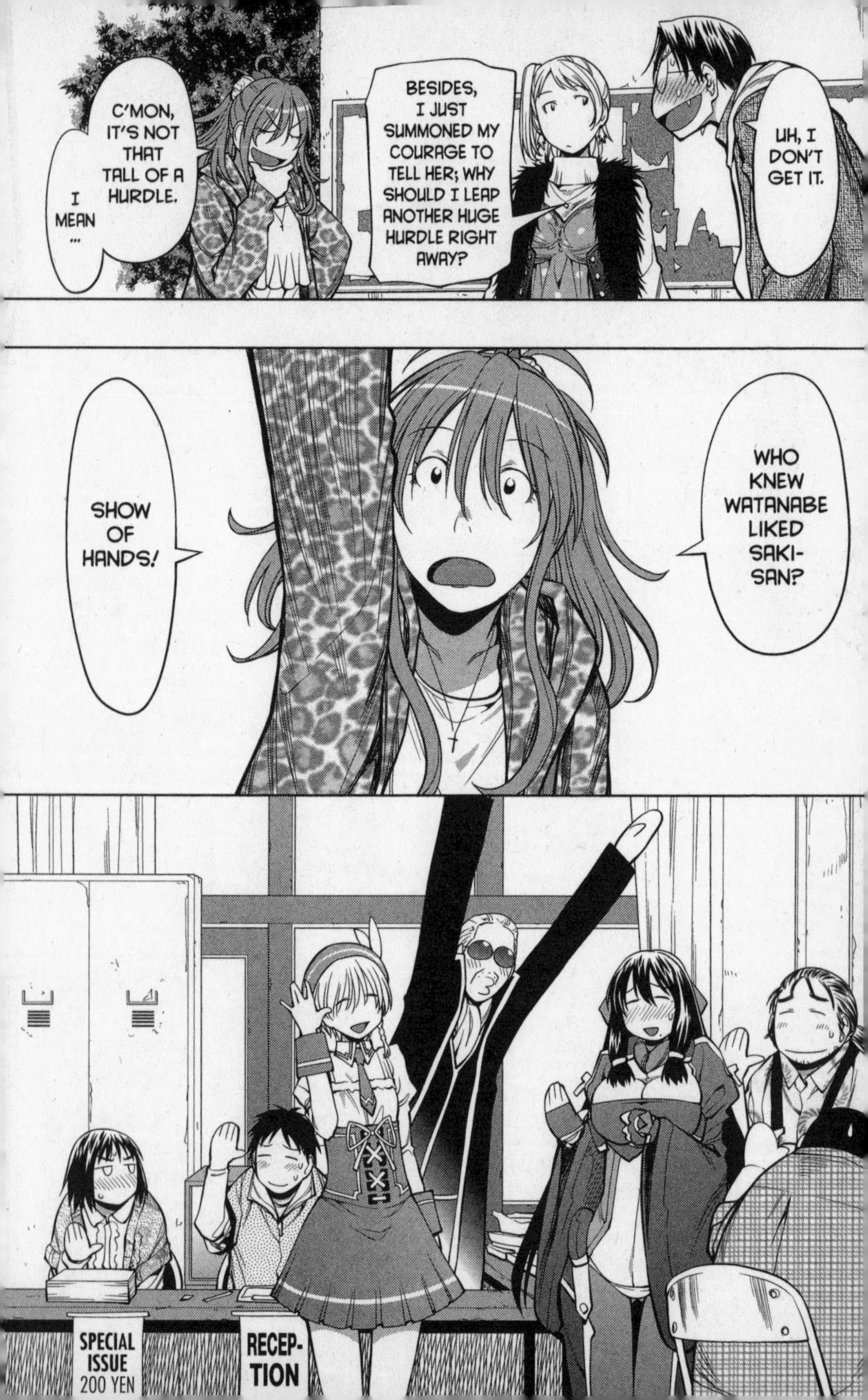
UH, I DON'T GET IT.
BESIDES, I JUST SUMMONED MY COURAGE TO TELL HER; WHY SHOULD I LEAP ANOTHER HUGE HURDLE RIGHT AWAY?
C'MON, IT'S NOT THAT TALL OF A HURDLE.
I MEAN ...
WHO KNEW WATANABE LIKED SAKI-SAN?
SHOW OF HANDS!
RECEP-TION
SPECIAL ISSUE 200 YEN

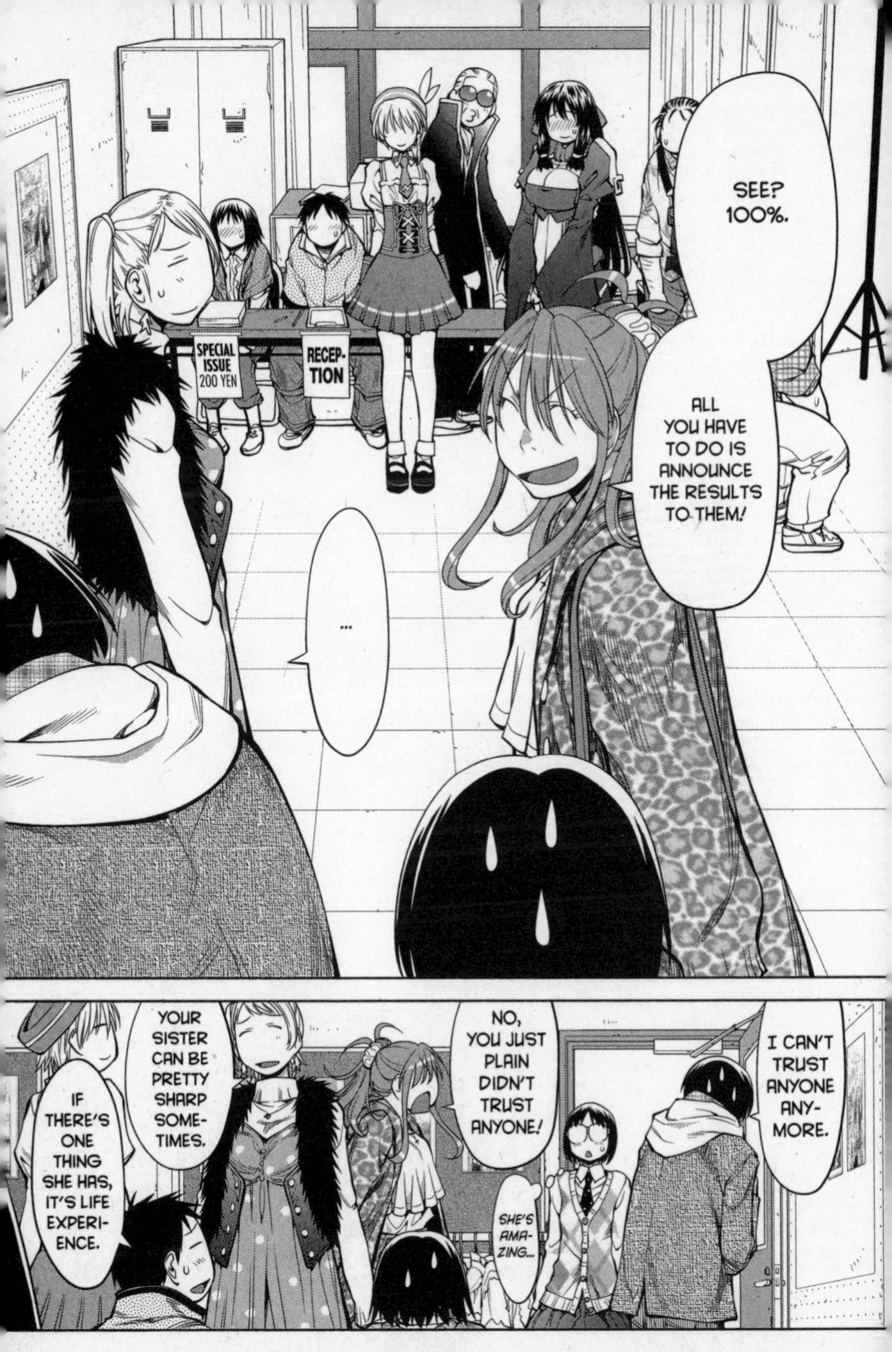
SPECIAL ISSUE 200 YEN
RECEPTION
SEE? 100%.
ALL YOU HAVE TO DO IS ANNOUNCE THE RESULTS TO THEM!
...
I CAN'T TRUST ANYONE ANYMORE.
NO, YOU JUST PLAIN DIDN'T TRUST ANYONE!
SHE'S AMAZING...
YOUR SISTER CAN BE PRETTY SHARP SOMETIMES.
IF THERE'S ONE THING SHE HAS, IT'S LIFE EXPERIENCE.

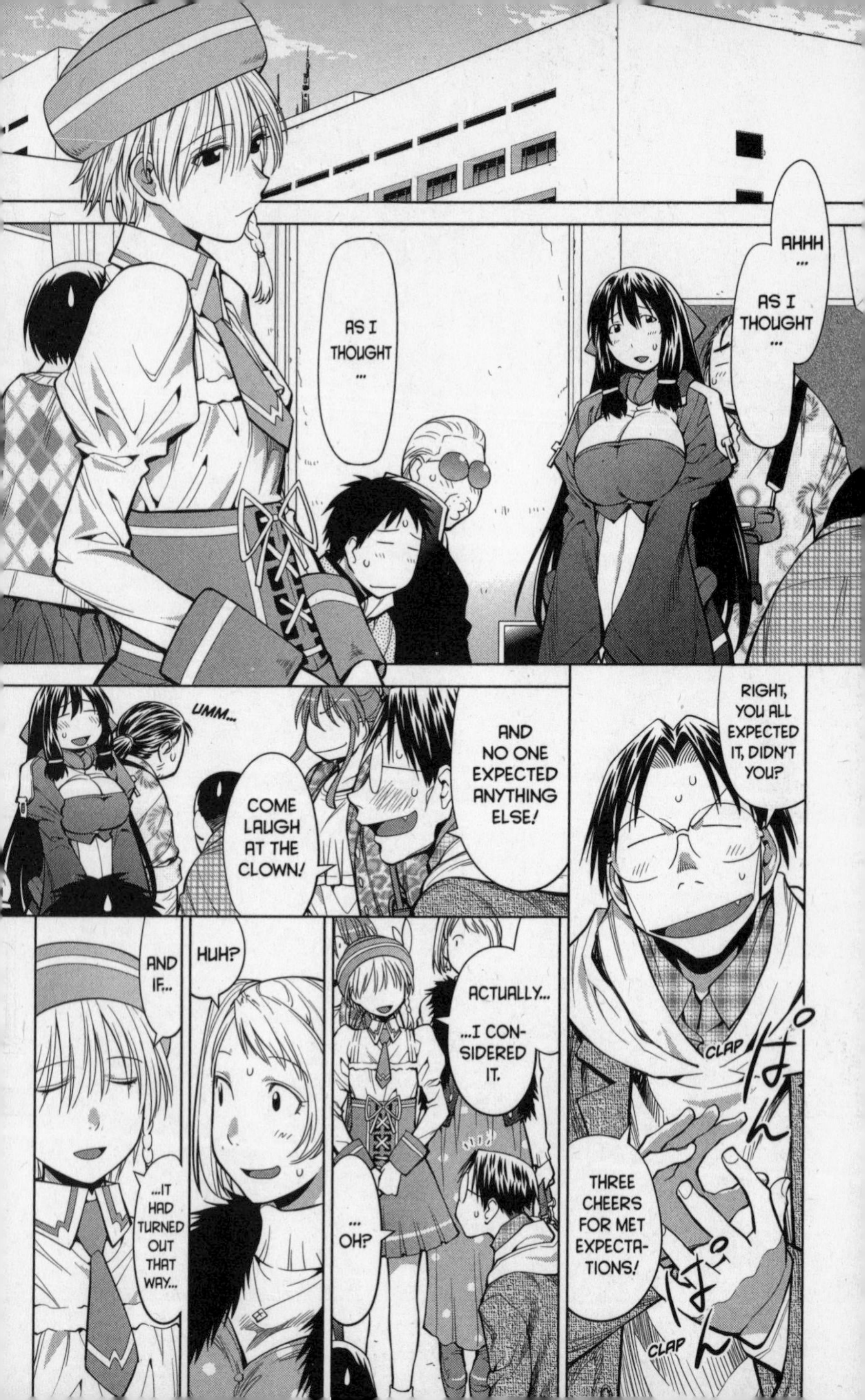
AHHH ... AS I THOUGHT ...
AS I THOUGHT ...
RIGHT, YOU ALL EXPECTED IT, DIDN'T YOU?
CLAP
ぱん
THREE CHEERS FOR MET EXPECTA-TIONS!
CLAP
ぱん
AND NO ONE EXPECTED ANYTHING ELSE!
COME LAUGH AT THE CLOWN!
UMM...
ACTUALLY...
...I CON-SIDERED IT.
... OH?
HUH?
AND IF...
...IT HAD TURNED OUT THAT WAY...

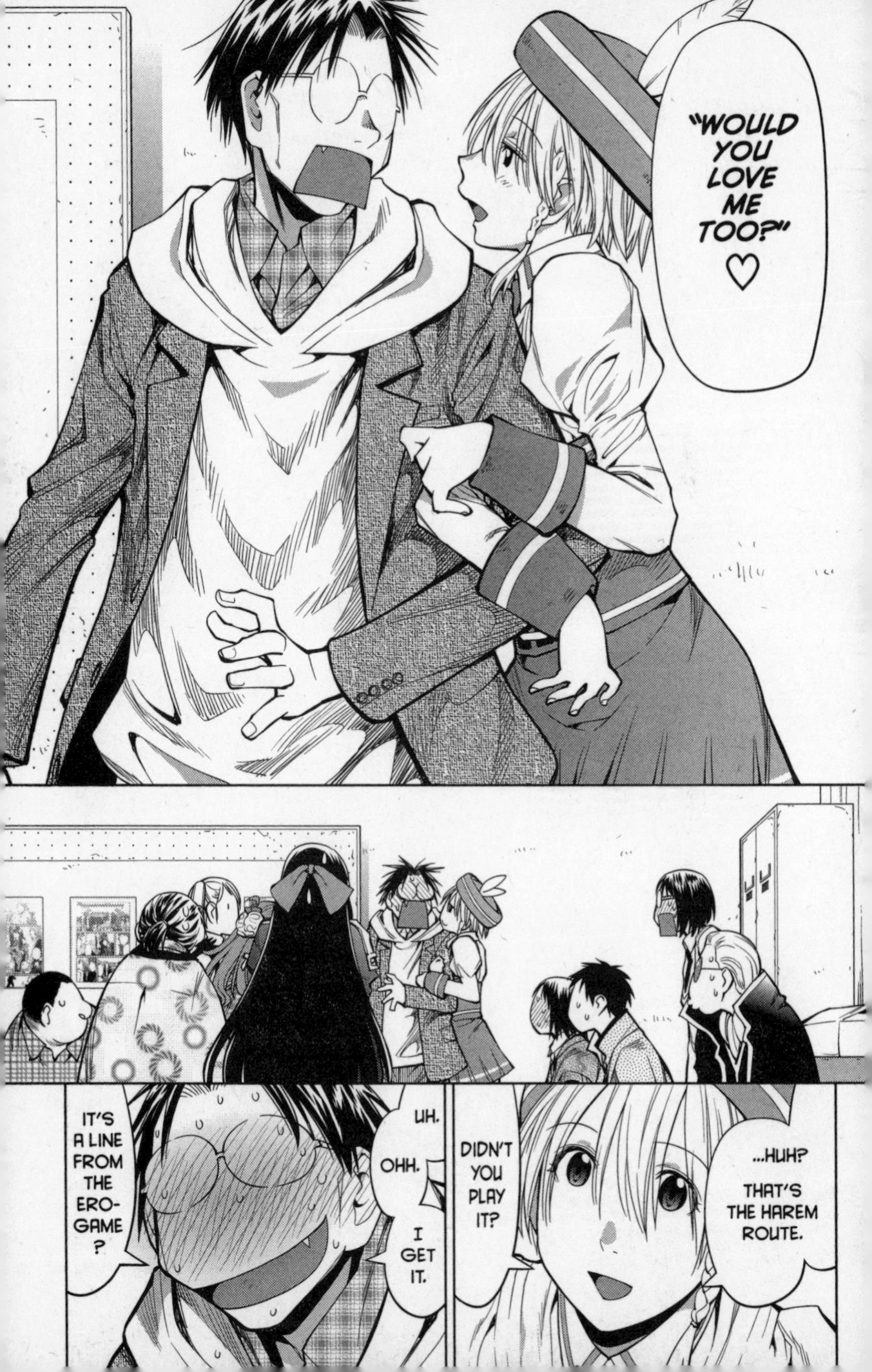
"WOULD YOU LOVE ME TOO?" ♡
...HUH? THAT'S THE HAREM ROUTE.
DIDN'T YOU PLAY IT?
UH.
OHH.
I GET IT.
IT'S A LINE FROM THE ERO-GAME?

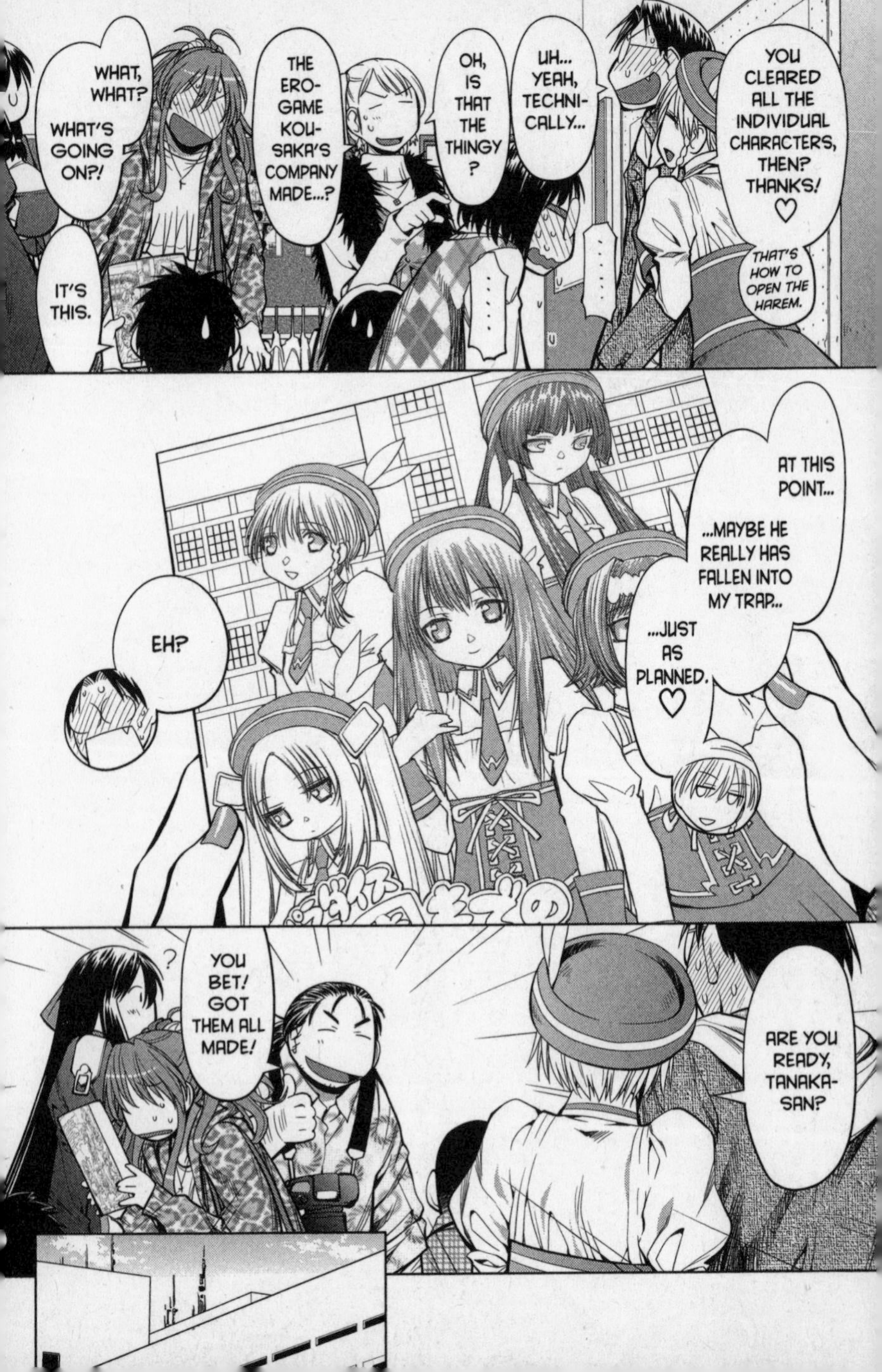
YOU CLEARED ALL THE INDIVIDUAL CHARACTERS, THEN? THANKS! ♡
THAT'S HOW TO OPEN THE HAREM.
UH... YEAH, TECHNICALLY...
OH, IS THAT THE THINGY?
THE ERO-GAME KOUSAKA'S COMPANY MADE...?
WHAT, WHAT?
WHAT'S GOING ON?!
IT'S THIS.
AT THIS POINT...
...MAYBE HE REALLY HAS FALLEN INTO MY TRAP...
...JUST AS PLANNED. ♡
EH?
ARE YOU READY, TANAKA-SAN?
YOU BET! GOT THEM ALL MADE!
?

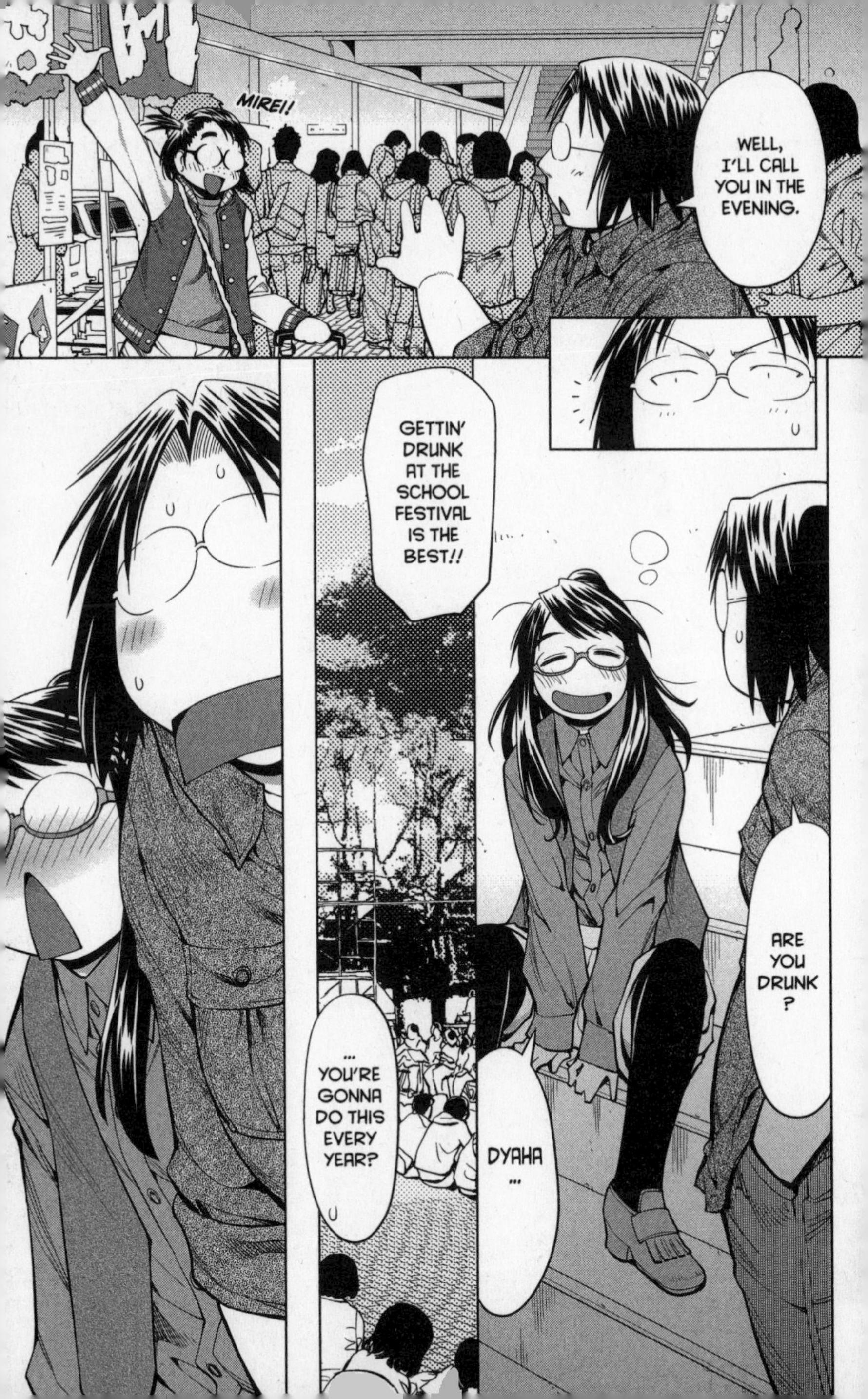
WELL, I'LL CALL YOU IN THE EVENING.
MIREI!
ARE YOU DRUNK ?
DYAHA ...
GETTIN' DRUNK AT THE SCHOOL FESTIVAL IS THE BEST!!
... YOU'RE GONNA DO THIS EVERY YEAR?

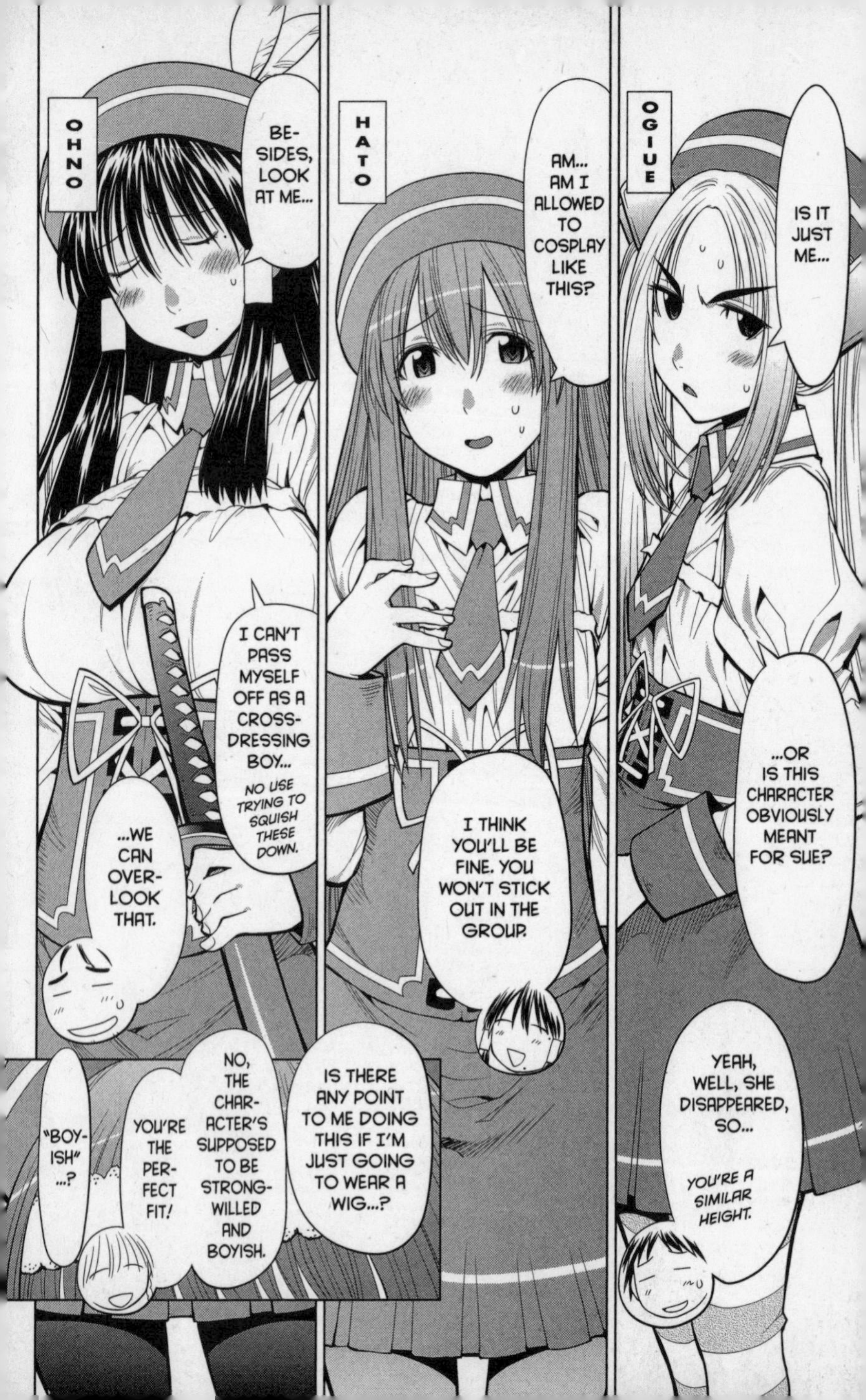
OGIUE
IS IT JUST ME...
...OR IS THIS CHARACTER OBVIOUSLY MEANT FOR SUE?
YEAH, WELL, SHE DISAPPEARED, SO...
YOU'RE A SIMILAR HEIGHT.
HATO
AM... AM I ALLOWED TO COSPLAY LIKE THIS?
I THINK YOU'LL BE FINE. YOU WON'T STICK OUT IN THE GROUP.
OHNO
BE-SIDES, LOOK AT ME...
I CAN'T PASS MYSELF OFF AS A CROSS-DRESSING BOY...
NO USE TRYING TO SQUISH THESE DOWN.
...WE CAN OVER-LOOK THAT.
IS THERE ANY POINT TO ME DOING THIS IF I'M JUST GOING TO WEAR A WIG...?
NO, THE CHAR-ACTER'S SUPPOSED TO BE STRONG-WILLED AND BOYISH.
YOU'RE THE PER-FECT FIT!
"BOY-ISH" ...?

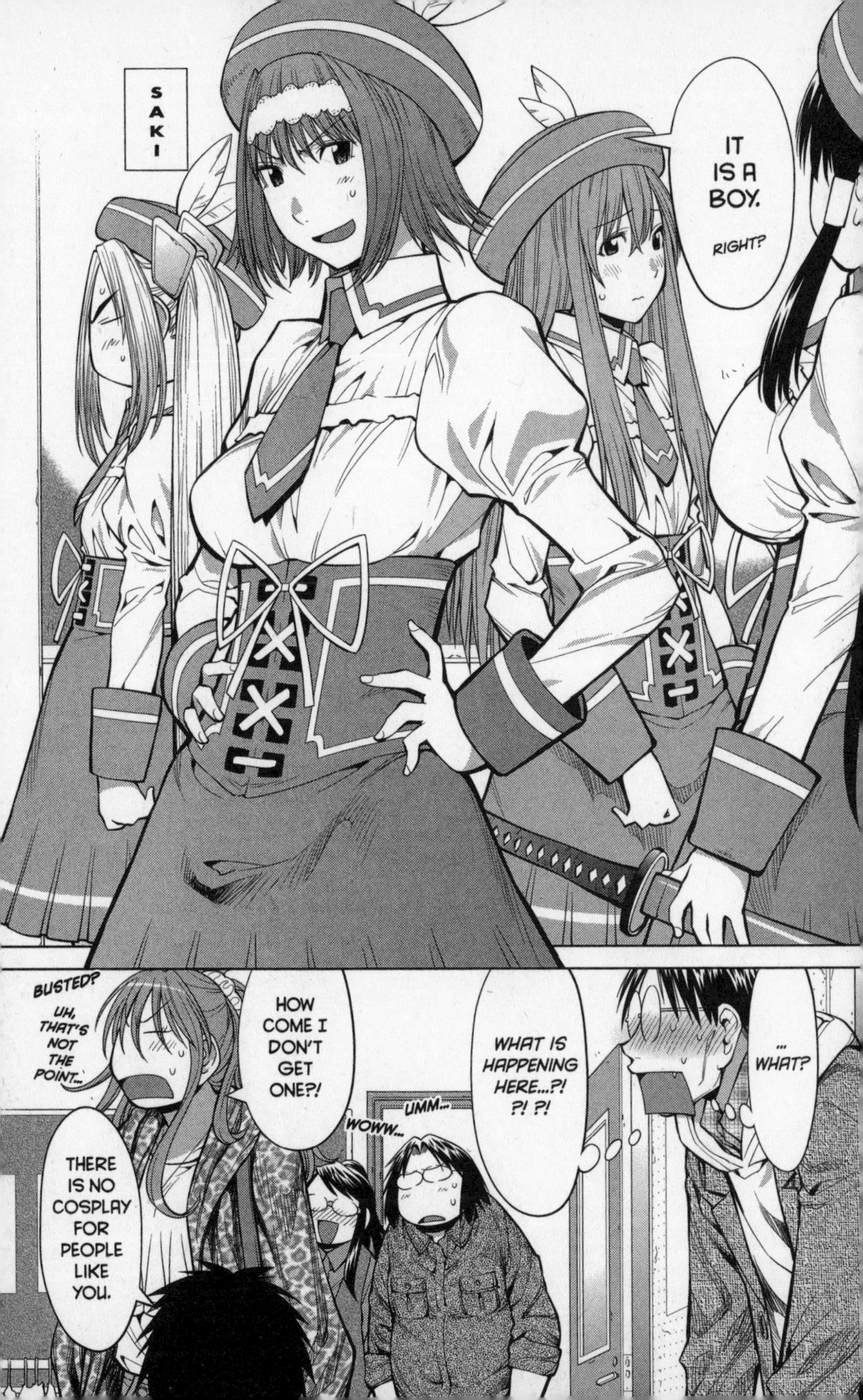
IT IS A BOY.
RIGHT?
SAKI
... WHAT?
WHAT IS HAPPENING HERE...?! ?! ?!
UMM...
WOWW...
HOW COME I DON'T GET ONE?!
BUSTED?
UH, THAT'S NOT THE POINT...
THERE IS NO COSPLAY FOR PEOPLE LIKE YOU.

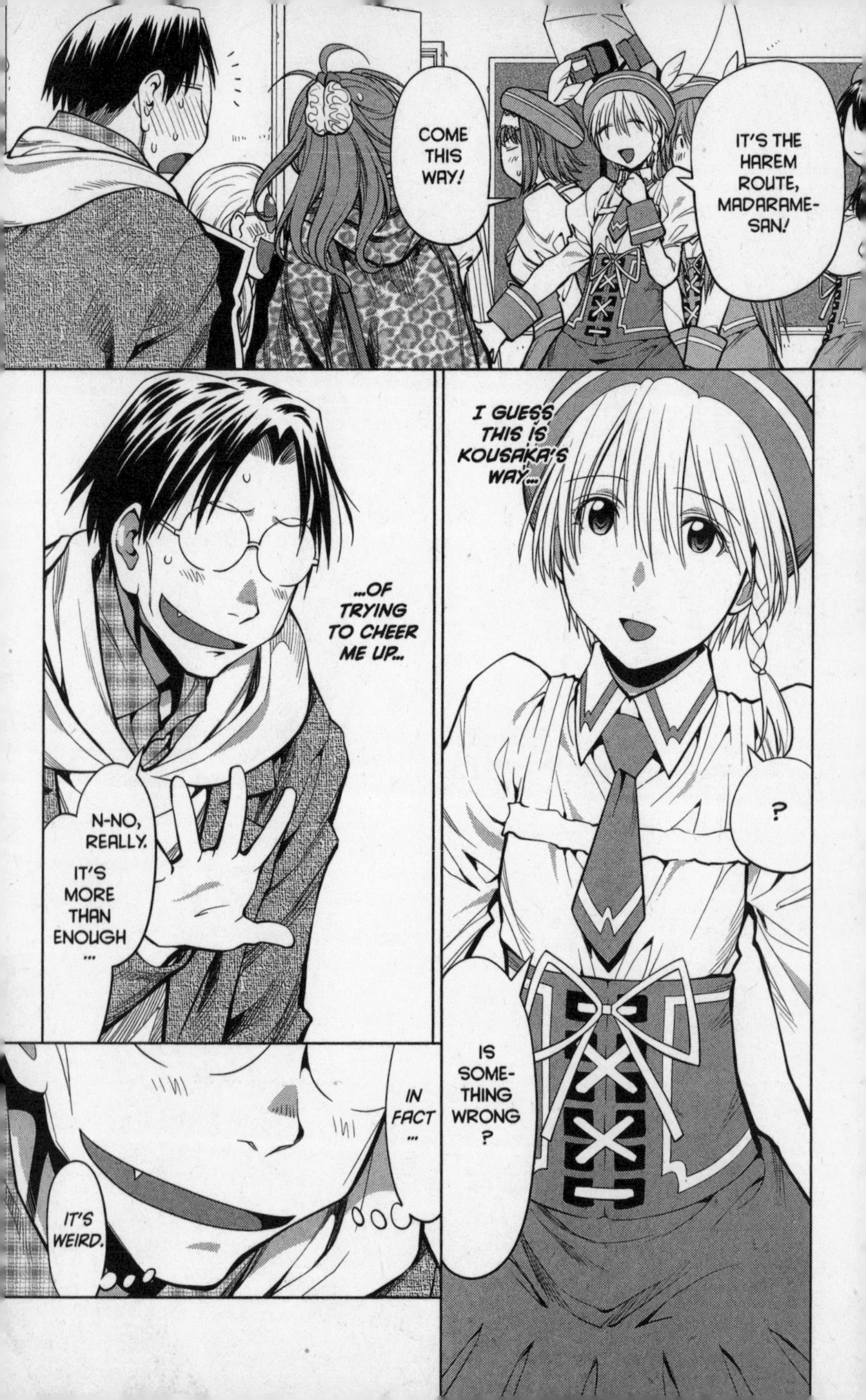
IT'S THE HAREM ROUTE, MADARAME-SAN!
COME THIS WAY!
I GUESS THIS IS KOUSAKA'S WAY...
?
IS SOMETHING WRONG?
...OF TRYING TO CHEER ME UP...
N-NO, REALLY.
IT'S MORE THAN ENOUGH...
IN FACT...
IT'S WEIRD.

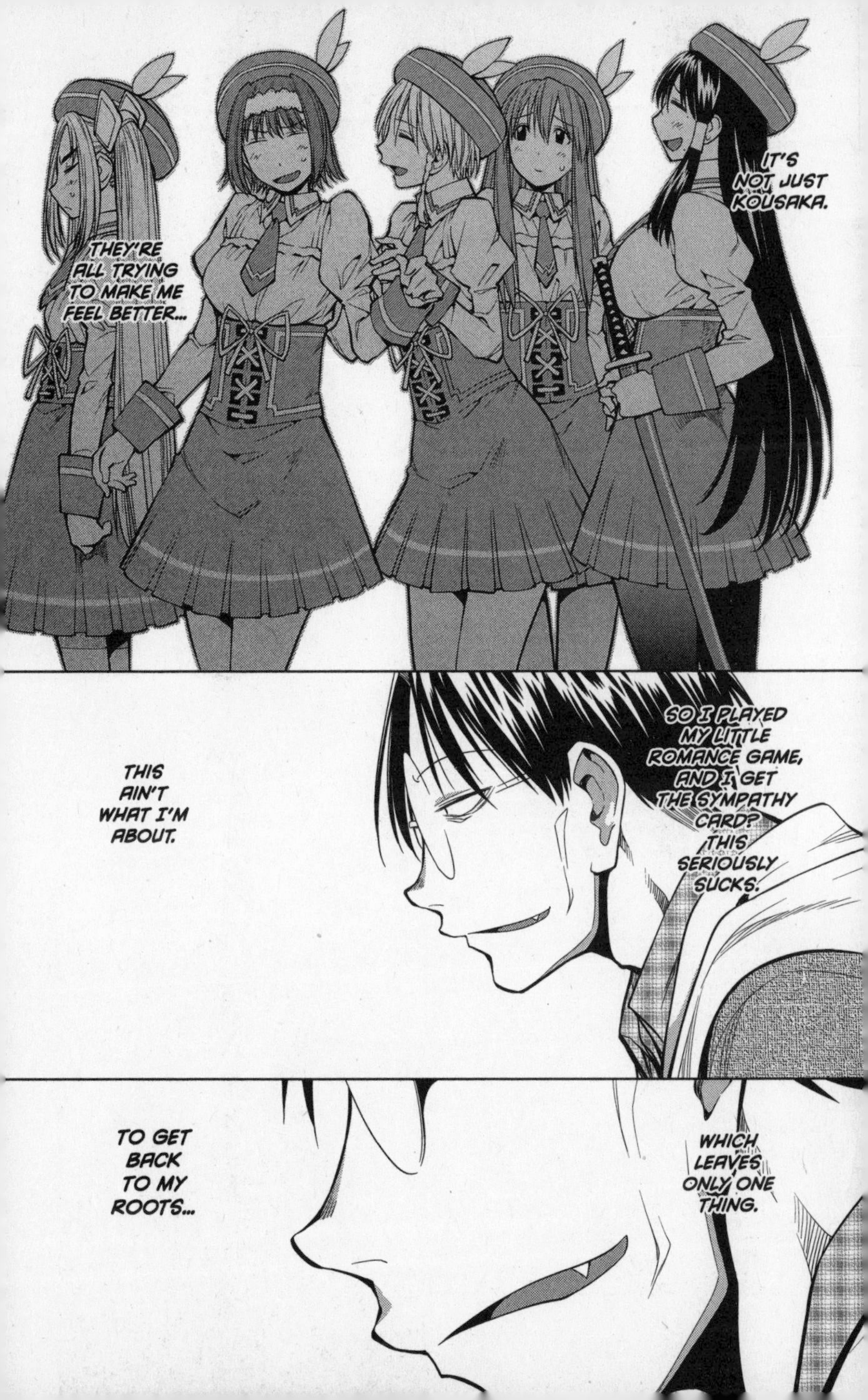
IT'S NOT JUST KOUSAKA.
THEY'RE ALL TRYING TO MAKE ME FEEL BETTER...
SO I PLAYED MY LITTLE ROMANCE GAME, AND I GET THE SYMPATHY CARD? THIS SERIOUSLY SUCKS.
THIS AIN'T WHAT I'M ABOUT.
WHICH LEAVES ONLY ONE THING.
TO GET BACK TO MY ROOTS...

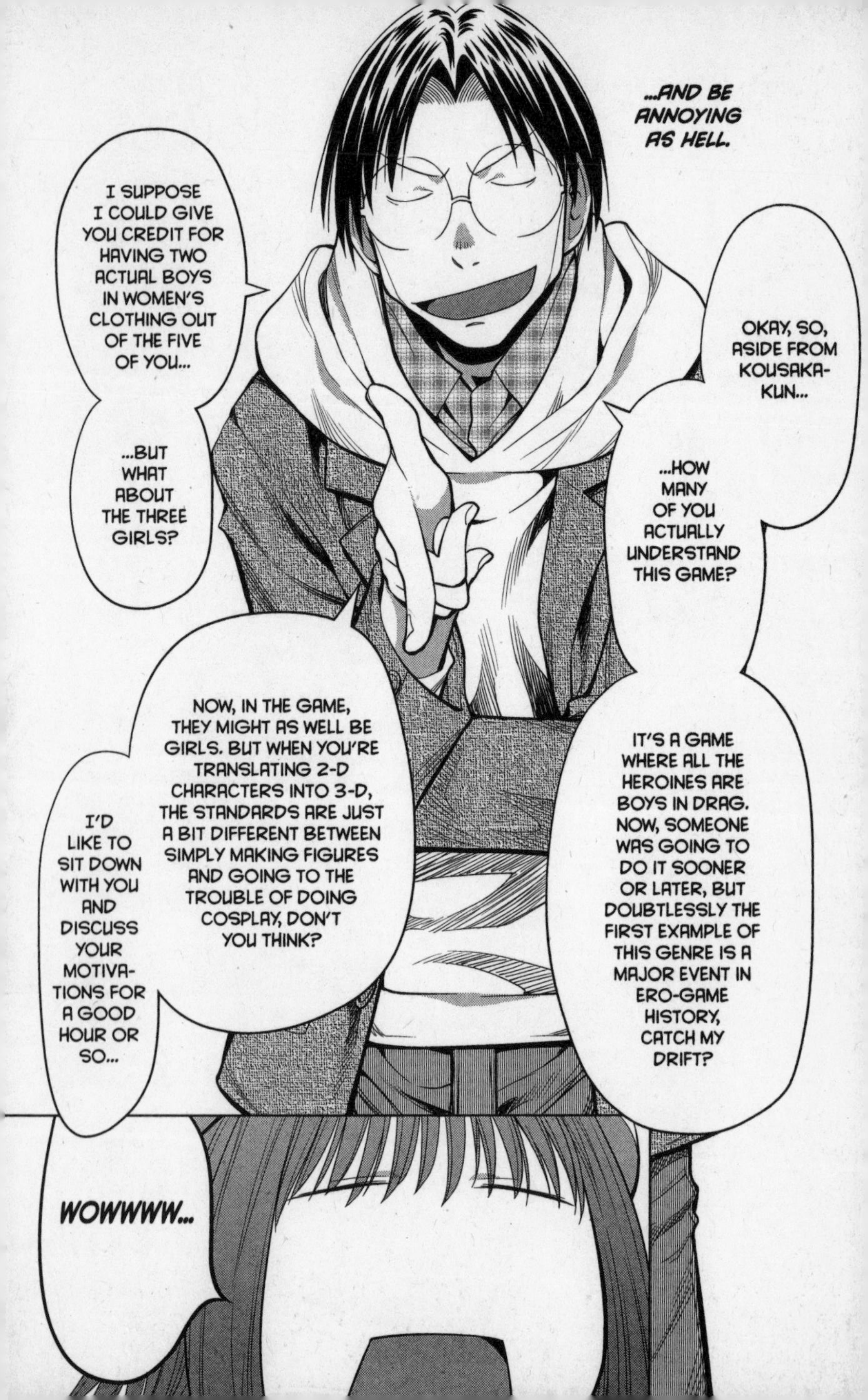
...AND BE ANNOYING AS HELL.
OKAY, SO, ASIDE FROM KOUSAKA-KUN...
...HOW MANY OF YOU ACTUALLY UNDERSTAND THIS GAME?
IT'S A GAME WHERE ALL THE HEROINES ARE BOYS IN DRAG. NOW, SOMEONE WAS GOING TO DO IT SOONER OR LATER, BUT DOUBTLESSLY THE FIRST EXAMPLE OF THIS GENRE IS A MAJOR EVENT IN ERO-GAME HISTORY, CATCH MY DRIFT?
I SUPPOSE I COULD GIVE YOU CREDIT FOR HAVING TWO ACTUAL BOYS IN WOMEN'S CLOTHING OUT OF THE FIVE OF YOU...
...BUT WHAT ABOUT THE THREE GIRLS?
NOW, IN THE GAME, THEY MIGHT AS WELL BE GIRLS. BUT WHEN YOU'RE TRANSLATING 2-D CHARACTERS INTO 3-D, THE STANDARDS ARE JUST A BIT DIFFERENT BETWEEN SIMPLY MAKING FIGURES AND GOING TO THE TROUBLE OF DOING COSPLAY, DON'T YOU THINK?
I'D LIKE TO SIT DOWN WITH YOU AND DISCUSS YOUR MOTIVATIONS FOR A GOOD HOUR OR SO...
WOWWWW...

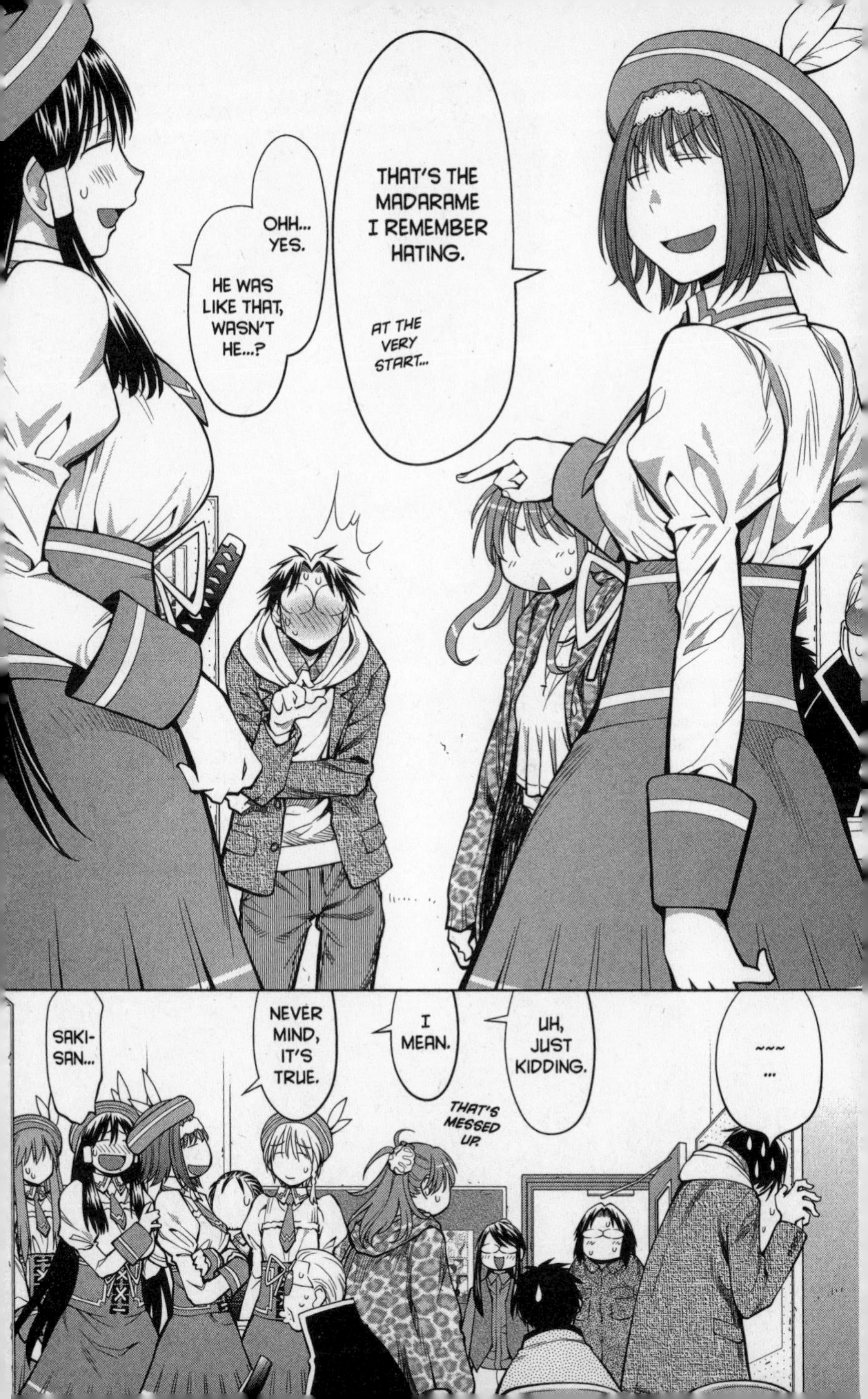
THAT'S THE MADARAME I REMEMBER HATING.
AT THE VERY START...
OHH... YES.
HE WAS LIKE THAT, WASN'T HE...?
...
UH, JUST KIDDING.
THAT'S MESSED UP.
I MEAN.
NEVER MIND, IT'S TRUE.
SAKI-SAN...

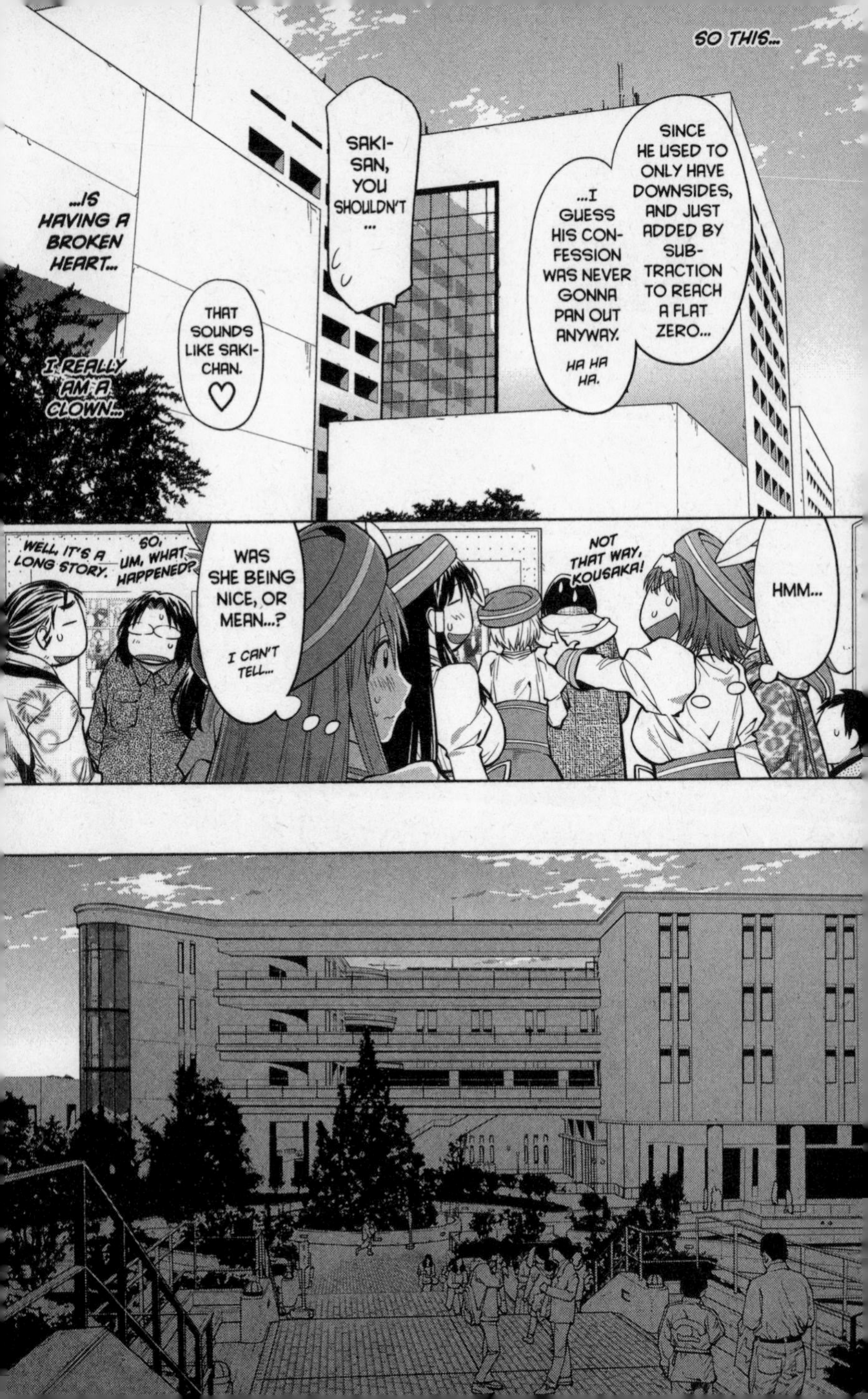
SO THIS...
SINCE HE USED TO ONLY HAVE DOWNSIDES, AND JUST ADDED BY SUBTRACTION TO REACH A FLAT ZERO...
SAKI-SAN, YOU SHOULDN'T ...
...I GUESS HIS CONFESSION WAS NEVER GONNA PAN OUT ANYWAY.
HA HA HA.
...IS HAVING A BROKEN HEART...
THAT SOUNDS LIKE SAKI-CHAN. ♡
I REALLY AM A CLOWN...
HMM...
NOT THAT WAY, KOUSAKA!
WAS SHE BEING NICE, OR MEAN...?
I CAN'T TELL...
SO, UM, WHAT HAPPENED?
WELL, IT'S A LONG STORY.

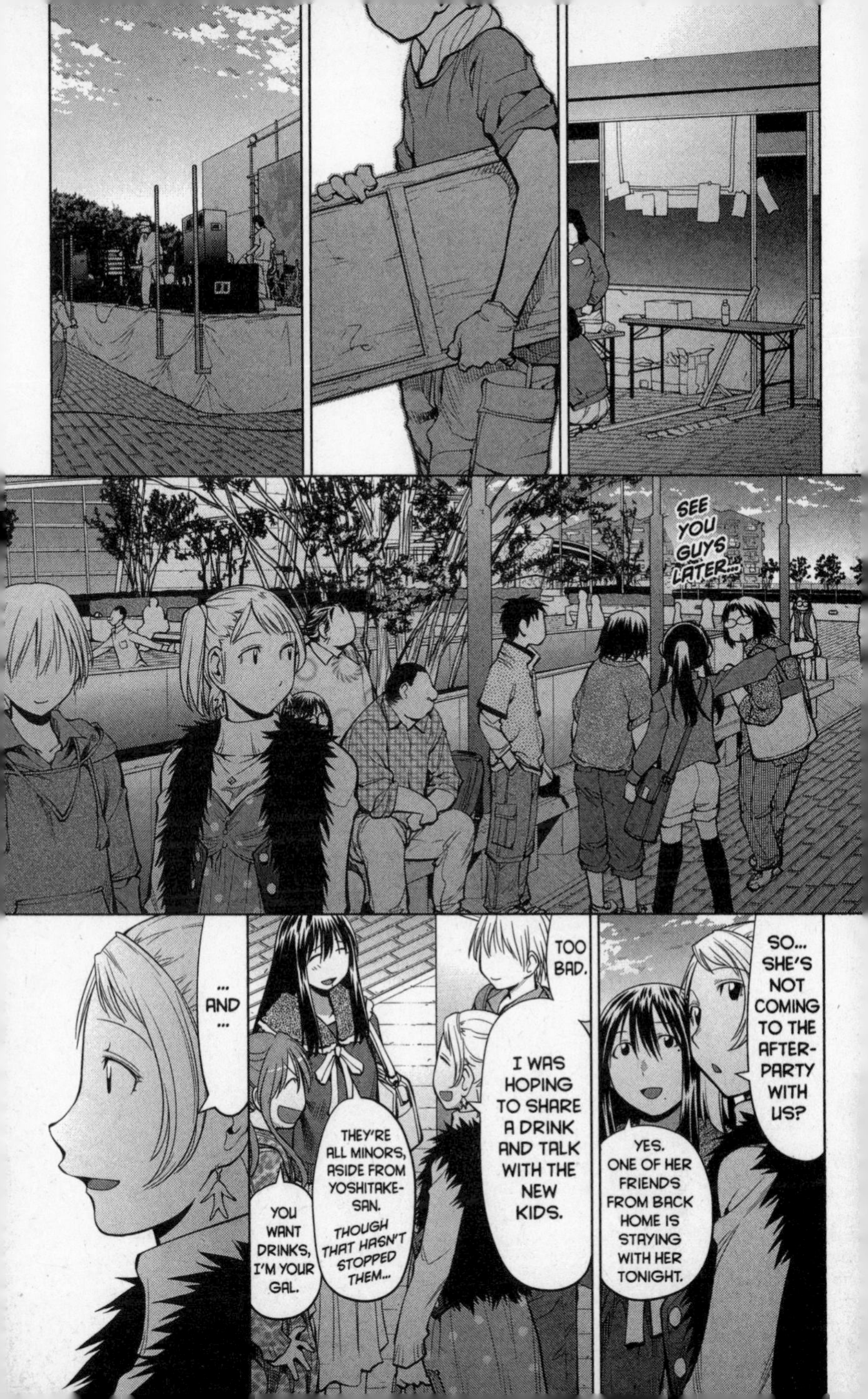
SEE YOU GUYS LATER...
SO... SHE'S NOT COMING TO THE AFTER-PARTY WITH US?
YES. ONE OF HER FRIENDS FROM BACK HOME IS STAYING WITH HER TONIGHT.
TOO BAD.
I WAS HOPING TO SHARE A DRINK AND TALK WITH THE NEW KIDS.
THEY'RE ALL MINORS, ASIDE FROM YOSHITAKE-SAN. *THOUGH THAT HASN'T STOPPED THEM...*
YOU WANT DRINKS, I'M YOUR GAL.
... AND ...

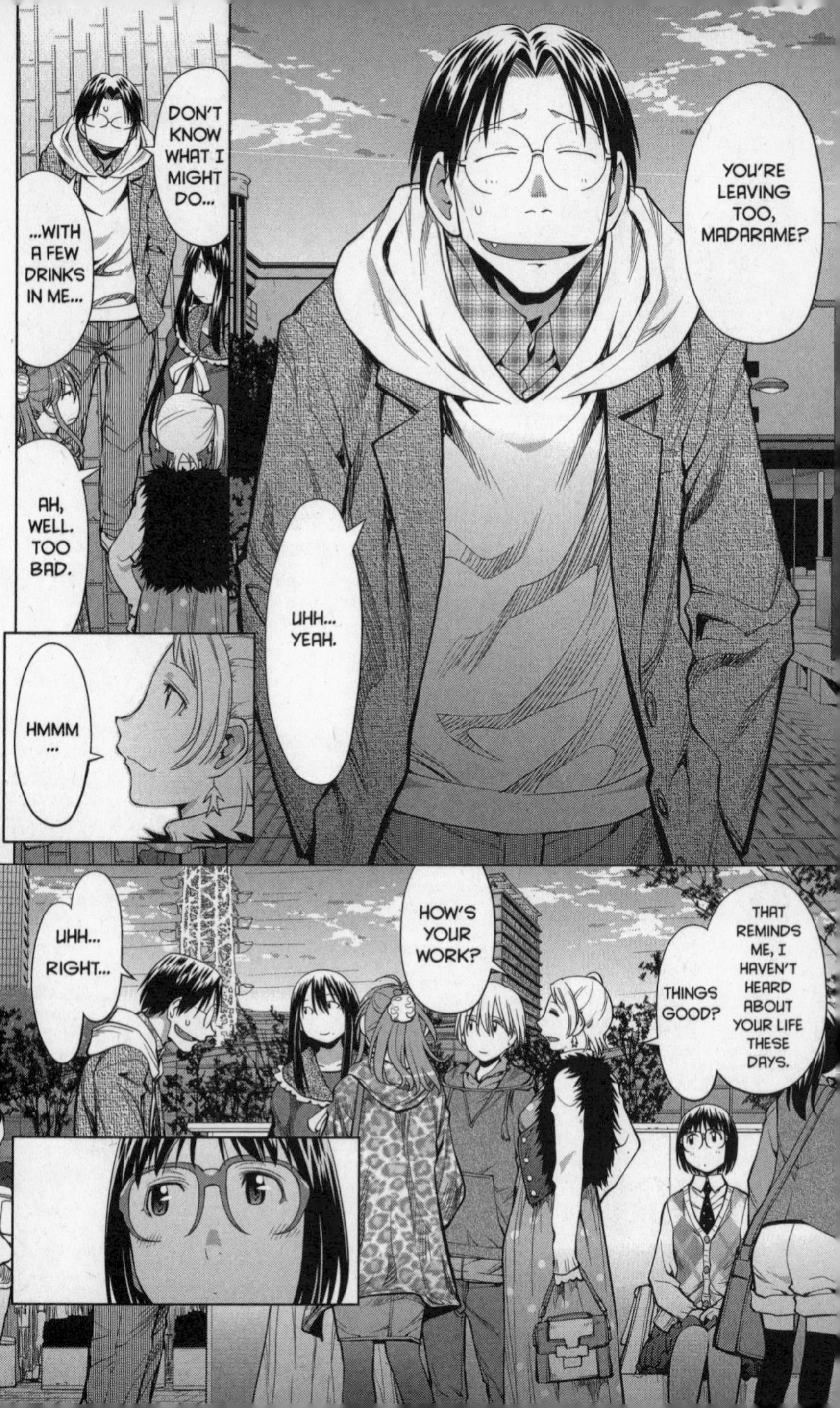
YOU'RE LEAVING TOO, MADARAME?
UHH... YEAH.
DON'T KNOW WHAT I MIGHT DO...
...WITH A FEW DRINKS IN ME...
AH, WELL. TOO BAD.
HMMM ...
THAT REMINDS ME, I HAVEN'T HEARD ABOUT YOUR LIFE THESE DAYS.
THINGS GOOD?
HOW'S YOUR WORK?
UHH... RIGHT...

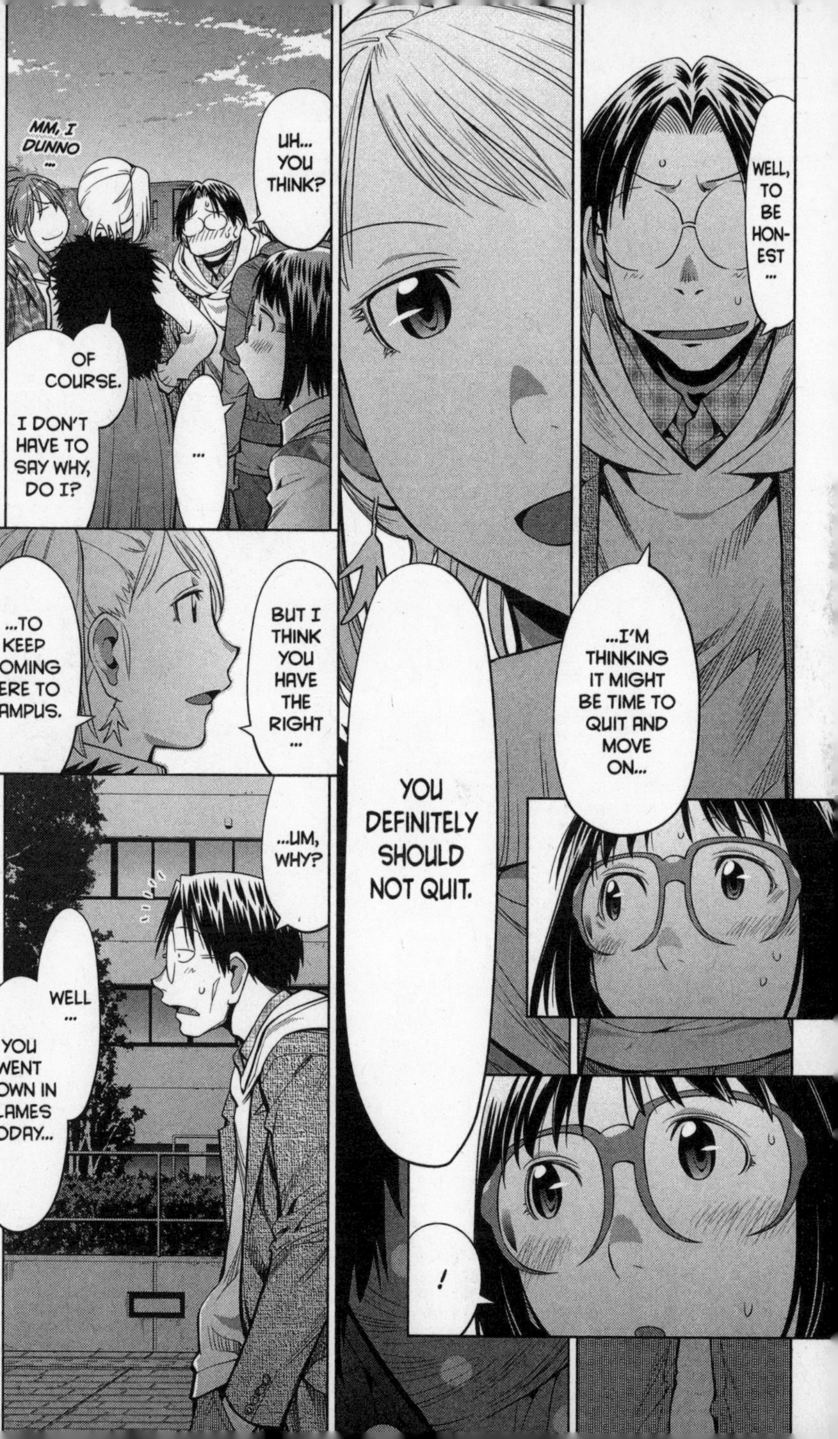
WELL, TO BE HON-EST ...
...I'M THINKING IT MIGHT BE TIME TO QUIT AND MOVE ON...
YOU DEFINITELY SHOULD NOT QUIT.
!
UH... YOU THINK?
MM, I DUNNO ...
OF COURSE.
I DON'T HAVE TO SAY WHY, DO I?
...
BUT I THINK YOU HAVE THE RIGHT ...
...TO KEEP COMING HERE TO CAMPUS.
...UM, WHY?
WELL ...
YOU WENT DOWN IN FLAMES TODAY...

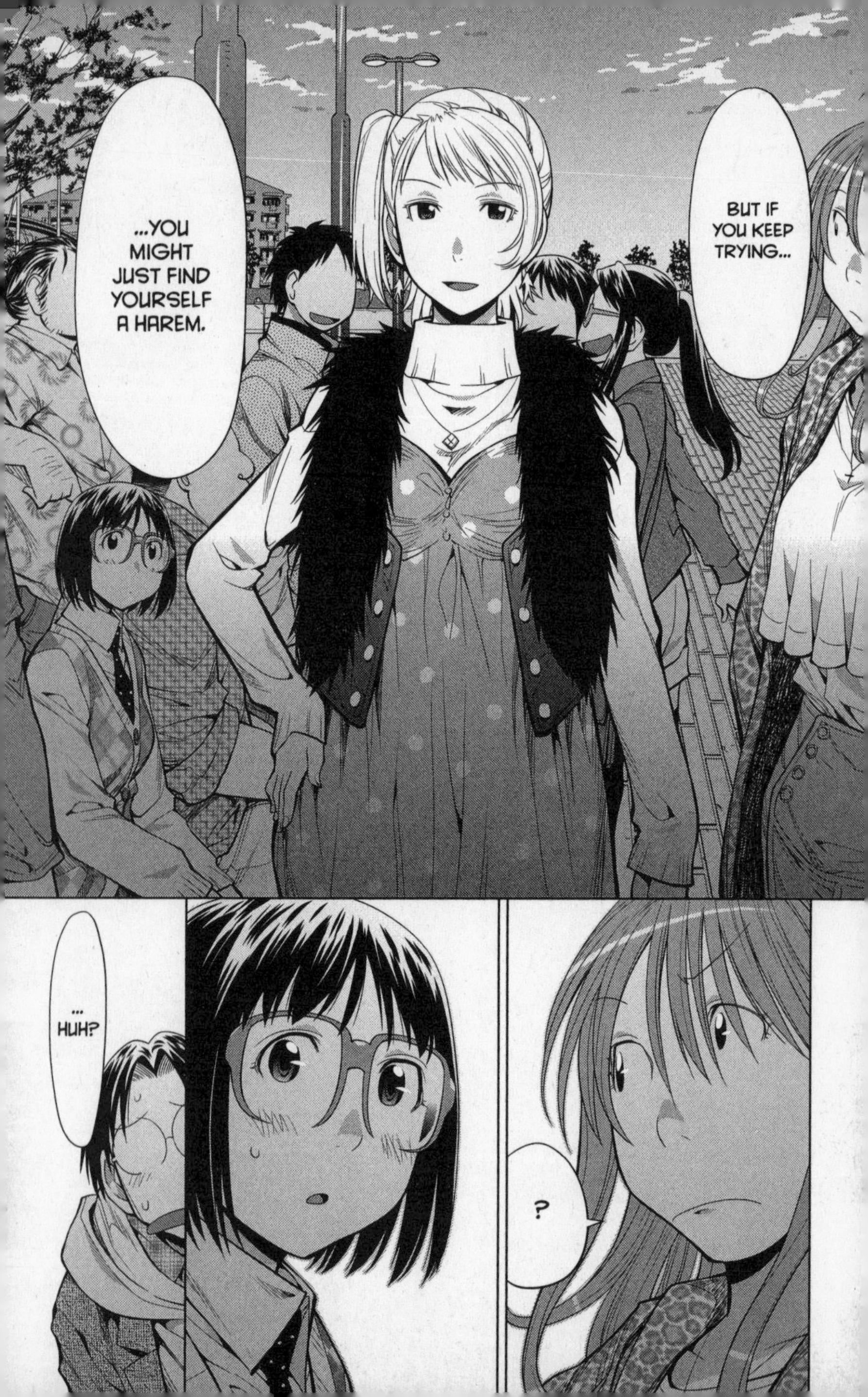
BUT IF YOU KEEP TRYING...
...YOU MIGHT JUST FIND YOURSELF A HAREM.
?
... HUH?

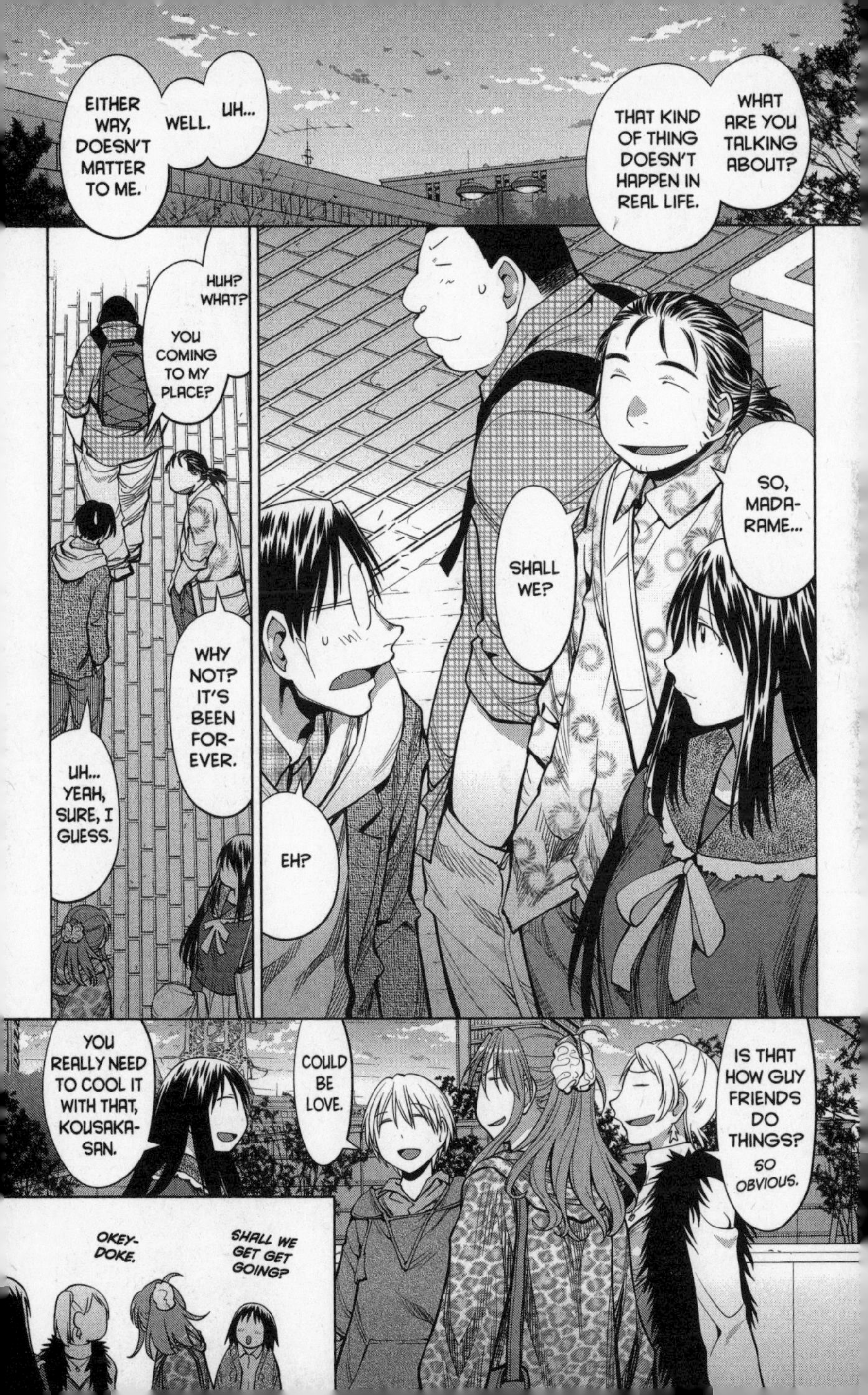
WHAT ARE YOU TALKING ABOUT?
THAT KIND OF THING DOESN'T HAPPEN IN REAL LIFE.
UH... WELL.
EITHER WAY, DOESN'T MATTER TO ME.
SO, MADA-RAME...
SHALL WE?
EH?
HUH? WHAT?
YOU COMING TO MY PLACE?
WHY NOT? IT'S BEEN FOR-EVER.
UH... YEAH, SURE, I GUESS.
IS THAT HOW GUY FRIENDS DO THINGS?
SO OBVIOUS.
COULD BE LOVE.
YOU REALLY NEED TO COOL IT WITH THAT, KOUSAKA-SAN.
SHALL WE GET GET GOING?
OKEY-DOKE.

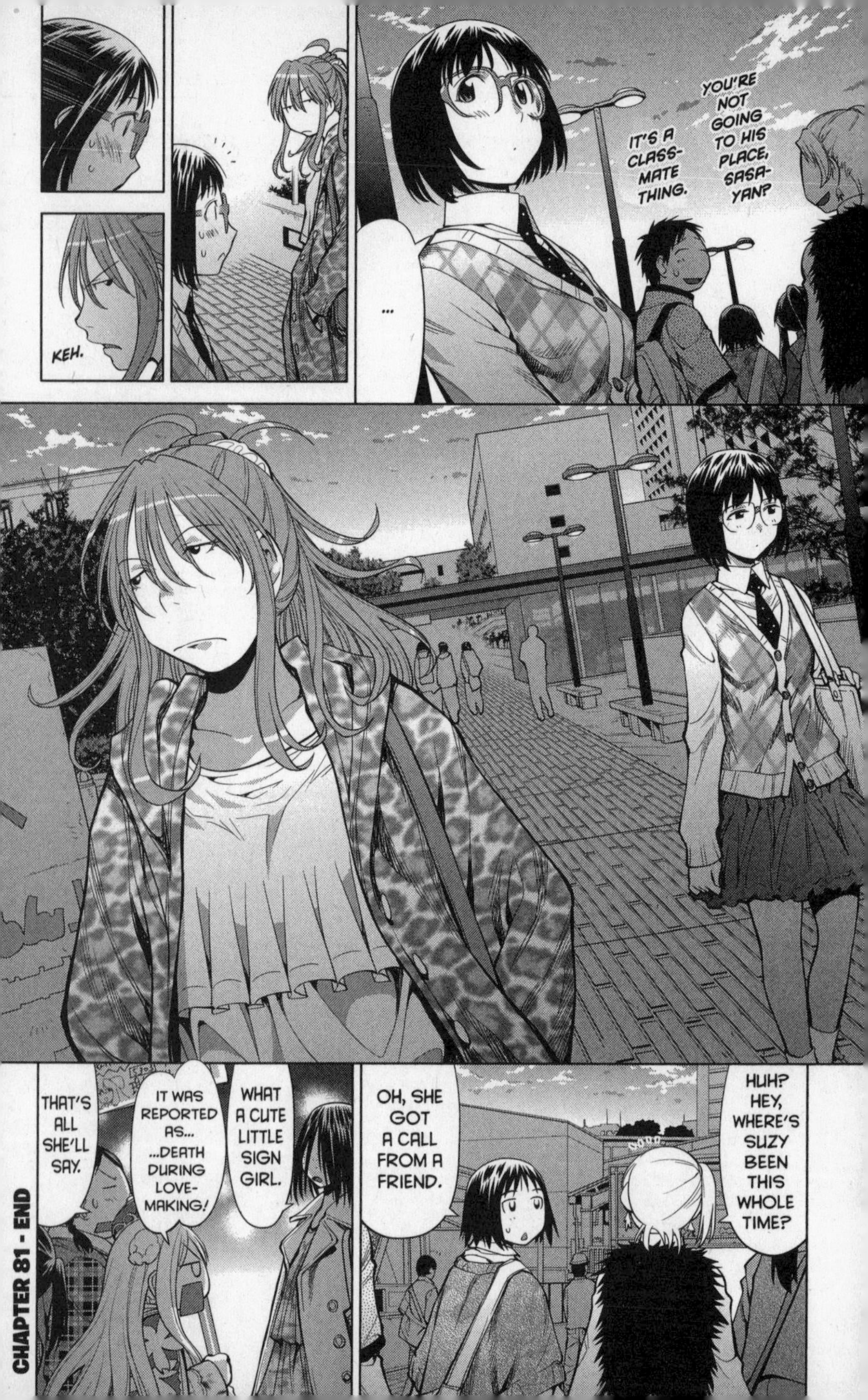
YOU'RE NOT GOING TO HIS PLACE, SASA-YAN?
IT'S A CLASS-MATE THING.
...
KEH.
HUH? HEY, WHERE'S SUZY BEEN THIS WHOLE TIME?
OH, SHE GOT A CALL FROM A FRIEND.
WHAT A CUTE LITTLE SIGN GIRL.
IT WAS REPORTED AS... ...DEATH DURING LOVE-MAKING!
THAT'S ALL SHE'LL SAY.

CHAPTER 81 - END

EVERYONE SAID...

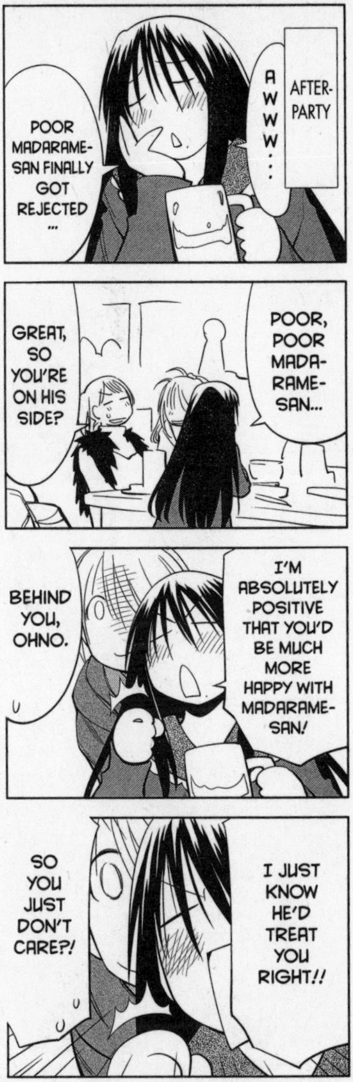
AFTER-PARTY
AWWW...
POOR MADARAME-SAN FINALLY GOT REJECTED...
POOR, POOR MADARAME-SAN...
GREAT, SO YOU'RE ON HIS SIDE?
I'M ABSOLUTELY POSITIVE THAT YOU'D BE MUCH MORE HAPPY WITH MADARAME-SAN!
BEHIND YOU, OHNO.
I JUST KNOW HE'D TREAT YOU RIGHT!!
SO YOU JUST DON'T CARE?!

THAT FUTURE DOES NOT EXIST

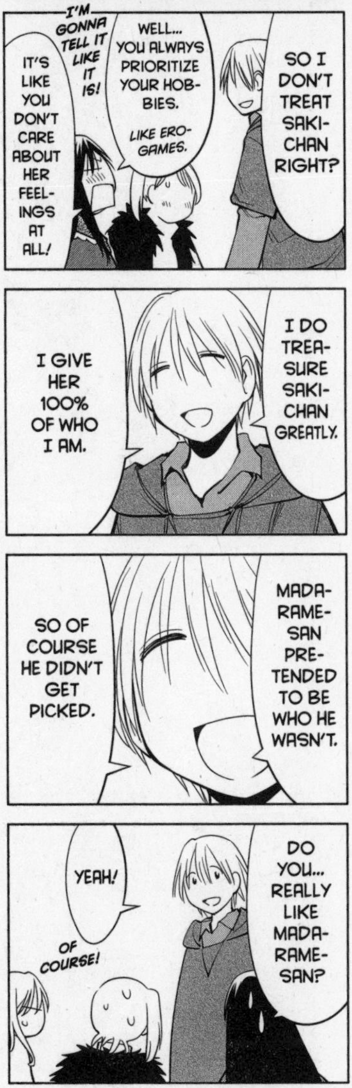
SO I DON'T TREAT SAKI-CHAN RIGHT?
WELL... YOU ALWAYS PRIORITIZE YOUR HOBBIES.
LIKE ERO-GAMES.
I'M GONNA TELL IT LIKE IT IS!
IT'S LIKE YOU DON'T CARE ABOUT HER FEELINGS AT ALL!
I DO TREASURE SAKI-CHAN GREATLY.
I GIVE HER 100% OF WHO I AM.
MADARAME-SAN PRETENDED TO BE WHO HE WASN'T.
SO OF COURSE HE DIDN'T GET PICKED.
DO YOU... REALLY LIKE MADARAME-SAN?
YEAH!
OF COURSE!

ME-FILTER

SO, HATO-CHAN.
I WANT YOU TO TELL ME WHAT HAPPENED TODAY AND IN THE PAST...
...IN EXCRUCIATING, VIVID DETAIL, NO STONE UNTURNED...
...WHETHER YOU WANT TO OR NOT!
UHH...
B-BUT... YAJIMA-SAN'S NOT HERE...
IT'S NOT REALLY FAIR.
CALLING FOR HELP, EH?
HAVE NO FEAR.
I'LL BE TELLING HER EVERYTHING I HEAR, ANYWAY!
JAB
OH, MAN...
SUCH A BAD FEELING ABOUT THIS...

SHOULDN'T HAVE TOLD HER

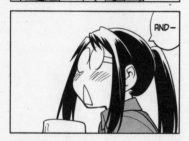

OHH, I SEE...
SO THAT'S WHAT HAPPENED...
AND—
THERE'S NO OTHER MEN IN THE STORY...
...ASIDE FROM YOUR BROTHER?
PARDON?
I THOUGHT MAYBE YOU GOT MUGGED BY A GANG OF THUGS WHILE YOU WERE OUTCAST...
...AND WHEN YOUR BEST FRIEND STEPPED IN TO BREAK IT UP, YOU WENT BEYOND THE BOUNDS OF FRIENDSHIP...!
NO, NO, NOTHING LIKE THAT AT ALL!!

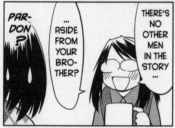

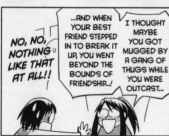

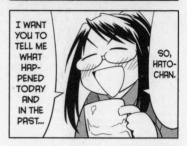

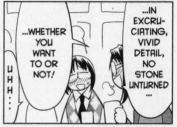

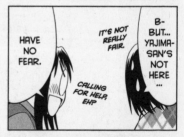

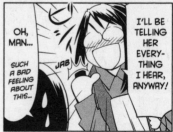

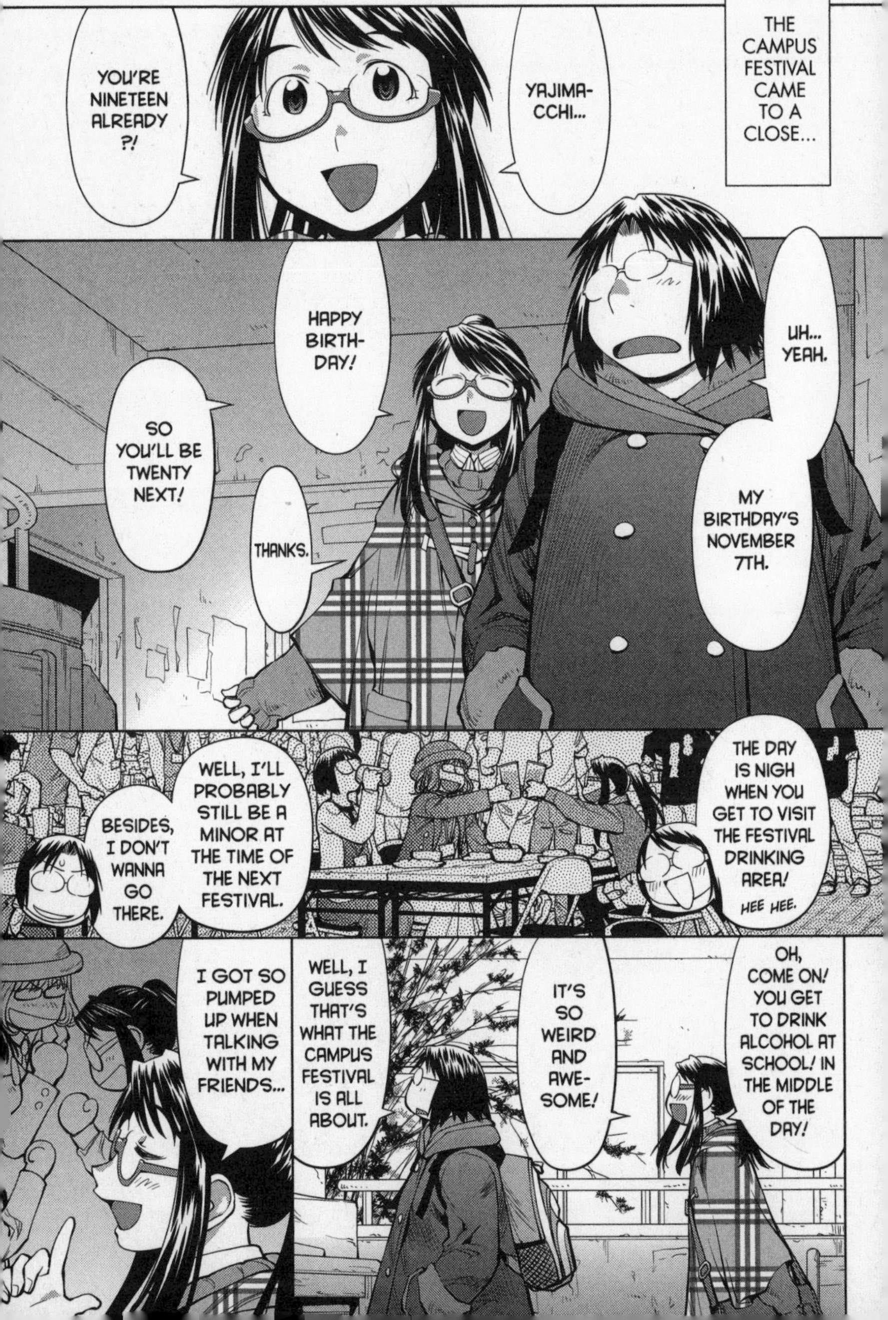
THE CAMPUS FESTIVAL CAME TO A CLOSE...
YAJIMA-CCHI...
YOU'RE NINETEEN ALREADY ?!
UH... YEAH.
MY BIRTHDAY'S NOVEMBER 7TH.
HAPPY BIRTH-DAY!
SO YOU'LL BE TWENTY NEXT!
THANKS.
THE DAY IS NIGH WHEN YOU GET TO VISIT THE FESTIVAL DRINKING AREA!
HEE HEE.
WELL, I'LL PROBABLY STILL BE A MINOR AT THE TIME OF THE NEXT FESTIVAL.
BESIDES, I DON'T WANNA GO THERE.
OH, COME ON! YOU GET TO DRINK ALCOHOL AT SCHOOL! IN THE MIDDLE OF THE DAY!
IT'S SO WEIRD AND AWE-SOME!
WELL, I GUESS THAT'S WHAT THE CAMPUS FESTIVAL IS ALL ABOUT.
I GOT SO PUMPED UP WHEN TALKING WITH MY FRIENDS...

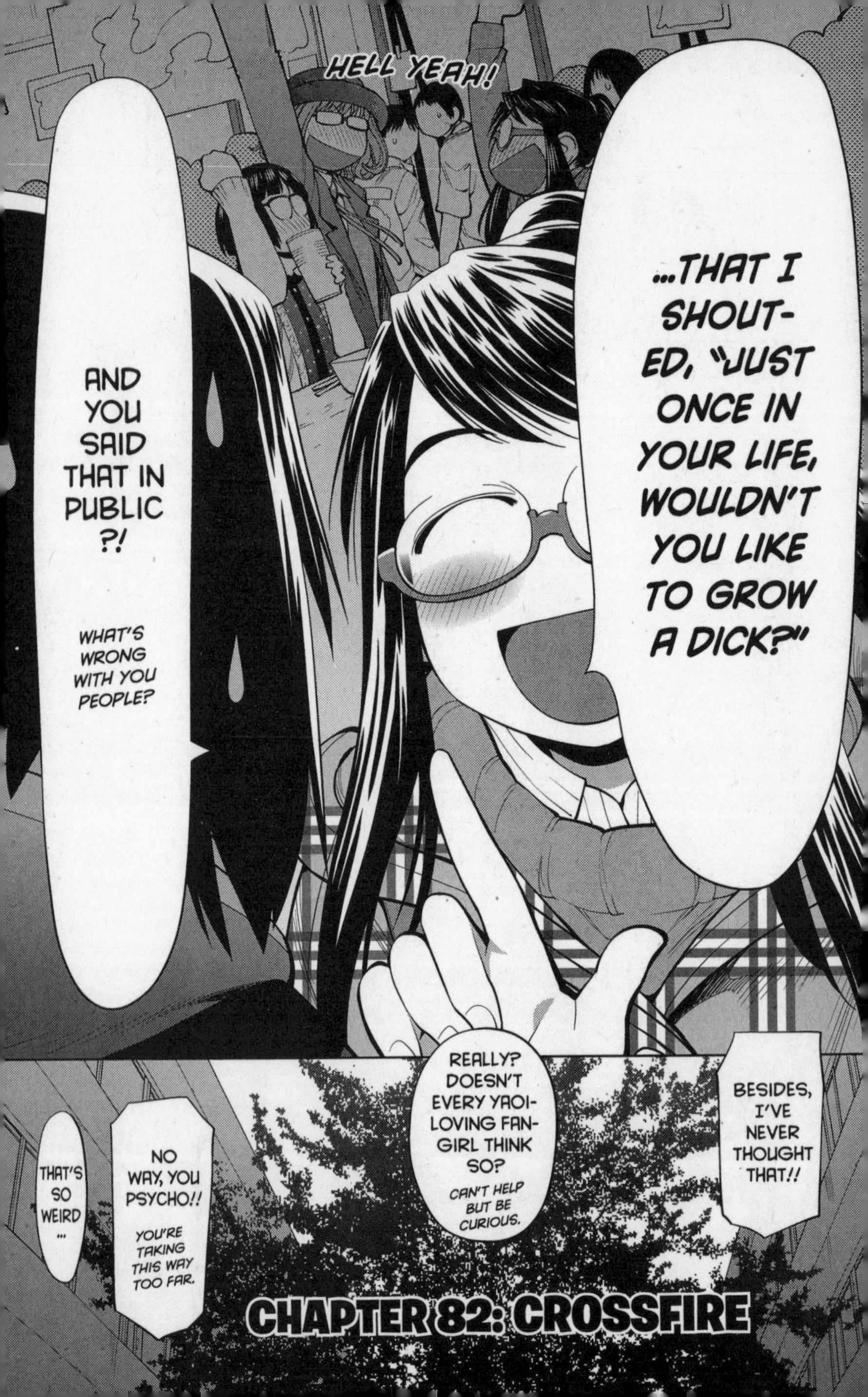
...THAT I SHOUTED, "JUST ONCE IN YOUR LIFE, WOULDN'T YOU LIKE TO GROW A DICK?"
HELL YEAH!
AND YOU SAID THAT IN PUBLIC?!
WHAT'S WRONG WITH YOU PEOPLE?
BESIDES, I'VE NEVER THOUGHT THAT!!
REALLY? DOESN'T EVERY YAOI-LOVING FANGIRL THINK SO?
CAN'T HELP BUT BE CURIOUS.
NO WAY, YOU PSYCHO!!
YOU'RE TAKING THIS WAY TOO FAR.
THAT'S SO WEIRD...
CHAPTER 82: CROSSFIRE

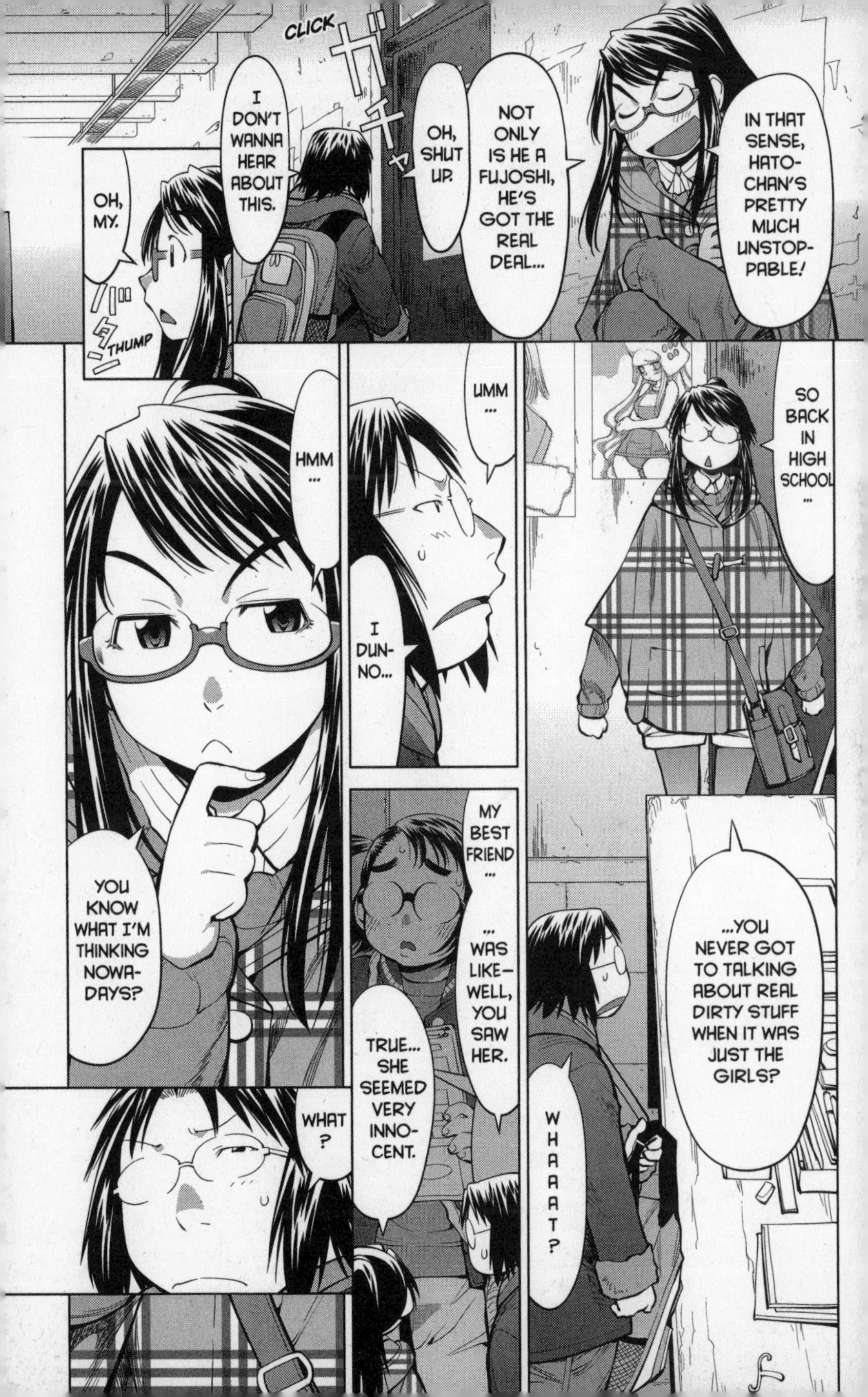
CLICK
IN THAT SENSE, HATO-CHAN'S PRETTY MUCH UNSTOP-PABLE!
NOT ONLY IS HE A FUJOSHI, HE'S GOT THE REAL DEAL...
OH, SHUT UP.
I DON'T WANNA HEAR ABOUT THIS.
OH, MY.
THUMP
SO BACK IN HIGH SCHOOL...
UMM...
I DUN-NO...
...YOU NEVER GOT TO TALKING ABOUT REAL DIRTY STUFF WHEN IT WAS JUST THE GIRLS?
WHAAAAT?
MY BEST FRIEND...
...WAS LIKE— WELL, YOU SAW HER.
TRUE... SHE SEEMED VERY INNO-CENT.
HMM...
YOU KNOW WHAT I'M THINKING NOWA-DAYS?
WHAT?

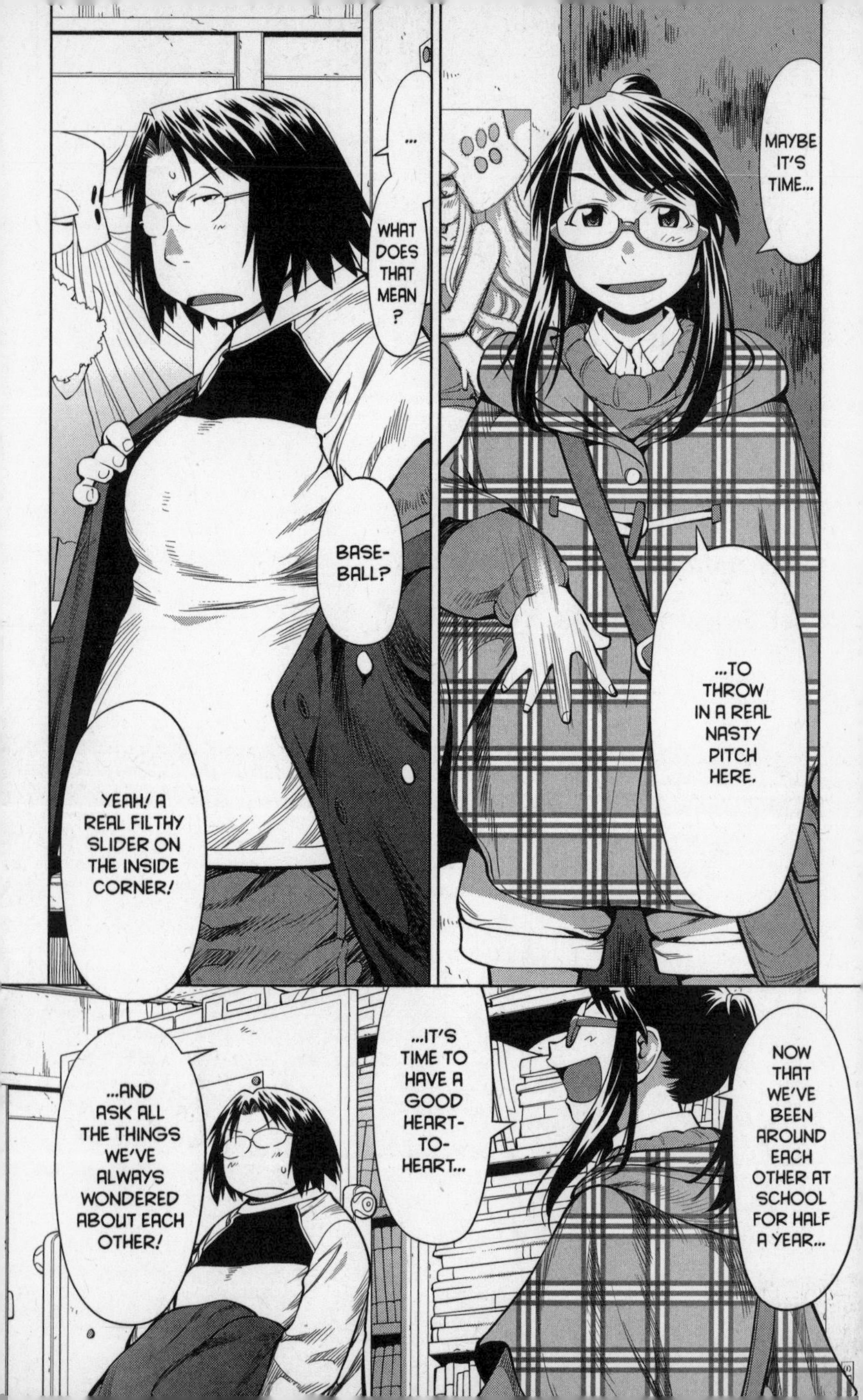
MAYBE IT'S TIME...
...TO THROW IN A REAL NASTY PITCH HERE.
...
WHAT DOES THAT MEAN?
BASE-BALL?
YEAH! A REAL FILTHY SLIDER ON THE INSIDE CORNER!
NOW THAT WE'VE BEEN AROUND EACH OTHER AT SCHOOL FOR HALF A YEAR...
...IT'S TIME TO HAVE A GOOD HEART-TO-HEART...
...AND ASK ALL THE THINGS WE'VE ALWAYS WONDERED ABOUT EACH OTHER!

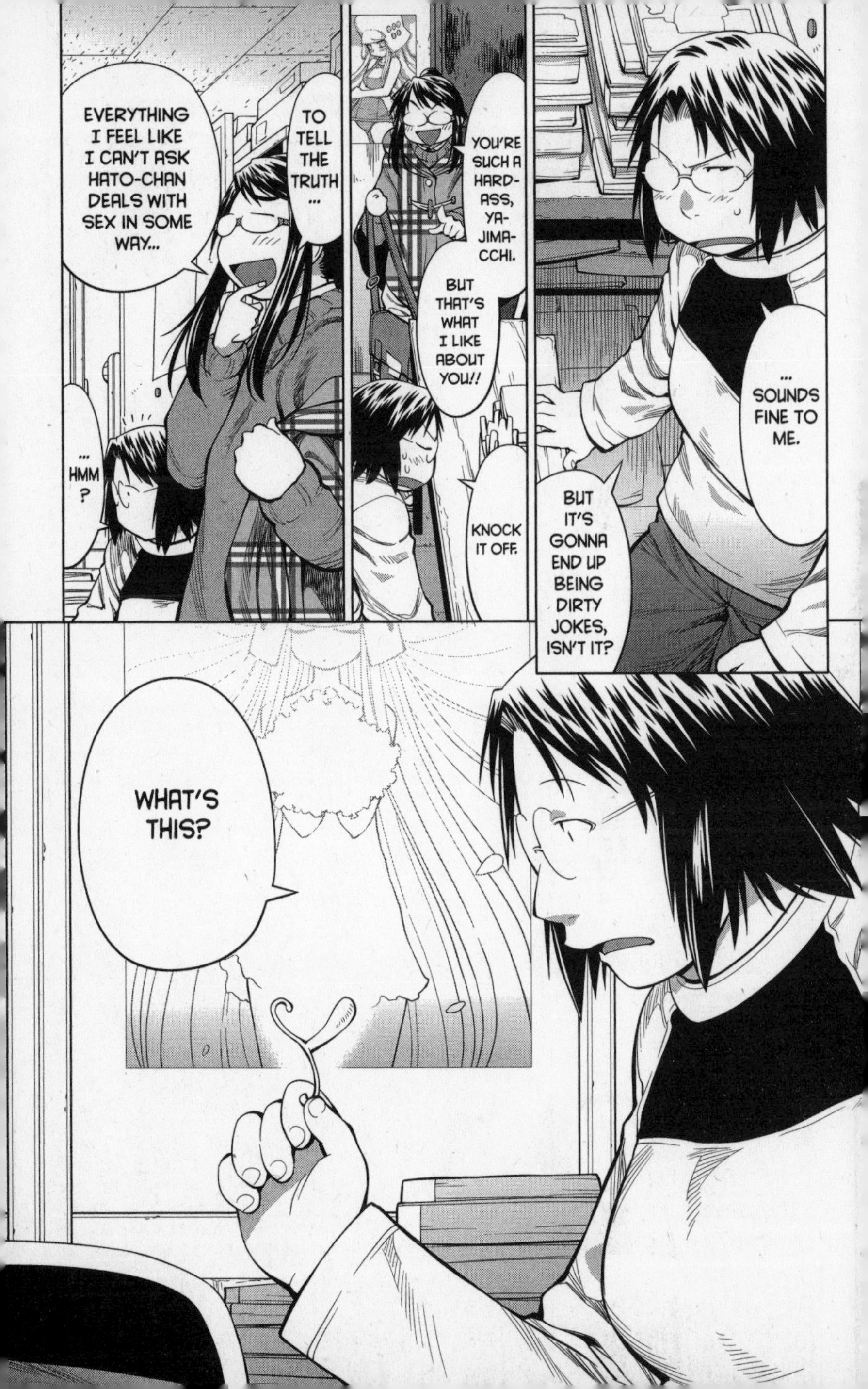
...SOUNDS FINE TO ME.
BUT IT'S GONNA END UP BEING DIRTY JOKES, ISN'T IT?
YOU'RE SUCH A HARD-ASS, YA-JIMA-CCHI.
BUT THAT'S WHAT I LIKE ABOUT YOU!!
KNOCK IT OFF.
TO TELL THE TRUTH...
EVERYTHING I FEEL LIKE I CAN'T ASK HATO-CHAN DEALS WITH SEX IN SOME WAY...
...HMM?
WHAT'S THIS?

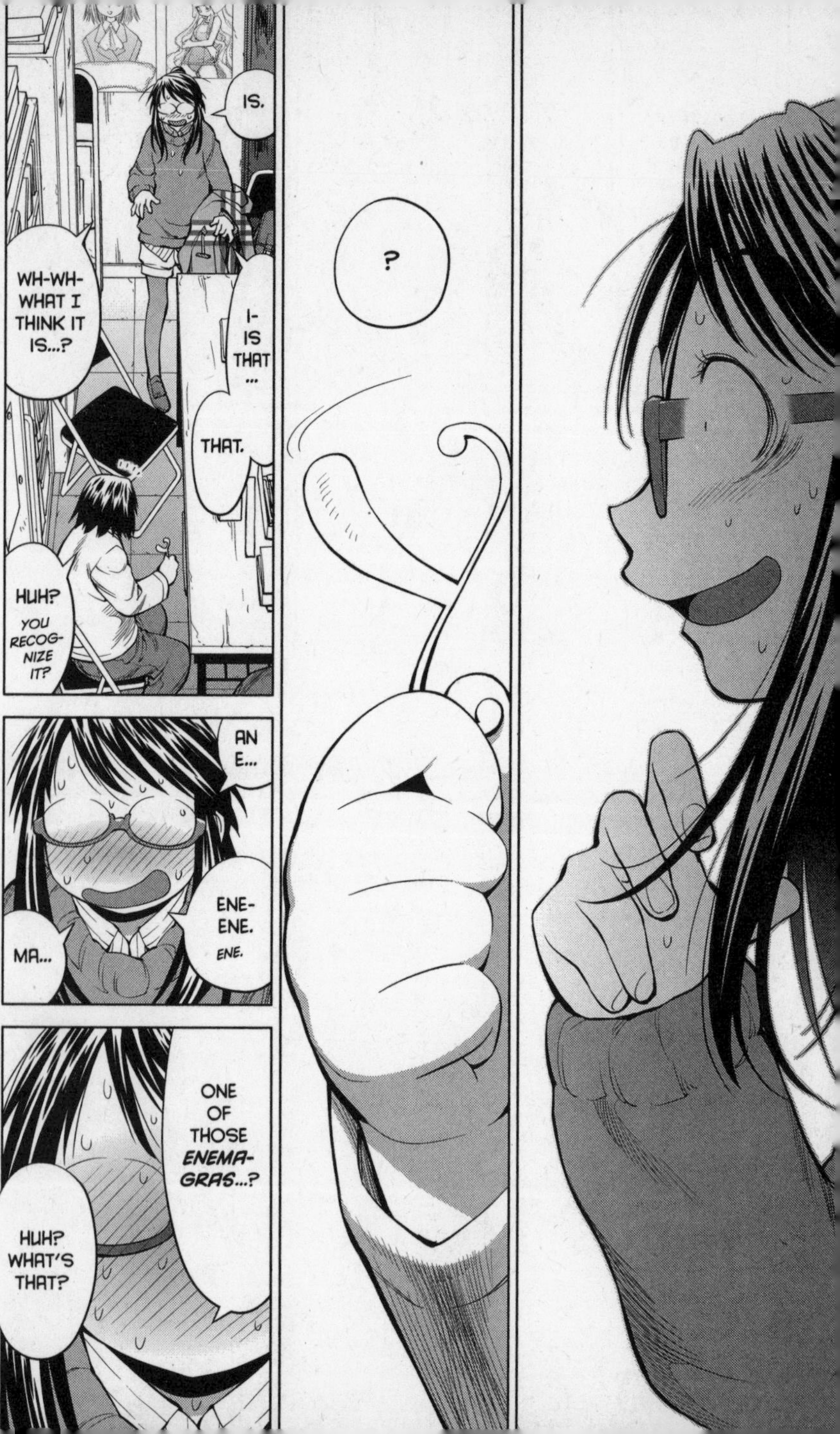
?
IS.
I-IS THAT...
WH-WH-WHAT I THINK IT IS...?
THAT.
HUH? YOU RECOGNIZE IT?
AN E...
ENE-ENE. ENE.
MA...
ONE OF THOSE ENEMAGRAS...?
HUH? WHAT'S THAT?

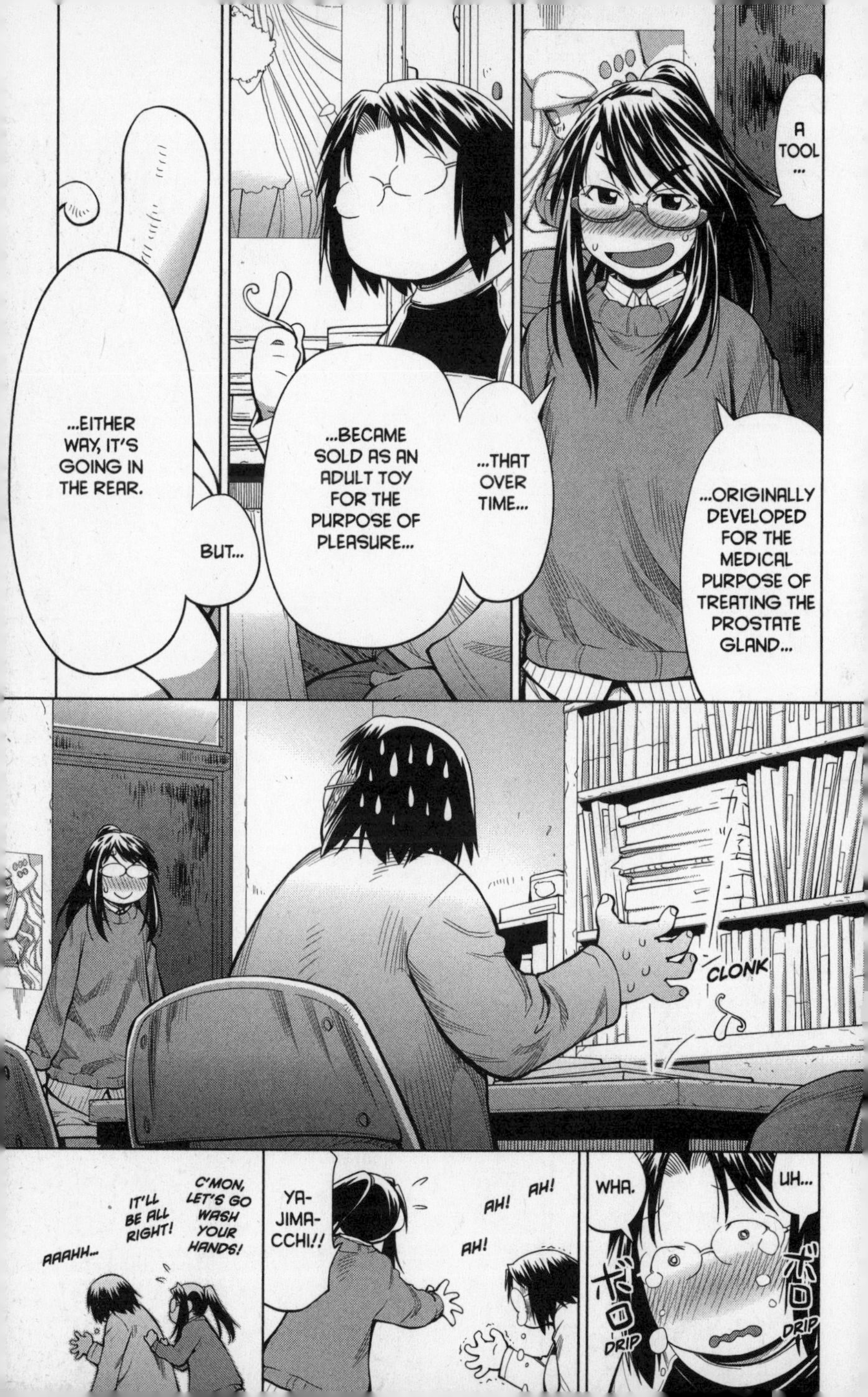
A TOOL ...
...ORIGINALLY DEVELOPED FOR THE MEDICAL PURPOSE OF TREATING THE PROSTATE GLAND...
...THAT OVER TIME...
...BECAME SOLD AS AN ADULT TOY FOR THE PURPOSE OF PLEASURE...
BUT...
...EITHER WAY, IT'S GOING IN THE REAR.
CLONK
UH...
WHA.
ボロ
DRIP
ボロ
DRIP
AH! AH!
AH!
YA-JIMA-CCHI!!
C'MON, LET'S GO WASH YOUR HANDS!
IT'LL BE ALL RIGHT!
AAAHH...

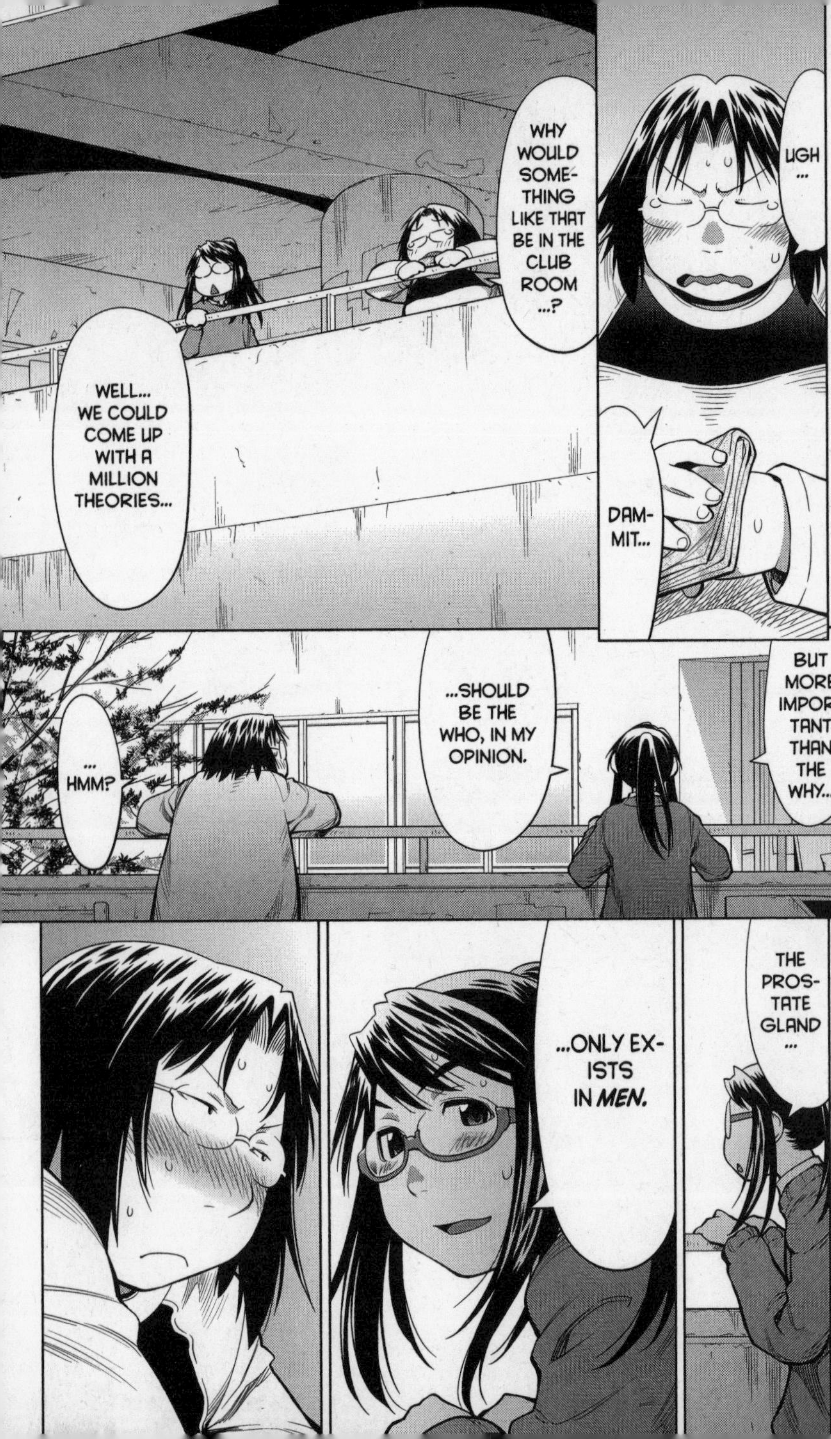
UGH ...
DAM-MIT...
WHY WOULD SOME-THING LIKE THAT BE IN THE CLUB ROOM ...?
WELL... WE COULD COME UP WITH A MILLION THEORIES...
BUT MORE IMPOR-TANT THAN THE WHY...
...SHOULD BE THE WHO, IN MY OPINION.
... HMM?
THE PROS-TATE GLAND ...
...ONLY EX-ISTS IN *MEN.*

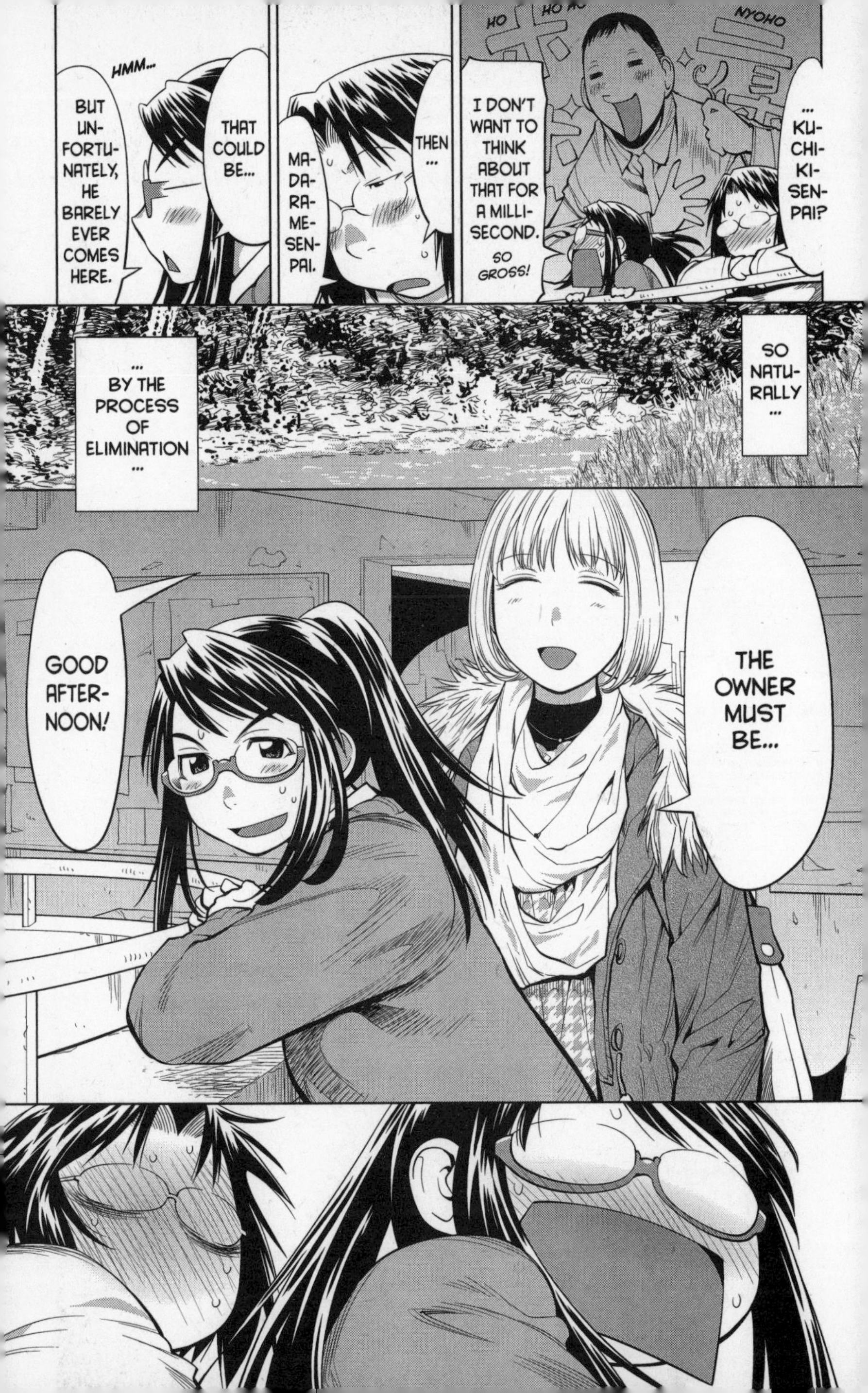
NYOHO
HO HO
HO
... KU-CHI-KI-SEN-PAI?
I DON'T WANT TO THINK ABOUT THAT FOR A MILLI-SECOND.
SO GROSS!
THEN ...
MA-DA-RA-ME-SEN-PAI.
HMM...
THAT COULD BE...
BUT UN-FORTU-NATELY, HE BARELY EVER COMES HERE.
SO NATU-RALLY ...
... BY THE PROCESS OF ELIMINATION ...
THE OWNER MUST BE...
GOOD AFTER-NOON!

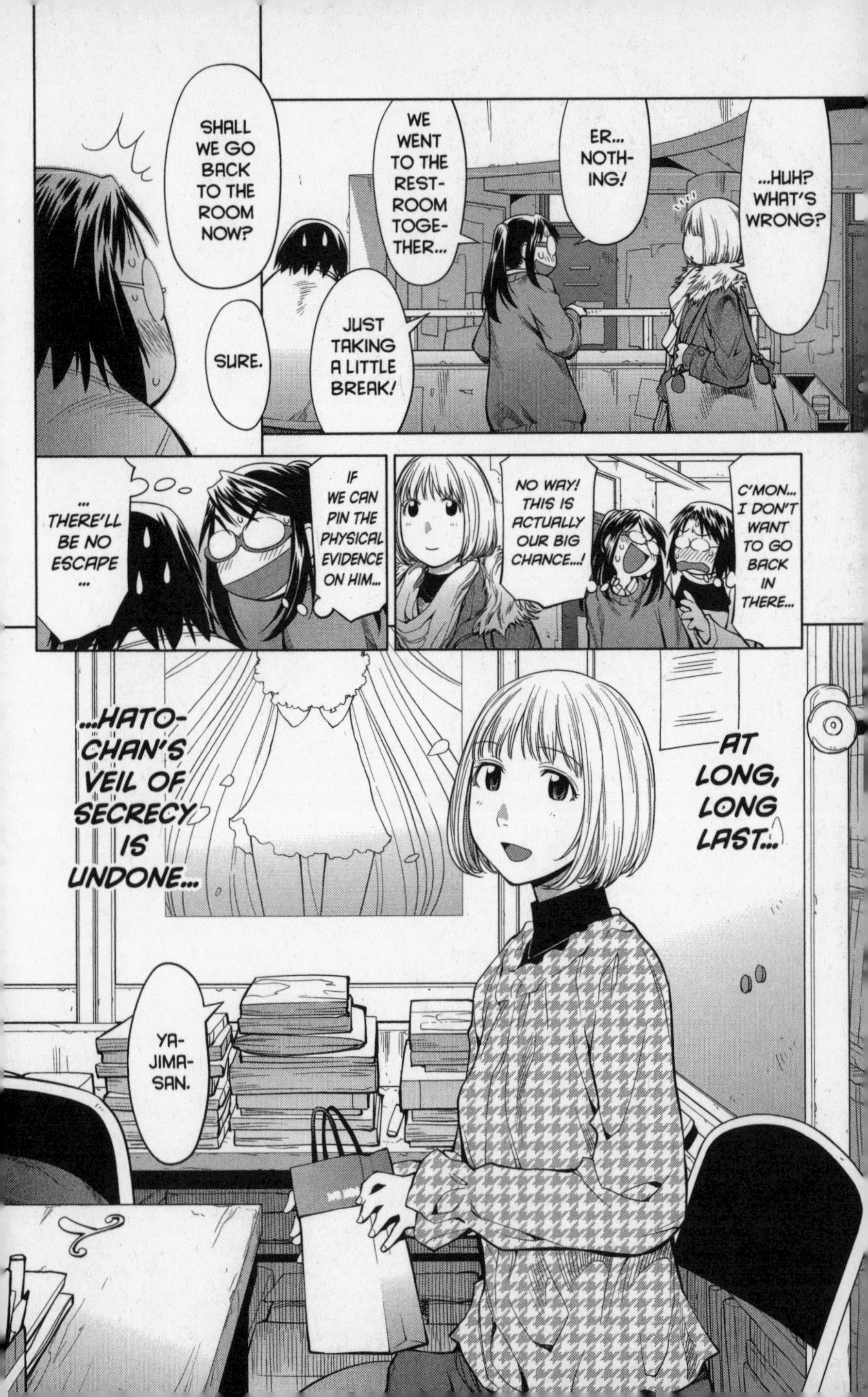
...HUH? WHAT'S WRONG?
ER... NOTHING!
WE WENT TO THE RESTROOM TOGETHER...
JUST TAKING A LITTLE BREAK!
SHALL WE GO BACK TO THE ROOM NOW?
SURE.
C'MON... I DON'T WANT TO GO BACK IN THERE...
NO WAY! THIS IS ACTUALLY OUR BIG CHANCE...!
IF WE CAN PIN THE PHYSICAL EVIDENCE ON HIM...
...THERE'LL BE NO ESCAPE...
AT LONG, LONG LAST...
...HATO-CHAN'S VEIL OF SECRECY IS UNDONE...
YAJIMA-SAN.

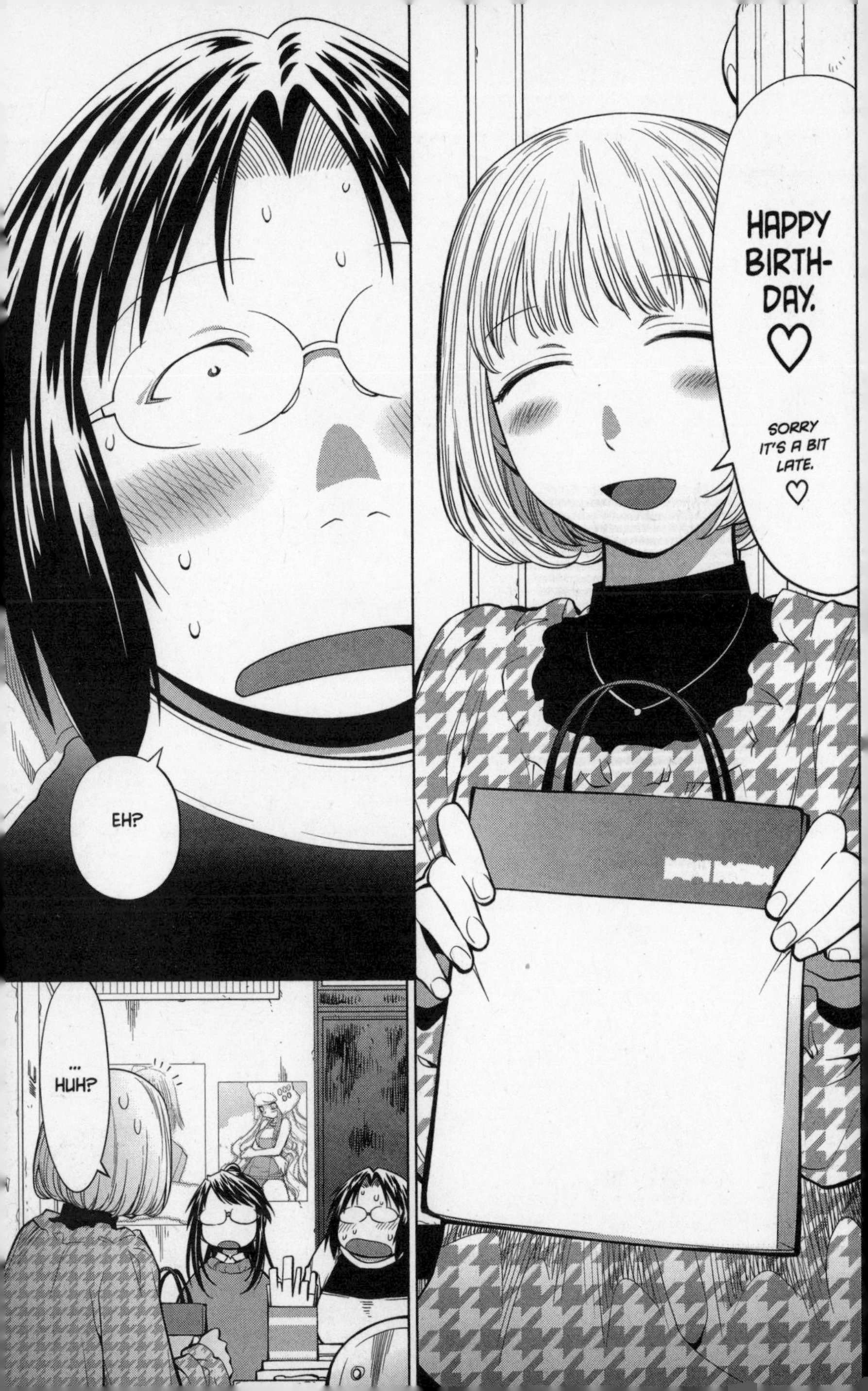
HAPPY BIRTH-DAY. ♡
SORRY IT'S A BIT LATE. ♡
EH?
... HUH?

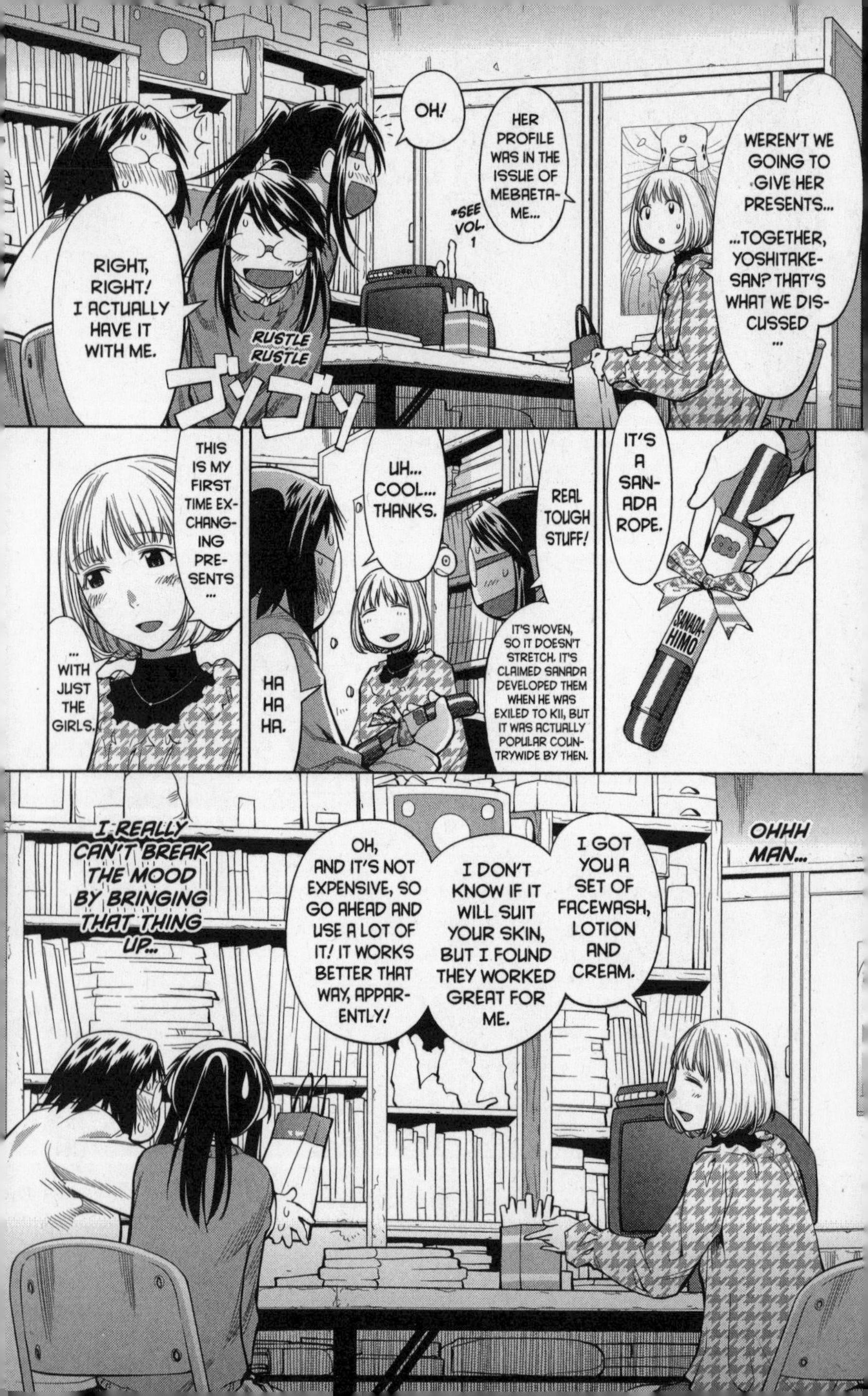
WEREN'T WE GOING TO GIVE HER PRESENTS... ...TOGETHER, YOSHITAKE-SAN? THAT'S WHAT WE DISCUSSED ...
HER PROFILE WAS IN THE ISSUE OF MEBAETA-ME...
*SEE VOL. 1
OH!
RUSTLE RUSTLE
RIGHT, RIGHT! I ACTUALLY HAVE IT WITH ME.
IT'S A SANADA ROPE.
SANADA-HIMO
REAL TOUGH STUFF!
IT'S WOVEN, SO IT DOESN'T STRETCH. IT'S CLAIMED SANADA DEVELOPED THEM WHEN HE WAS EXILED TO KII, BUT IT WAS ACTUALLY POPULAR COUNTRYWIDE BY THEN.
UH... COOL... THANKS.
HA HA HA.
THIS IS MY FIRST TIME EXCHANGING PRESENTS ...
... WITH JUST THE GIRLS.
OHHH MAN...
I GOT YOU A SET OF FACEWASH, LOTION AND CREAM.
I DON'T KNOW IF IT WILL SUIT YOUR SKIN, BUT I FOUND THEY WORKED GREAT FOR ME.
OH, AND IT'S NOT EXPENSIVE, SO GO AHEAD AND USE A LOT OF IT! IT WORKS BETTER THAT WAY, APPARENTLY!
I REALLY CAN'T BREAK THE MOOD BY BRINGING THAT THING UP...

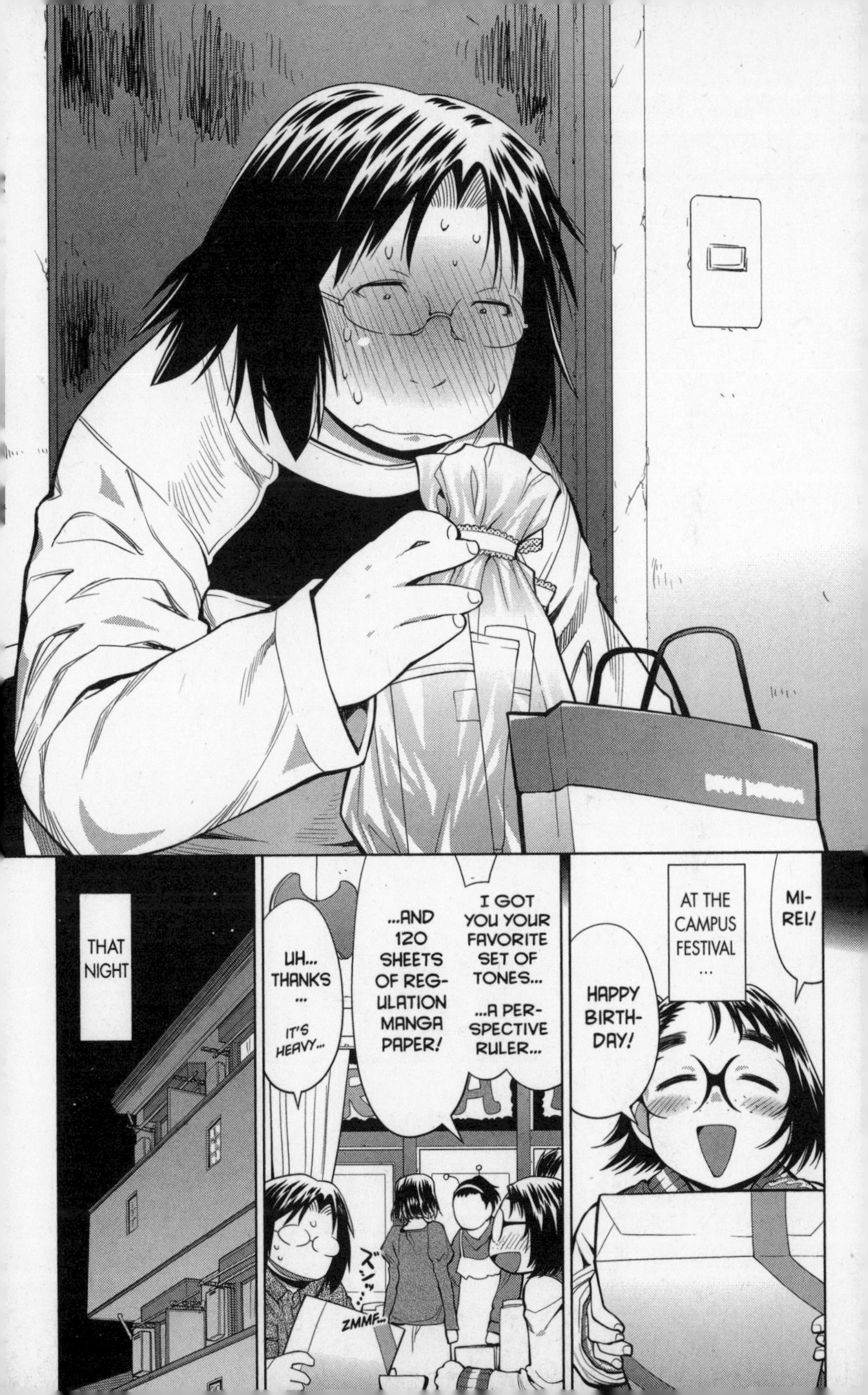
MI-REI!
AT THE CAMPUS FESTIVAL ...
HAPPY BIRTHDAY!
I GOT YOU YOUR FAVORITE SET OF TONES... ...A PERSPECTIVE RULER...
...AND 120 SHEETS OF REGULATION MANGA PAPER!
UH... THANKS ...
IT'S HEAVY...
ZMMF...
THAT NIGHT

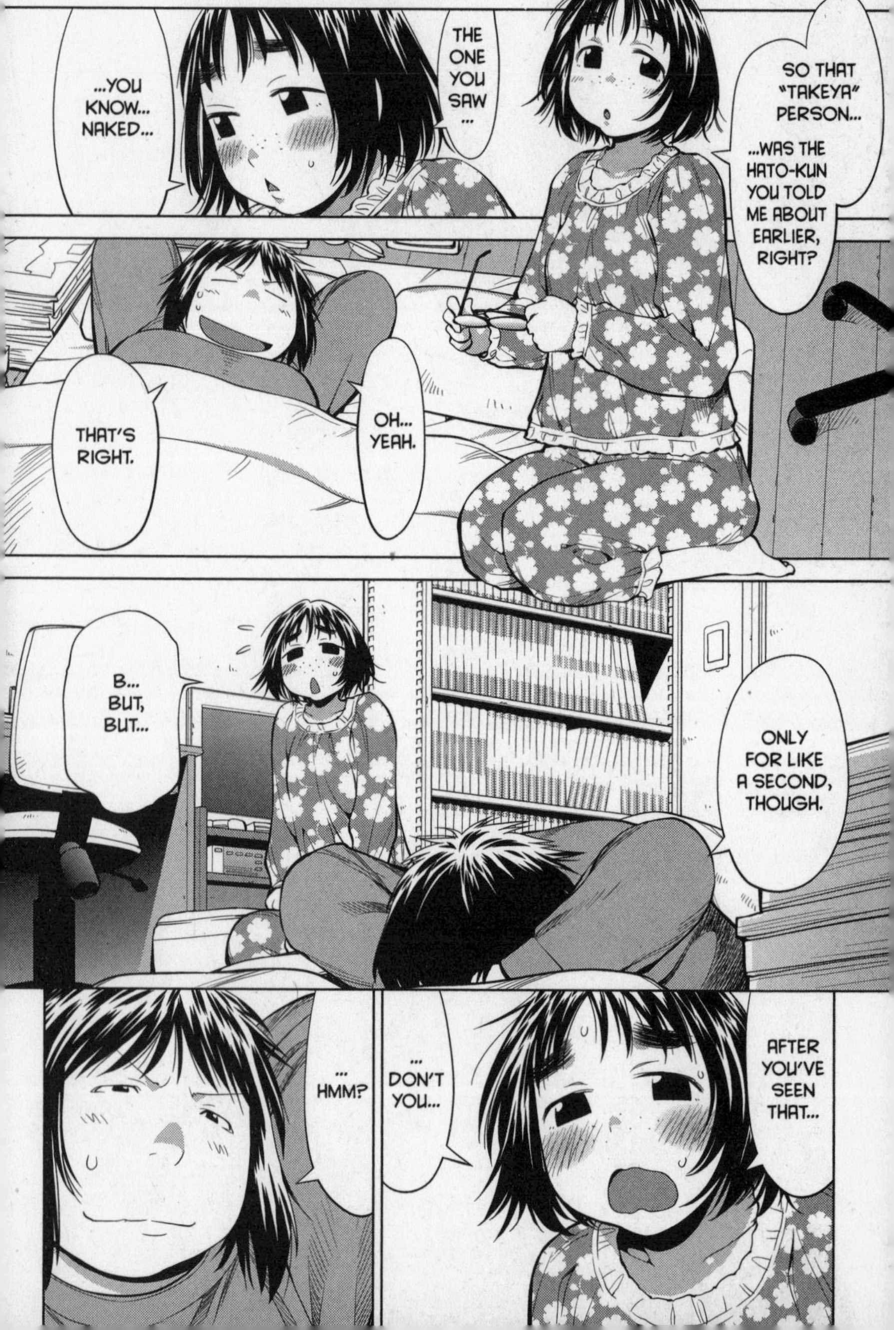
SO THAT "TAKEYA" PERSON... ...WAS THE HATO-KUN YOU TOLD ME ABOUT EARLIER, RIGHT?
THE ONE YOU SAW ...
...YOU KNOW... NAKED...
OH... YEAH.
THAT'S RIGHT.
ONLY FOR LIKE A SECOND, THOUGH.
B... BUT, BUT...
AFTER YOU'VE SEEN THAT...
... DON'T YOU...
... HMM?

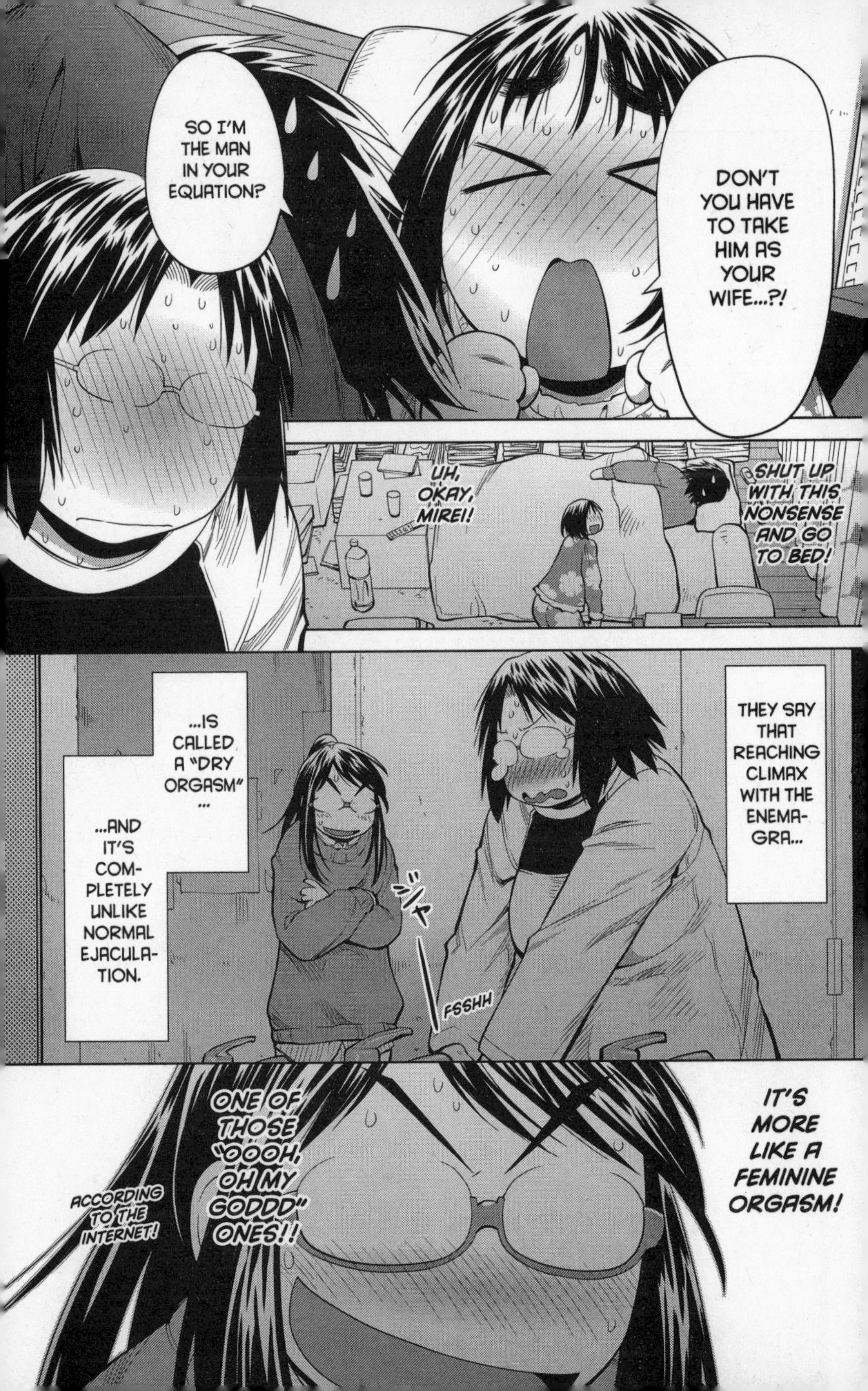
DON'T YOU HAVE TO TAKE HIM AS YOUR WIFE...?!
SO I'M THE MAN IN YOUR EQUATION?
SHUT UP WITH THIS NONSENSE AND GO TO BED!
UH, OKAY, MIREI!
THEY SAY THAT REACHING CLIMAX WITH THE ENEMA-GRA...
...IS CALLED A "DRY ORGASM"...
...AND IT'S COMPLETELY UNLIKE NORMAL EJACULATION.
ジャー
FSSHH
IT'S MORE LIKE A FEMININE ORGASM!
ONE OF THOSE "OOOH, OH MY GODDD" ONES!!
ACCORDING TO THE INTERNET!

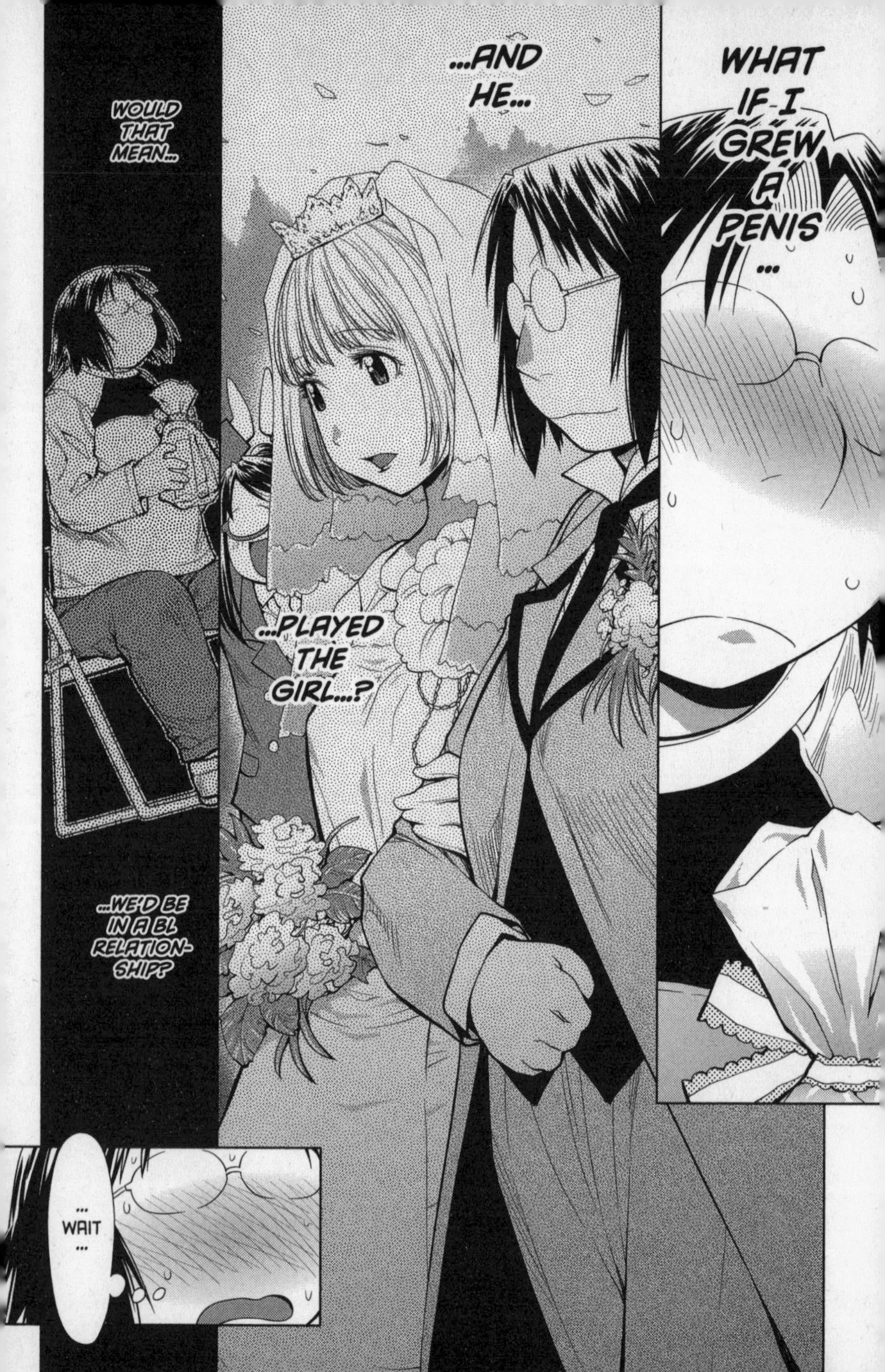
WHAT IF I GREW A PENIS...
...AND HE...
...PLAYED THE GIRL...?
WOULD THAT MEAN...
...WE'D BE IN A BL RELATION-SHIP?
...WAIT...

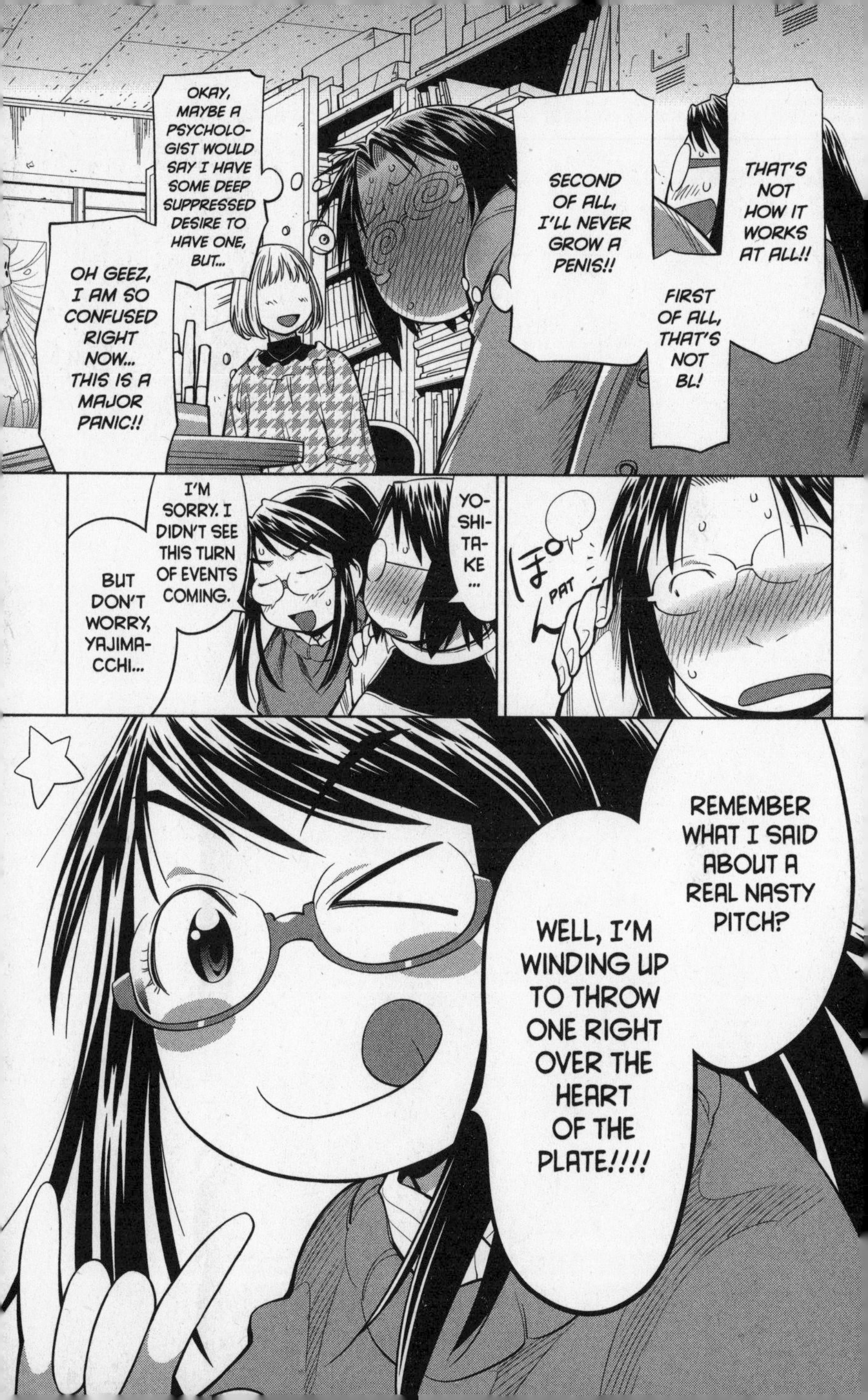
THAT'S NOT HOW IT WORKS AT ALL!!
FIRST OF ALL, THAT'S NOT BL!
SECOND OF ALL, I'LL NEVER GROW A PENIS!!
OKAY, MAYBE A PSYCHOLO-GIST WOULD SAY I HAVE SOME DEEP SUPPRESSED DESIRE TO HAVE ONE, BUT...
OH GEEZ, I AM SO CONFUSED RIGHT NOW... THIS IS A MAJOR PANIC!!
ぽん
PAT
YO-SHI-TA-KE...
I'M SORRY. I DIDN'T SEE THIS TURN OF EVENTS COMING.
BUT DON'T WORRY, YAJIMA-CCHI...
REMEMBER WHAT I SAID ABOUT A REAL NASTY PITCH?
WELL, I'M WINDING UP TO THROW ONE RIGHT OVER THE HEART OF THE PLATE!!!!

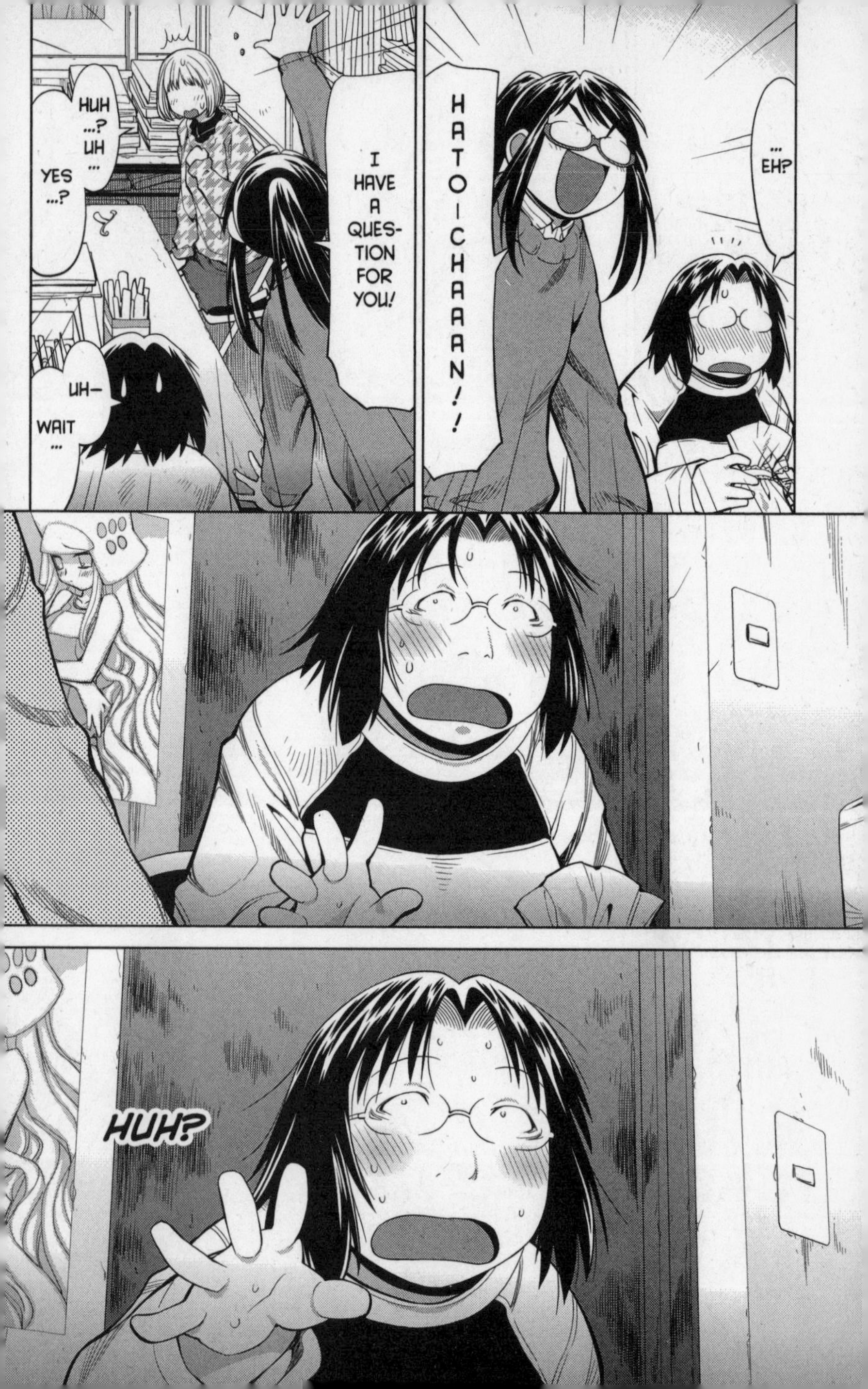
HATO-ICHAAAAN!!
...EH?
I HAVE A QUESTION FOR YOU!
HUH ...? UH ... YES ...?
UH— WAIT ...
HUH?

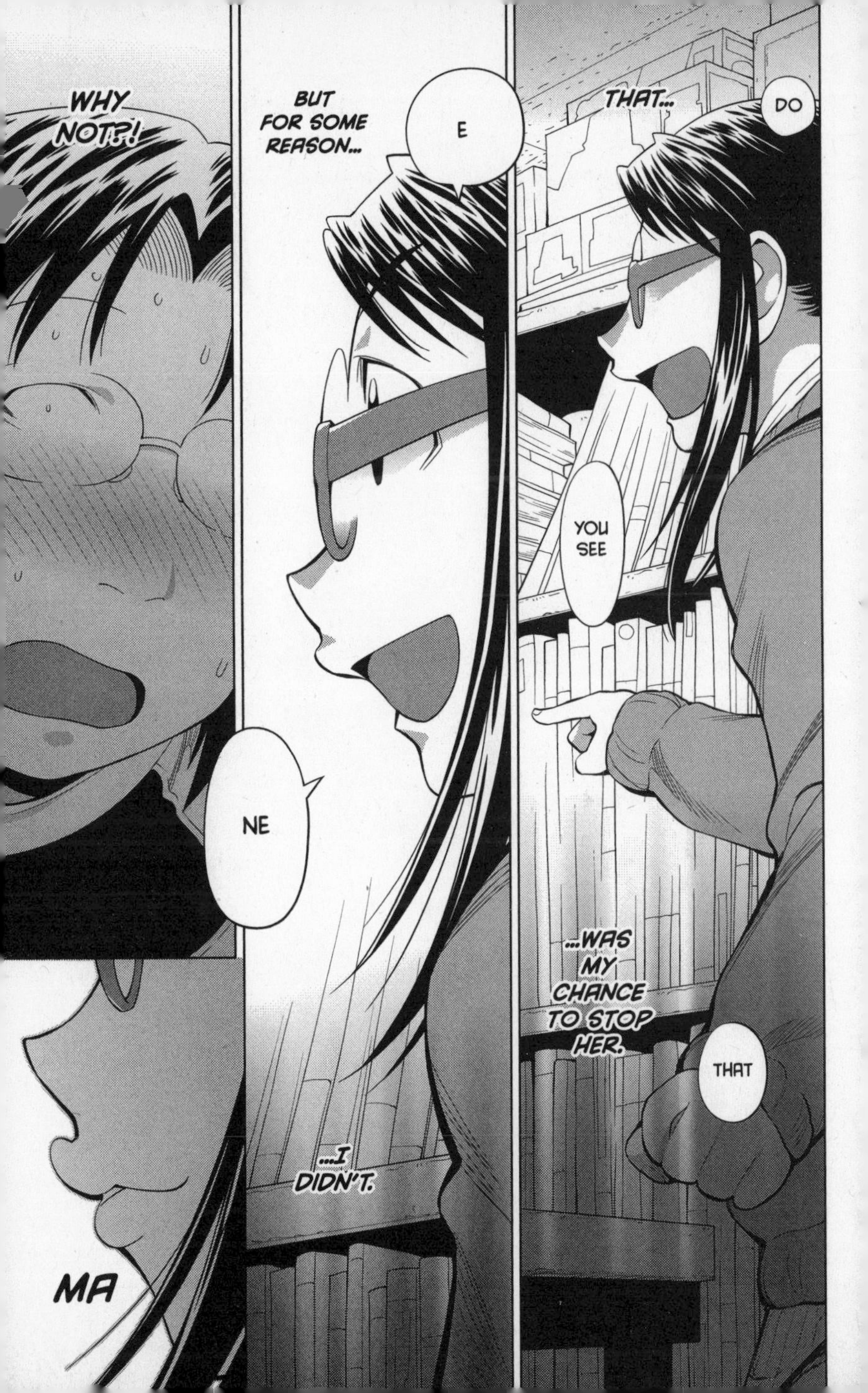
DO
THAT...
YOU SEE
...WAS MY CHANCE TO STOP HER.
THAT
E
BUT FOR SOME REASON...
NE
...I DIDN'T.
WHY NOT?!
MA

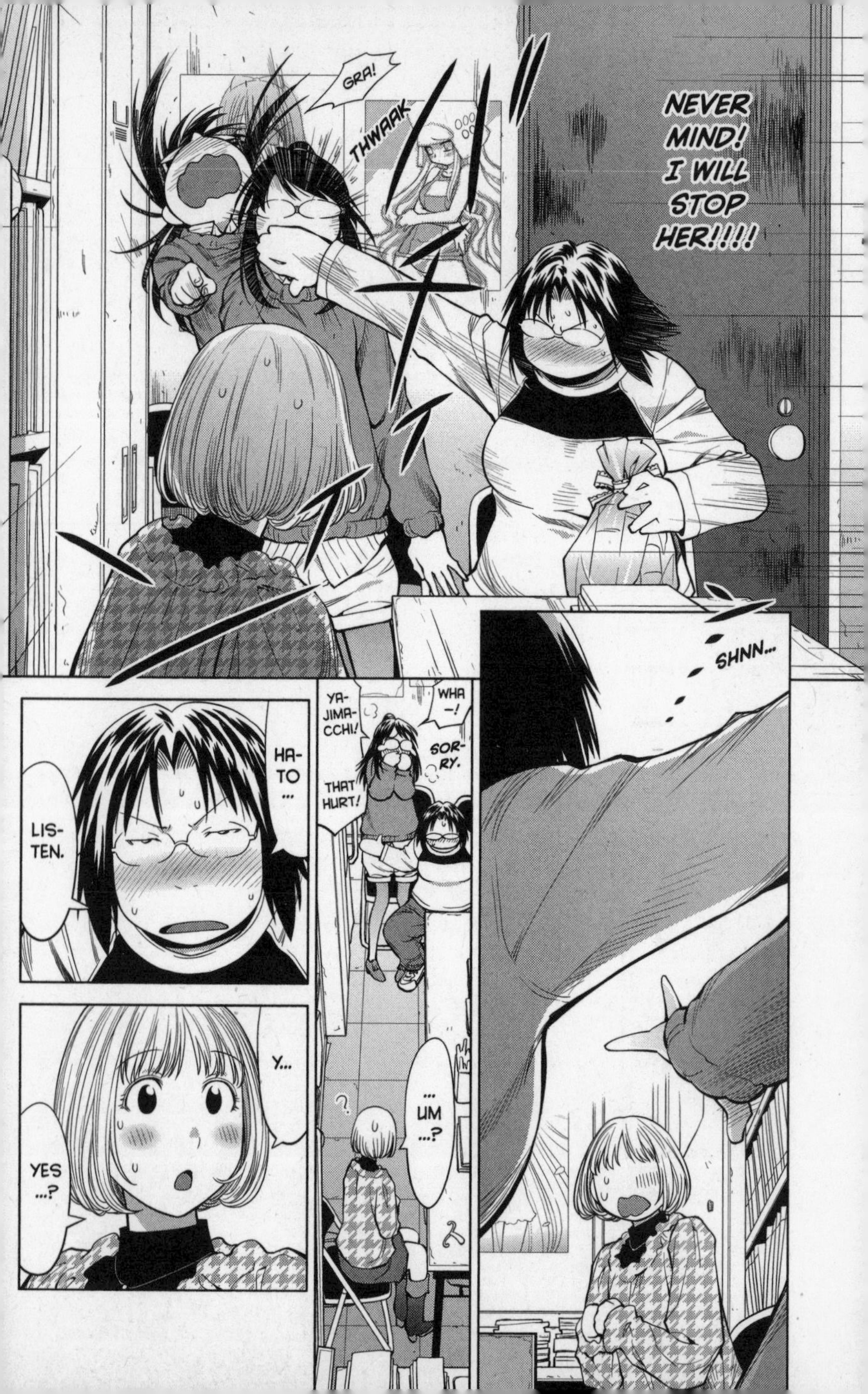
NEVER MIND! I WILL STOP HER!!!!
GRA!
THWAAK
SHNN...
WHA-!
SOR-RY.
YA-JIMA-CCHI!
THAT HURT!
...UM...?
HA-TO...
LIS-TEN.
Y...
YES...?

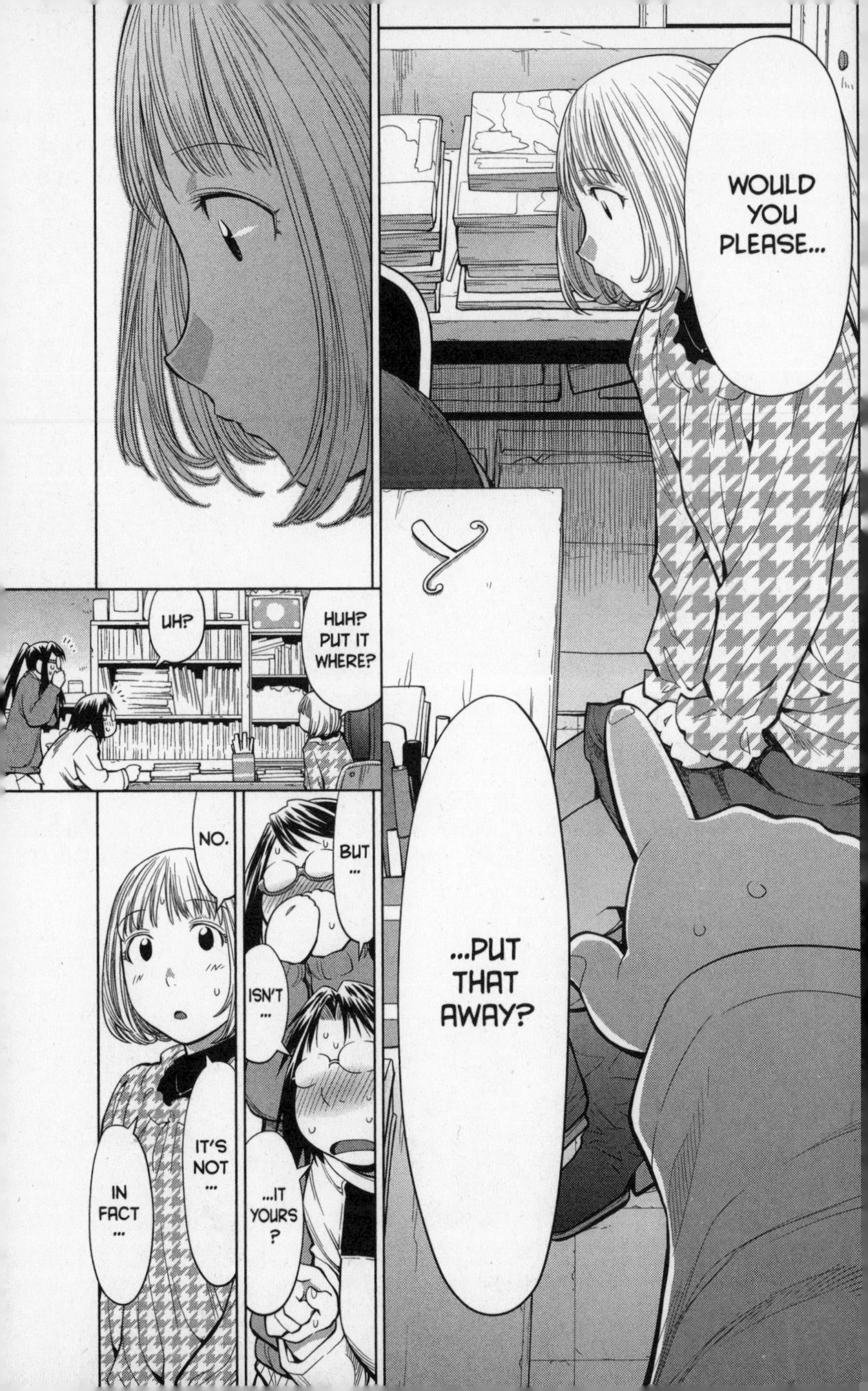
WOULD YOU PLEASE...
...PUT THAT AWAY?
HUH? PUT IT WHERE?
UH?
BUT...
ISN'T...
...IT YOURS?
NO.
IT'S NOT...
IN FACT...

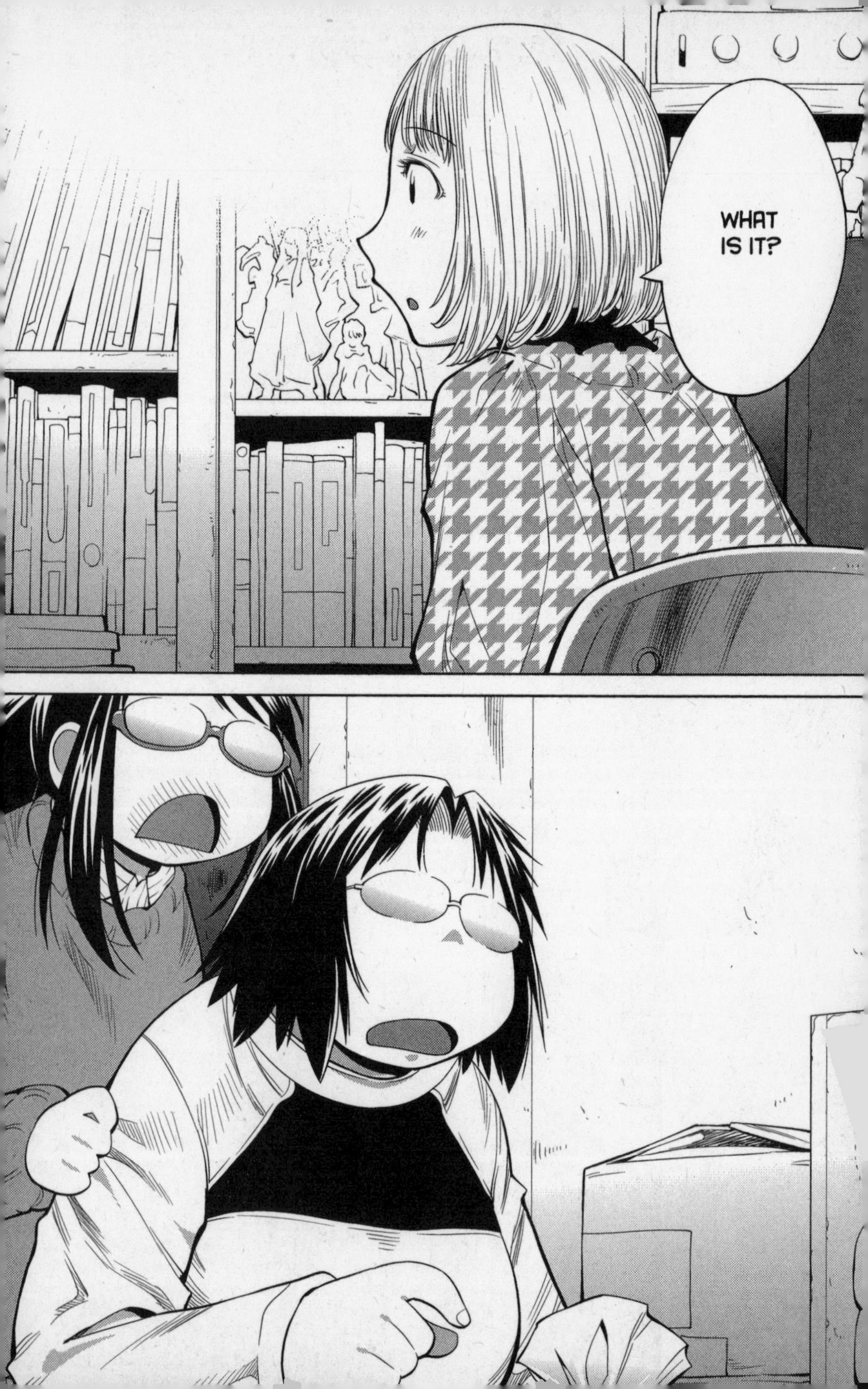
WHAT IS IT?

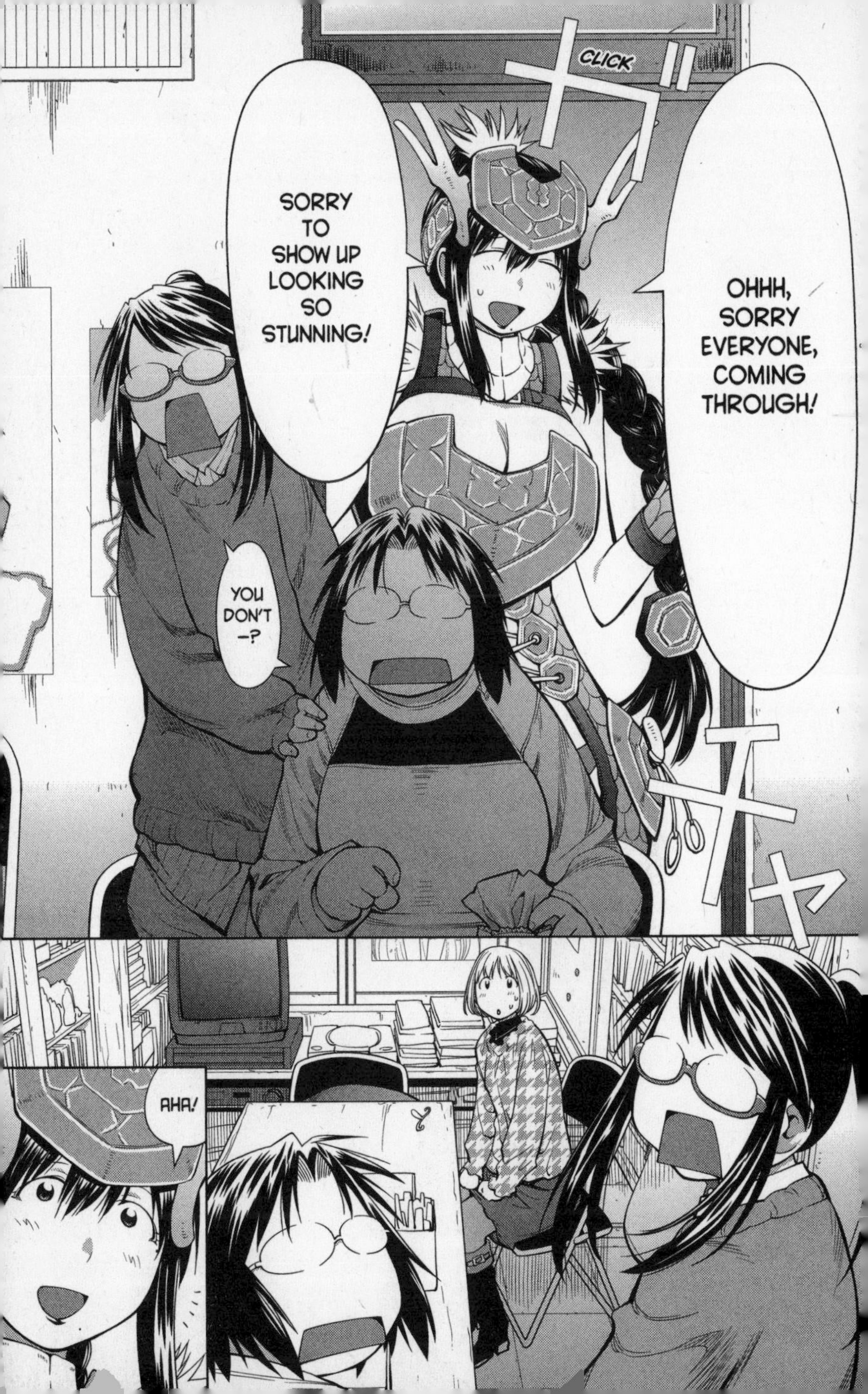
CLICK
OHHH, SORRY EVERYONE, COMING THROUGH!
SORRY TO SHOW UP LOOKING SO STUNNING!
YOU DON'T -?
AHA!

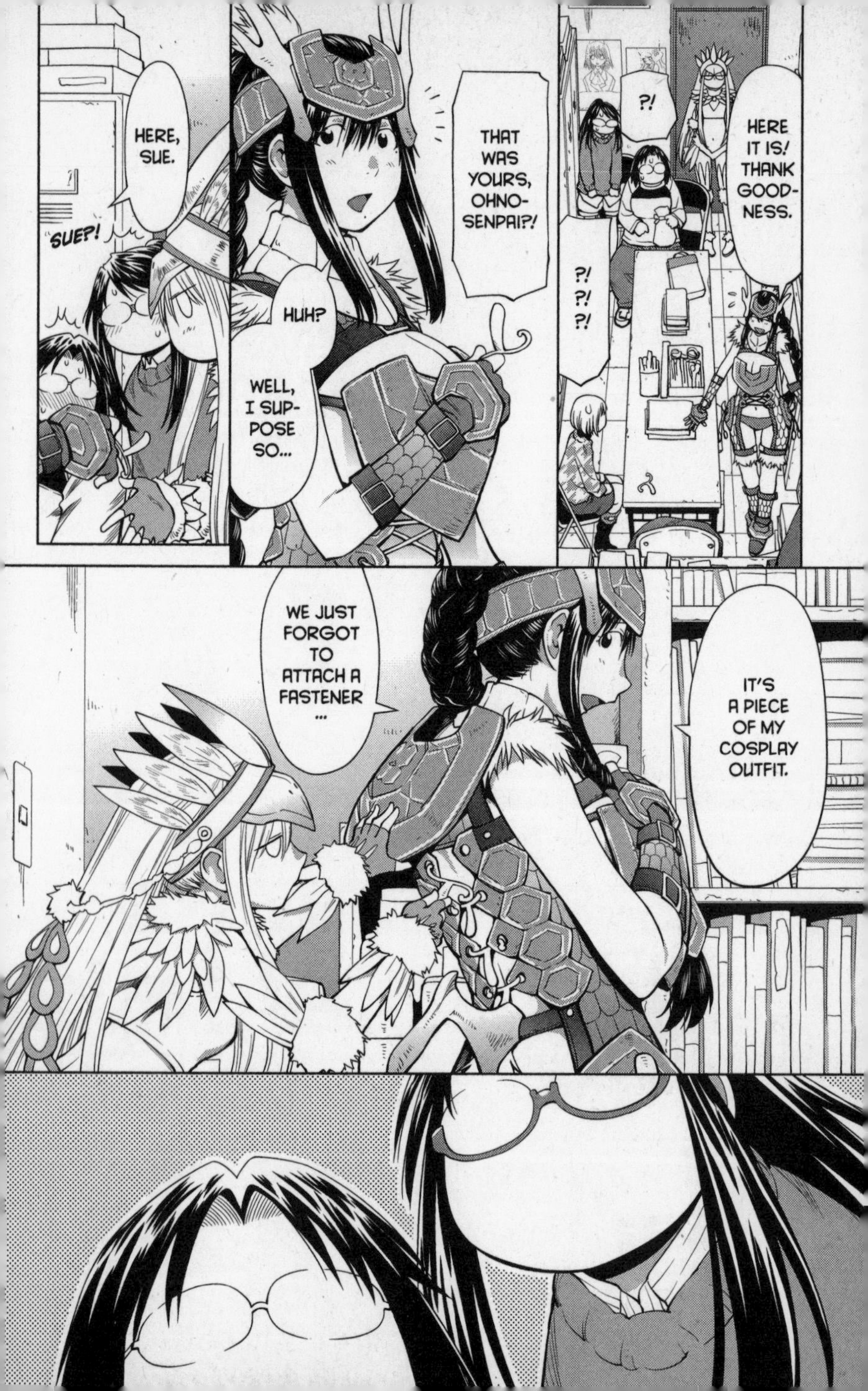
HERE IT IS! THANK GOODNESS.
?!
?! ?! ?!
THAT WAS YOURS, OHNO-SENPAI?!
HUH?
WELL, I SUPPOSE SO...
HERE, SUE.
SUEP!
IT'S A PIECE OF MY COSPLAY OUTFIT.
WE JUST FORGOT TO ATTACH A FASTENER ...

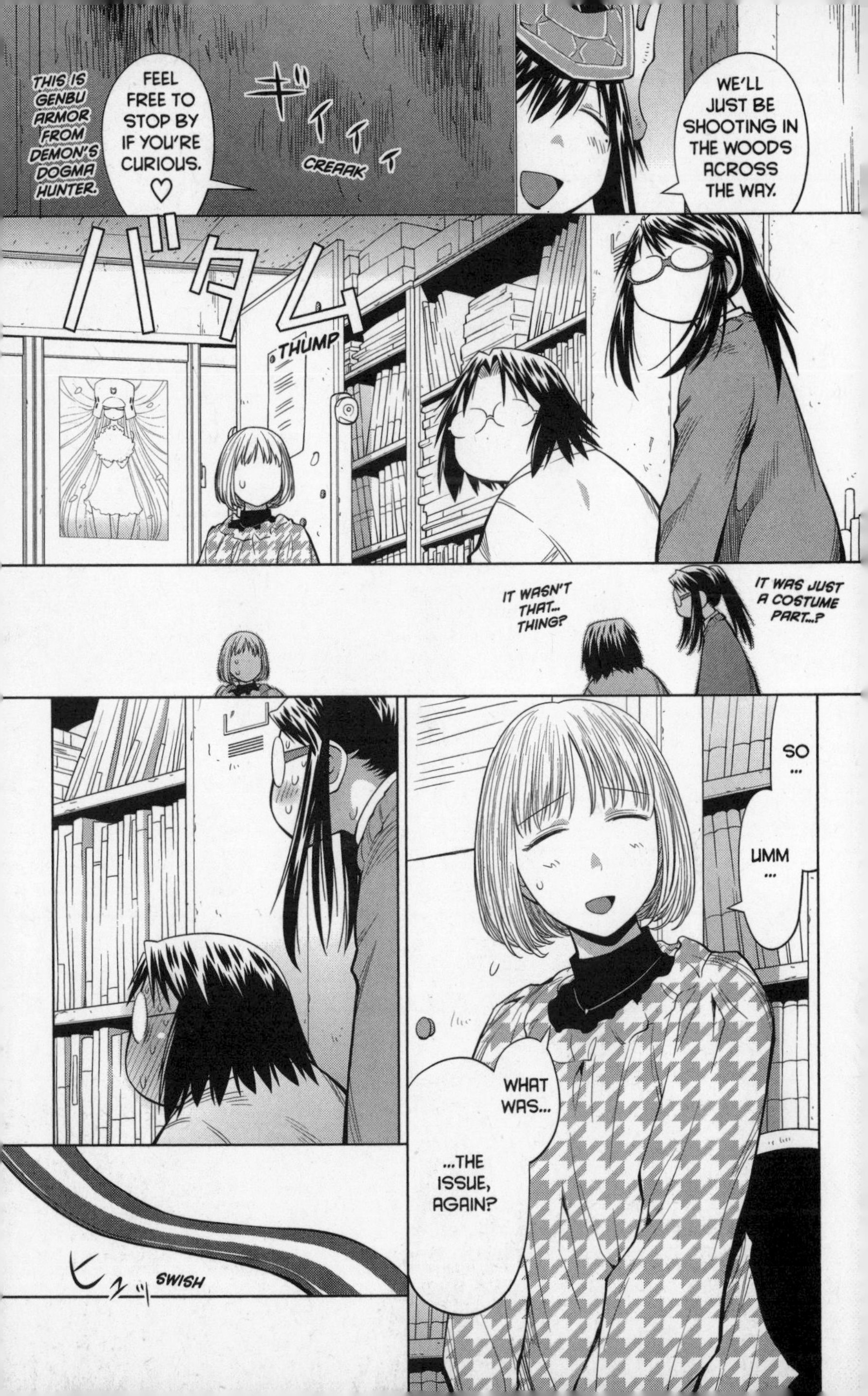
WE'LL JUST BE SHOOTING IN THE WOODS ACROSS THE WAY.
ギィィィ
CREAAK
FEEL FREE TO STOP BY IF YOU'RE CURIOUS. ♡
THIS IS GENBU ARMOR FROM DEMON'S DOGMA HUNTER.
バタム
THUMP
IT WAS JUST A COSTUME PART...?
IT WASN'T THAT... THING?
SO ...
UMM ...
WHAT WAS...
...THE ISSUE, AGAIN?
ヒュッ
SWISH

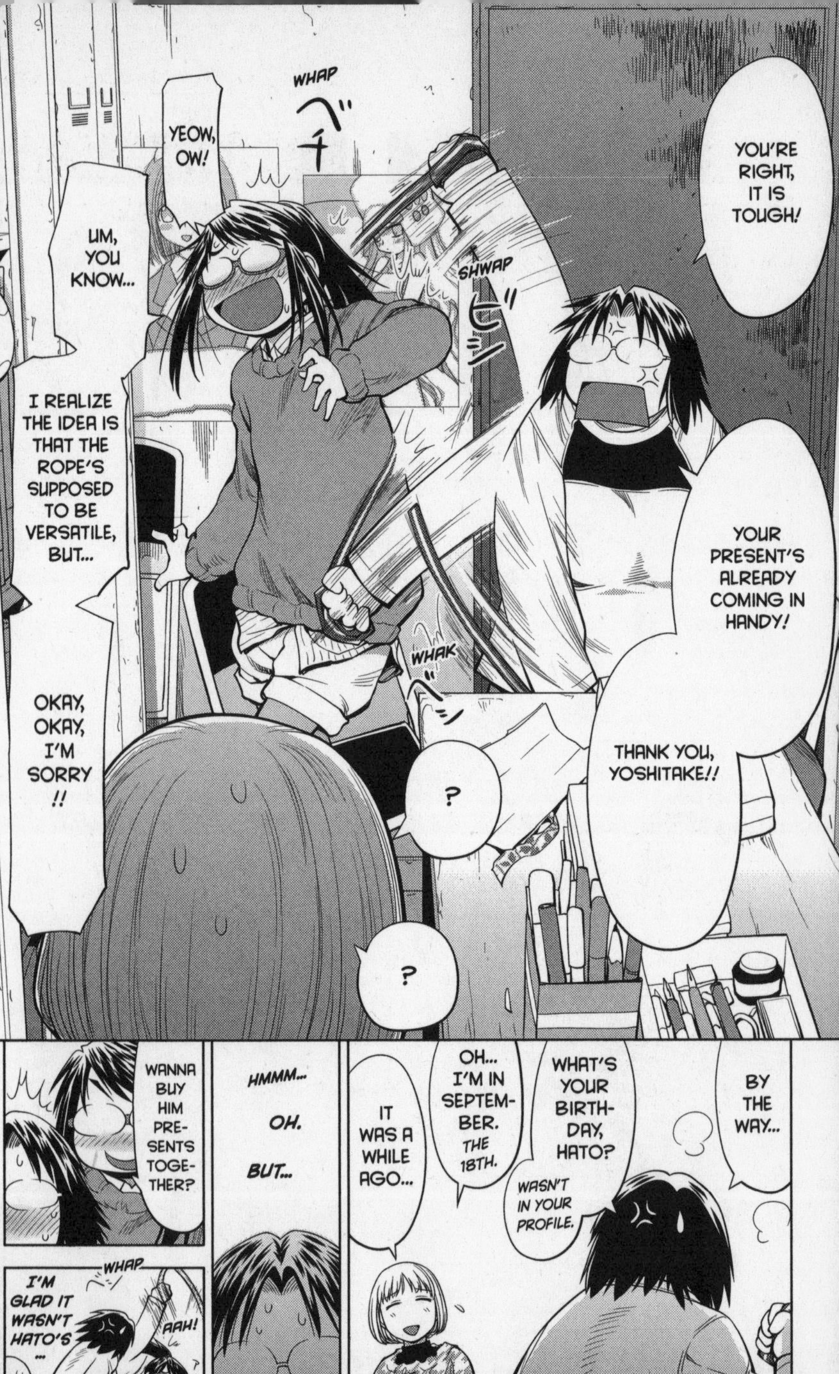
YOU'RE RIGHT, IT IS TOUGH!
WHAP
YEOW, OW!
SHWAP
UM, YOU KNOW...
YOUR PRESENT'S ALREADY COMING IN HANDY!
I REALIZE THE IDEA IS THAT THE ROPE'S SUPPOSED TO BE VERSATILE, BUT...
WHAK
THANK YOU, YOSHITAKE!!
OKAY, OKAY, I'M SORRY!!
?
?
BY THE WAY...
WHAT'S YOUR BIRTH-DAY, HATO?
WASN'T IN YOUR PROFILE.
OH... I'M IN SEPTEM-BER. THE 18TH.
IT WAS A WHILE AGO...
HMMM...
OH.
BUT...
WANNA BUY HIM PRE-SENTS TOGE-THER?
WHAP
I'M GLAD IT WASN'T HATO'S ...
AAH!
BWAP

CHAPTER 82 - END

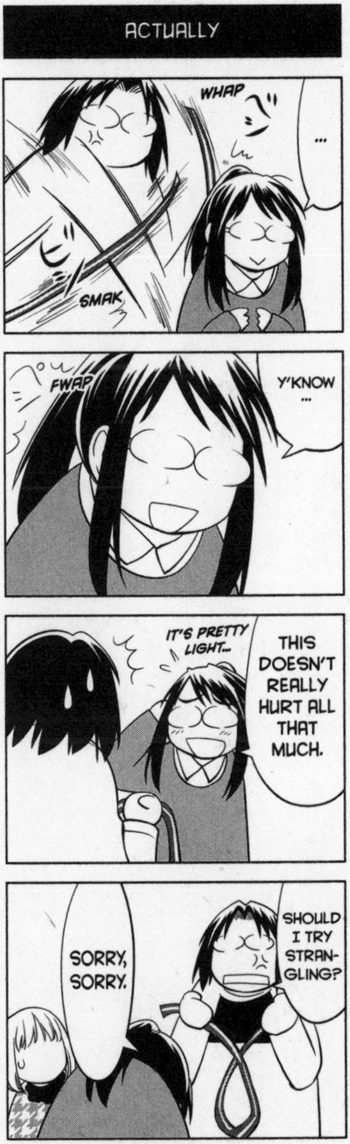
ACTUALLY
WHAP
...
SMAK
FWAP
Y'KNOW ...
IT'S PRETTY LIGHT...
THIS DOESN'T REALLY HURT ALL THAT MUCH.
SHOULD I TRY STRANGLING?
SORRY, SORRY.

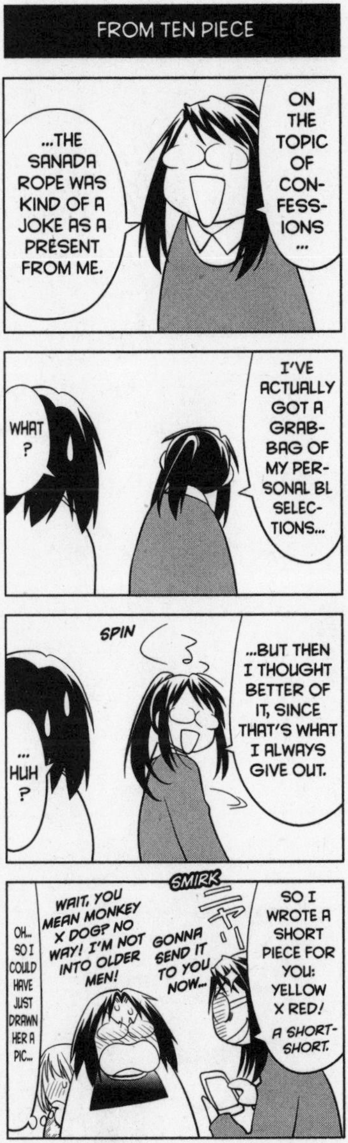
FROM TEN PIECE
ON THE TOPIC OF CONFESSIONS ...
...THE SANADA ROPE WAS KIND OF A JOKE AS A PRESENT FROM ME.
I'VE ACTUALLY GOT A GRAB-BAG OF MY PERSONAL BL SELECTIONS...
WHAT?
SPIN
...BUT THEN I THOUGHT BETTER OF IT, SINCE THAT'S WHAT I ALWAYS GIVE OUT.
... HUH?
SO I WROTE A SHORT PIECE FOR YOU: YELLOW X RED!
A SHORT-SHORT.
SMIRK
GONNA SEND IT TO YOU NOW...
WAIT, YOU MEAN MONKEY X DOG? NO WAY! I'M NOT INTO OLDER MEN!
OH... SO I COULD HAVE JUST DRAWN HER A PIC...

INEVITABLE

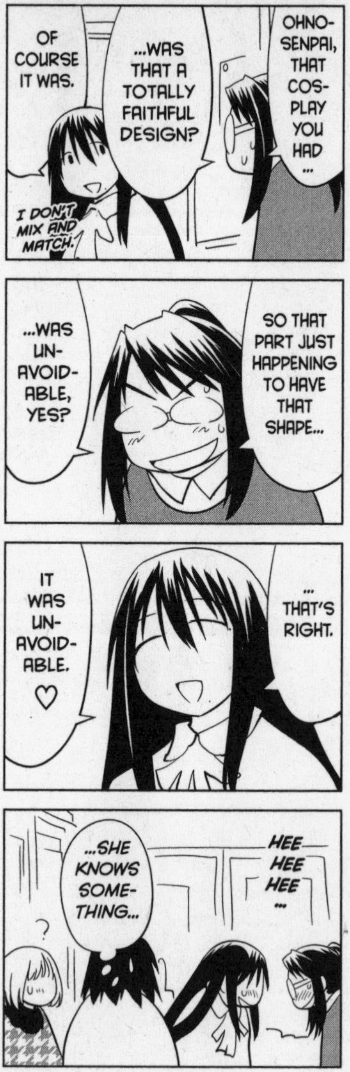
OHNO-SENPAI, THAT COS-PLAY YOU HAD ...
...WAS THAT A TOTALLY FAITHFUL DESIGN?
OF COURSE IT WAS.
I DON'T MIX AND MATCH.
SO THAT PART JUST HAPPENING TO HAVE THAT SHAPE...
...WAS UN-AVOID-ABLE, YES?
... THAT'S RIGHT.
IT WAS UN-AVOID-ABLE. ♡
HEE HEE HEE ...
...SHE KNOWS SOME-THING...
?

HATO PRESENTS

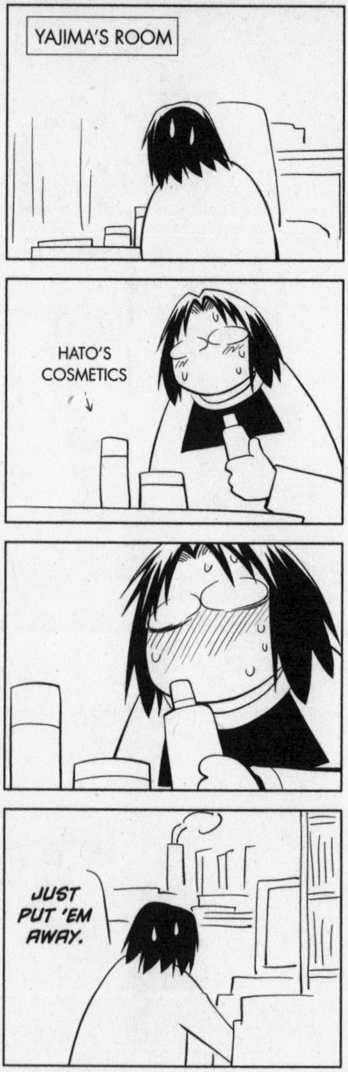
YAJIMA'S ROOM
HATO'S COSMETICS
JUST PUT 'EM AWAY.

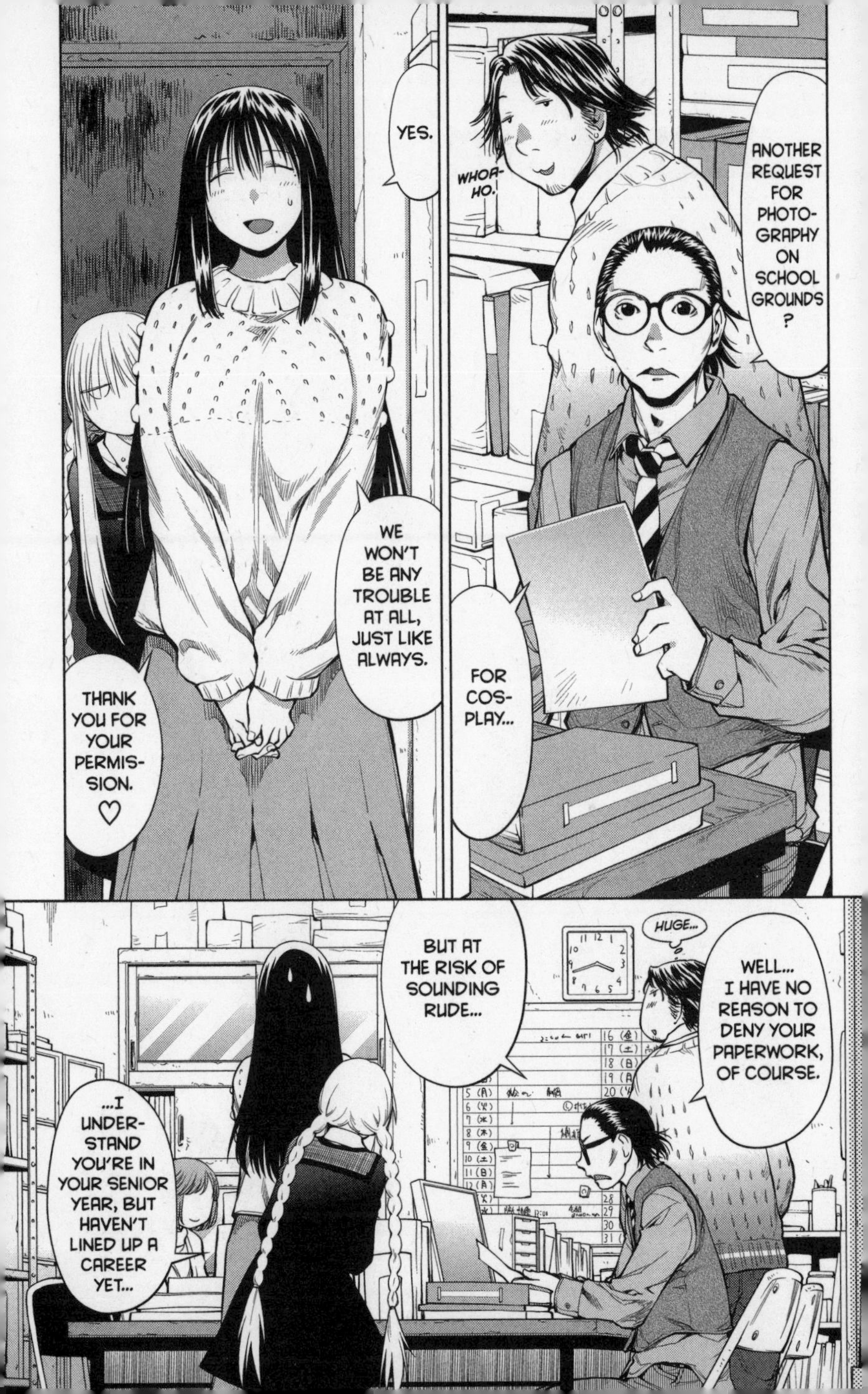
ANOTHER REQUEST FOR PHOTOGRAPHY ON SCHOOL GROUNDS?
WHOA-HO.
FOR COSPLAY...
YES.
WE WON'T BE ANY TROUBLE AT ALL, JUST LIKE ALWAYS.
THANK YOU FOR YOUR PERMISSION. ♡
HUGE...
WELL... I HAVE NO REASON TO DENY YOUR PAPERWORK, OF COURSE.
BUT AT THE RISK OF SOUNDING RUDE...
...I UNDERSTAND YOU'RE IN YOUR SENIOR YEAR, BUT HAVEN'T LINED UP A CAREER YET...

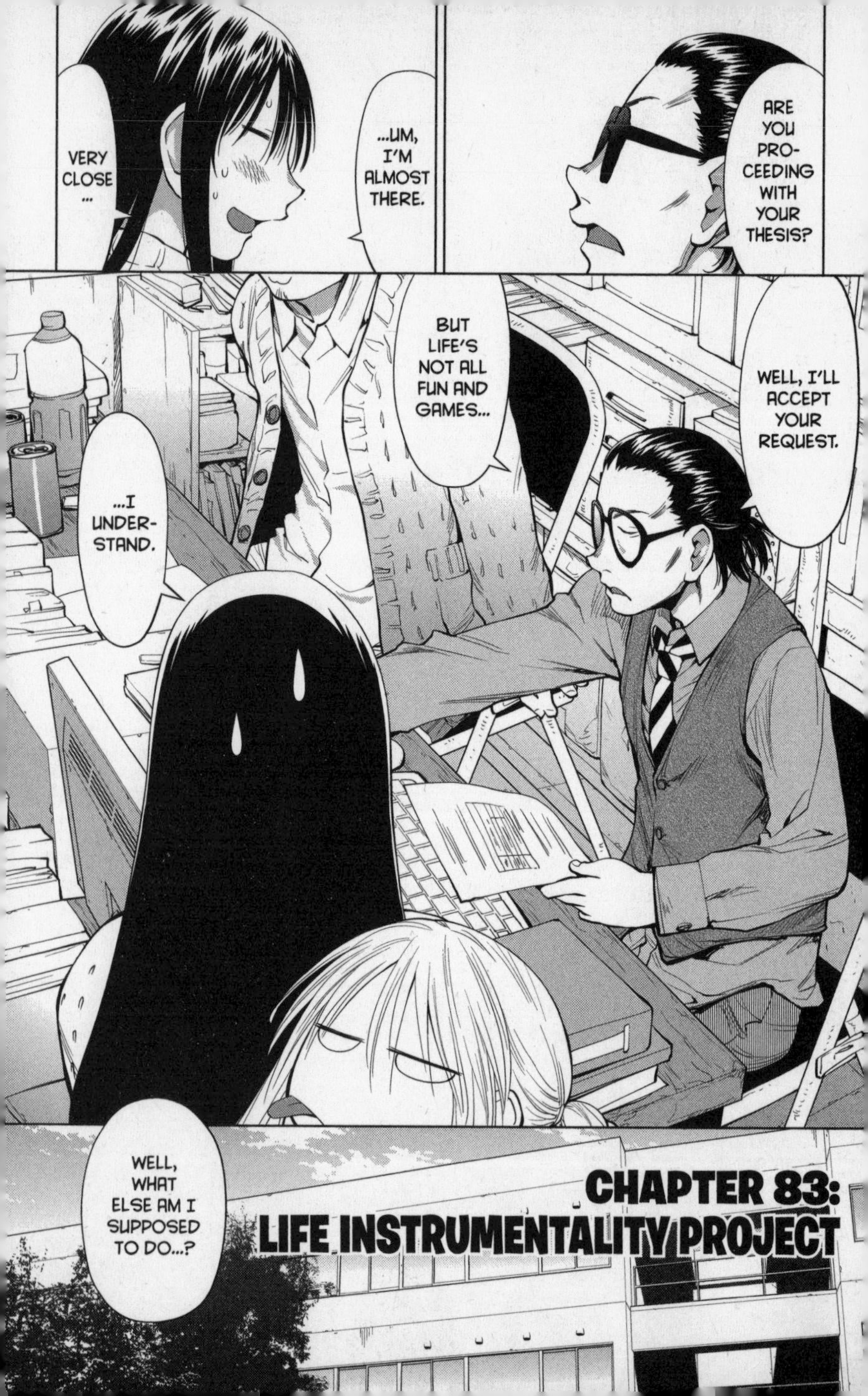
ARE YOU PRO-CEEDING WITH YOUR THESIS?
...UM, I'M ALMOST THERE.
VERY CLOSE ...
WELL, I'LL ACCEPT YOUR REQUEST.
BUT LIFE'S NOT ALL FUN AND GAMES...
...I UNDER-STAND.
CHAPTER 83: LIFE INSTRUMENTALITY PROJECT
WELL, WHAT ELSE AM I SUPPOSED TO DO...?

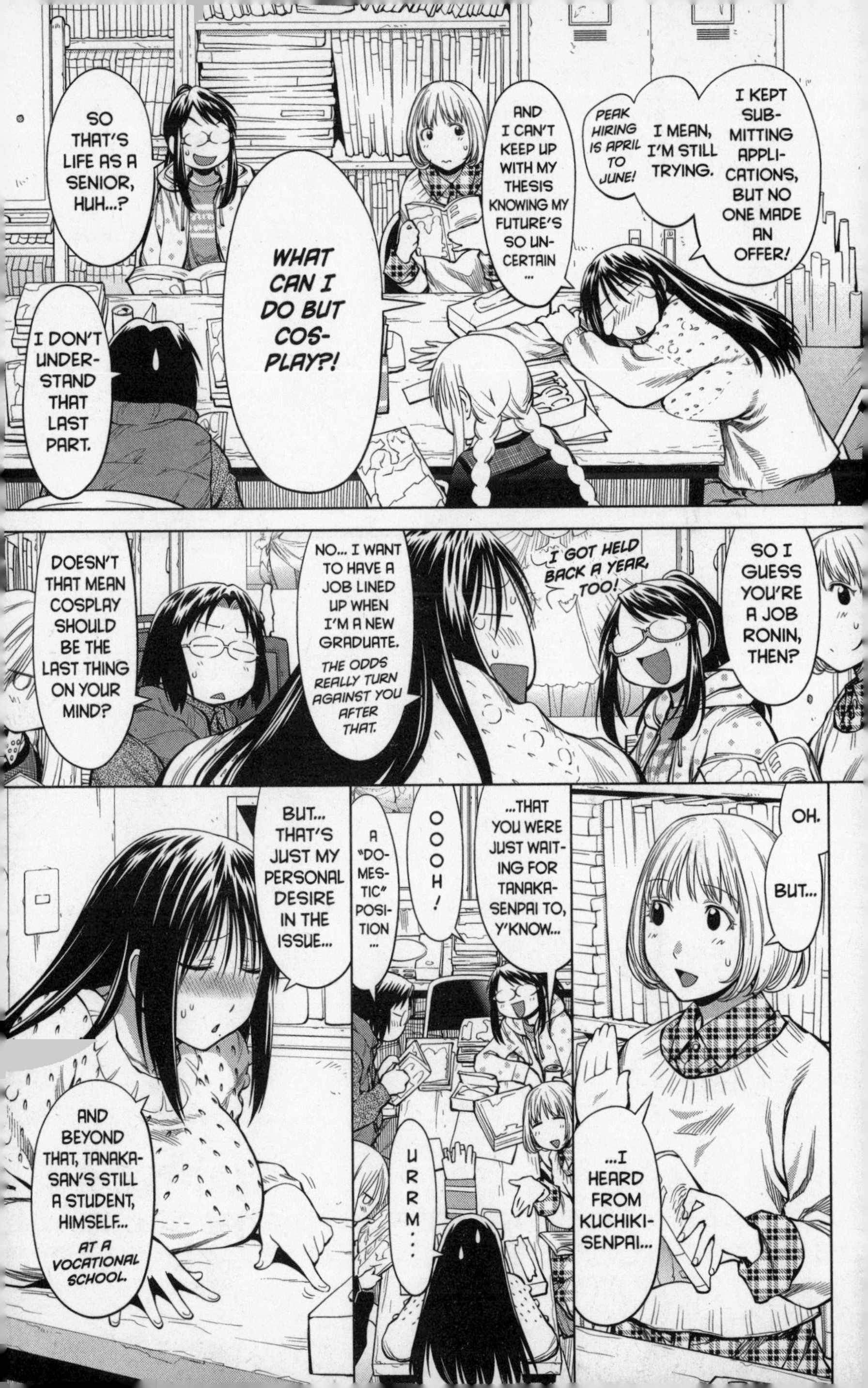
I KEPT SUBMITTING APPLICATIONS, BUT NO ONE MADE AN OFFER!
I MEAN, I'M STILL TRYING.
PEAK HIRING IS APRIL TO JUNE!
AND I CAN'T KEEP UP WITH MY THESIS KNOWING MY FUTURE'S SO UNCERTAIN...
WHAT CAN I DO BUT COSPLAY?!
SO THAT'S LIFE AS A SENIOR, HUH...?
I DON'T UNDERSTAND THAT LAST PART.
SO I GUESS YOU'RE A JOB RONIN, THEN?
I GOT HELD BACK A YEAR, TOO!
NO... I WANT TO HAVE A JOB LINED UP WHEN I'M A NEW GRADUATE.
THE ODDS REALLY TURN AGAINST YOU AFTER THAT.
DOESN'T THAT MEAN COSPLAY SHOULD BE THE LAST THING ON YOUR MIND?
OH.
BUT...
...I HEARD FROM KUCHIKI-SENPAI...
...THAT YOU WERE JUST WAITING FOR TANAKA-SENPAI TO, Y'KNOW...
OOOH!
A "DOMESTIC" POSITION...
URRM...
BUT... THAT'S JUST MY PERSONAL DESIRE IN THE ISSUE...
AND BEYOND THAT, TANAKA-SAN'S STILL A STUDENT, HIMSELF...
AT A VOCATIONAL SCHOOL.

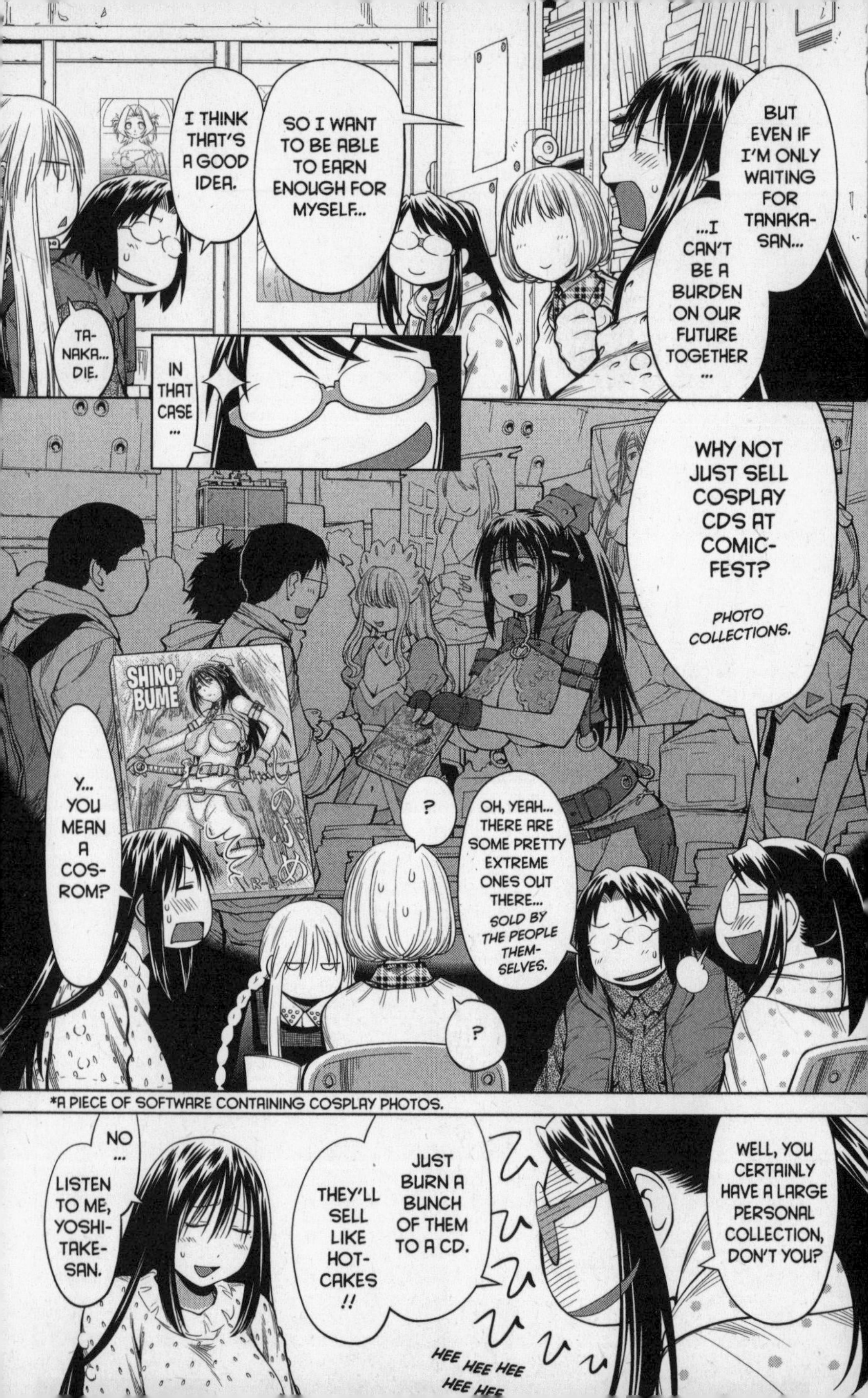
BUT EVEN IF I'M ONLY WAITING FOR TANAKA-SAN...
...I CAN'T BE A BURDEN ON OUR FUTURE TOGETHER...
SO I WANT TO BE ABLE TO EARN ENOUGH FOR MYSELF...
I THINK THAT'S A GOOD IDEA.
TA-NAKA... DIE.
IN THAT CASE...
WHY NOT JUST SELL COSPLAY CDS AT COMIC-FEST?
PHOTO COLLECTIONS.
SHINO-BUME
OH, YEAH... THERE ARE SOME PRETTY EXTREME ONES OUT THERE...
SOLD BY THE PEOPLE THEMSELVES.
?
Y... YOU MEAN A COS-ROM?
?
WELL, YOU CERTAINLY HAVE A LARGE PERSONAL COLLECTION, DON'T YOU?
HEE HEE HEE HEE HEE
JUST BURN A BUNCH OF THEM TO A CD.
THEY'LL SELL LIKE HOT-CAKES!!
NO... LISTEN TO ME, YOSHI-TAKE-SAN.

*A PIECE OF SOFTWARE CONTAINING COSPLAY PHOTOS.

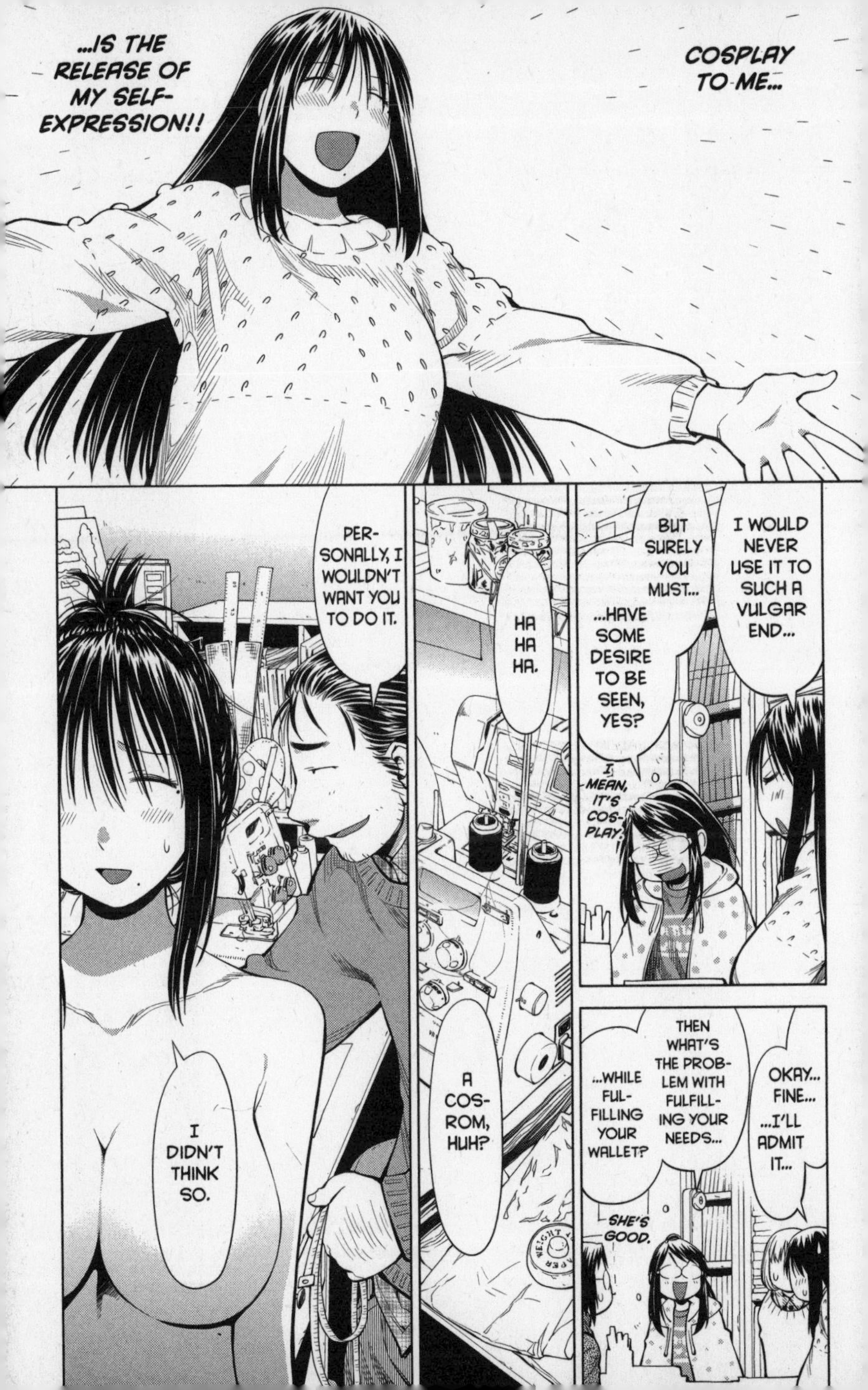
COSPLAY TO ME...
...IS THE RELEASE OF MY SELF-EXPRESSION!!
I WOULD NEVER USE IT TO SUCH A VULGAR END...
BUT SURELY YOU MUST... ...HAVE SOME DESIRE TO BE SEEN, YES?
I MEAN, IT'S COSPLAY.
OKAY... FINE... ...I'LL ADMIT IT...
THEN WHAT'S THE PROBLEM WITH FULFILLING YOUR NEEDS...
...WHILE FULFILLING YOUR WALLET?
SHE'S GOOD.
HA HA HA.
A COS-ROM, HUH?
PERSONALLY, I WOULDN'T WANT YOU TO DO IT.
I DIDN'T THINK SO.

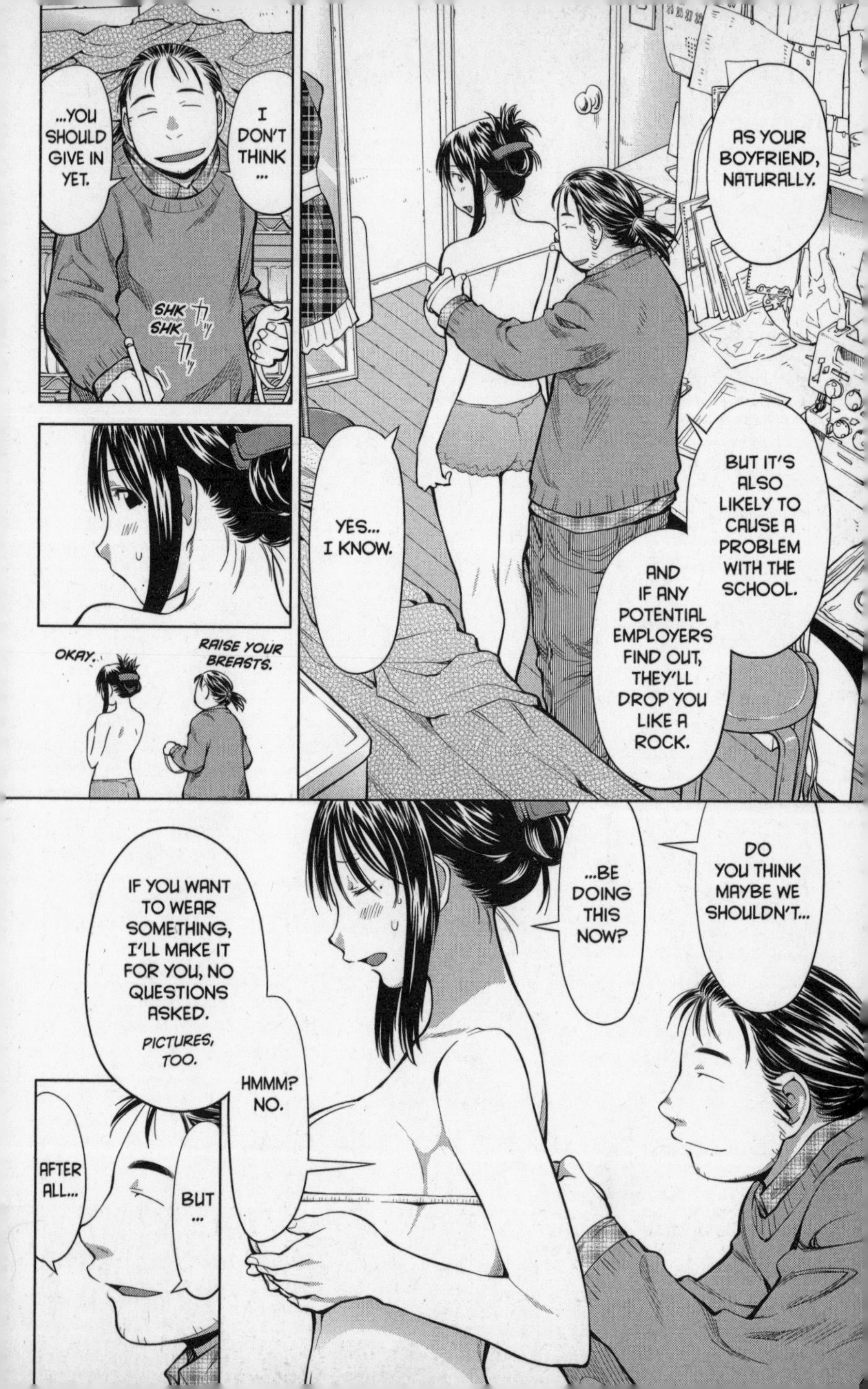
AS YOUR BOYFRIEND, NATURALLY.
BUT IT'S ALSO LIKELY TO CAUSE A PROBLEM WITH THE SCHOOL.
AND IF ANY POTENTIAL EMPLOYERS FIND OUT, THEY'LL DROP YOU LIKE A ROCK.
YES... I KNOW.
I DON'T THINK...
...YOU SHOULD GIVE IN YET.
SHK SHK
RAISE YOUR BREASTS.
OKAY.
DO YOU THINK MAYBE WE SHOULDN'T...
...BE DOING THIS NOW?
IF YOU WANT TO WEAR SOMETHING, I'LL MAKE IT FOR YOU, NO QUESTIONS ASKED.
PICTURES, TOO.
HMMM? NO.
BUT...
AFTER ALL...

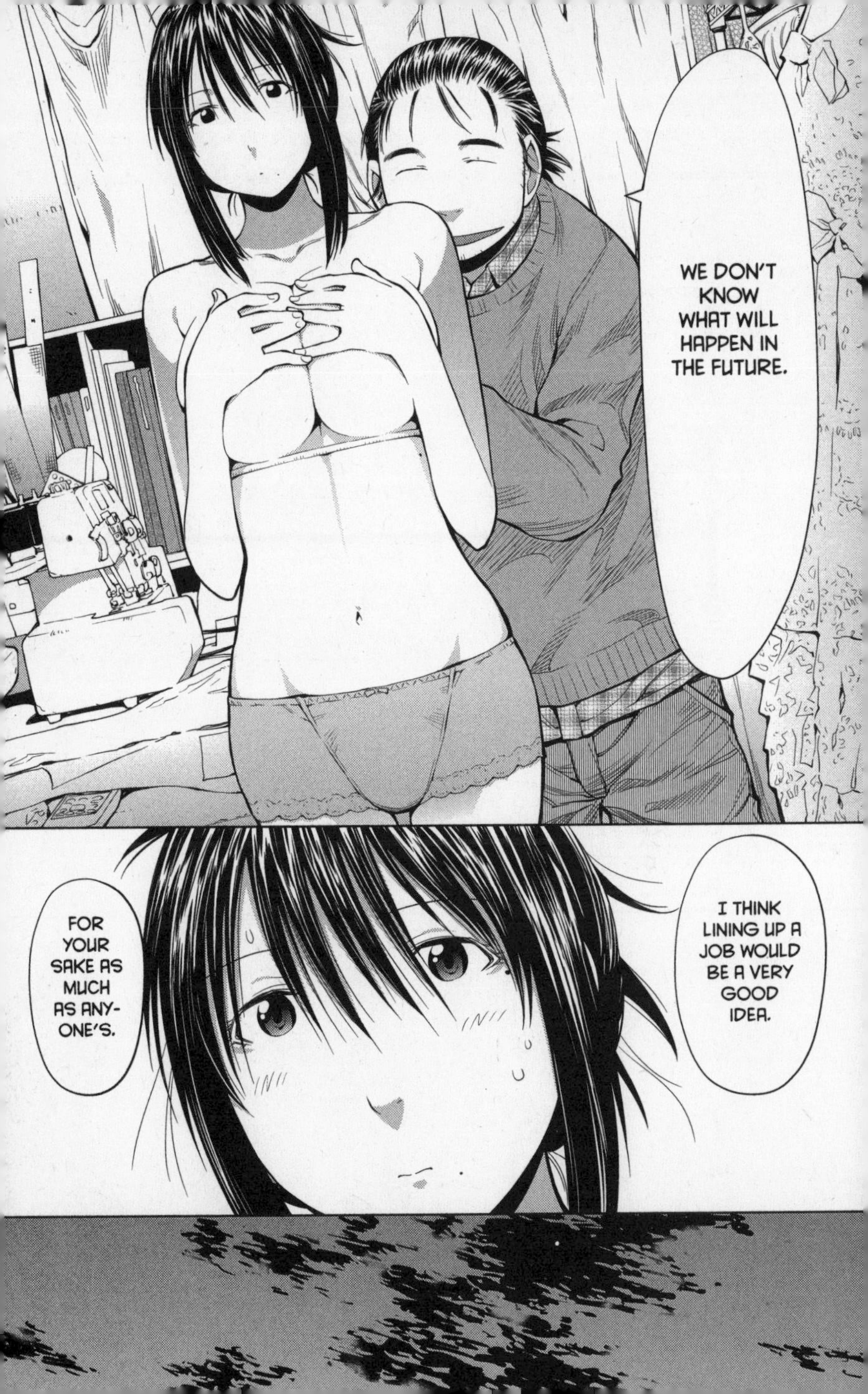
WE DON'T KNOW WHAT WILL HAPPEN IN THE FUTURE.
I THINK LINING UP A JOB WOULD BE A VERY GOOD IDEA.
FOR YOUR SAKE AS MUCH AS ANY-ONE'S.

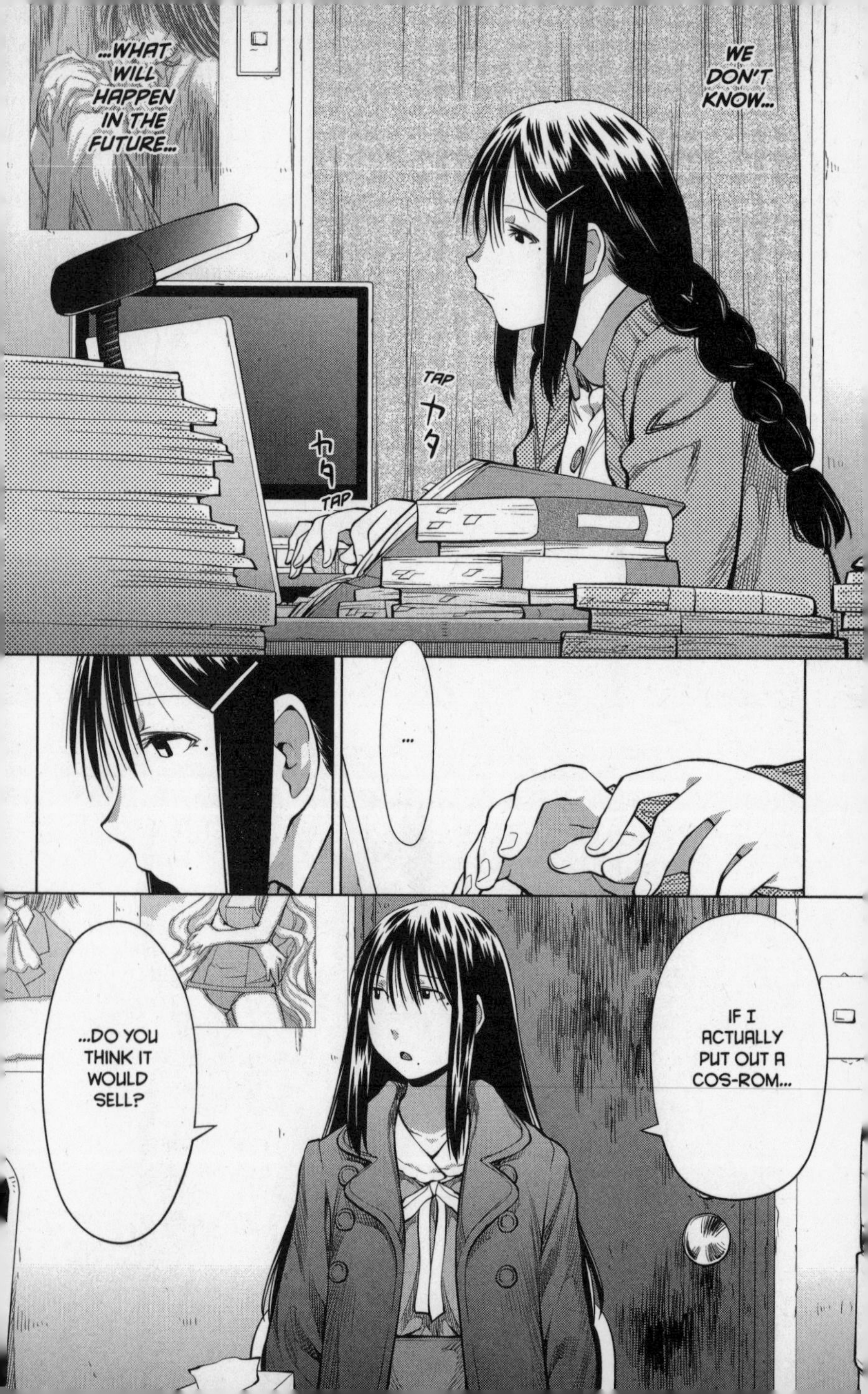
WE DON'T KNOW...
...WHAT WILL HAPPEN IN THE FUTURE...
TAP カタ
カタ TAP
...
IF I ACTUALLY PUT OUT A COS-ROM...
...DO YOU THINK IT WOULD SELL?

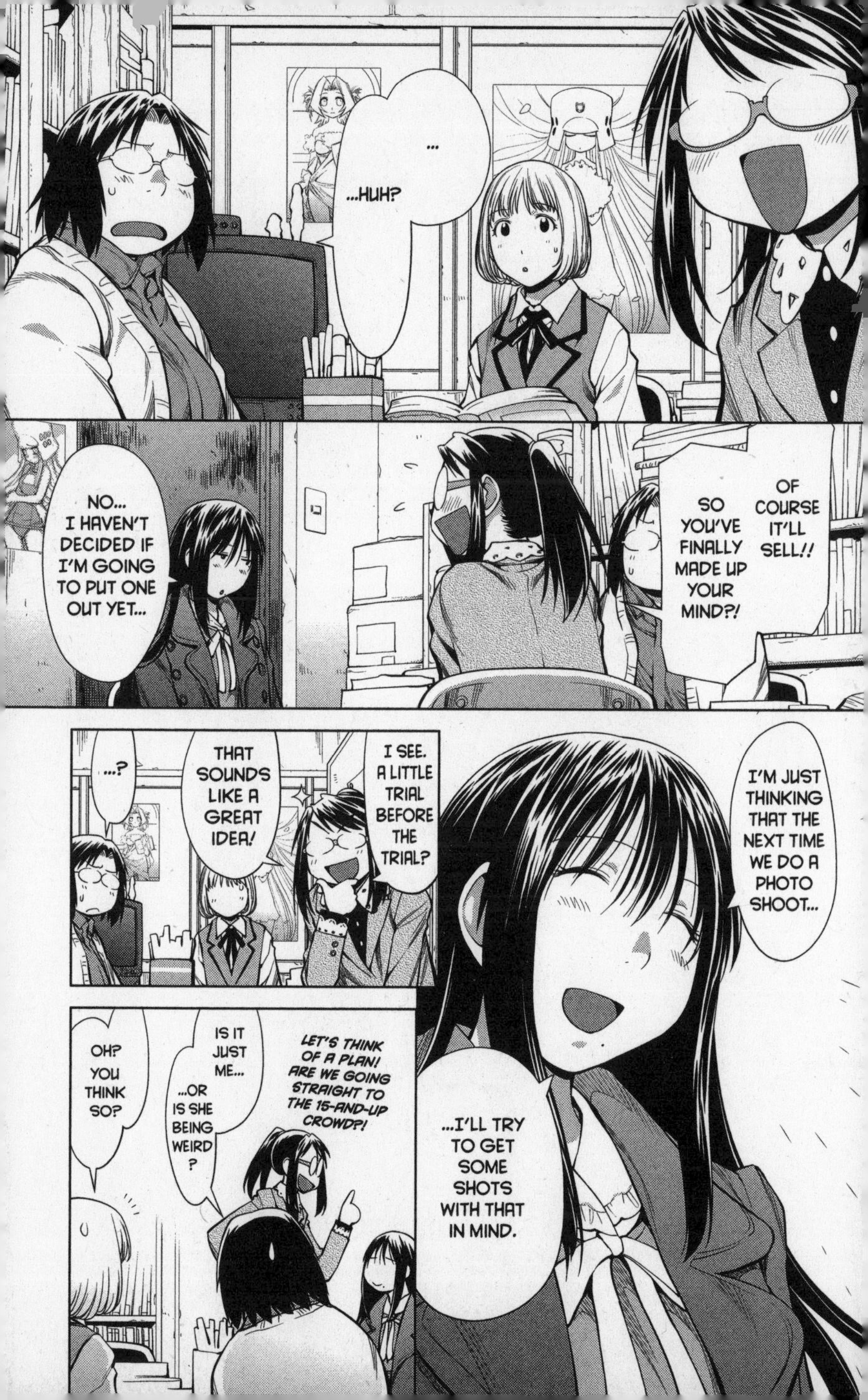
...
...HUH?
SO YOU'VE FINALLY MADE UP YOUR MIND?! OF COURSE IT'LL SELL!!
NO... I HAVEN'T DECIDED IF I'M GOING TO PUT ONE OUT YET...
I'M JUST THINKING THAT THE NEXT TIME WE DO A PHOTO SHOOT...
...I'LL TRY TO GET SOME SHOTS WITH THAT IN MIND.
I SEE. A LITTLE TRIAL BEFORE THE TRIAL?
THAT SOUNDS LIKE A GREAT IDEA!
...?
LET'S THINK OF A PLAN! ARE WE GOING STRAIGHT TO THE 15-AND-UP CROWD?!
IS IT JUST ME...
...OR IS SHE BEING WEIRD?
OH? YOU THINK SO?

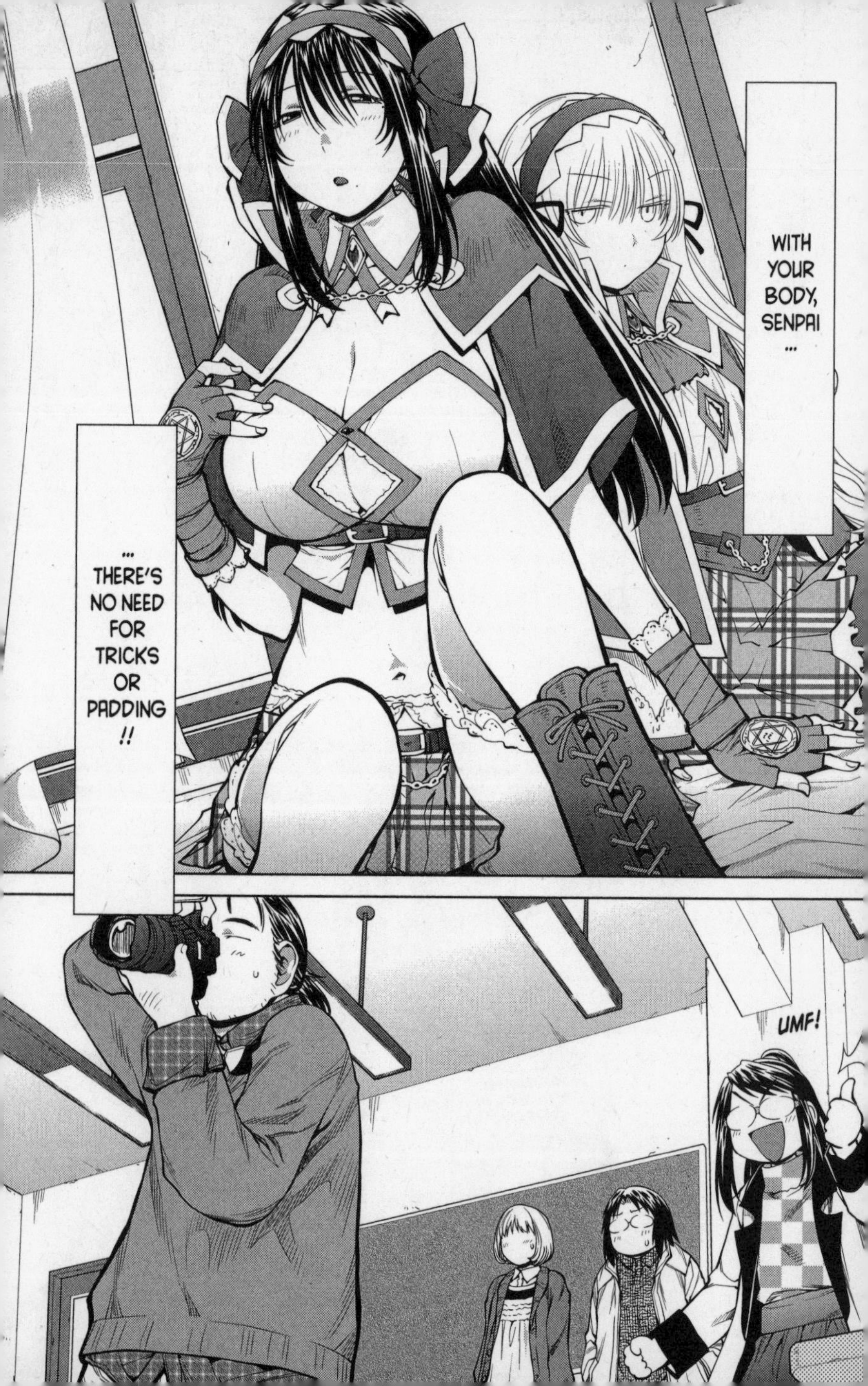
WITH YOUR BODY, SENPAI ...
... THERE'S NO NEED FOR TRICKS OR PADDING !!
UMF!

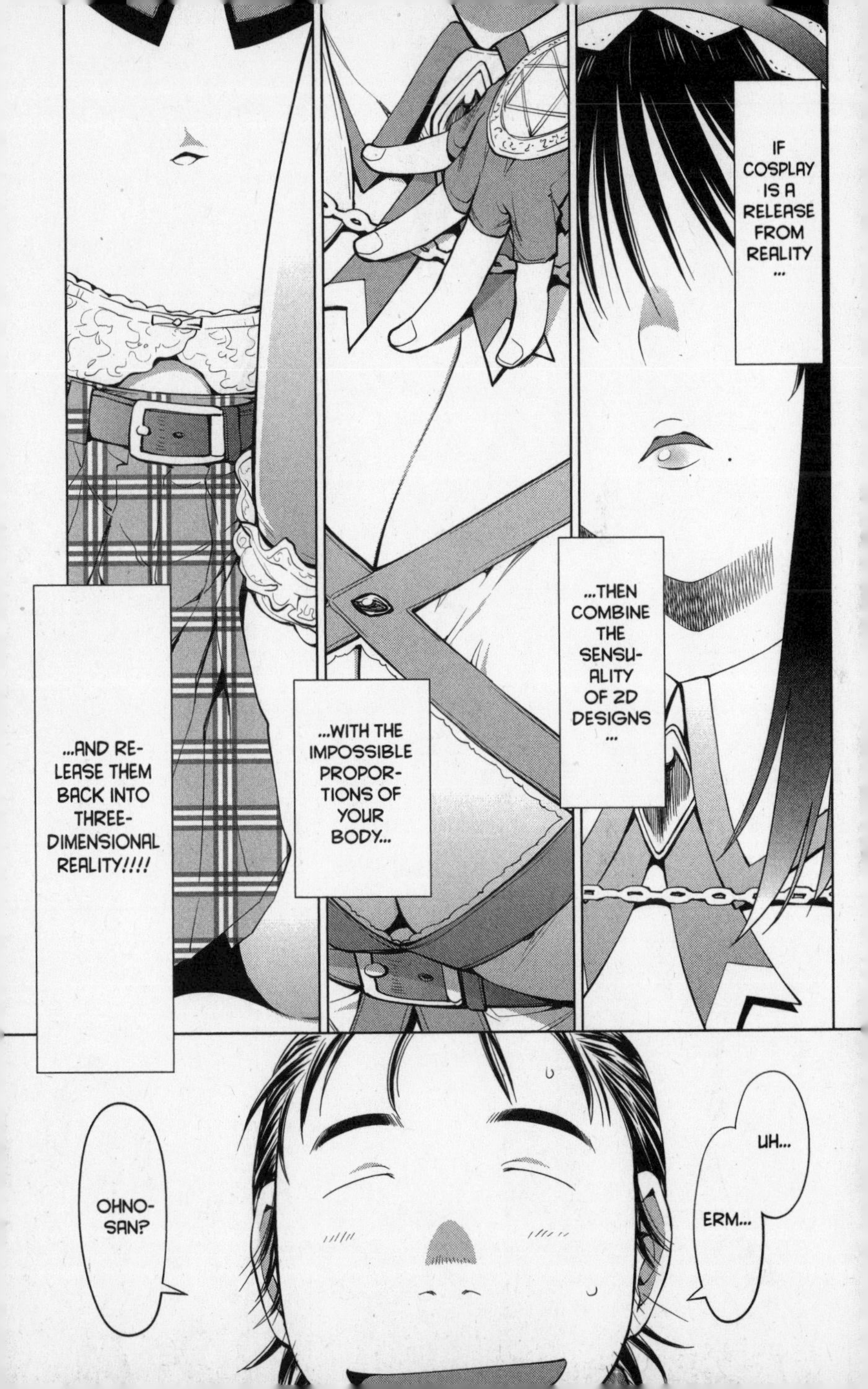
IF COSPLAY IS A RELEASE FROM REALITY...
...THEN COMBINE THE SENSU-ALITY OF 2D DESIGNS...
...WITH THE IMPOSSIBLE PROPOR-TIONS OF YOUR BODY...
...AND RE-LEASE THEM BACK INTO THREE-DIMENSIONAL REALITY!!!!
UH...
ERM...
OHNO-SAN?

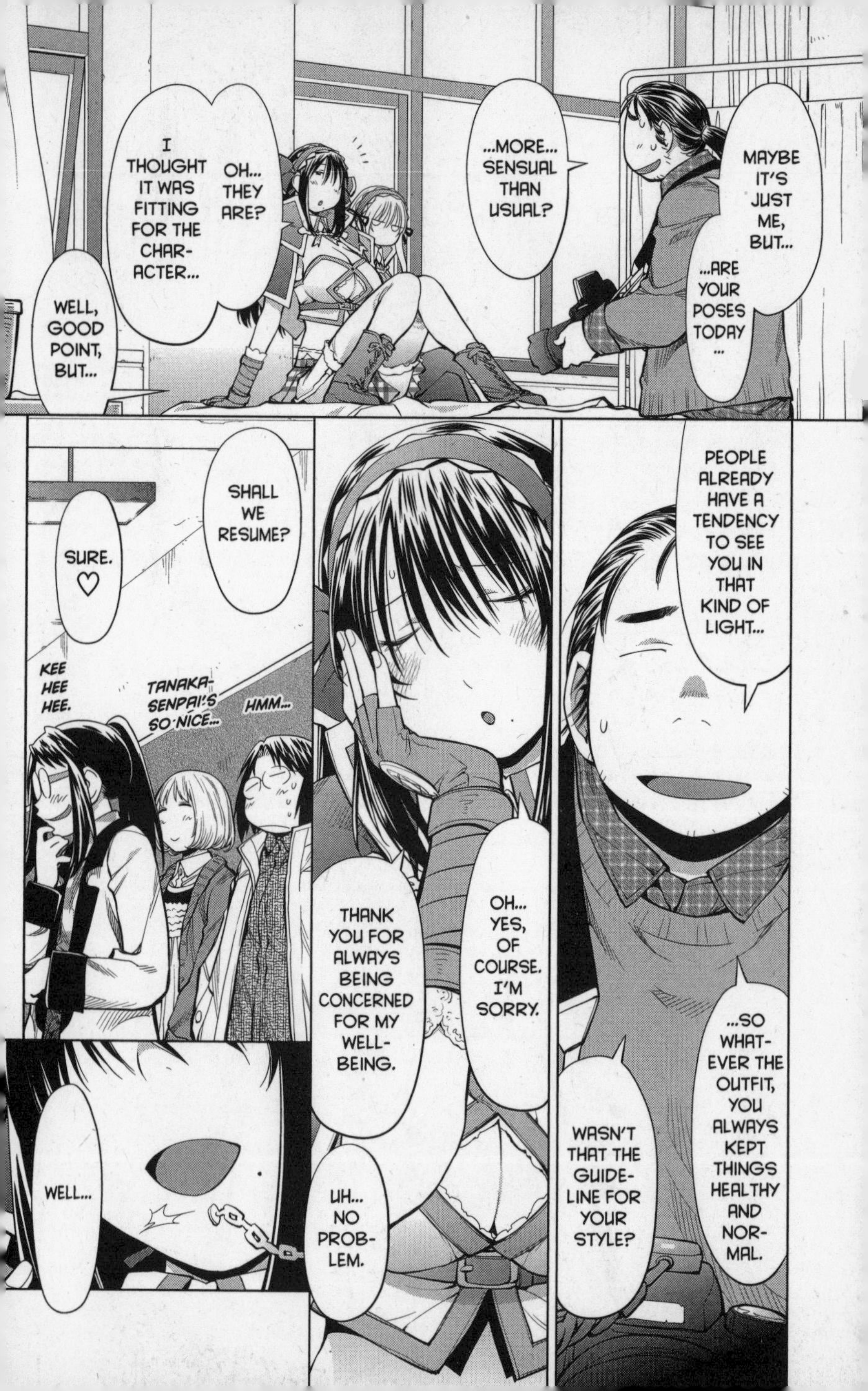
MAYBE IT'S JUST ME, BUT...
...ARE YOUR POSES TODAY...
...MORE... SENSUAL THAN USUAL?
OH... THEY ARE?
I THOUGHT IT WAS FITTING FOR THE CHAR-ACTER...
WELL, GOOD POINT, BUT...
PEOPLE ALREADY HAVE A TENDENCY TO SEE YOU IN THAT KIND OF LIGHT...
...SO WHAT-EVER THE OUTFIT, YOU ALWAYS KEPT THINGS HEALTHY AND NOR-MAL.
WASN'T THAT THE GUIDE-LINE FOR YOUR STYLE?
OH... YES, OF COURSE. I'M SORRY.
THANK YOU FOR ALWAYS BEING CONCERNED FOR MY WELL-BEING.
UH... NO PROB-LEM.
SHALL WE RESUME?
SURE. ♡
HMM...
TANAKA-SENPAI'S SO NICE...
KEE HEE HEE.
WELL...

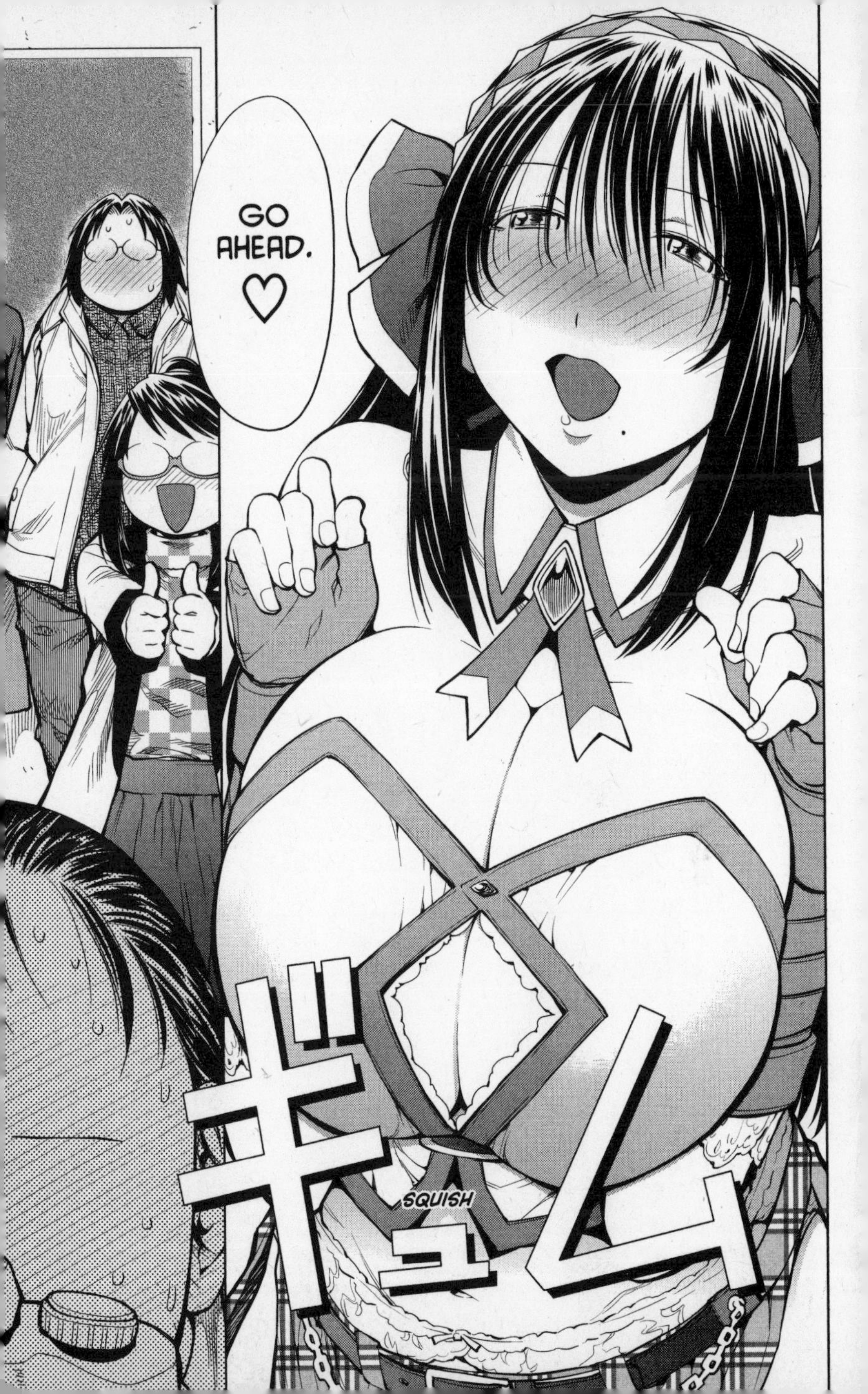
GO AHEAD. ♡
ギュム
SQUISH

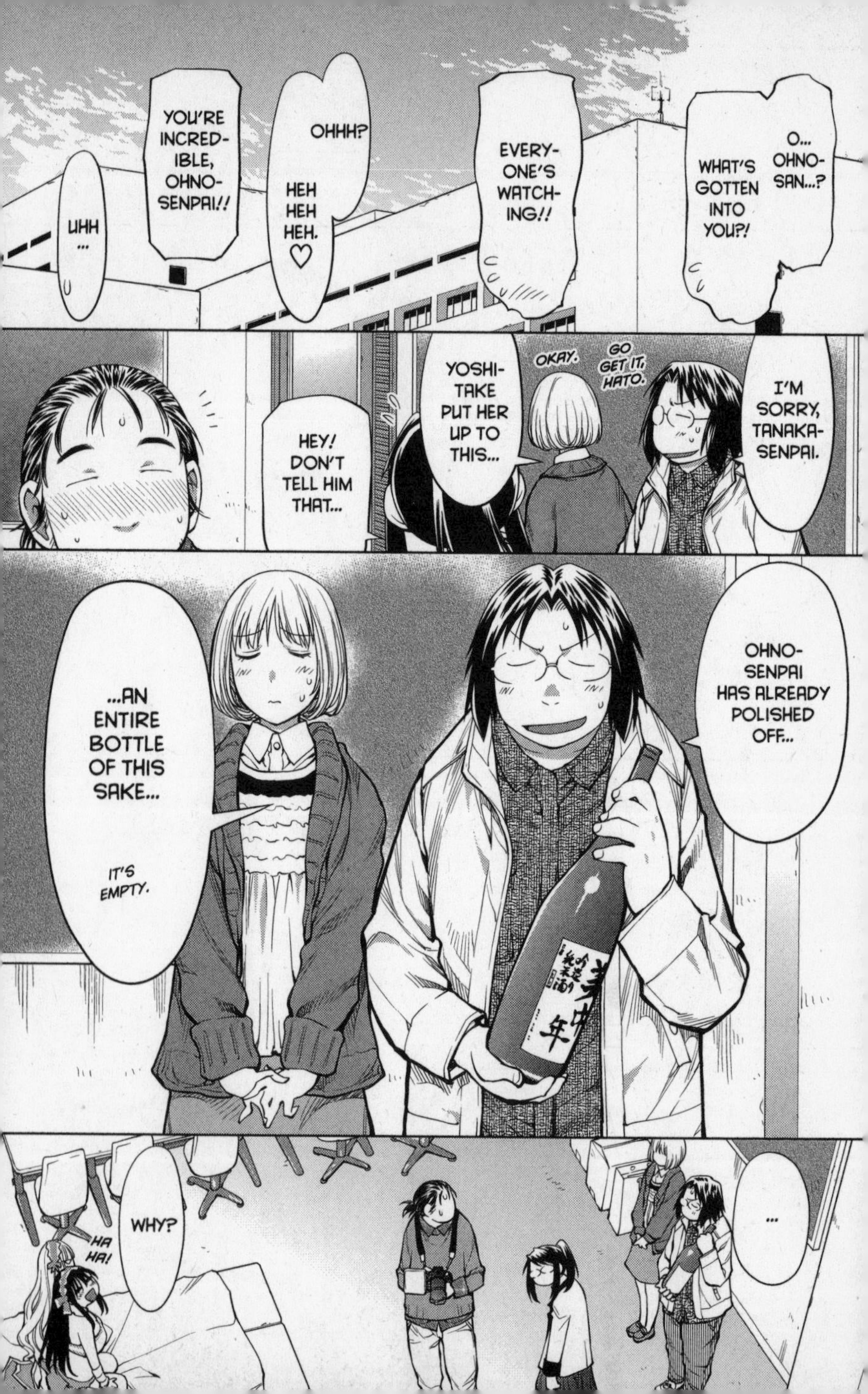
O... OHNO-SAN...?
WHAT'S GOTTEN INTO YOU?!
EVERY-ONE'S WATCHING!!
OHHH?
HEH HEH HEH. ♡
YOU'RE INCRED-IBLE, OHNO-SENPAI!!
UHH ...
I'M SORRY, TANAKA-SENPAI.
GO GET IT, HATO.
OKAY.
YOSHI-TAKE PUT HER UP TO THIS...
HEY! DON'T TELL HIM THAT...
OHNO-SENPAI HAS ALREADY POLISHED OFF...
...AN ENTIRE BOTTLE OF THIS SAKE...
IT'S EMPTY.
...
WHY?
HA HA!

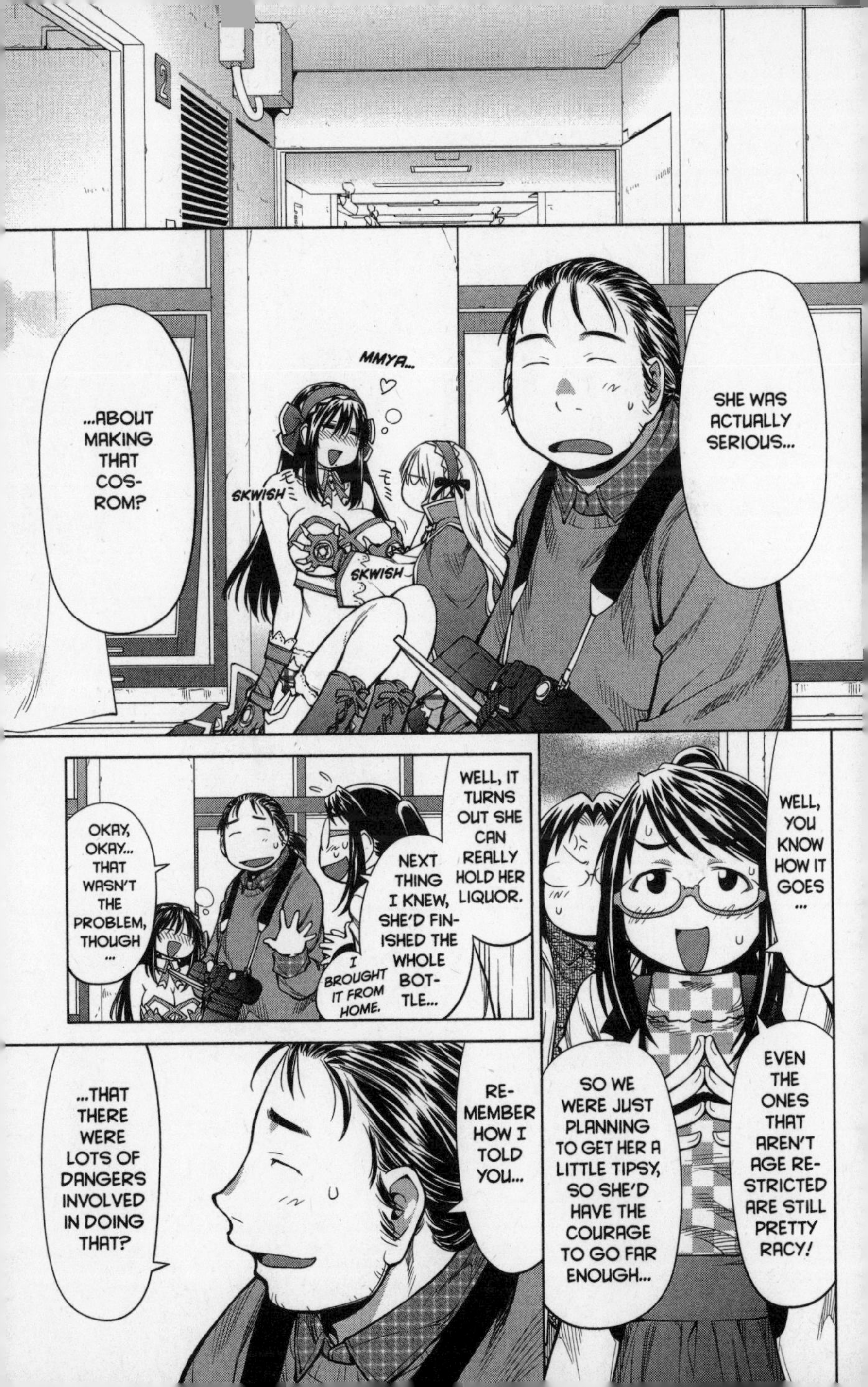
SHE WAS ACTUALLY SERIOUS...
MMYA...
SKWISH
SKWISH
...ABOUT MAKING THAT COS-ROM?
WELL, YOU KNOW HOW IT GOES...
EVEN THE ONES THAT AREN'T AGE RE-STRICTED ARE STILL PRETTY RACY!
SO WE WERE JUST PLANNING TO GET HER A LITTLE TIPSY, SO SHE'D HAVE THE COURAGE TO GO FAR ENOUGH...
WELL, IT TURNS OUT SHE CAN REALLY HOLD HER LIQUOR.
NEXT THING I KNEW, SHE'D FIN-ISHED THE WHOLE BOT-TLE...
I BROUGHT IT FROM HOME.
OKAY, OKAY... THAT WASN'T THE PROBLEM, THOUGH...
RE-MEMBER HOW I TOLD YOU...
...THAT THERE WERE LOTS OF DANGERS INVOLVED IN DOING THAT?

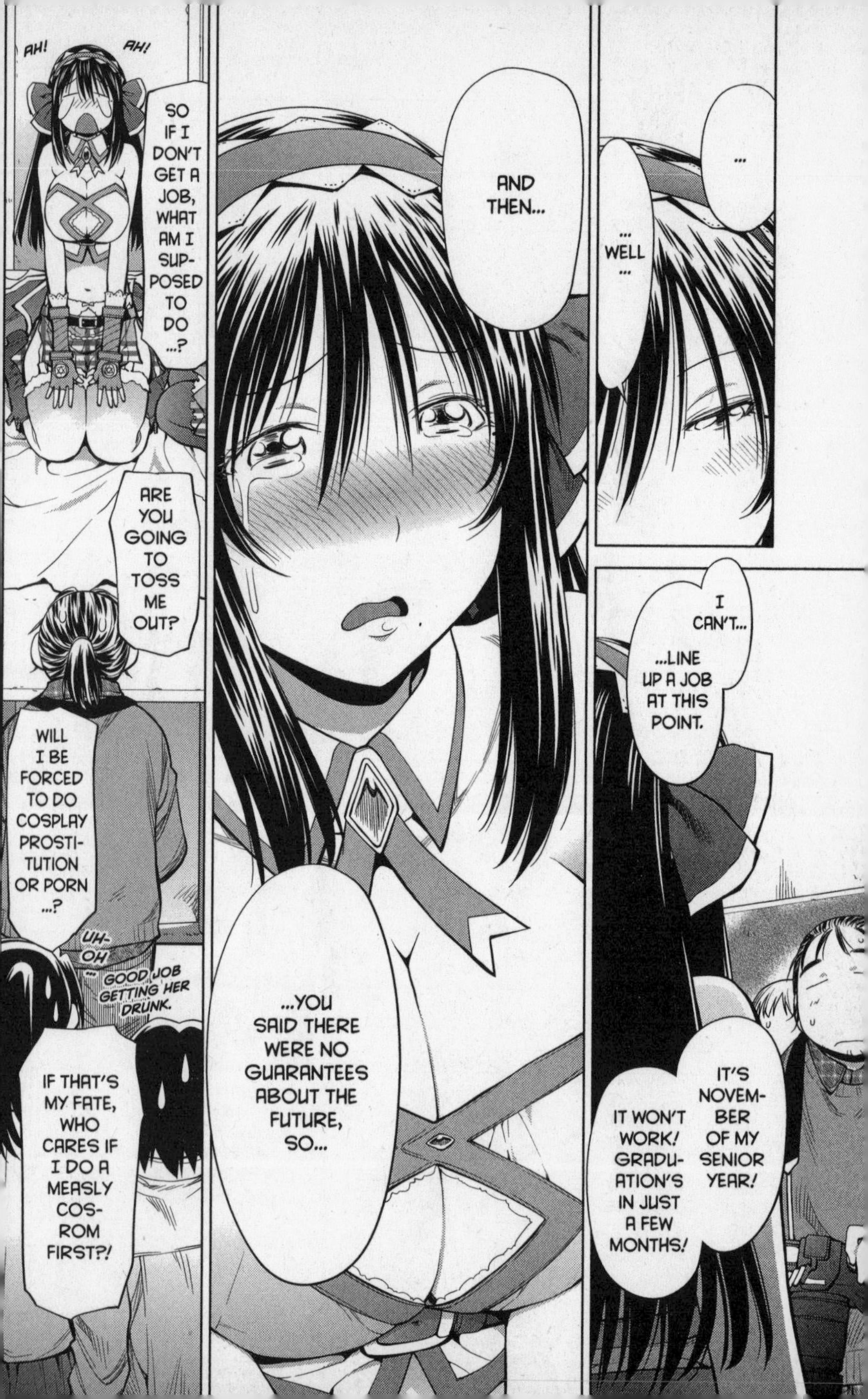
...
... WELL ...
I CAN'T...
...LINE UP A JOB AT THIS POINT.
IT'S NOVEMBER OF MY SENIOR YEAR!
IT WON'T WORK! GRADUATION'S IN JUST A FEW MONTHS!
AND THEN...
...YOU SAID THERE WERE NO GUARANTEES ABOUT THE FUTURE, SO...
AH! AH!
SO IF I DON'T GET A JOB, WHAT AM I SUPPOSED TO DO ...?
ARE YOU GOING TO TOSS ME OUT?
WILL I BE FORCED TO DO COSPLAY PROSTITUTION OR PORN ...?
UH-OH ...
GOOD JOB GETTING HER DRUNK.
IF THAT'S MY FATE, WHO CARES IF I DO A MEASLY COS-ROM FIRST?!

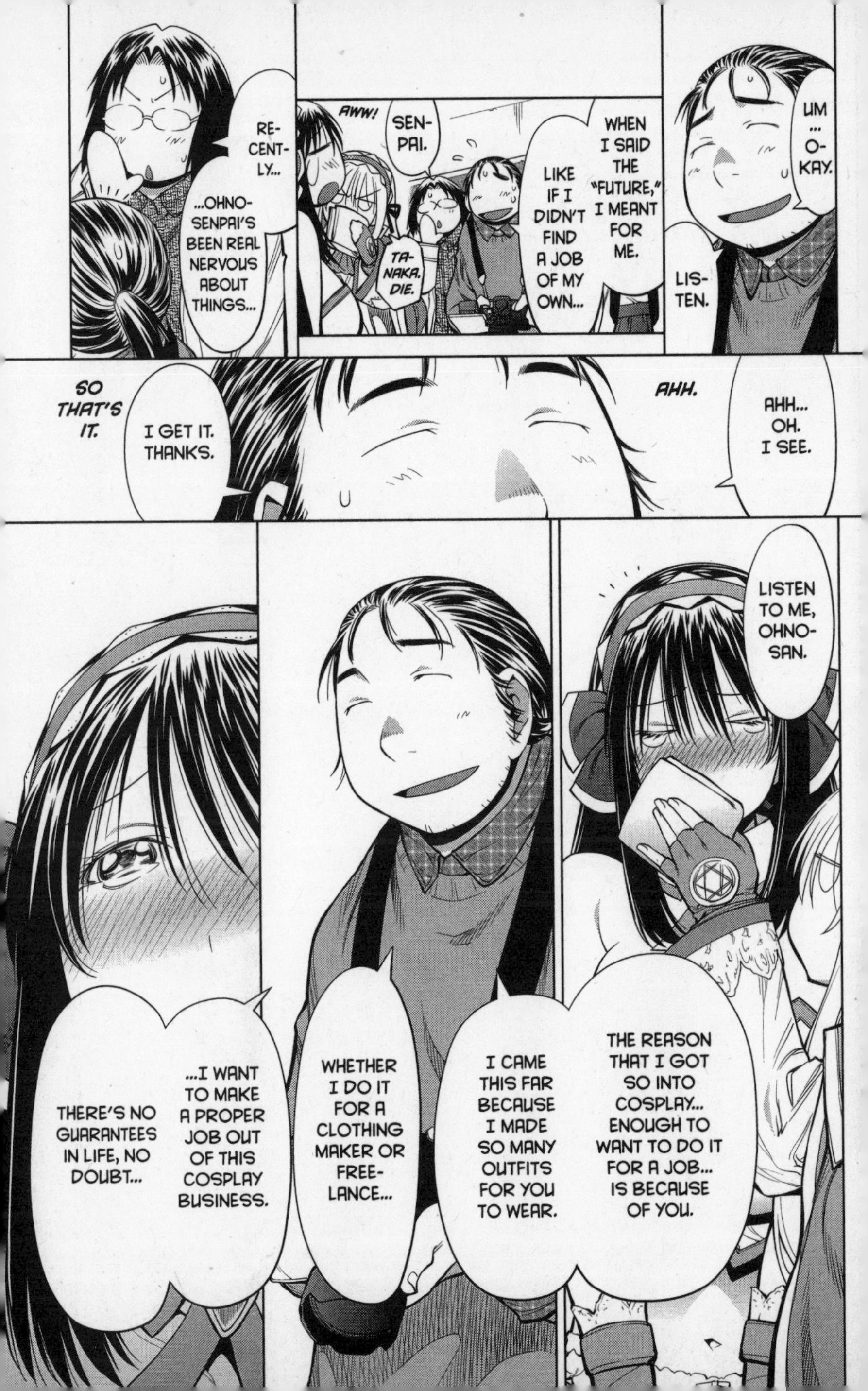
UM... O-KAY.
LISTEN.
WHEN I SAID THE "FUTURE," I MEANT FOR ME.
LIKE IF I DIDN'T FIND A JOB OF MY OWN...
SEN-PAI.
AWW!
TA-NAKA. DIE.
RE-CENTLY...
...OHNO-SENPAI'S BEEN REAL NERVOUS ABOUT THINGS...
AHH... OH. I SEE.
AHH.
I GET IT. THANKS.
SO THAT'S IT.
LISTEN TO ME, OHNO-SAN.
THE REASON THAT I GOT SO INTO COSPLAY... ENOUGH TO WANT TO DO IT FOR A JOB... IS BECAUSE OF YOU.
I CAME THIS FAR BECAUSE I MADE SO MANY OUTFITS FOR YOU TO WEAR.
WHETHER I DO IT FOR A CLOTHING MAKER OR FREE-LANCE...
...I WANT TO MAKE A PROPER JOB OUT OF THIS COSPLAY BUSINESS.
THERE'S NO GUARANTEES IN LIFE, NO DOUBT...

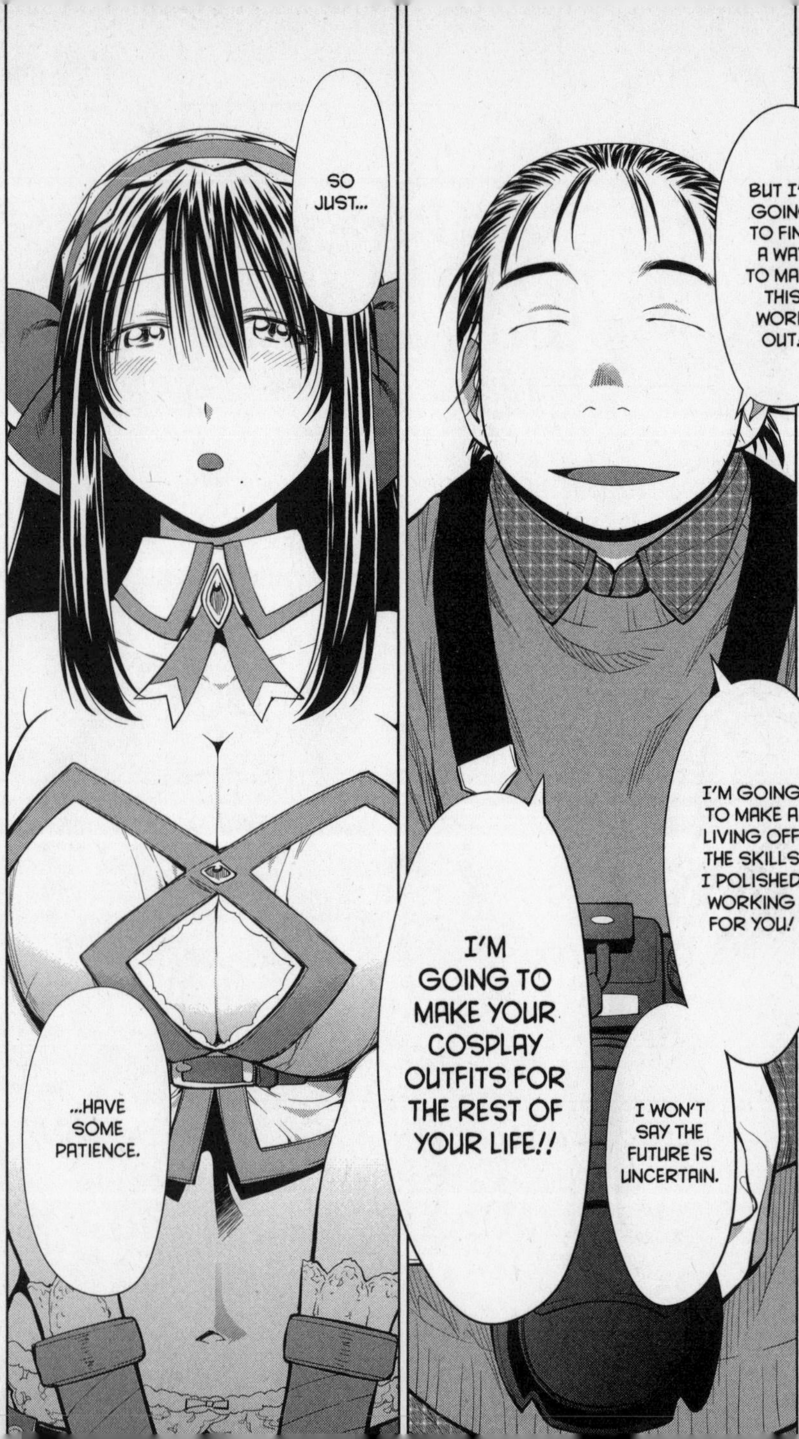
BUT I'M GOING TO FIND A WAY TO MAKE THIS WORK OUT!
I'M GOING TO MAKE A LIVING OFF THE SKILLS I POLISHED WORKING FOR YOU!
I WON'T SAY THE FUTURE IS UNCERTAIN.
I'M GOING TO MAKE YOUR COSPLAY OUTFITS FOR THE REST OF YOUR LIFE!!
SO JUST...
...HAVE SOME PATIENCE.

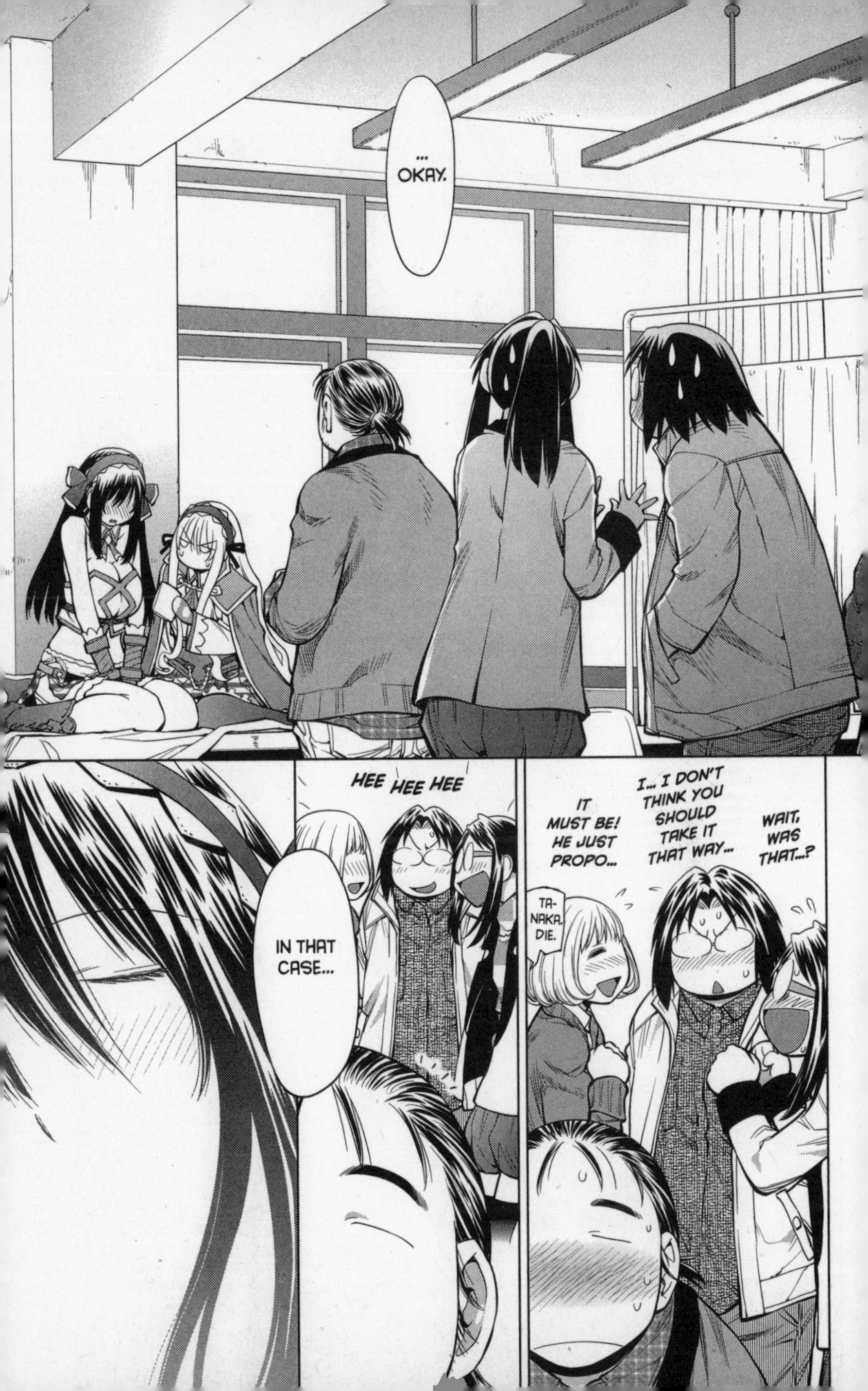
... OKAY.
WAIT, WAS THAT...?
I... I DON'T THINK YOU SHOULD TAKE IT THAT WAY...
IT MUST BE! HE JUST PROPO...
TA-NAKA. DIE.
HEE HEE HEE
IN THAT CASE...

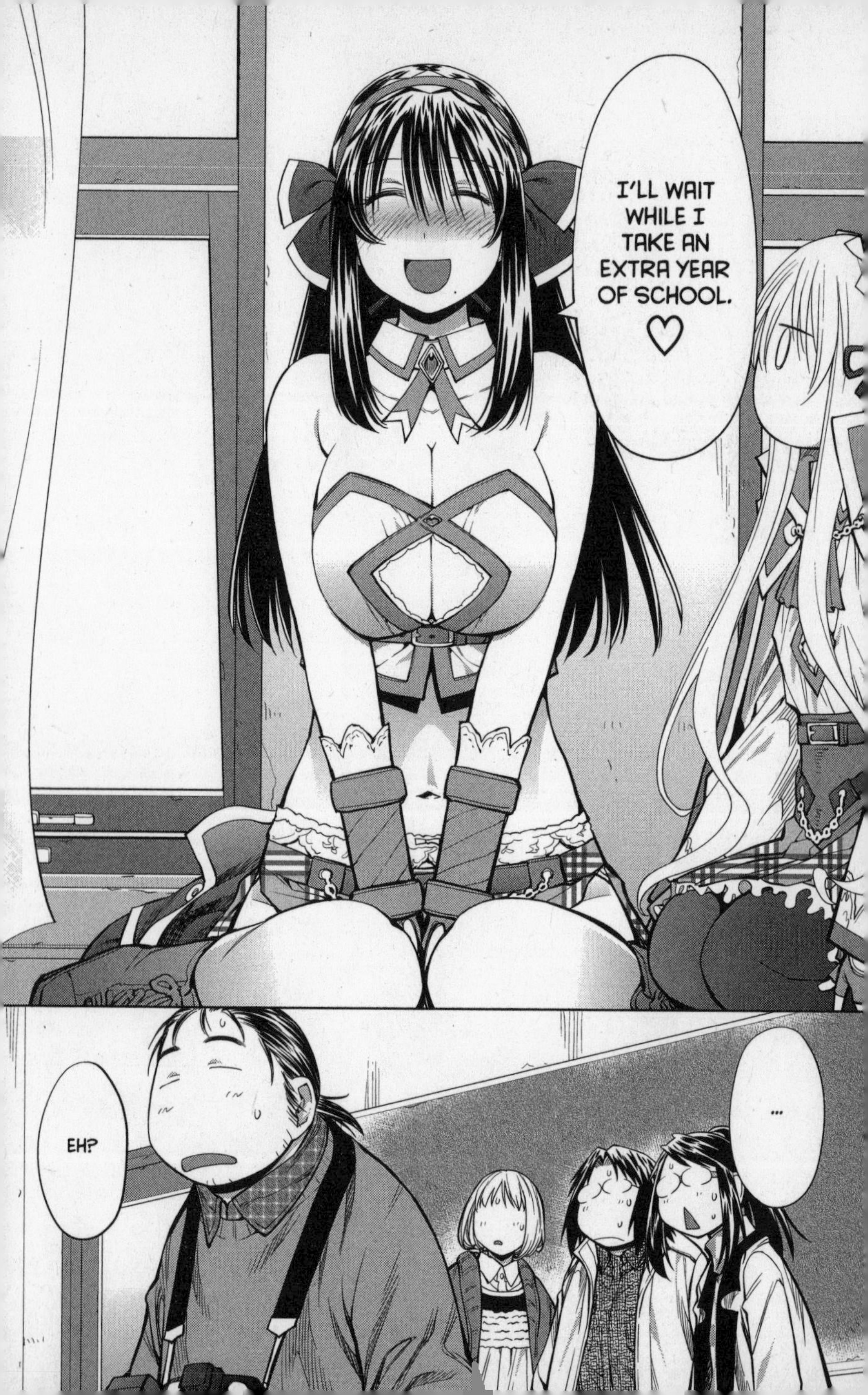
I'LL WAIT WHILE I TAKE AN EXTRA YEAR OF SCHOOL. ♡
...
EH?

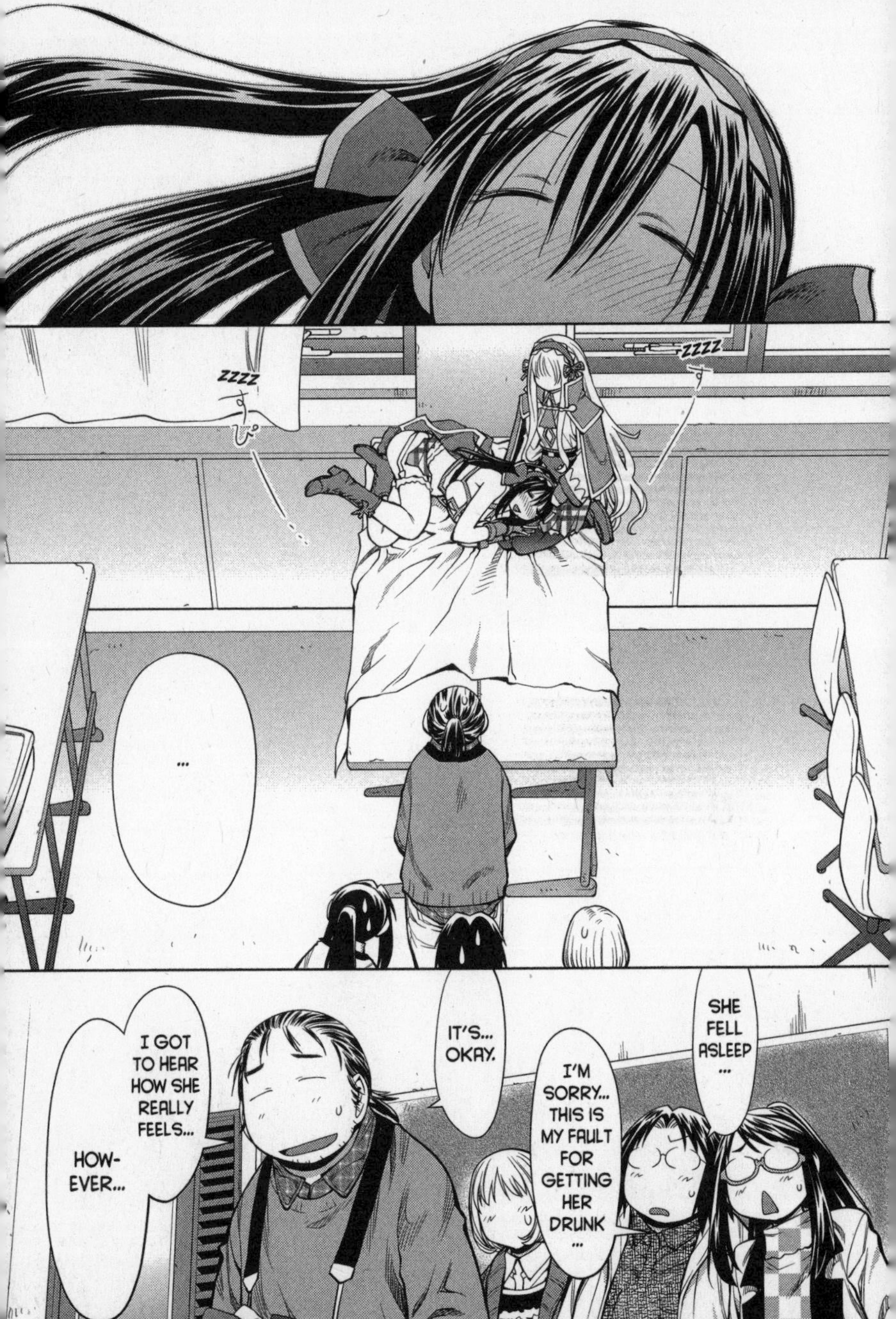

ZZZZ
ZZZZ
...
SHE FELL ASLEEP ...
I'M SORRY... THIS IS MY FAULT FOR GETTING HER DRUNK ...
IT'S... OKAY.
I GOT TO HEAR HOW SHE REALLY FEELS...
HOW-EVER...

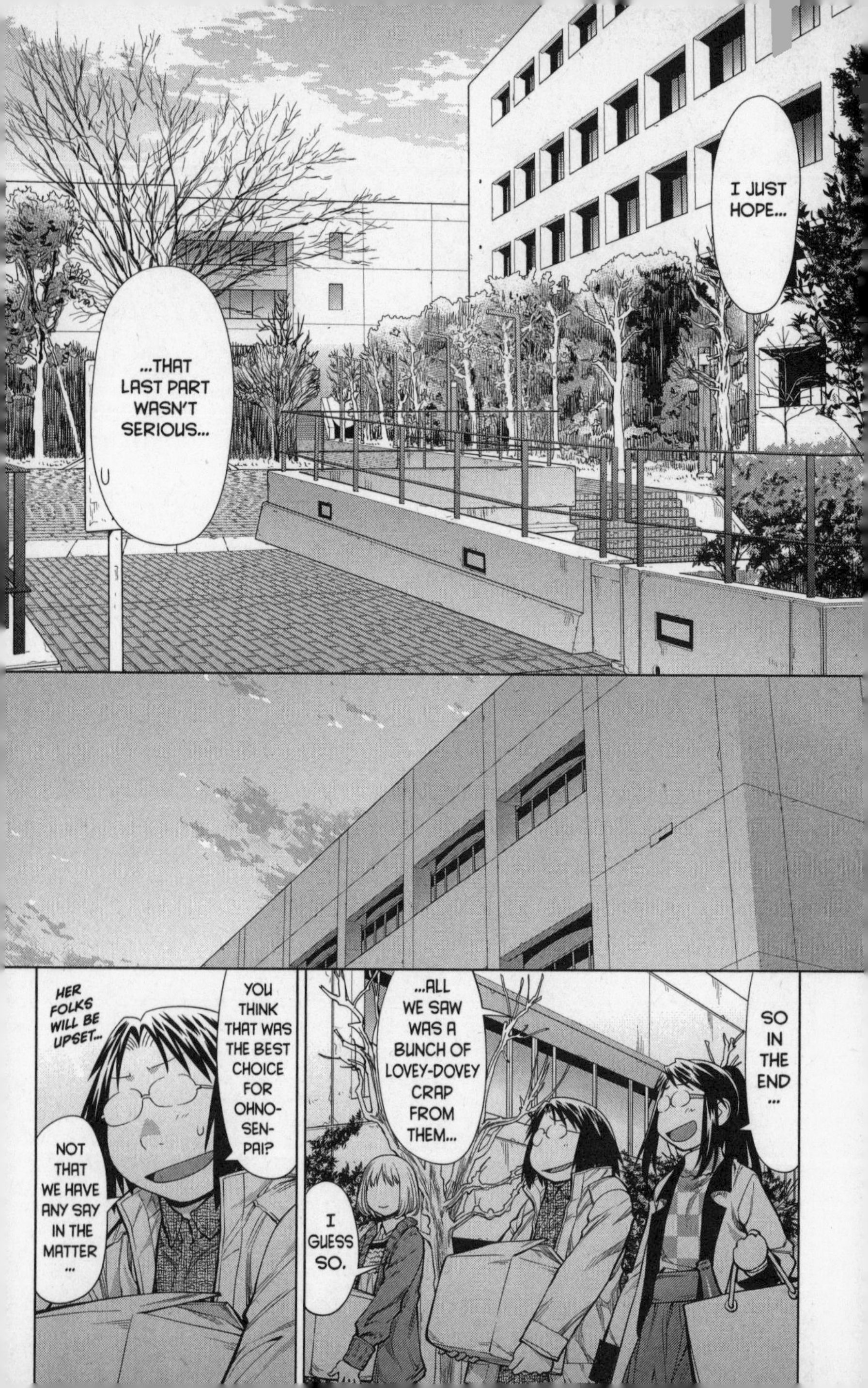
I JUST HOPE...
...THAT LAST PART WASN'T SERIOUS...
SO IN THE END ...
...ALL WE SAW WAS A BUNCH OF LOVEY-DOVEY CRAP FROM THEM...
I GUESS SO.
YOU THINK THAT WAS THE BEST CHOICE FOR OHNO-SEN-PAI?
HER FOLKS WILL BE UPSET...
NOT THAT WE HAVE ANY SAY IN THE MATTER ...

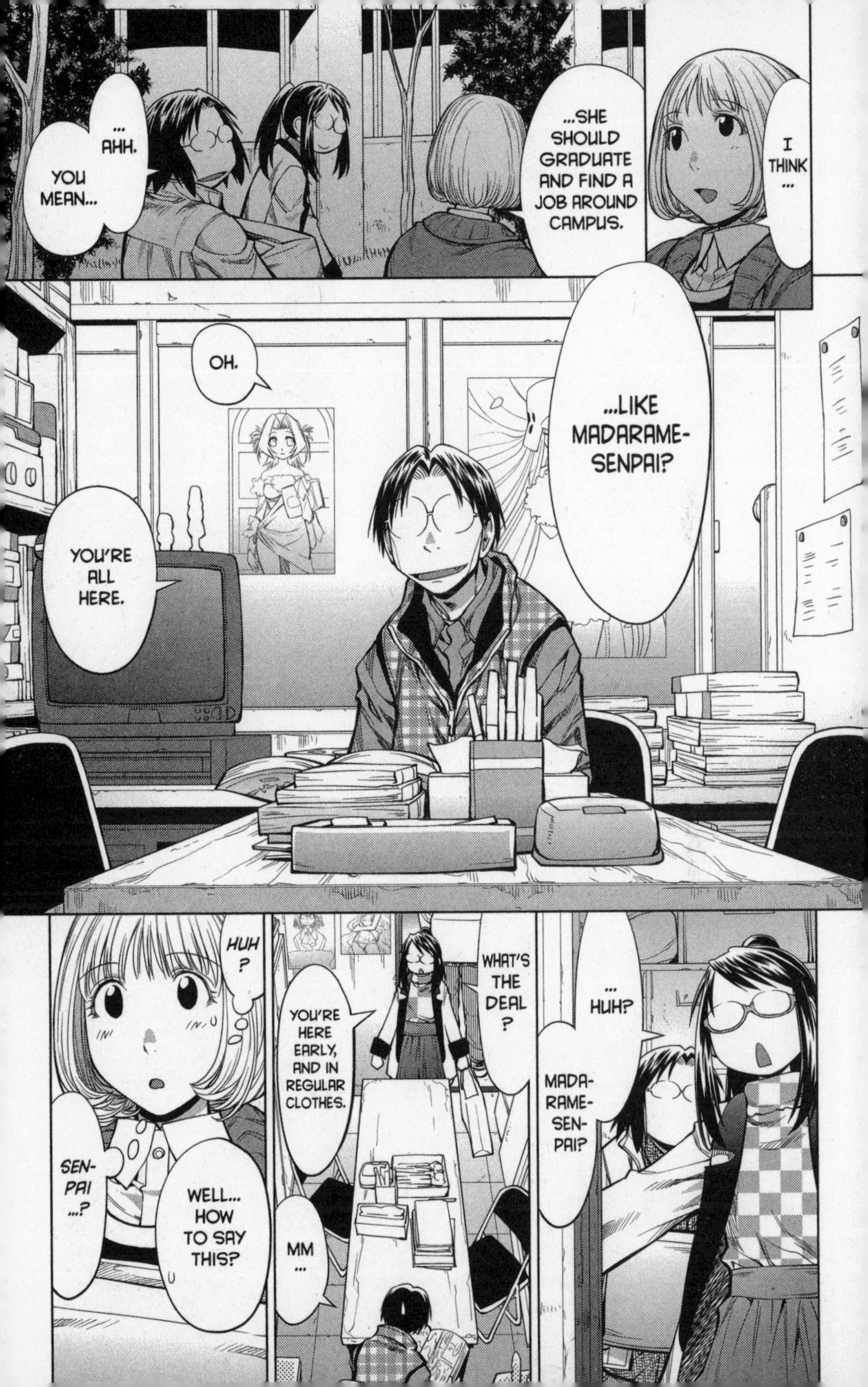
I THINK...
...SHE SHOULD GRADUATE AND FIND A JOB AROUND CAMPUS.
...AHH.
YOU MEAN...
...LIKE MADARAME-SENPAI?
OH.
YOU'RE ALL HERE.
...HUH?
MADA-RAME-SEN-PAI?
WHAT'S THE DEAL?
YOU'RE HERE EARLY, AND IN REGULAR CLOTHES.
MM...
HUH?
SEN-PAI...?
WELL... HOW TO SAY THIS?

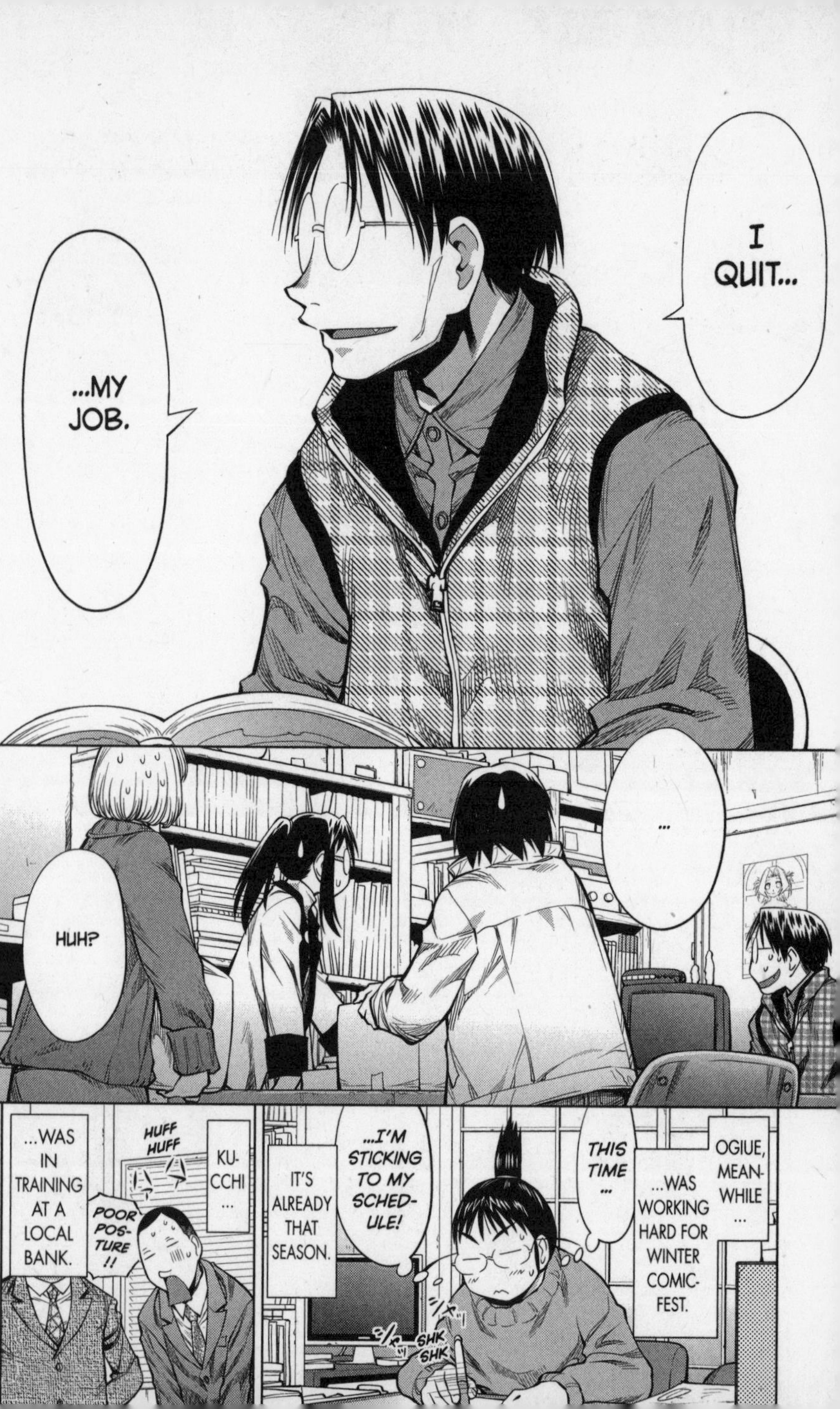
I QUIT...
...MY JOB.
...
HUH?
OGIUE, MEANWHILE ...
...WAS WORKING HARD FOR WINTER COMIC-FEST.
THIS TIME ...
...I'M STICKING TO MY SCHEDULE!
SHK SHK
IT'S ALREADY THAT SEASON.
KU-CCHI ...
HUFF HUFF
...WAS IN TRAINING AT A LOCAL BANK.
POOR POSTURE !!

CHAPTER 83 - END

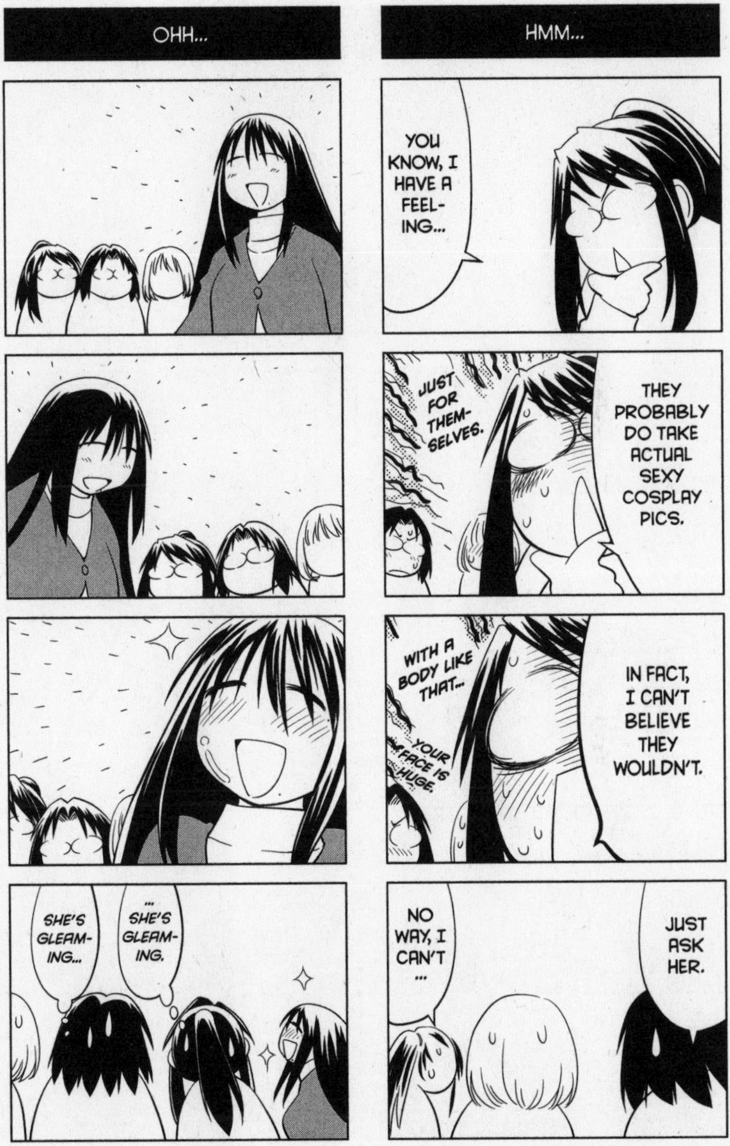
HMM...
YOU KNOW, I HAVE A FEEL-ING...
THEY PROBABLY DO TAKE ACTUAL SEXY COSPLAY PICS.
JUST FOR THEM-SELVES.
IN FACT, I CAN'T BELIEVE THEY WOULDN'T.
WITH A BODY LIKE THAT...
YOUR FACE IS HUGE.
JUST ASK HER.
NO WAY, I CAN'T ...
OHH...
... SHE'S GLEAM-ING.
SHE'S GLEAM-ING...

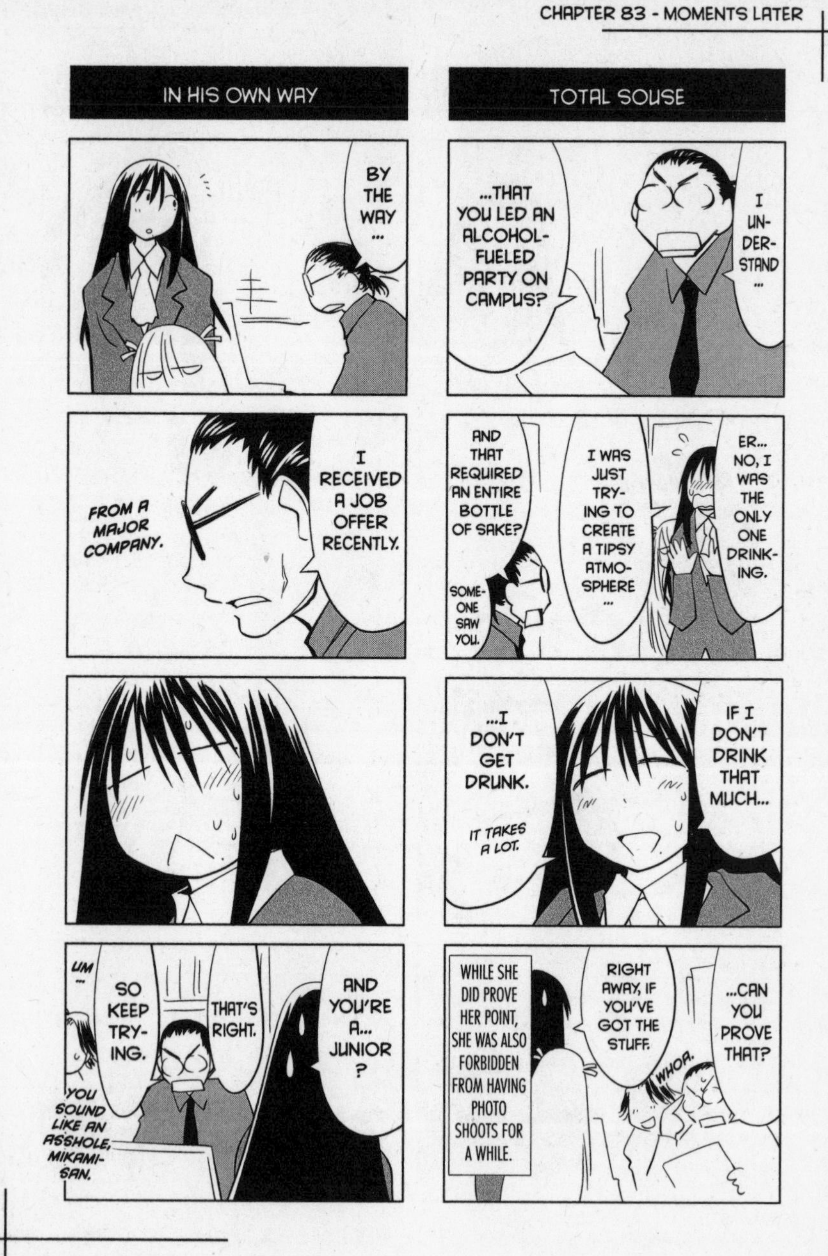
TOTAL SOUSE
I UNDERSTAND...
...THAT YOU LED AN ALCOHOL-FUELED PARTY ON CAMPUS?
ER... NO, I WAS THE ONLY ONE DRINKING.
I WAS JUST TRYING TO CREATE A TIPSY ATMOSPHERE...
AND THAT REQUIRED AN ENTIRE BOTTLE OF SAKE?
SOMEONE SAW YOU.
IF I DON'T DRINK THAT MUCH...
...I DON'T GET DRUNK.
IT TAKES A LOT.
...CAN YOU PROVE THAT?
WHOA.
RIGHT AWAY, IF YOU'VE GOT THE STUFF.
WHILE SHE DID PROVE HER POINT, SHE WAS ALSO FORBIDDEN FROM HAVING PHOTO SHOOTS FOR A WHILE.
IN HIS OWN WAY
BY THE WAY...
I RECEIVED A JOB OFFER RECENTLY.
FROM A MAJOR COMPANY.
AND YOU'RE A... JUNIOR?
THAT'S RIGHT.
SO KEEP TRYING.
UM...
YOU SOUND LIKE AN ASSHOLE, MIKAMI-SAN.

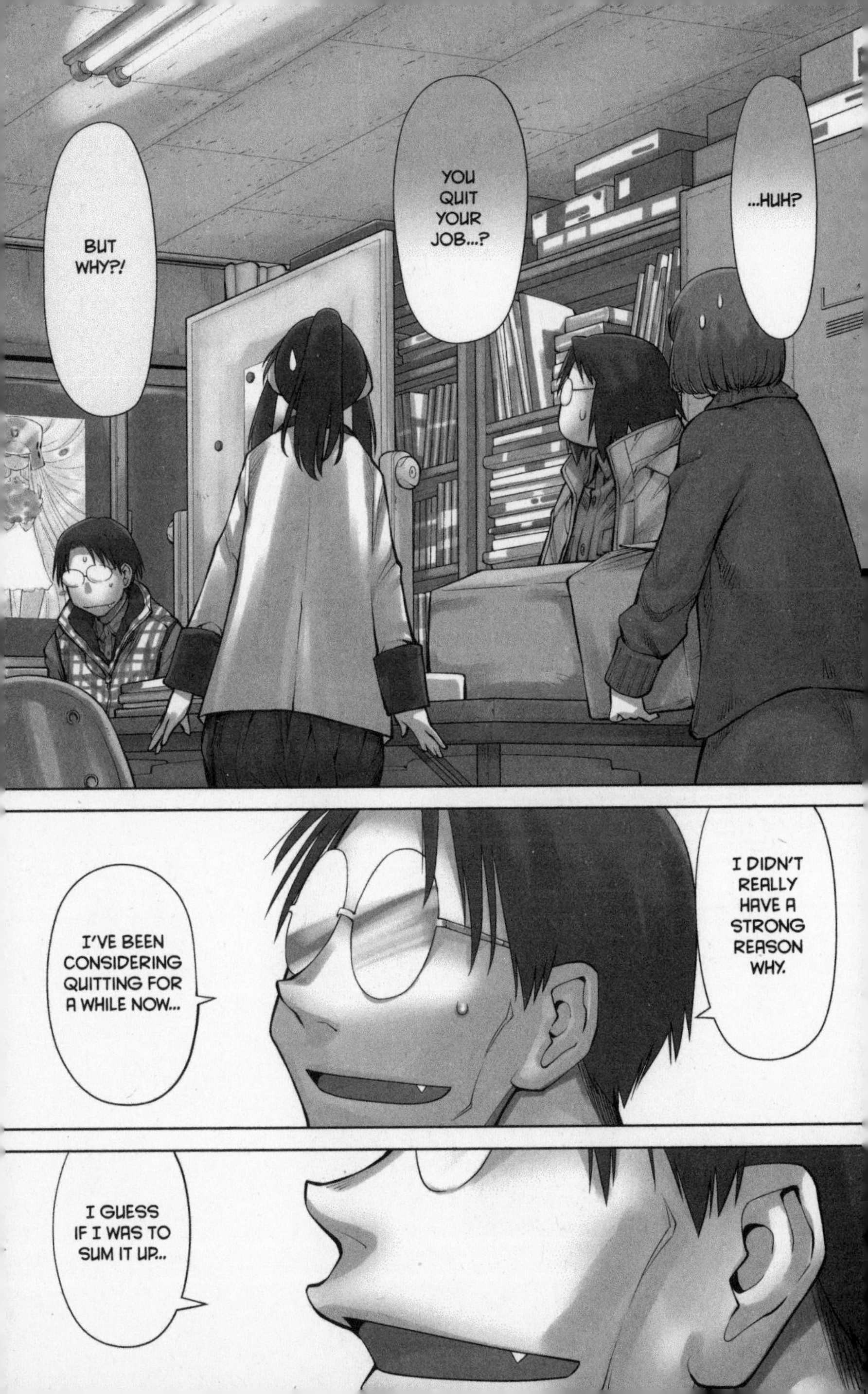
...HUH?
YOU QUIT YOUR JOB...?
BUT WHY?!
I DIDN'T REALLY HAVE A STRONG REASON WHY.
I'VE BEEN CONSIDERING QUITTING FOR A WHILE NOW...
I GUESS IF I WAS TO SUM IT UP...

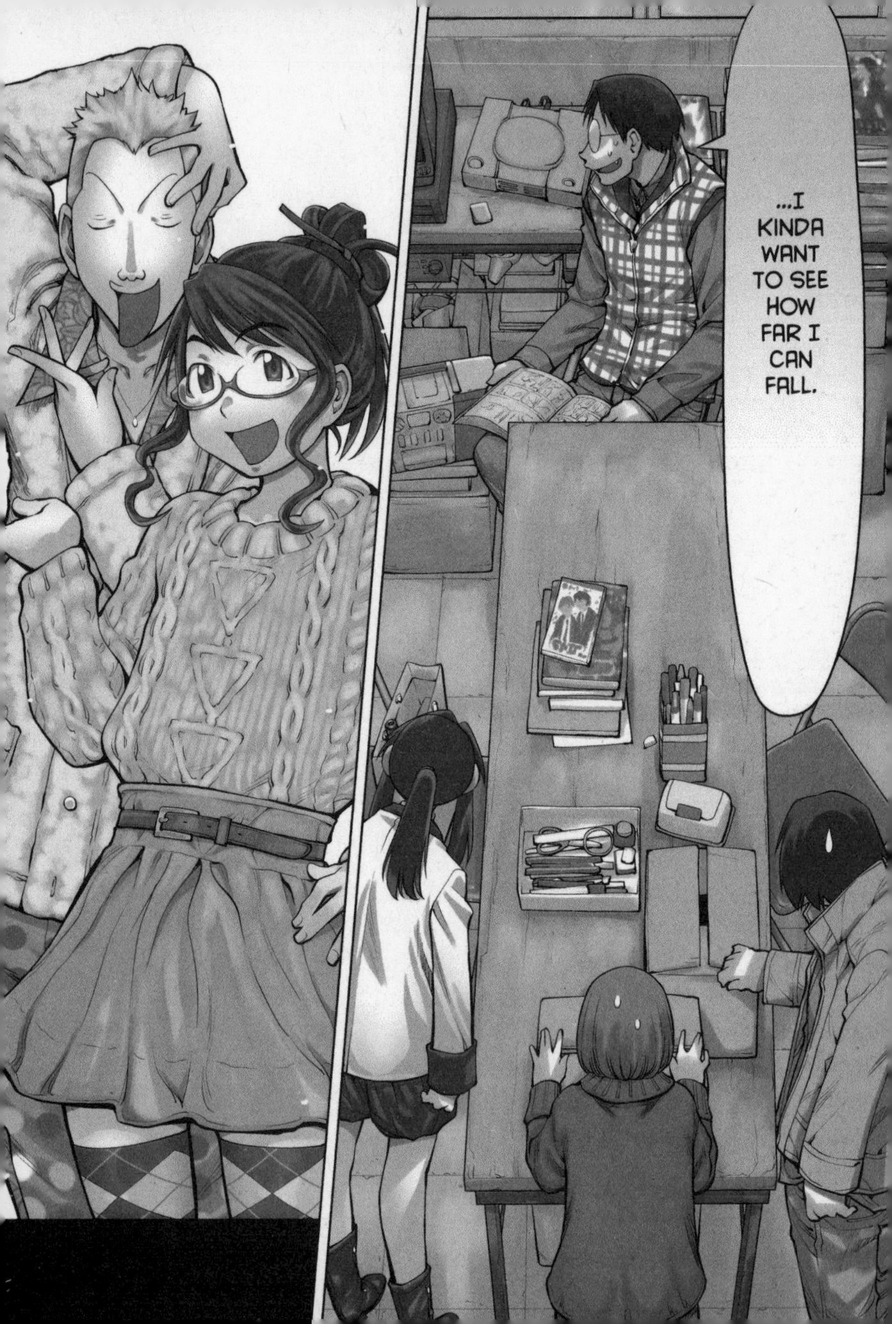
...I KINDA WANT TO SEE HOW FAR I CAN FALL.

CHAPTER 84: RED (FACE) KING

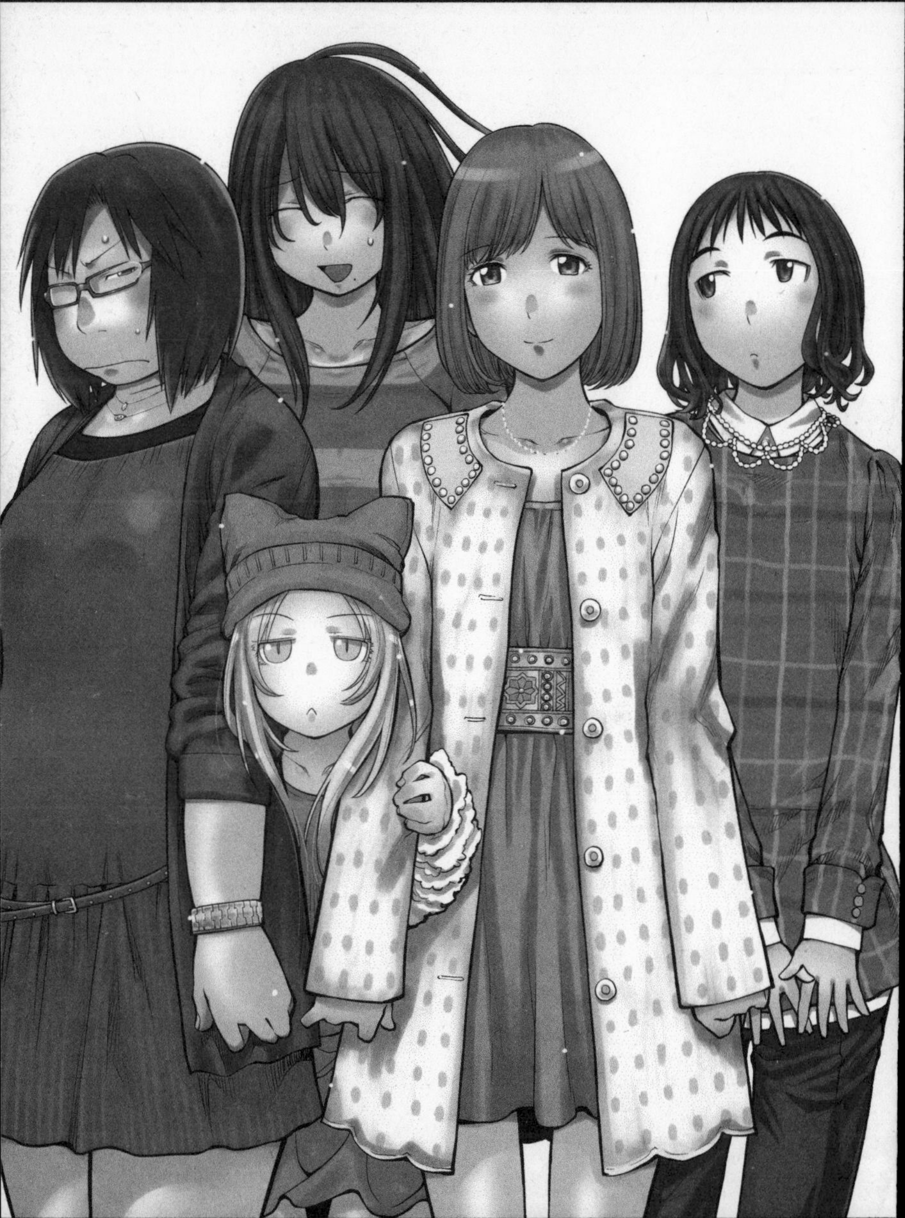

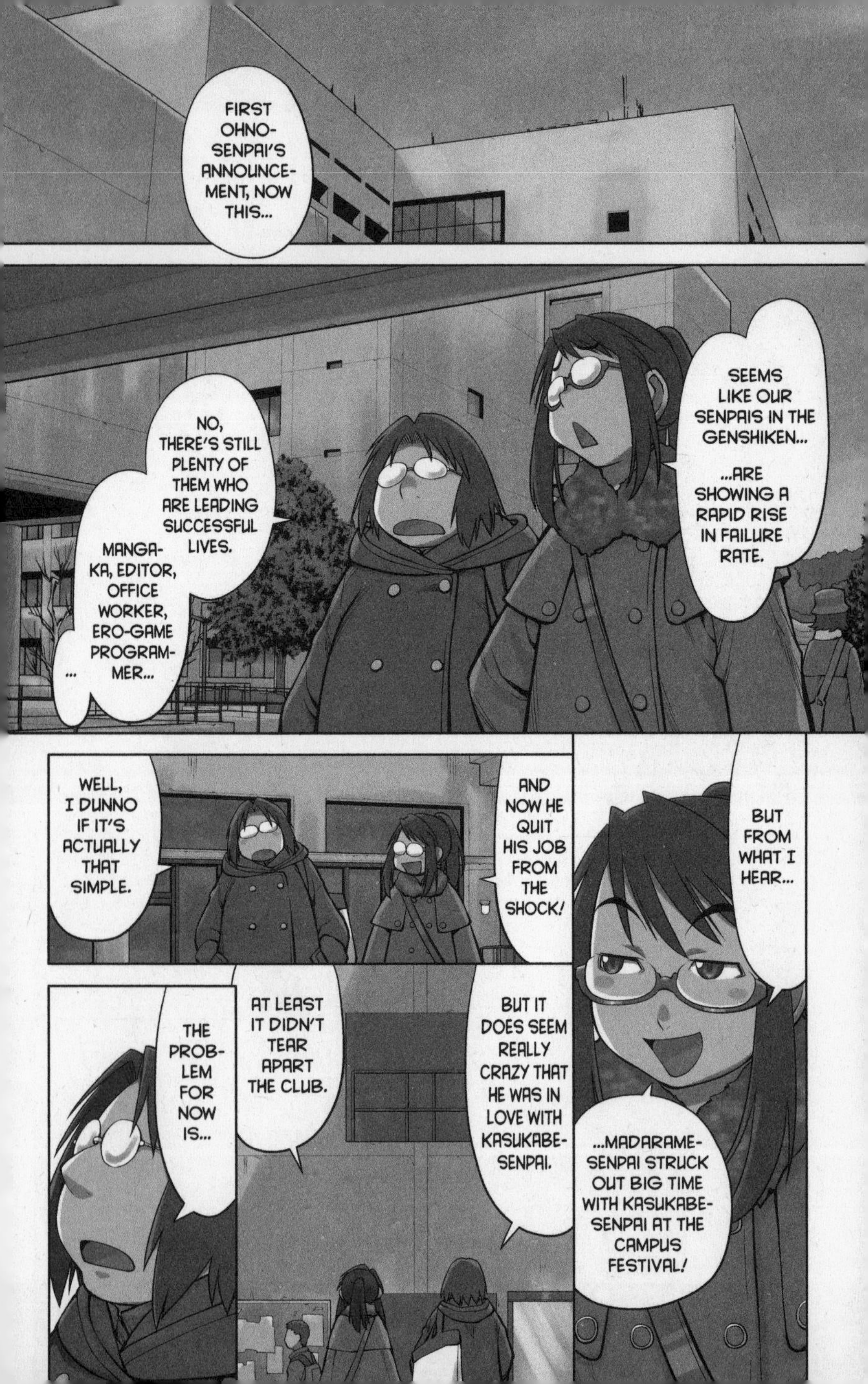
FIRST OHNO-SENPAI'S ANNOUNCEMENT, NOW THIS...
SEEMS LIKE OUR SENPAIS IN THE GENSHIKEN...
...ARE SHOWING A RAPID RISE IN FAILURE RATE.
NO, THERE'S STILL PLENTY OF THEM WHO ARE LEADING SUCCESSFUL LIVES.
MANGA-KA, EDITOR, OFFICE WORKER, ERO-GAME PROGRAMMER... ...
BUT FROM WHAT I HEAR...
...MADARAME-SENPAI STRUCK OUT BIG TIME WITH KASUKABE-SENPAI AT THE CAMPUS FESTIVAL!
AND NOW HE QUIT HIS JOB FROM THE SHOCK!
WELL, I DUNNO IF IT'S ACTUALLY THAT SIMPLE.
BUT IT DOES SEEM REALLY CRAZY THAT HE WAS IN LOVE WITH KASUKABE-SENPAI.
AT LEAST IT DIDN'T TEAR APART THE CLUB.
THE PROBLEM FOR NOW IS...

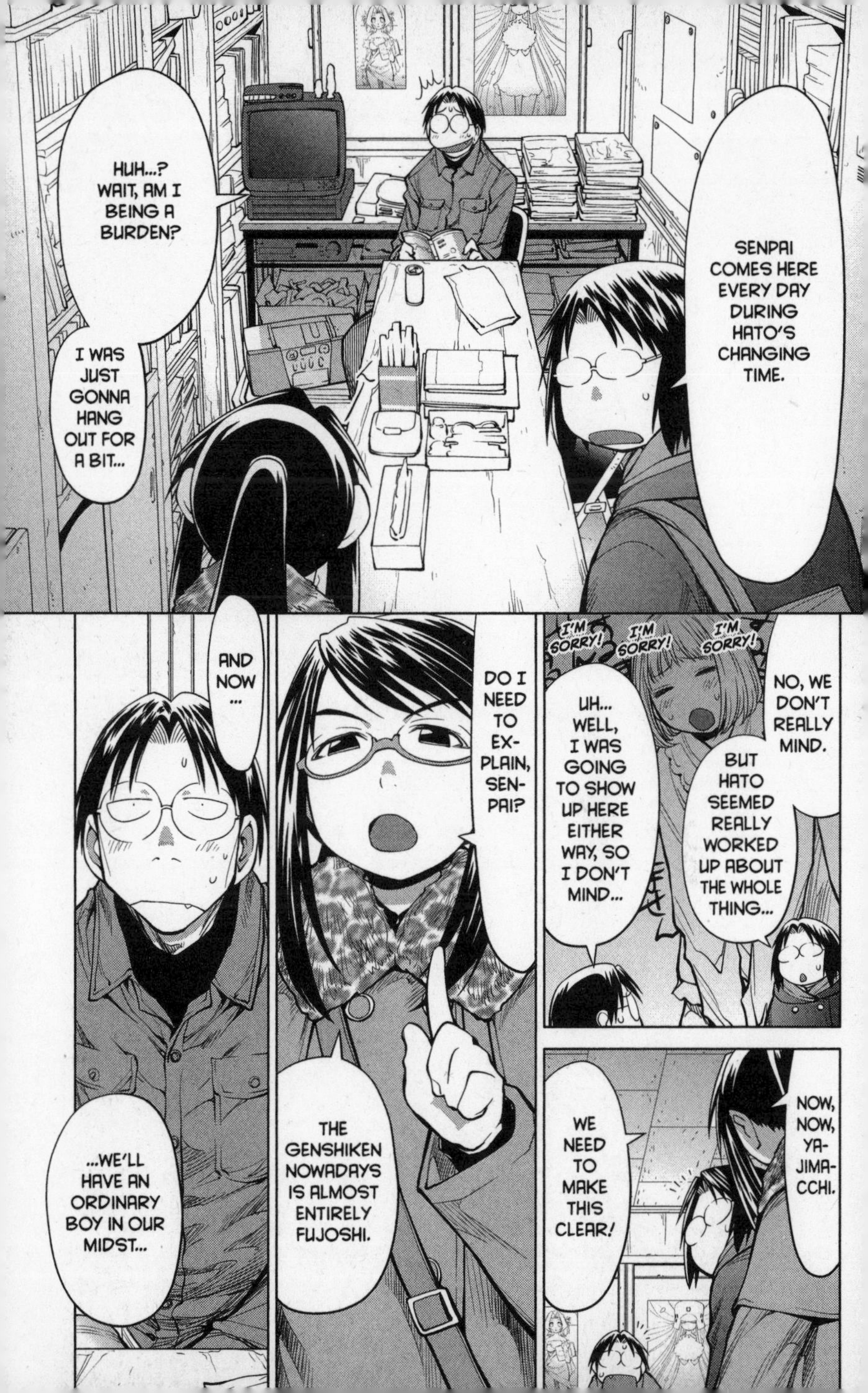
SENPAI COMES HERE EVERY DAY DURING HATO'S CHANGING TIME.
HUH...? WAIT, AM I BEING A BURDEN?
I WAS JUST GONNA HANG OUT FOR A BIT...
I'M SORRY!
I'M SORRY!
I'M SORRY!
NO, WE DON'T REALLY MIND.
BUT HATO SEEMED REALLY WORKED UP ABOUT THE WHOLE THING...
UH... WELL, I WAS GOING TO SHOW UP HERE EITHER WAY, SO I DON'T MIND...
NOW, NOW, YA-JIMA-CCHI.
WE NEED TO MAKE THIS CLEAR!
DO I NEED TO EX-PLAIN, SEN-PAI?
THE GENSHIKEN NOWADAYS IS ALMOST ENTIRELY FUJOSHI.
AND NOW...
...WE'LL HAVE AN ORDINARY BOY IN OUR MIDST...

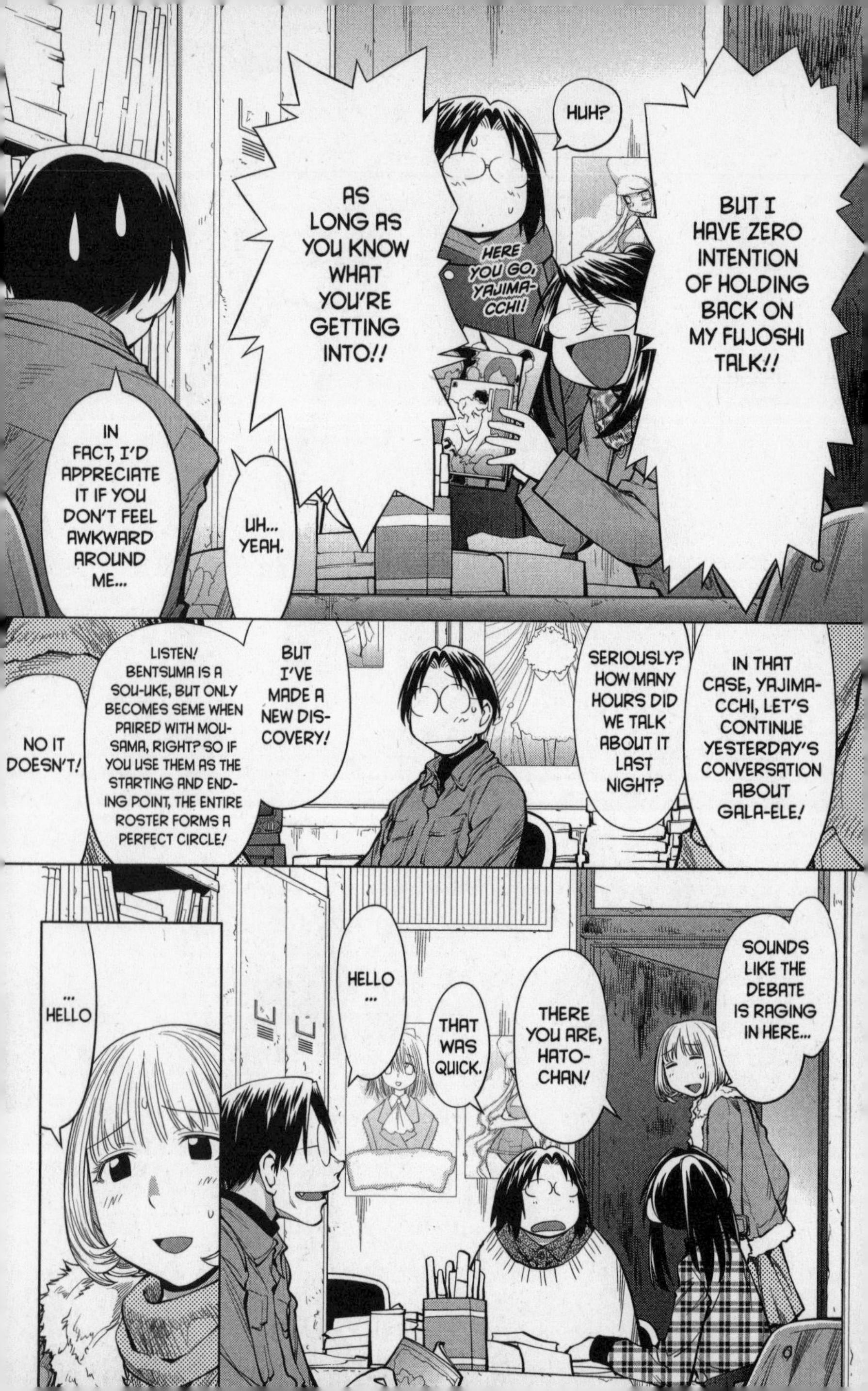

BUT I HAVE ZERO INTENTION OF HOLDING BACK ON MY FUJOSHI TALK!!
HUH?
AS LONG AS YOU KNOW WHAT YOU'RE GETTING INTO!!
HERE YOU GO, YAJIMA-CCHI!
IN FACT, I'D APPRECIATE IT IF YOU DON'T FEEL AWKWARD AROUND ME...
UH... YEAH.
IN THAT CASE, YAJIMA-CCHI, LET'S CONTINUE YESTERDAY'S CONVERSATION ABOUT GALA-ELE!
SERIOUSLY? HOW MANY HOURS DID WE TALK ABOUT IT LAST NIGHT?
BUT I'VE MADE A NEW DIS-COVERY!
LISTEN! BENTSUMA IS A SOU-UKE, BUT ONLY BECOMES SEME WHEN PAIRED WITH MOU-SAMA, RIGHT? SO IF YOU USE THEM AS THE STARTING AND END-ING POINT, THE ENTIRE ROSTER FORMS A PERFECT CIRCLE!
NO IT DOESN'T!
SOUNDS LIKE THE DEBATE IS RAGING IN HERE...
THERE YOU ARE, HATO-CHAN!
THAT WAS QUICK.
HELLO...
... HELLO

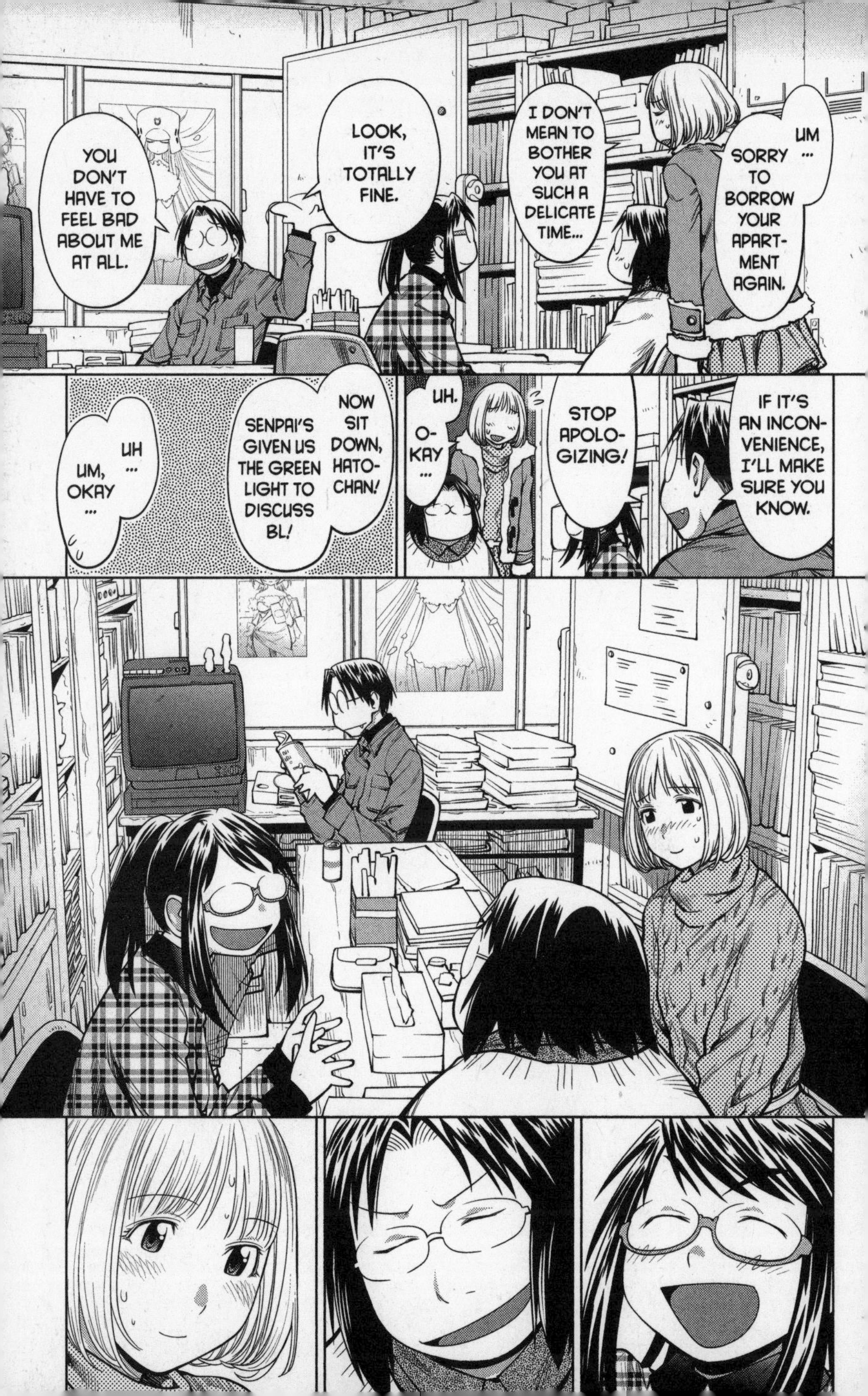
UM ... SORRY TO BORROW YOUR APARTMENT AGAIN.
I DON'T MEAN TO BOTHER YOU AT SUCH A DELICATE TIME...
LOOK, IT'S TOTALLY FINE.
YOU DON'T HAVE TO FEEL BAD ABOUT ME AT ALL.
IF IT'S AN INCONVENIENCE, I'LL MAKE SURE YOU KNOW.
STOP APOLOGIZING!
UH. O-KAY ...
NOW SIT DOWN, HATO-CHAN!
SENPAI'S GIVEN US THE GREEN LIGHT TO DISCUSS BL!
UH ... UM, OKAY ...

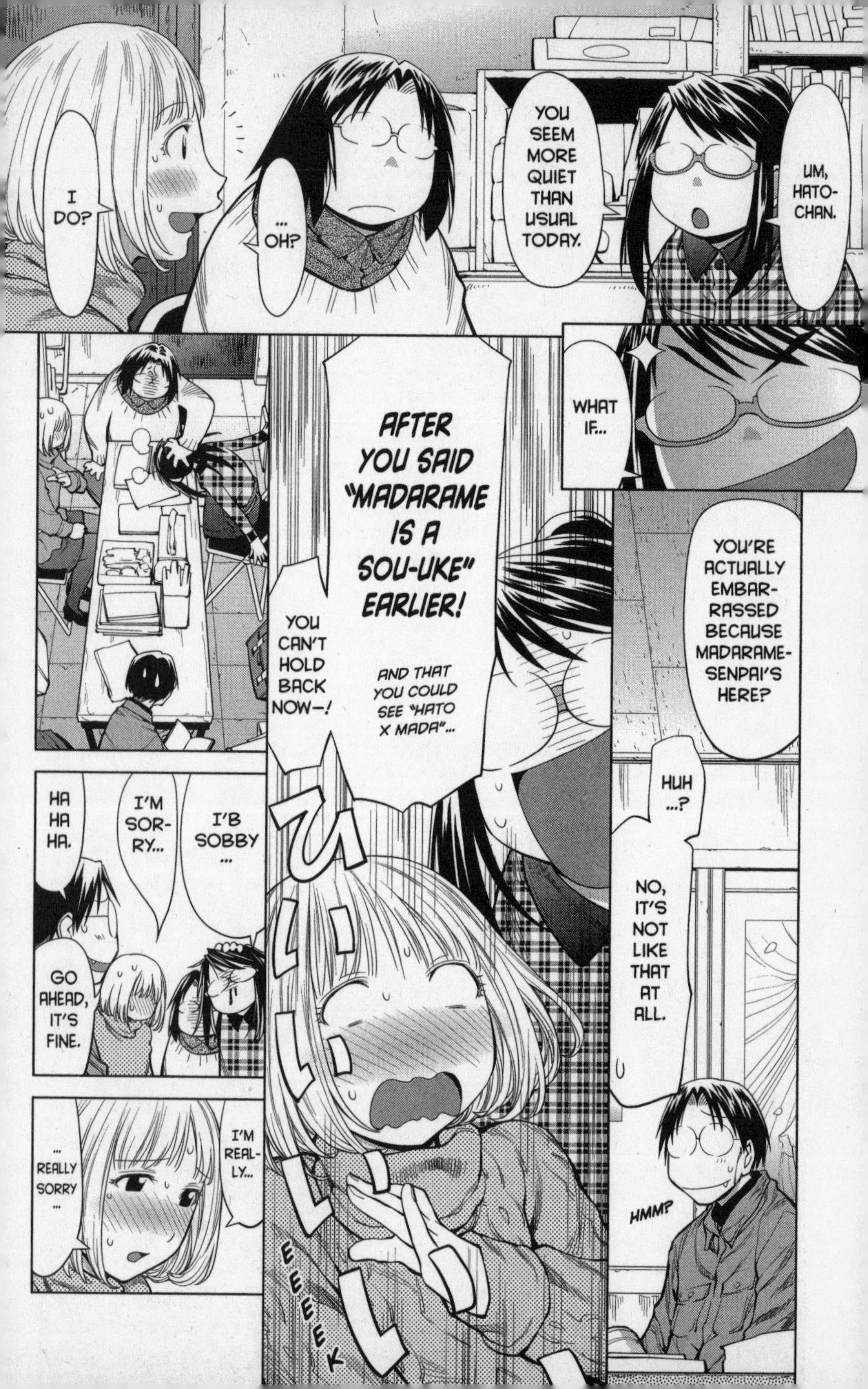
UM, HATO-CHAN.
YOU SEEM MORE QUIET THAN USUAL TODAY.
...OH?
I DO?
WHAT IF...
YOU'RE ACTUALLY EMBARRASSED BECAUSE MADARAME-SENPAI'S HERE?
HUH...?
NO, IT'S NOT LIKE THAT AT ALL.
HMM?
AFTER YOU SAID "MADARAME IS A SOU-UKE" EARLIER!
AND THAT YOU COULD SEE "HATO X MADA"...
YOU CAN'T HOLD BACK NOW—!
EEEEEK
I'B SOBBY...
I'M SORRY...
HA HA HA.
GO AHEAD, IT'S FINE.
I'M REALLY...
...REALLY SORRY...

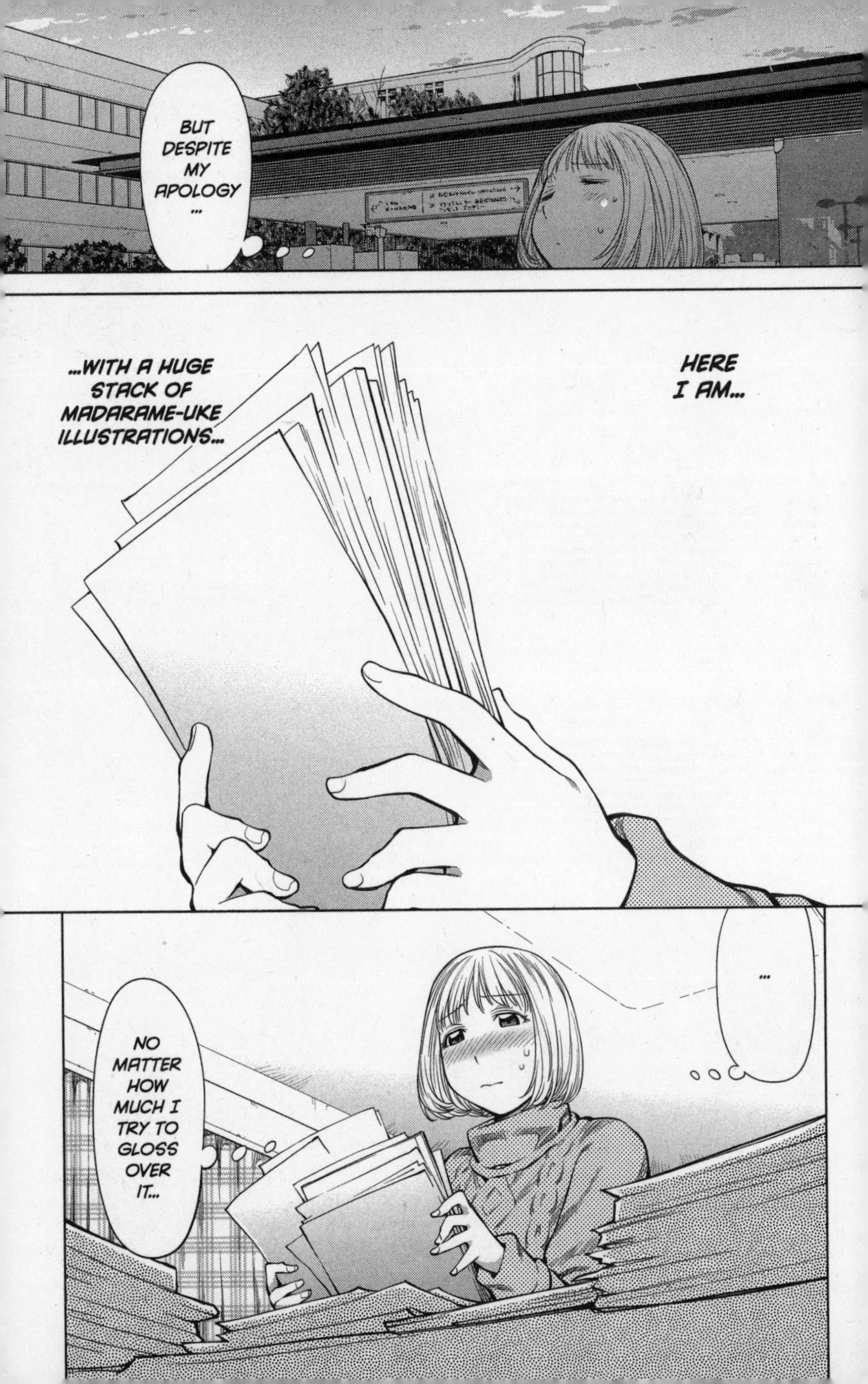
BUT DESPITE MY APOLOGY ...
HERE I AM...
...WITH A HUGE STACK OF MADARAME-UKE ILLUSTRATIONS...
...
NO MATTER HOW MUCH I TRY TO GLOSS OVER IT...

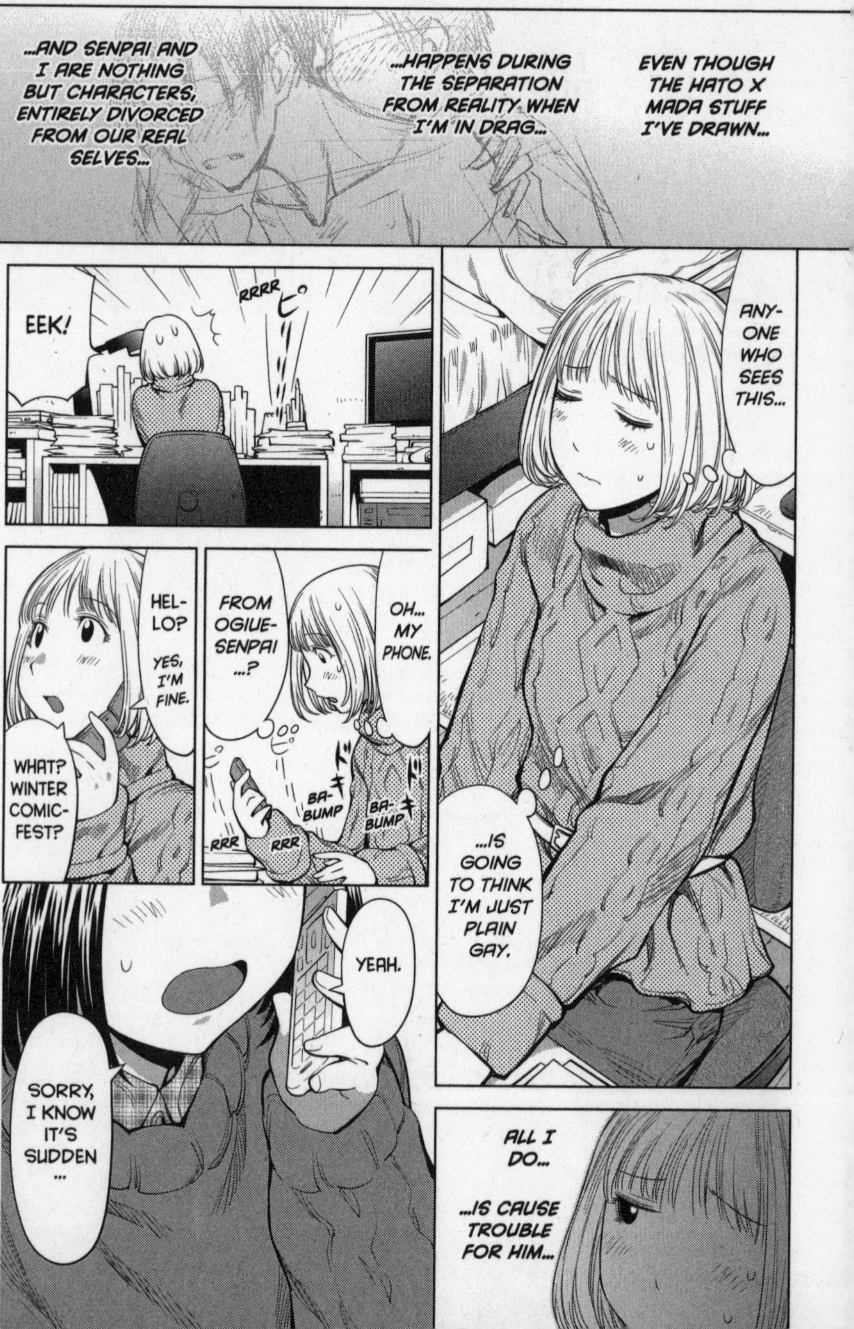
EVEN THOUGH THE HATO X MADA STUFF I'VE DRAWN...
...HAPPENS DURING THE SEPARATION FROM REALITY WHEN I'M IN DRAG...
...AND SENPAI AND I ARE NOTHING BUT CHARACTERS, ENTIRELY DIVORCED FROM OUR REAL SELVES...
ANY-ONE WHO SEES THIS...
...IS GOING TO THINK I'M JUST PLAIN GAY.
RRRR
ピ
EEK!
OH... MY PHONE.
FROM OGIUE-SENPAI ...?
ドキ
BA-BUMP
ドキ
BA-BUMP
RRR
RRR
HEL-LO?
YES, I'M FINE.
WHAT? WINTER COMIC-FEST?
YEAH.
SORRY, I KNOW IT'S SUDDEN ...
ALL I DO...
...IS CAUSE TROUBLE FOR HIM...

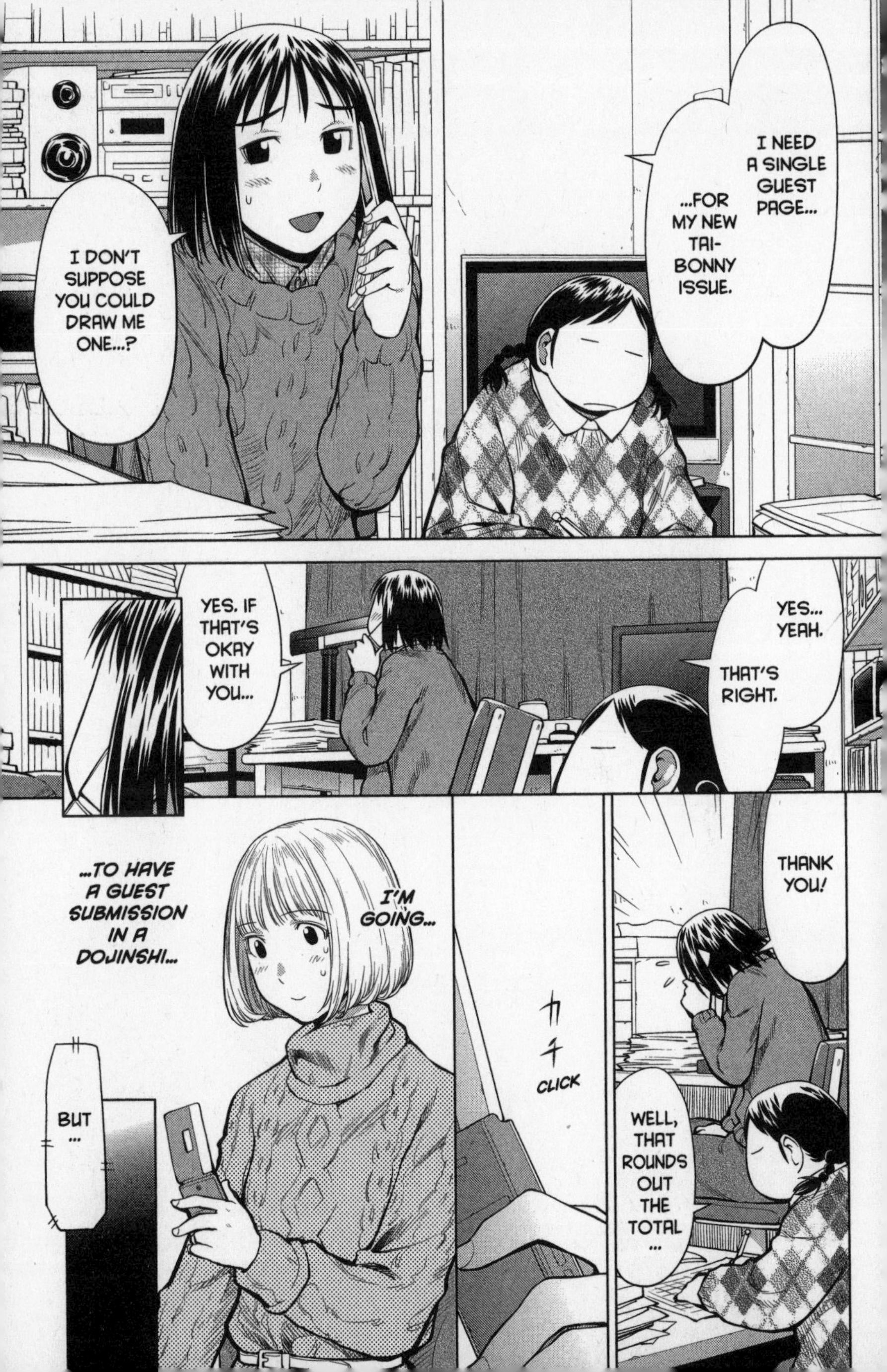
I NEED A SINGLE GUEST PAGE...
...FOR MY NEW TAI-BONNY ISSUE.
I DON'T SUPPOSE YOU COULD DRAW ME ONE...?
YES... YEAH.
THAT'S RIGHT.
YES. IF THAT'S OKAY WITH YOU...
THANK YOU!
WELL, THAT ROUNDS OUT THE TOTAL ...
カチ
CLICK
I'M GOING...
...TO HAVE A GUEST SUBMISSION IN A DOJINSHI...
BUT ...

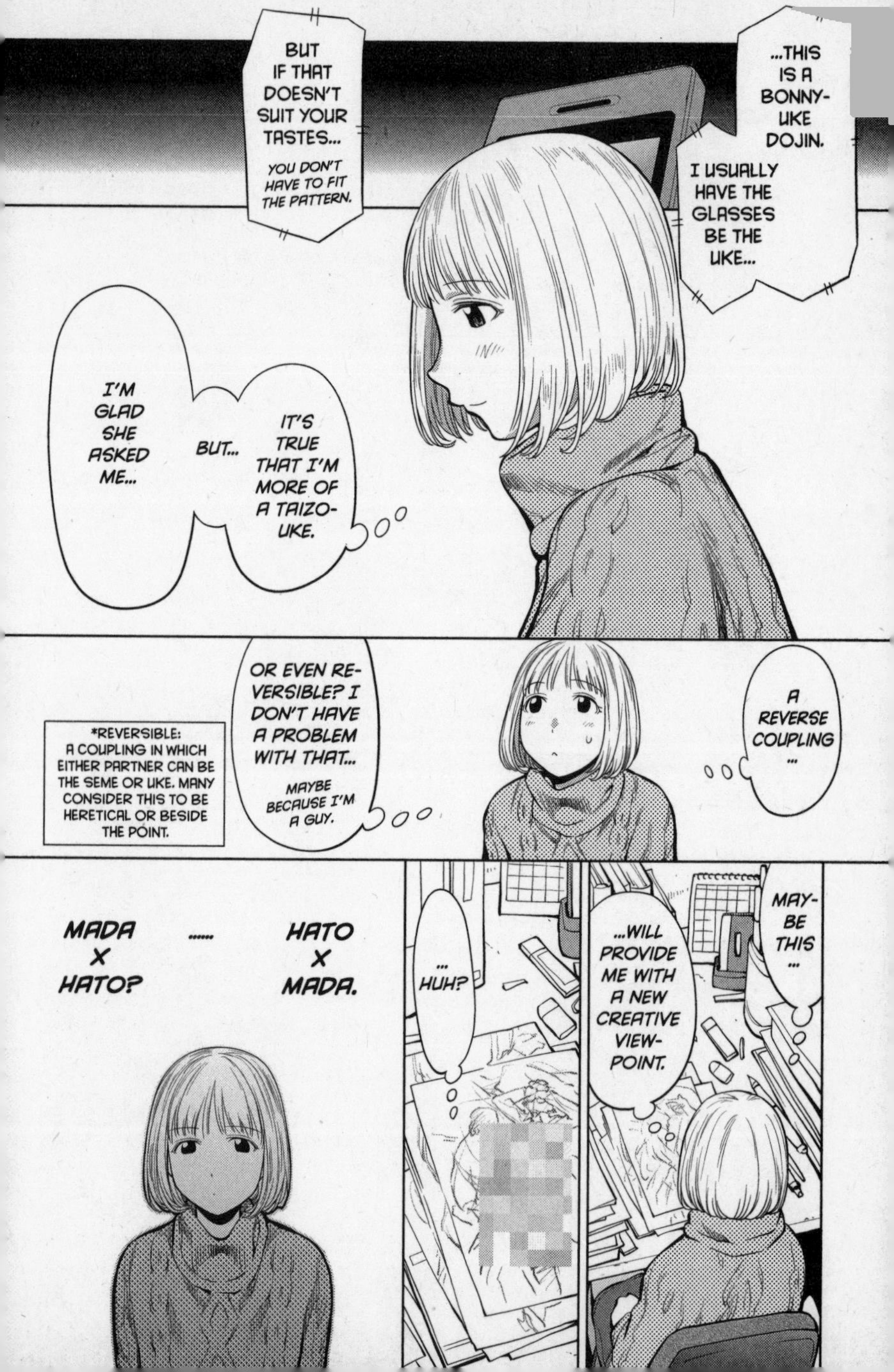
...THIS IS A BONNY-UKE DOJIN.
I USUALLY HAVE THE GLASSES BE THE UKE...
BUT IF THAT DOESN'T SUIT YOUR TASTES...
YOU DON'T HAVE TO FIT THE PATTERN.
I'M GLAD SHE ASKED ME...
BUT...
IT'S TRUE THAT I'M MORE OF A TAIZO-UKE.
A REVERSE COUPLING...
OR EVEN RE-VERSIBLE? I DON'T HAVE A PROBLEM WITH THAT...
MAYBE BECAUSE I'M A GUY.
*REVERSIBLE: A COUPLING IN WHICH EITHER PARTNER CAN BE THE SEME OR UKE. MANY CONSIDER THIS TO BE HERETICAL OR BESIDE THE POINT.
MAY-BE THIS...
...WILL PROVIDE ME WITH A NEW CREATIVE VIEW-POINT.
... HUH?
HATO X MADA.
......
MADA X HATO?

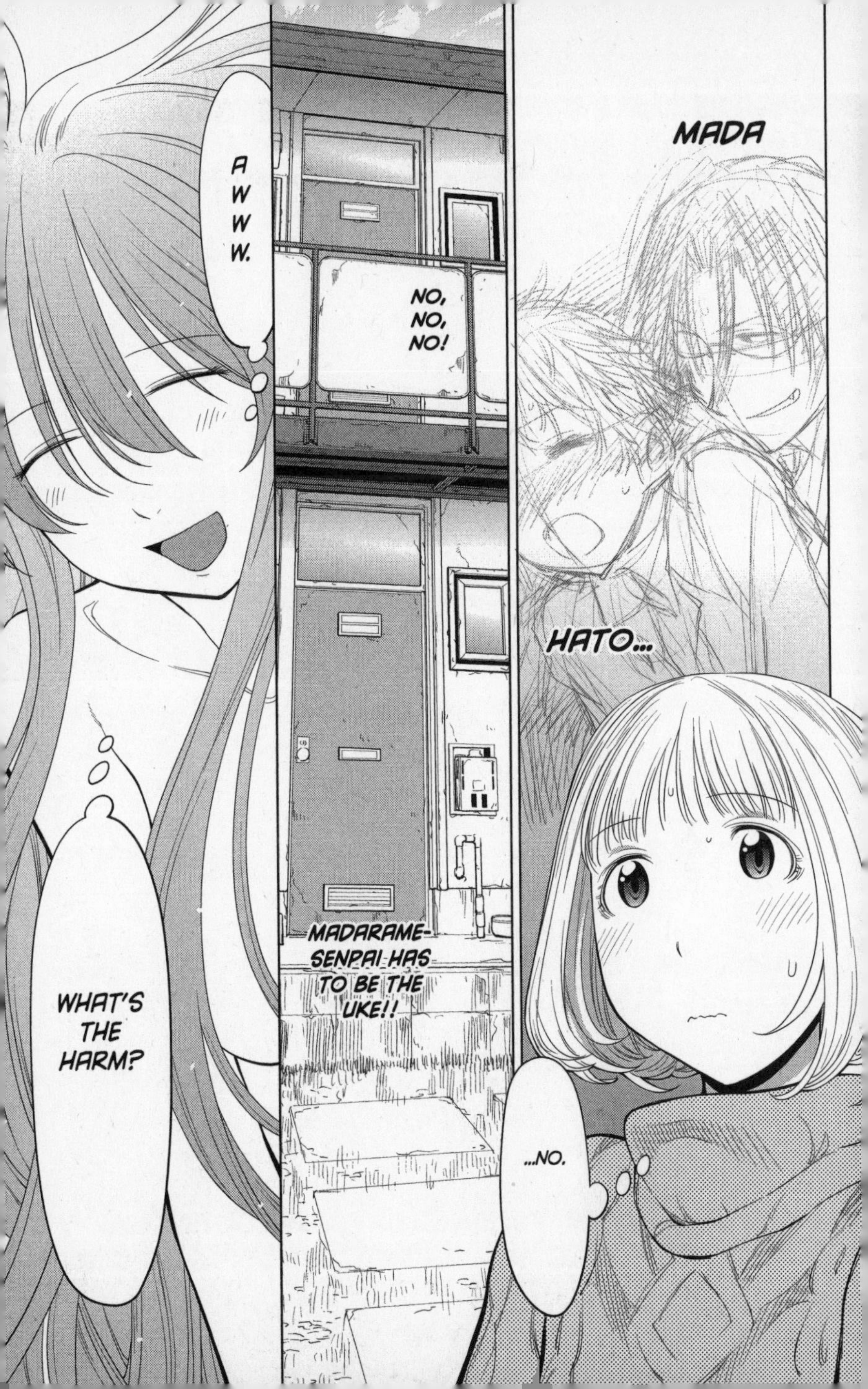
MADA
HATO...
...NO.
NO, NO, NO!
MADARAME-SENPAI HAS TO BE THE UKE!!
AWWW.
WHAT'S THE HARM?

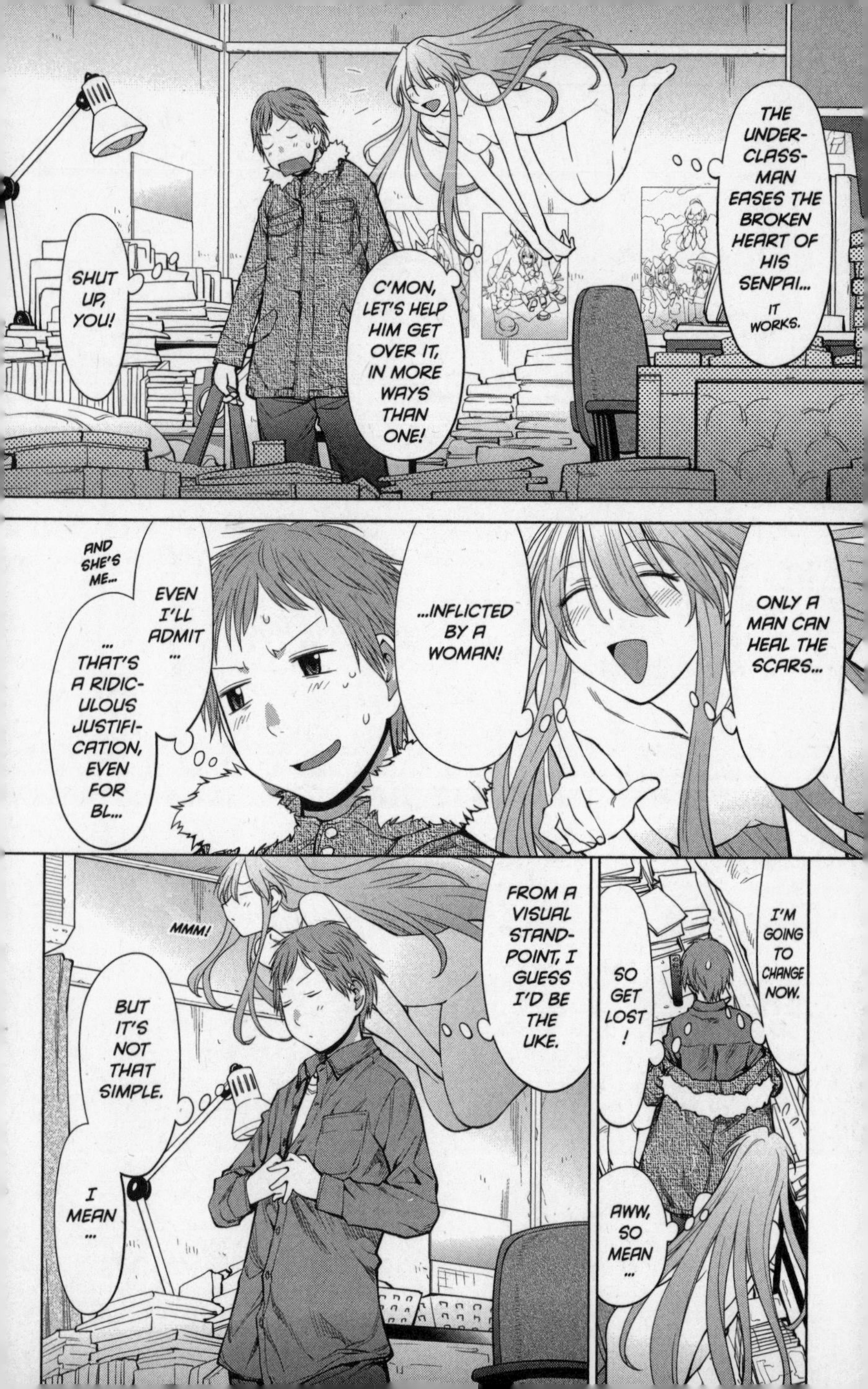
THE UNDER-CLASS-MAN EASES THE BROKEN HEART OF HIS SENPAI...
IT WORKS.
C'MON, LET'S HELP HIM GET OVER IT, IN MORE WAYS THAN ONE!
SHUT UP, YOU!
ONLY A MAN CAN HEAL THE SCARS...
...INFLICTED BY A WOMAN!
EVEN I'LL ADMIT ...
... THAT'S A RIDICULOUS JUSTIFICATION, EVEN FOR BL...
AND SHE'S ME...
I'M GOING TO CHANGE NOW.
SO GET LOST!
AWW, SO MEAN ...
FROM A VISUAL STANDPOINT, I GUESS I'D BE THE UKE.
MMM!
BUT IT'S NOT THAT SIMPLE.
I MEAN ...

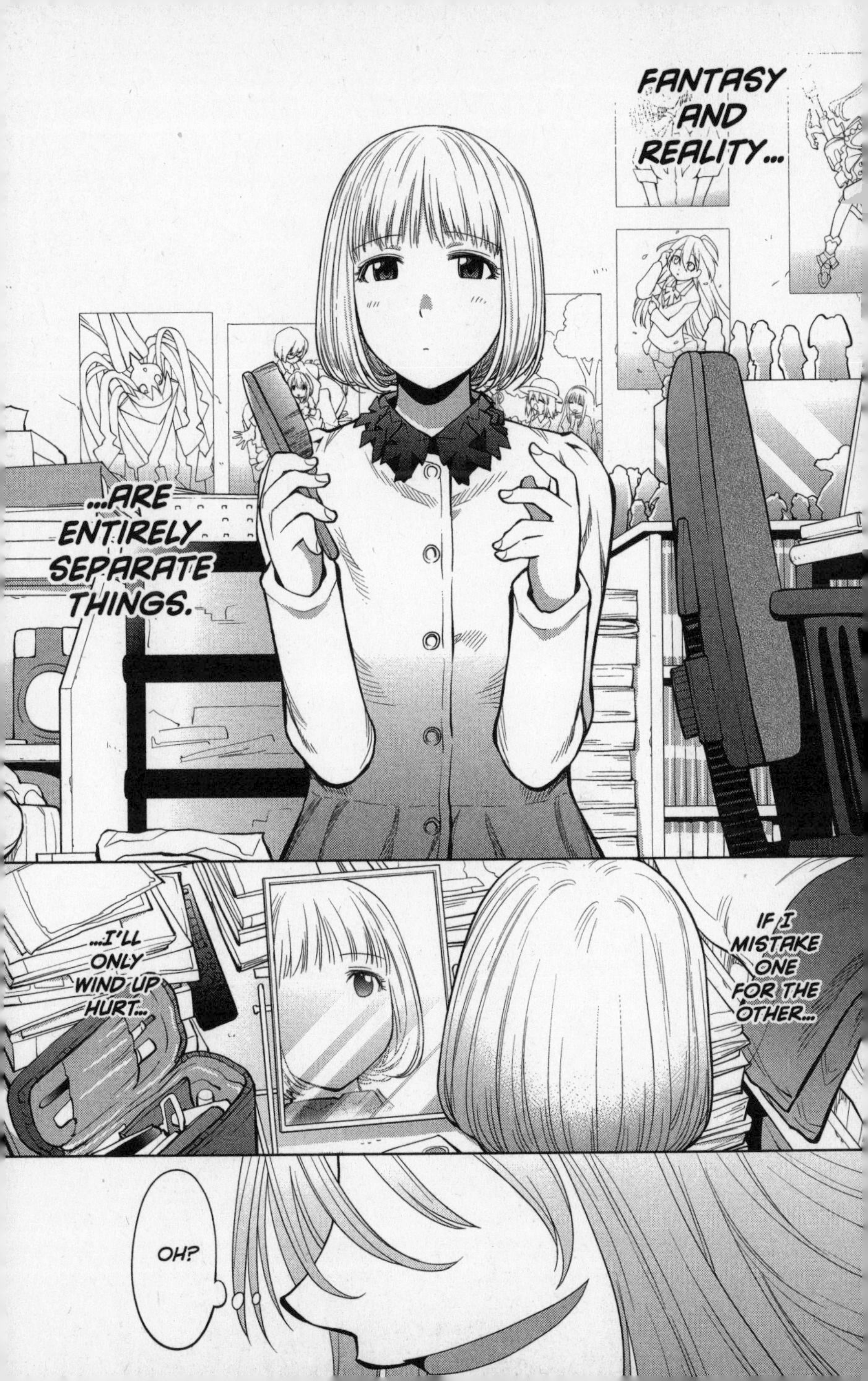
FANTASY AND REALITY...
...ARE ENTIRELY SEPARATE THINGS.
IF I MISTAKE ONE FOR THE OTHER...
...I'LL ONLY WIND UP HURT...
OH?

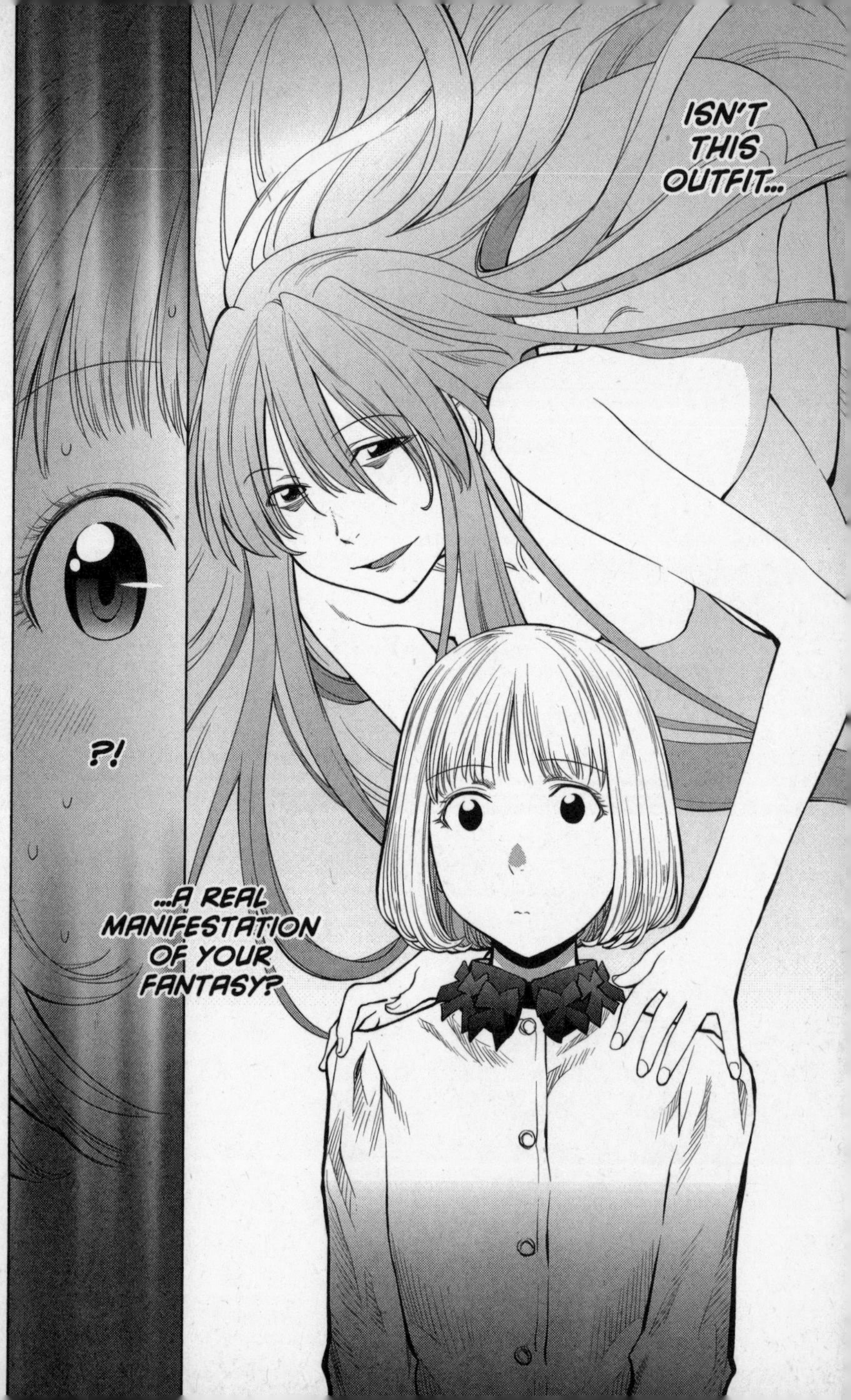
ISN'T THIS OUTFIT...
...A REAL MANIFESTATION OF YOUR FANTASY?
?!

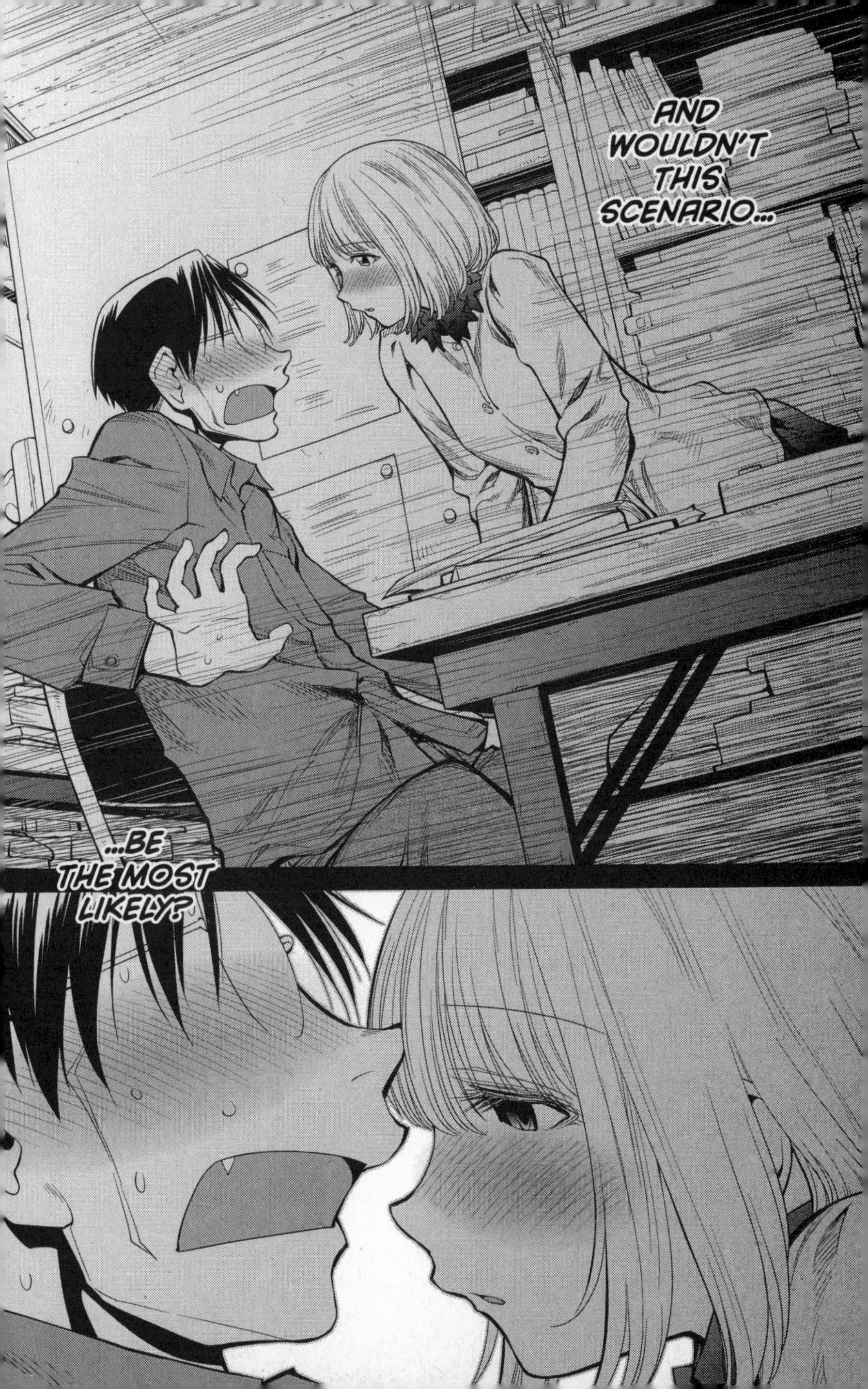
AND WOULDN'T THIS SCENARIO...
...BE THE MOST LIKELY?

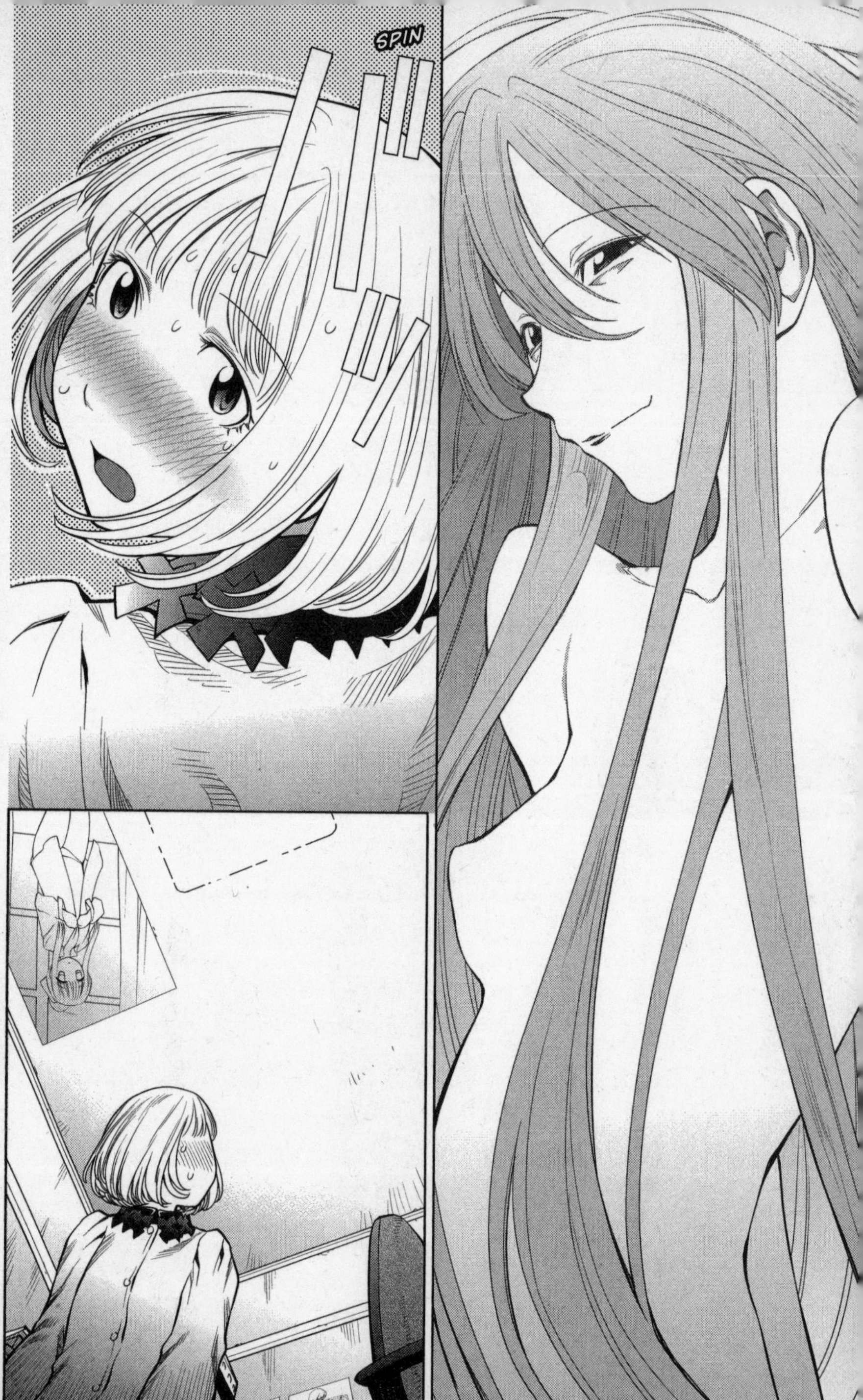
SPIN

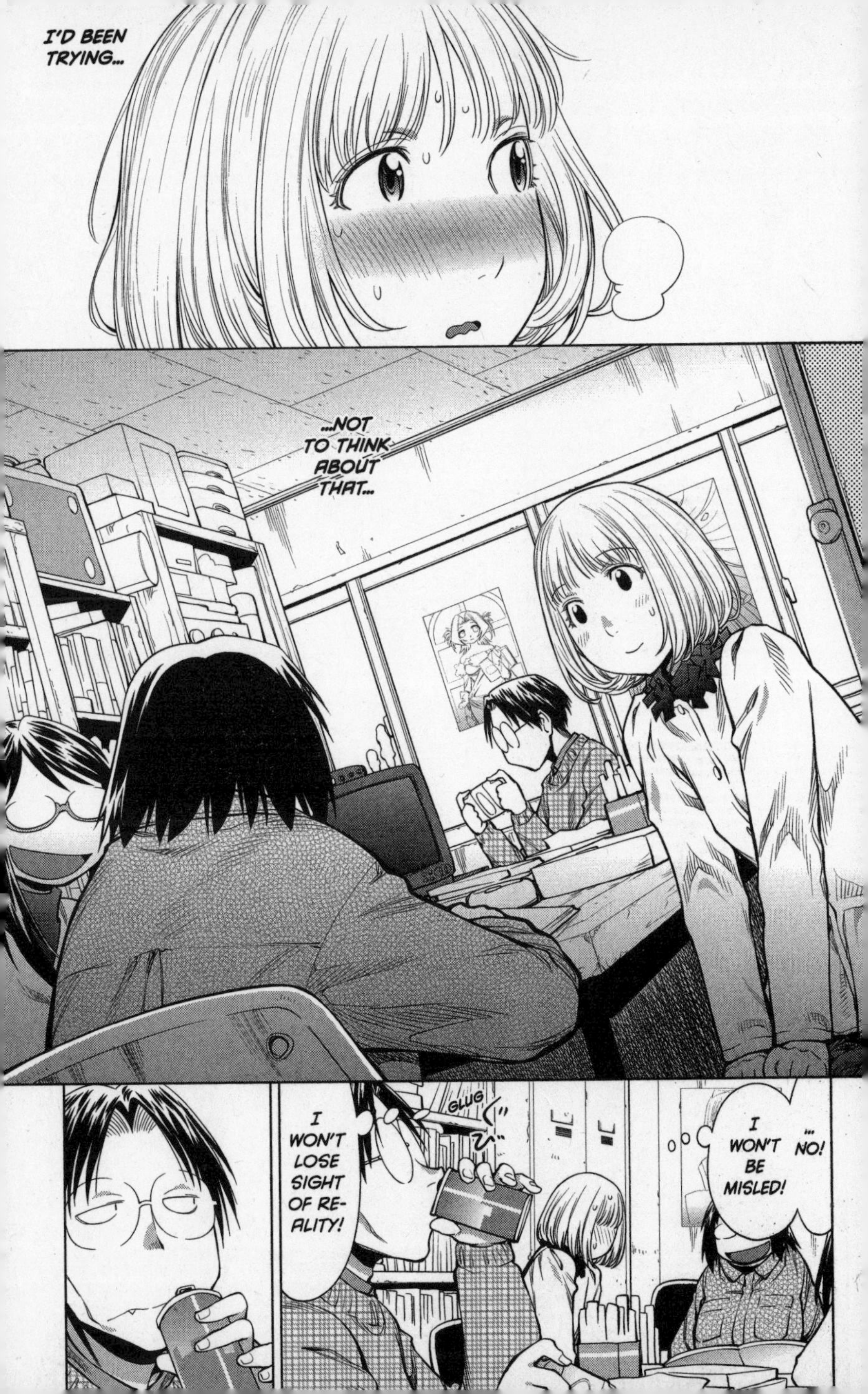
I'D BEEN TRYING...
...NOT TO THINK ABOUT THAT...
... NO!
I WON'T BE MISLED!
GLUG
I WON'T LOSE SIGHT OF RE-ALITY!

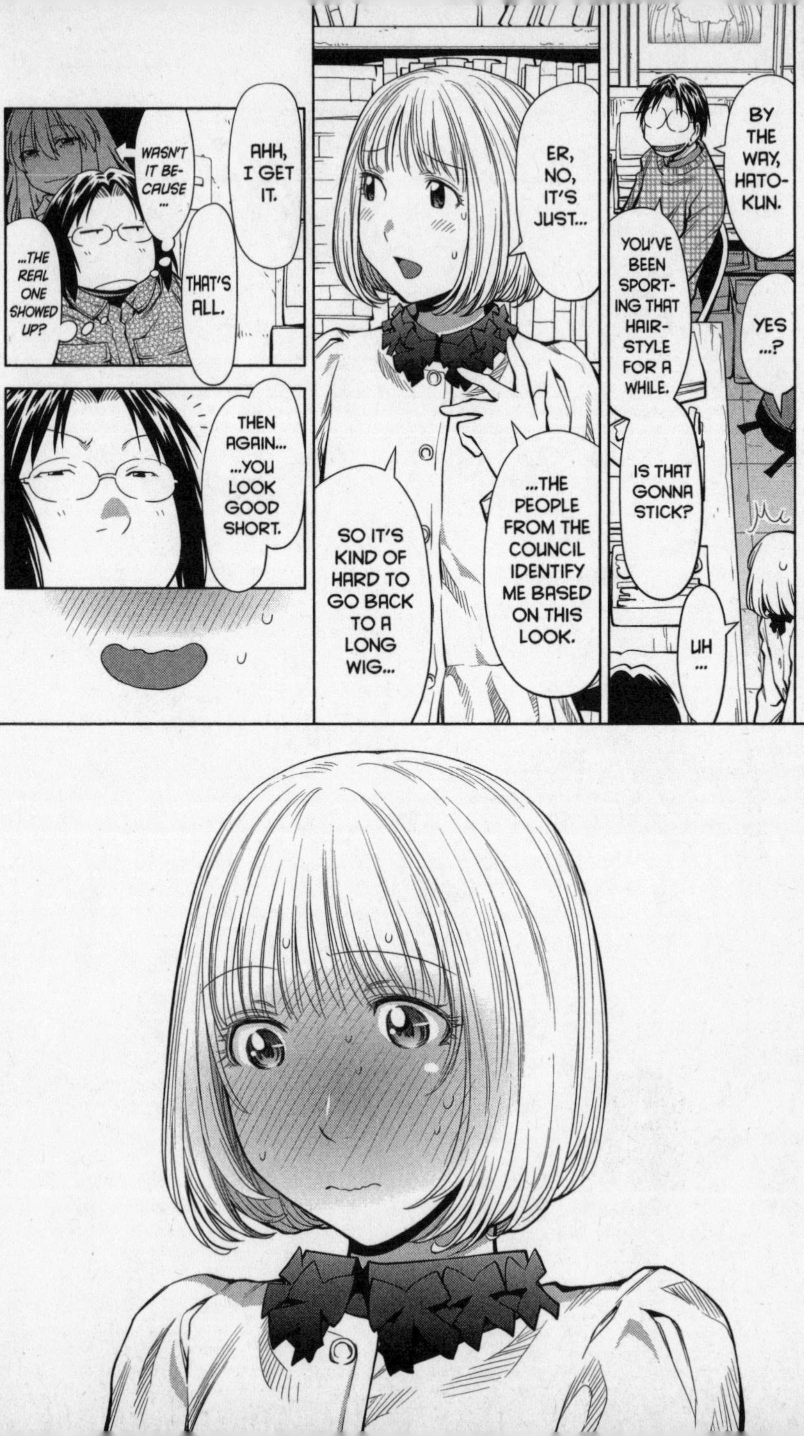

BY THE WAY, HATO-KUN.
YES ...?
YOU'VE BEEN SPORTING THAT HAIRSTYLE FOR A WHILE.
IS THAT GONNA STICK?
UH ...
ER, NO, IT'S JUST...
...THE PEOPLE FROM THE COUNCIL IDENTIFY ME BASED ON THIS LOOK.
SO IT'S KIND OF HARD TO GO BACK TO A LONG WIG...
AHH, I GET IT.
THAT'S ALL.
WASN'T IT BECAUSE ...
...THE REAL ONE SHOWED UP?
THEN AGAIN... ...YOU LOOK GOOD SHORT.

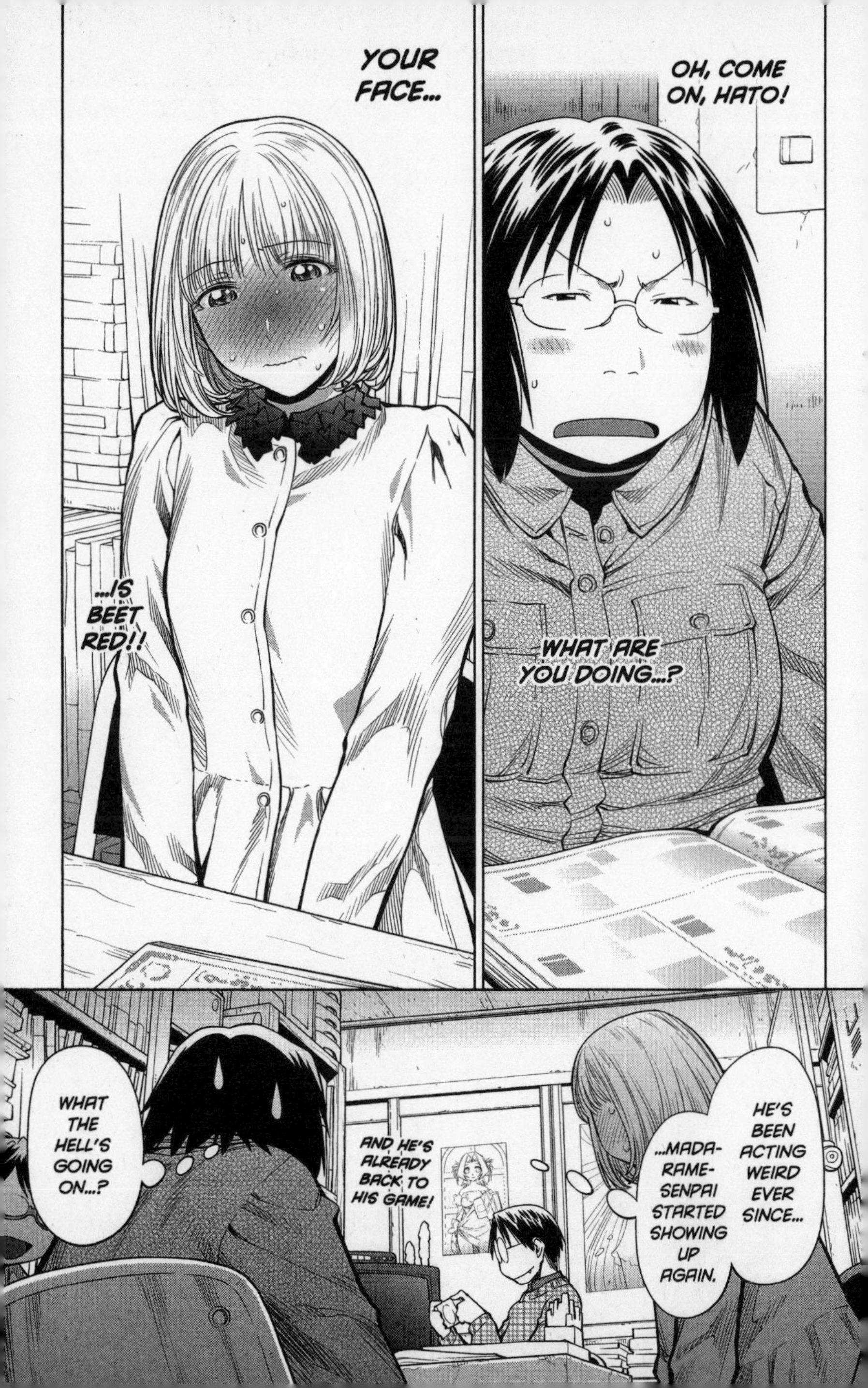
OH, COME ON, HATO!
WHAT ARE YOU DOING...?
YOUR FACE...
...IS BEET RED!!
HE'S BEEN ACTING WEIRD EVER SINCE...
...MADARAME-SENPAI STARTED SHOWING UP AGAIN.
AND HE'S ALREADY BACK TO HIS GAME!
WHAT THE HELL'S GOING ON...?

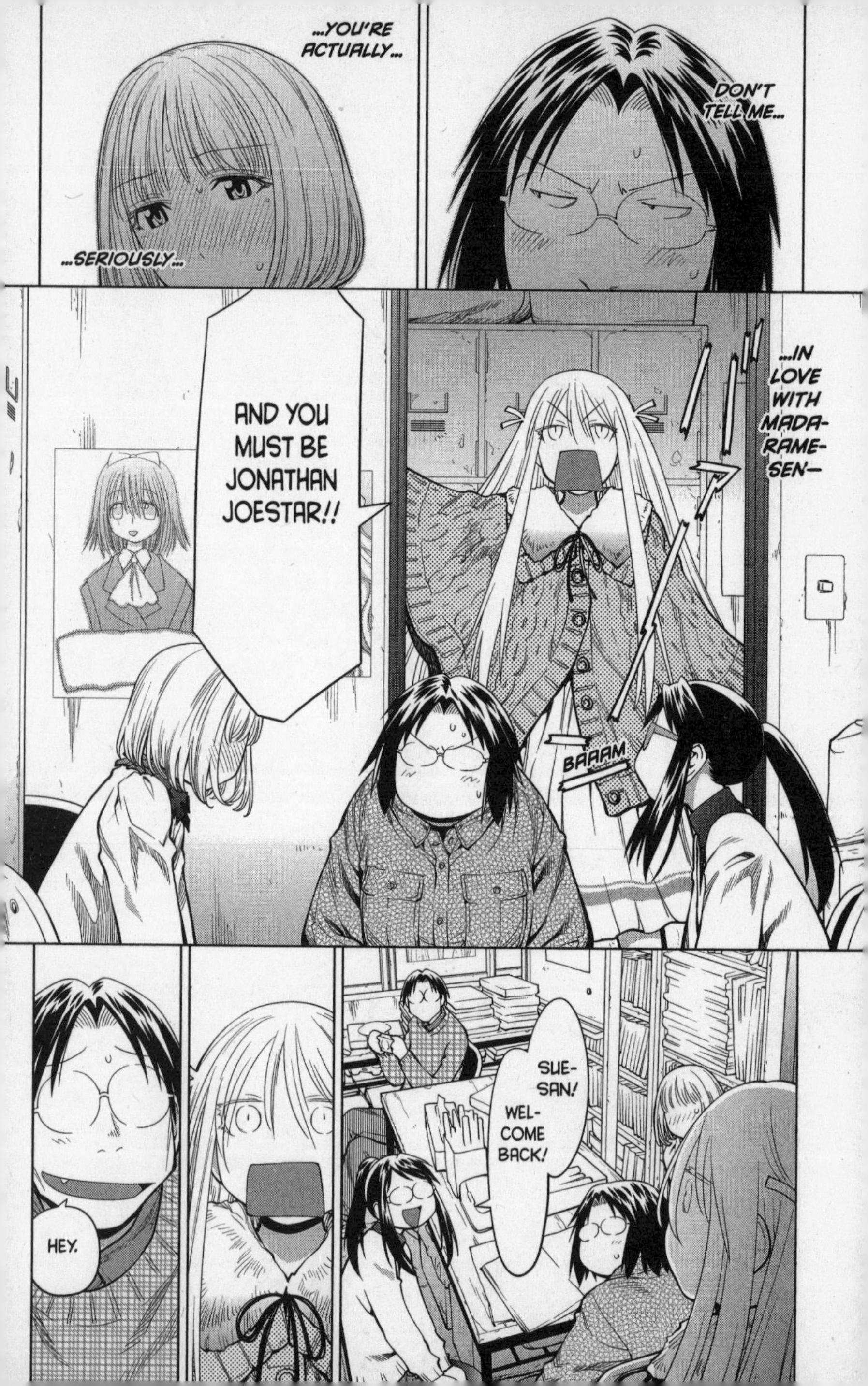
DON'T TELL ME...
...YOU'RE ACTUALLY...
...SERIOUSLY...
...IN LOVE WITH MADA-RAME-SEN—
BAAAM
AND YOU MUST BE JONATHAN JOESTAR!!
SUE-SAN! WEL-COME BACK!
HEY.

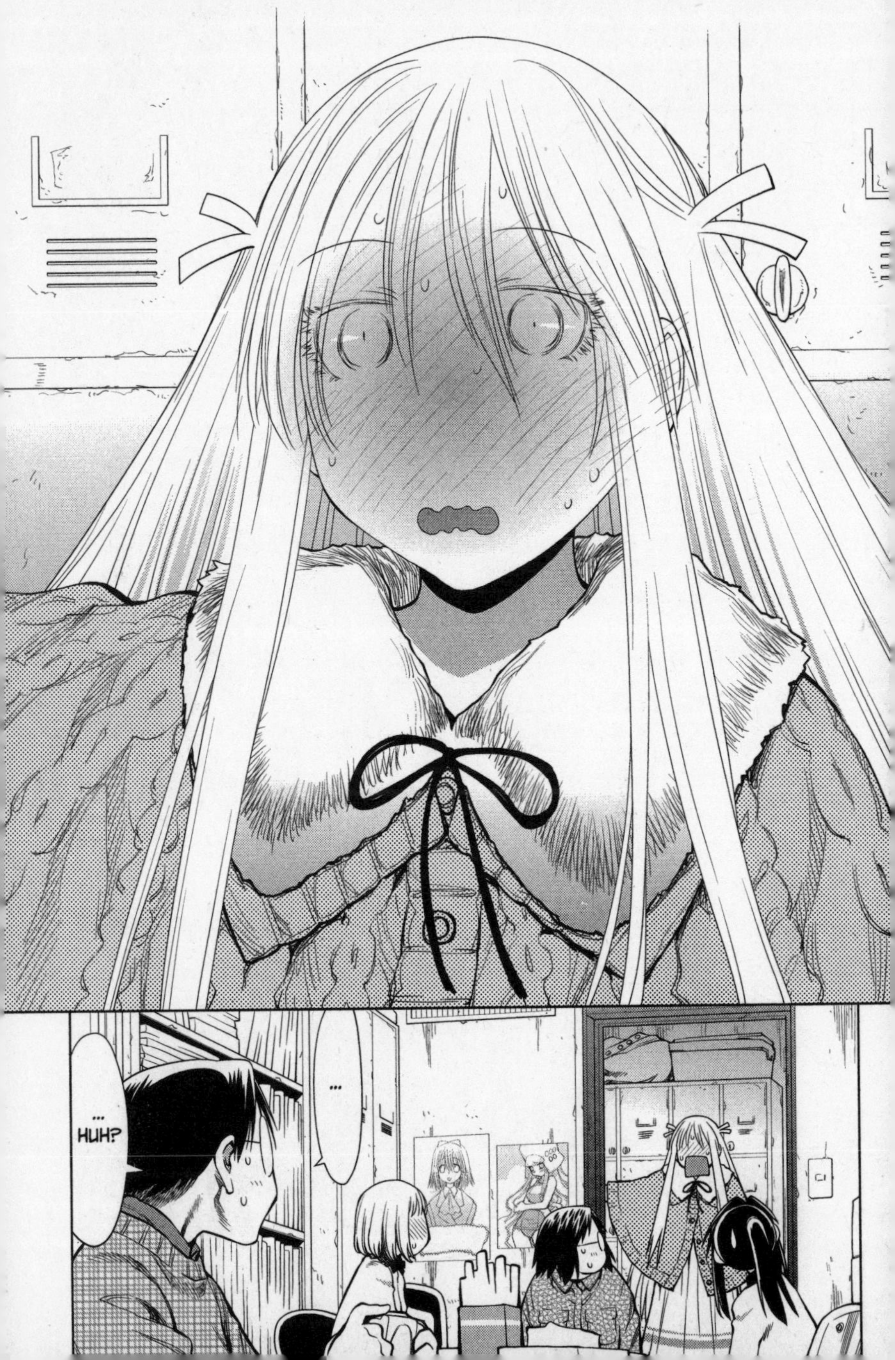
...
...
HUH?

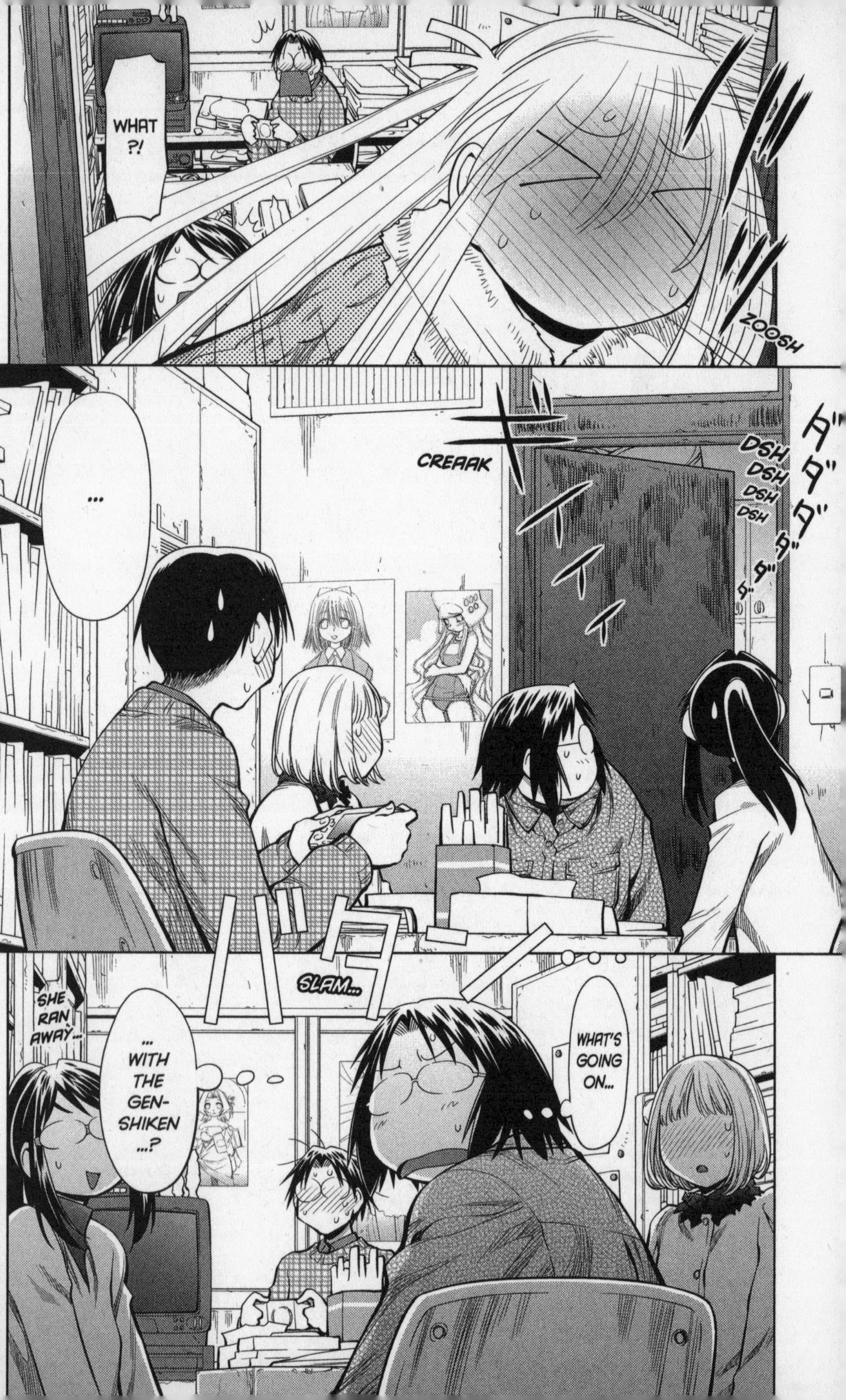
WHAT ?!
ZOOSH
ダダダダダダ
DSH DSH DSH DSH
ギイイイイ
CREAAK
...
バタ
SLAM...
WHAT'S GOING ON...
... WITH THE GEN-SHIKEN ...?
SHE RAN AWAY...

CHAPTER 84 - END

THE BIGGEST PROBLEM

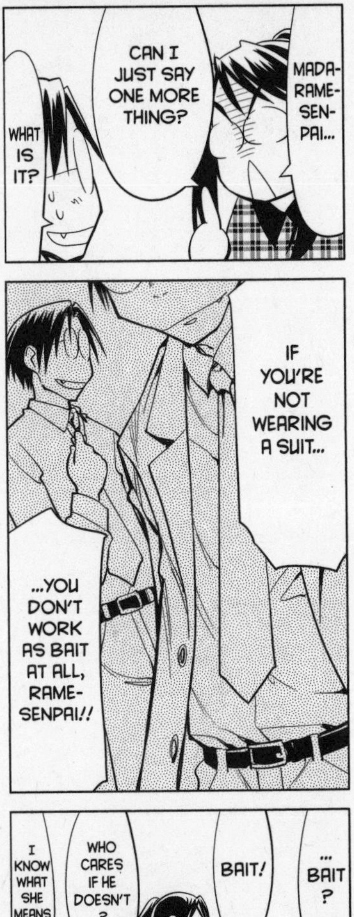
MADARAME-SENPAI...
CAN I JUST SAY ONE MORE THING?
WHAT IS IT?
IF YOU'RE NOT WEARING A SUIT...
...YOU DON'T WORK AS BAIT AT ALL, RAME-SENPAI!!
... BAIT?
BAIT!
WHO CARES IF HE DOESN'T?
I KNOW WHAT SHE MEANS ...
"RAME-SENPAI"?

FIGURE IT OUT YOURSELF

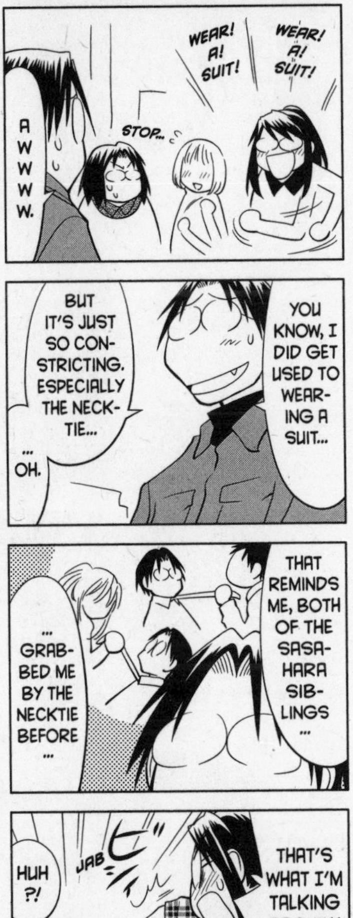
WEAR! A! SUIT!
WEAR! A! SUIT!
STOP...
AWWWWW.
YOU KNOW, I DID GET USED TO WEARING A SUIT...
BUT IT'S JUST SO CONSTRICTING. ESPECIALLY THE NECKTIE...
... OH.
THAT REMINDS ME, BOTH OF THE SASAHARA SIBLINGS ...
... GRABBED ME BY THE NECKTIE BEFORE ...
THAT'S WHAT I'M TALKING ABOUT!!
BAIT, BAIT!!
JAB
BOTH OF THEM?
HUH ?!

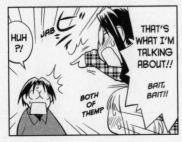

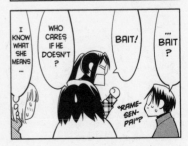

SAME DIFFERENCE

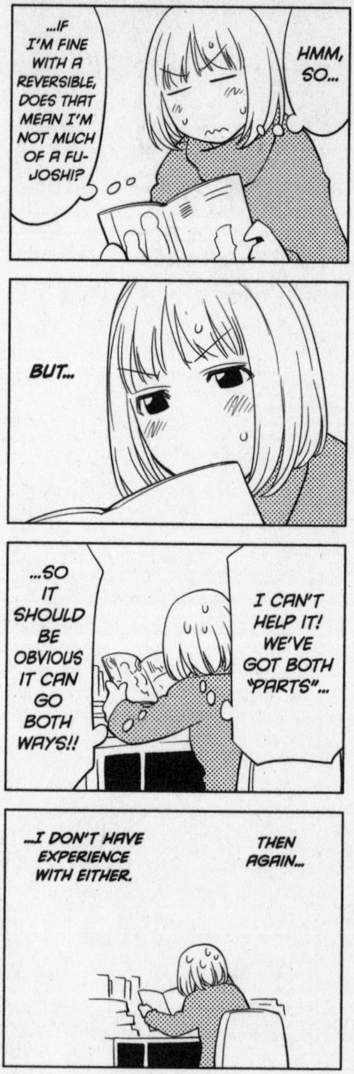
HMM, SO...
...IF I'M FINE WITH A REVERSIBLE, DOES THAT MEAN I'M NOT MUCH OF A FU-JOSHI?
BUT...
I CAN'T HELP IT! WE'VE GOT BOTH "PARTS"...
...SO IT SHOULD BE OBVIOUS IT CAN GO BOTH WAYS!!
THEN AGAIN...
...I DON'T HAVE EXPERIENCE WITH EITHER.

I WANTED ALL THE SOUND EFFECTS...

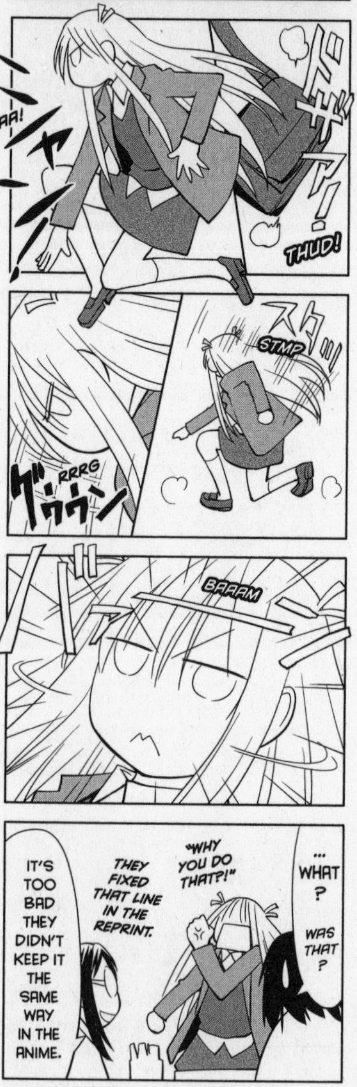
THUD!
SHAA!
STMP
RRRG
BAAAM
... WHAT? WAS THAT?
"WHY YOU DO THAT?!"
THEY FIXED THAT LINE IN THE REPRINT.
IT'S TOO BAD THEY DIDN'T KEEP IT THE SAME WAY IN THE ANIME.

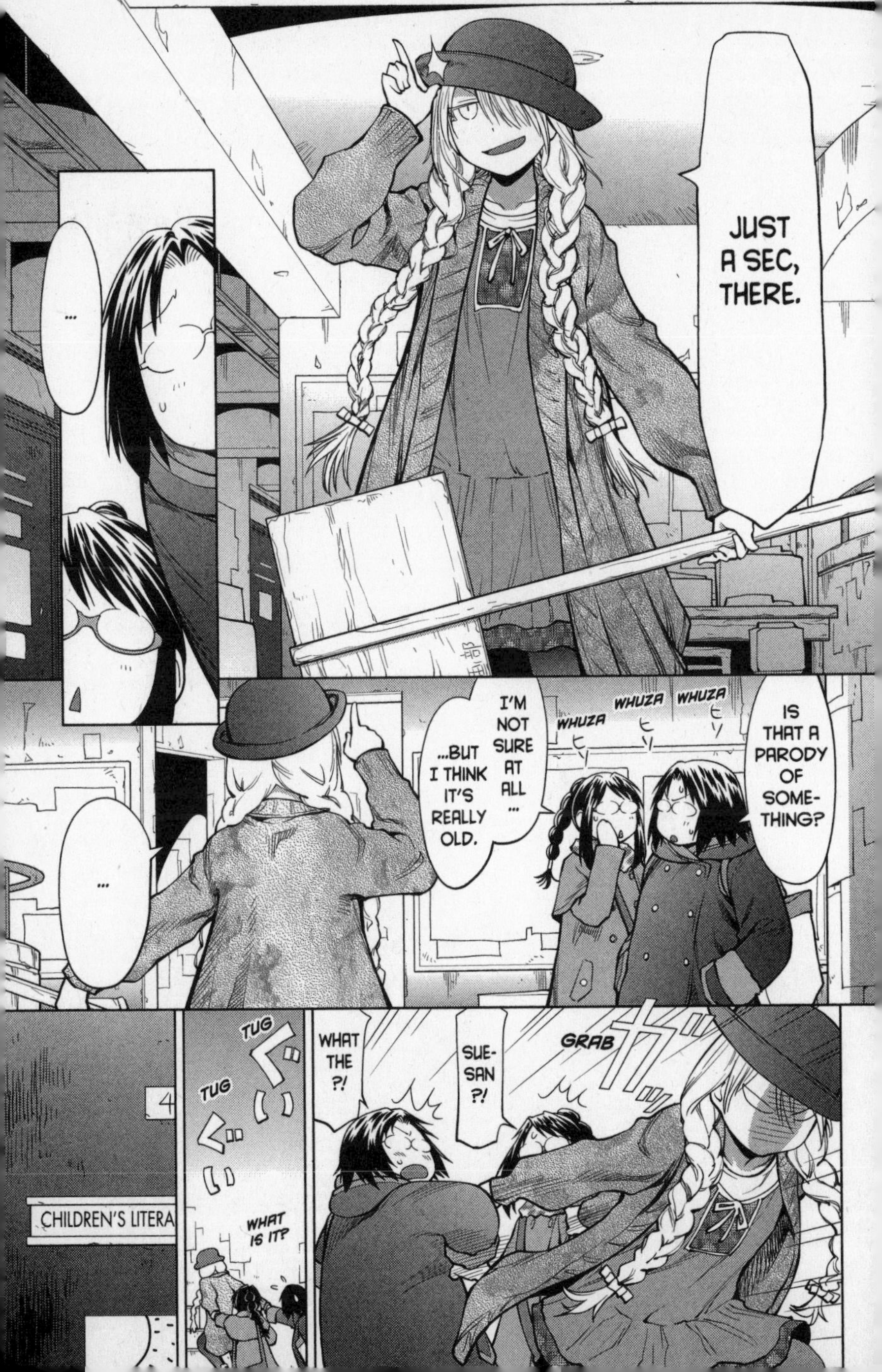
JUST A SEC, THERE.
...
IS THAT A PARODY OF SOME-THING?
WHUZA
WHUZA
WHUZA
I'M NOT SURE AT ALL ...
...BUT I THINK IT'S REALLY OLD.
...
GRAB
SUE-SAN?!
WHAT THE ?!
TUG
TUG
WHAT IS IT?
4
CHILDREN'S LITERA

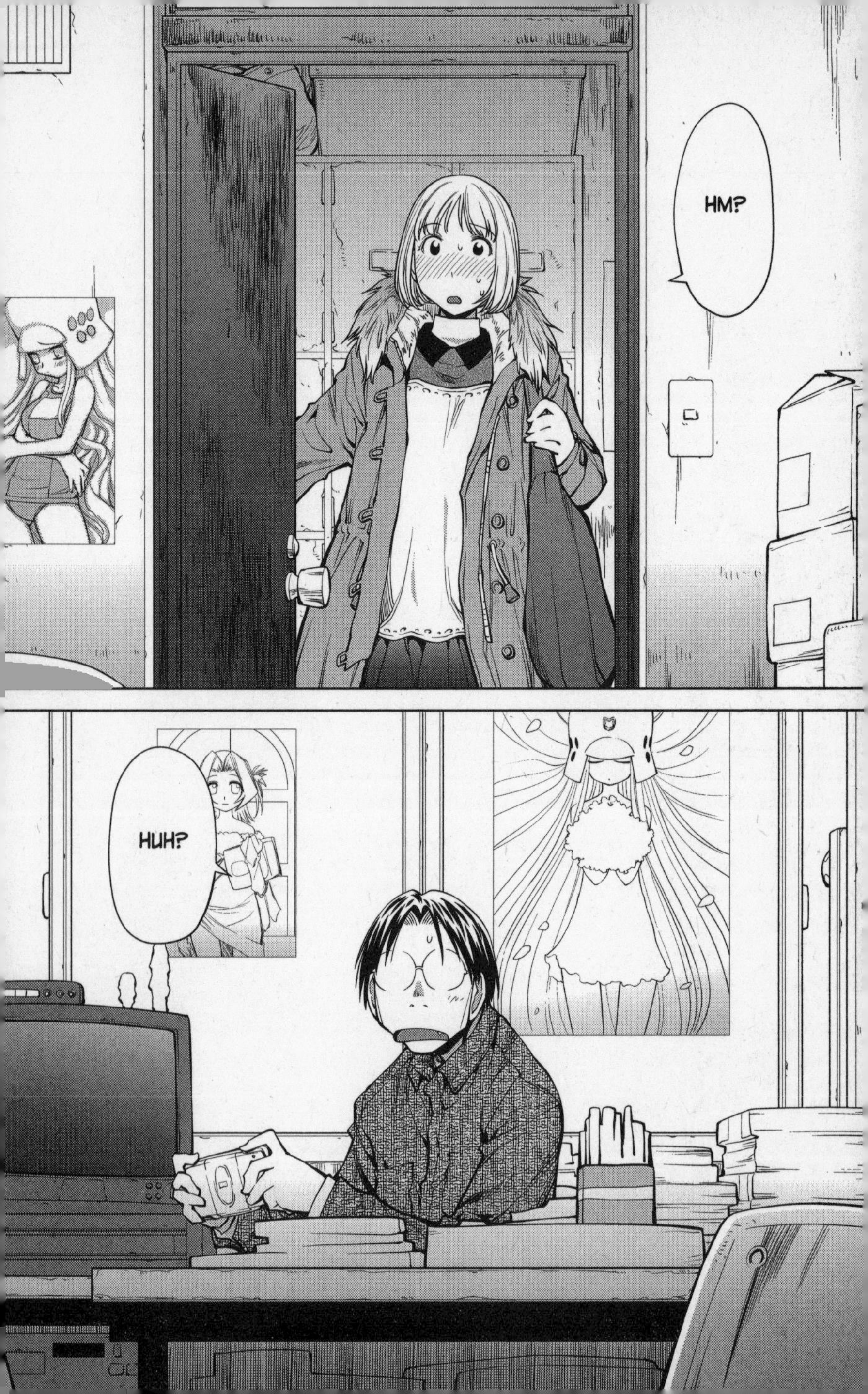
HM?
HUH?

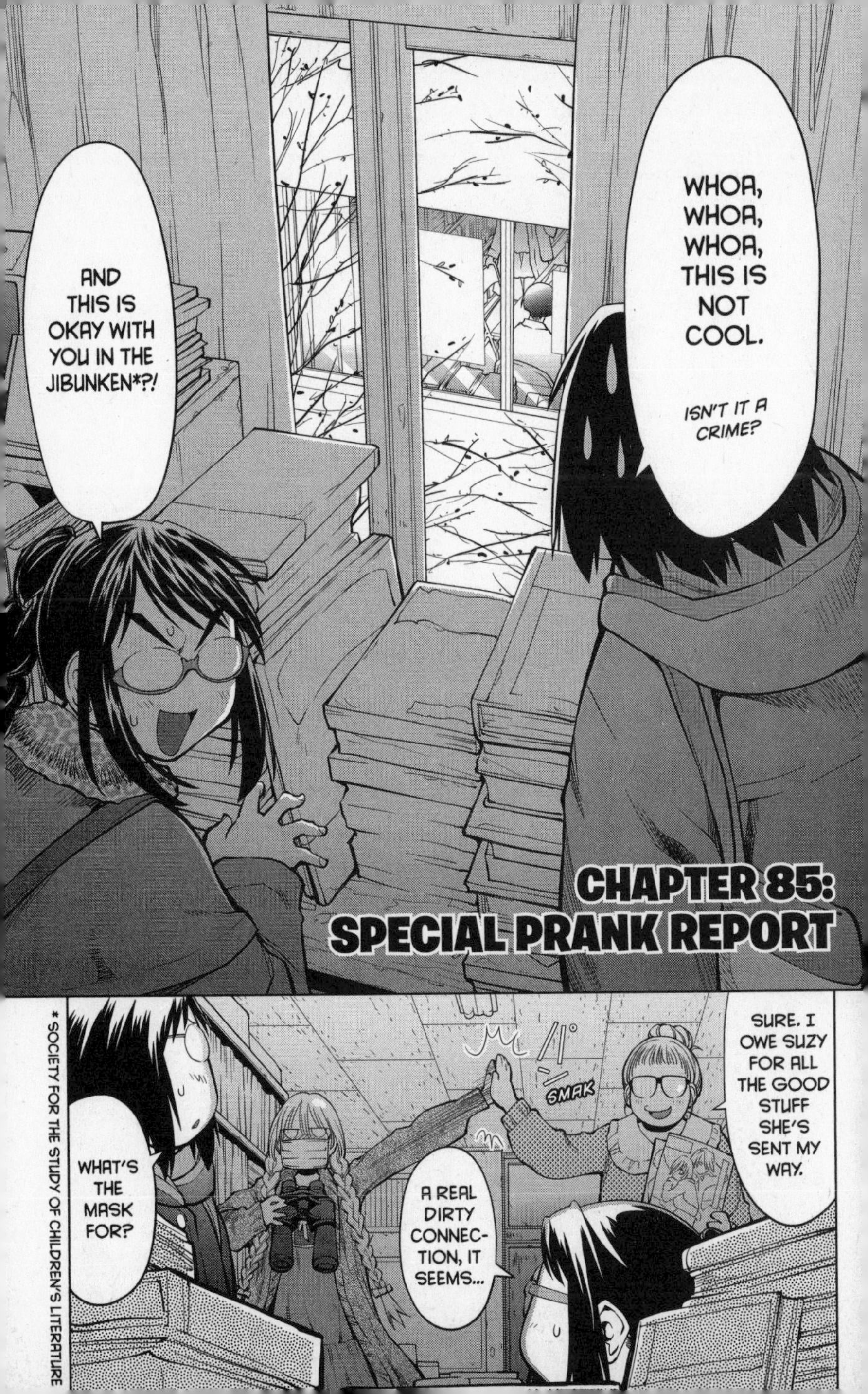
WHOA, WHOA, WHOA, THIS IS NOT COOL.
ISN'T IT A CRIME?
AND THIS IS OKAY WITH YOU IN THE JIBUNKEN*?!
CHAPTER 85: SPECIAL PRANK REPORT
SURE. I OWE SUZY FOR ALL THE GOOD STUFF SHE'S SENT MY WAY.
SMAK
A REAL DIRTY CONNECTION, IT SEEMS...
WHAT'S THE MASK FOR?

* SOCIETY FOR THE STUDY OF CHILDREN'S LITERATURE

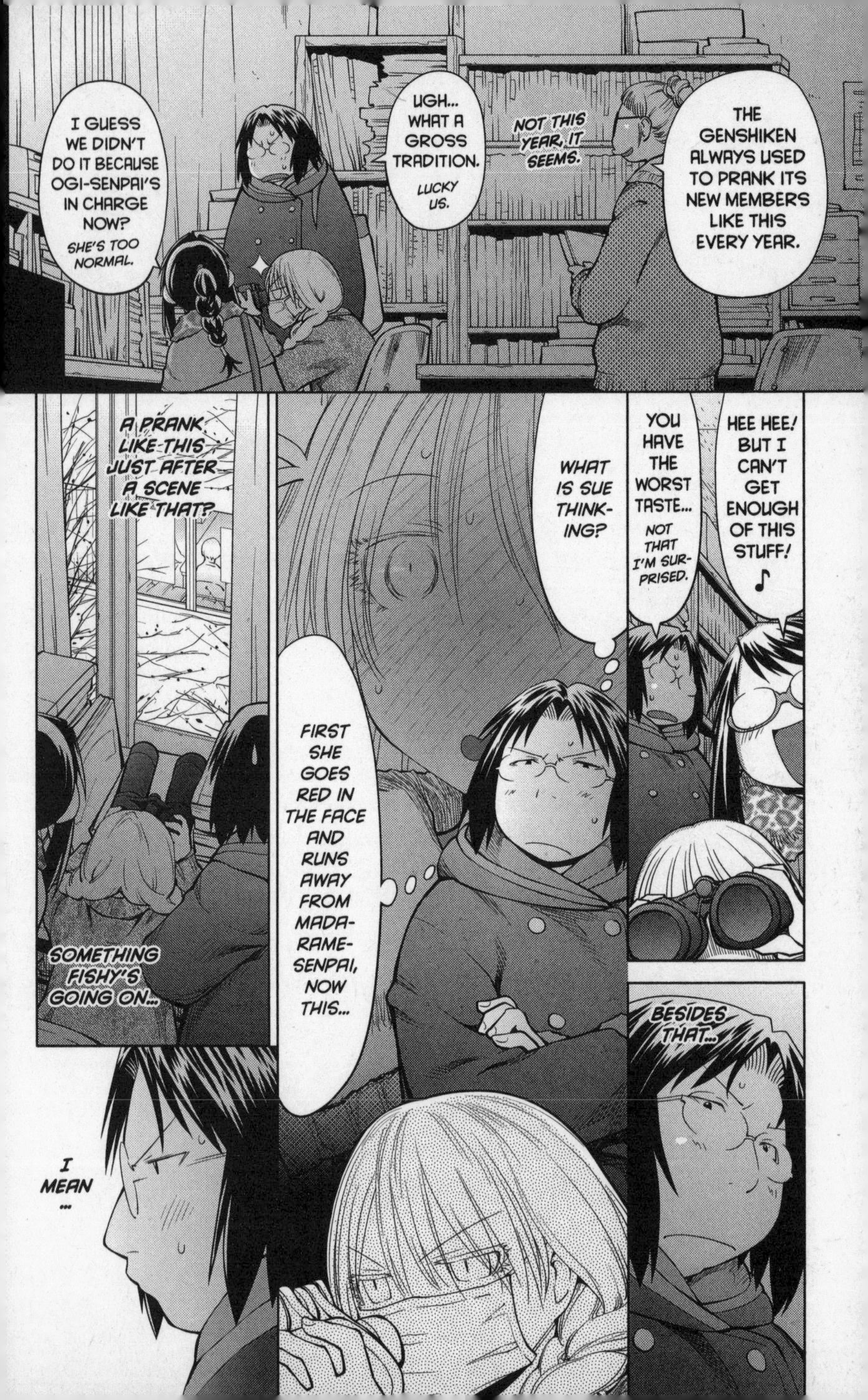
THE GENSHIKEN ALWAYS USED TO PRANK ITS NEW MEMBERS LIKE THIS EVERY YEAR.
NOT THIS YEAR, IT SEEMS.
UGH... WHAT A GROSS TRADITION.
LUCKY US.
I GUESS WE DIDN'T DO IT BECAUSE OGI-SENPAI'S IN CHARGE NOW?
SHE'S TOO NORMAL.
HEE HEE! BUT I CAN'T GET ENOUGH OF THIS STUFF! ♪
YOU HAVE THE WORST TASTE...
NOT THAT I'M SURPRISED.
BESIDES THAT...
WHAT IS SUE THINKING?
FIRST SHE GOES RED IN THE FACE AND RUNS AWAY FROM MADA-RAME-SENPAI, NOW THIS...
A PRANK LIKE THIS JUST AFTER A SCENE LIKE THAT?
SOMETHING FISHY'S GOING ON...
I MEAN...

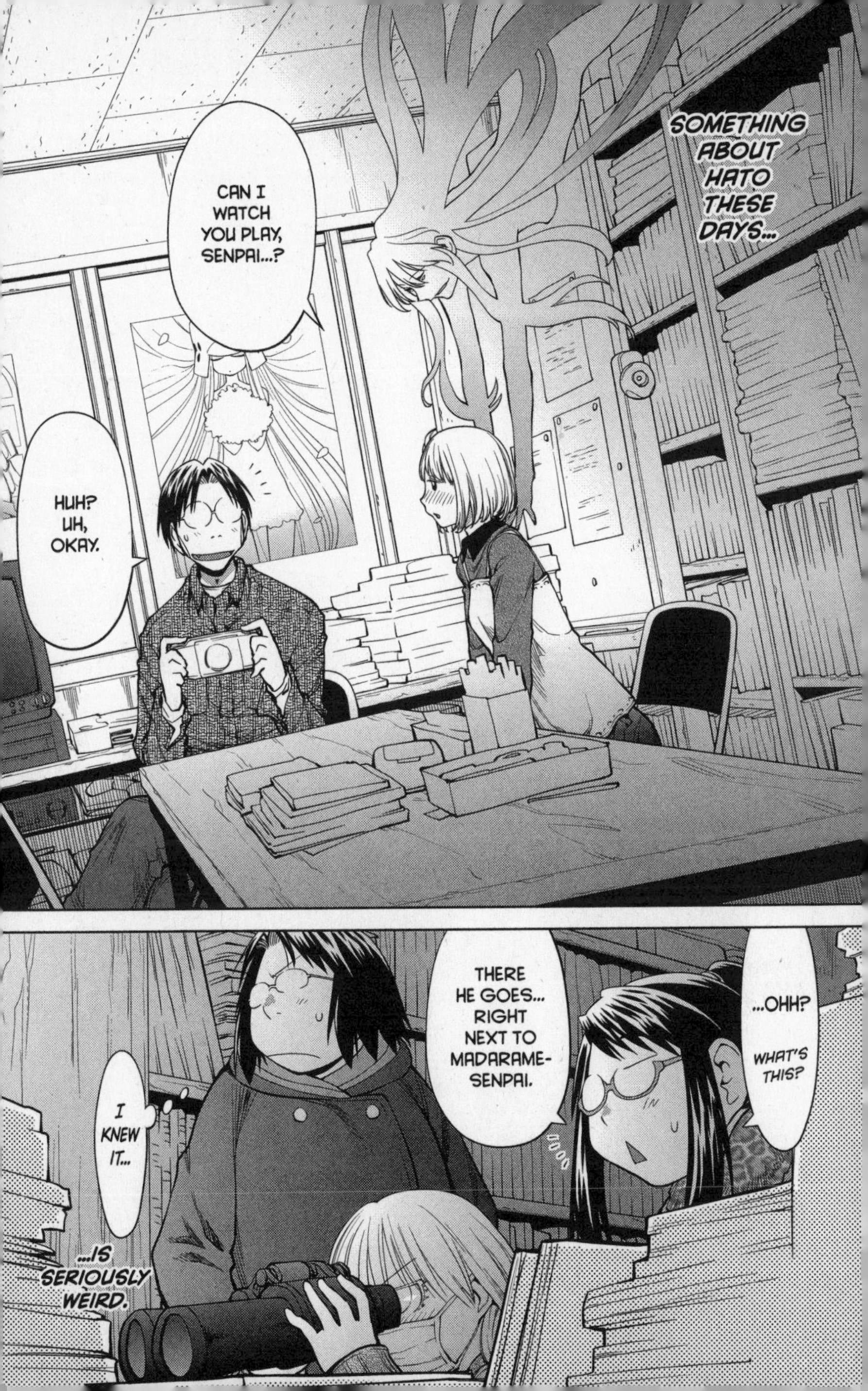
SOMETHING ABOUT HATO THESE DAYS...
CAN I WATCH YOU PLAY, SENPAI...?
HUH? UH, OKAY.
...OHH?
WHAT'S THIS?
THERE HE GOES... RIGHT NEXT TO MADARAME-SENPAI.
I KNEW IT...
...IS SERIOUSLY WEIRD.

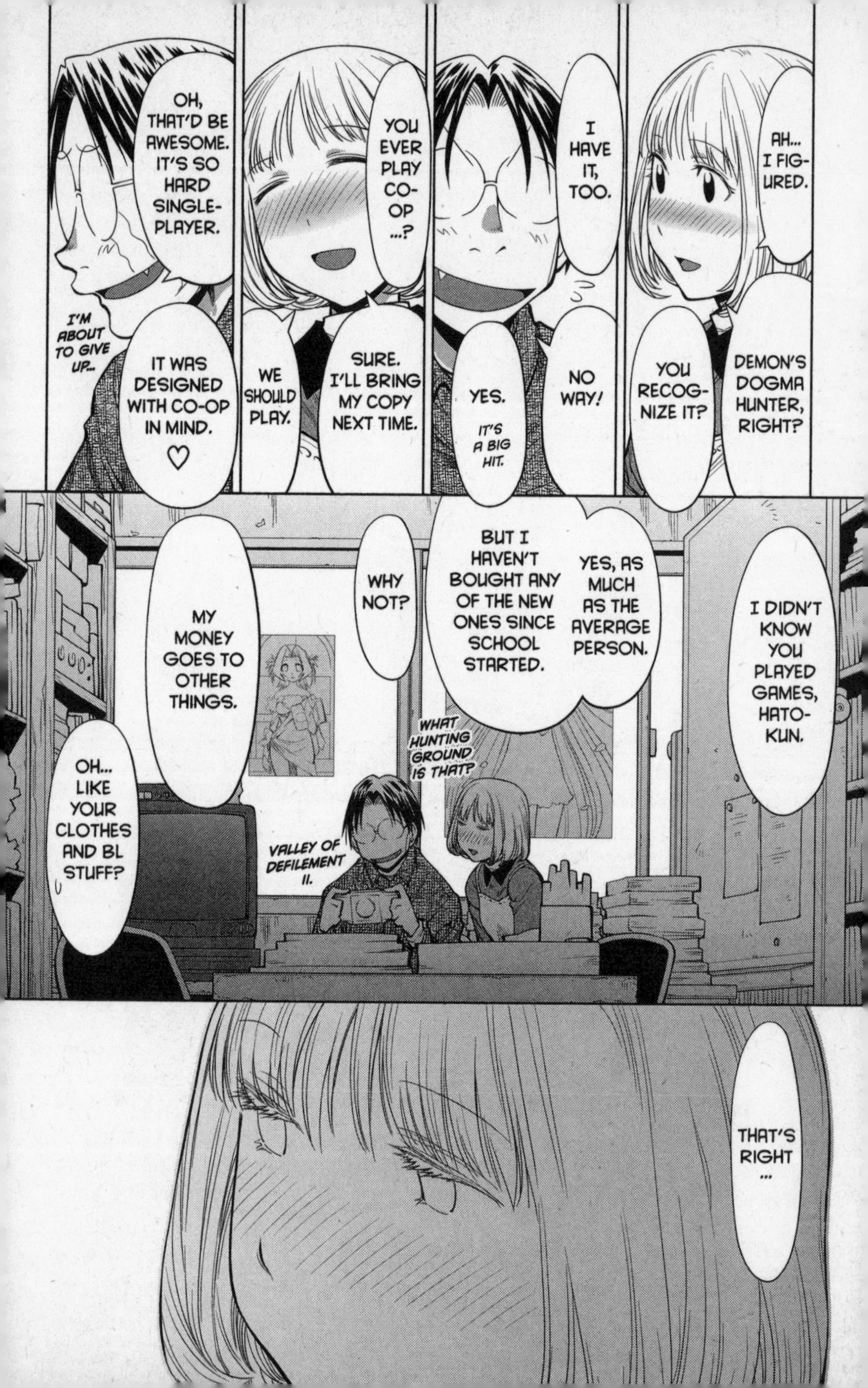
AH... I FIG-URED.
DEMON'S DOGMA HUNTER, RIGHT?
YOU RECOG-NIZE IT?
I HAVE IT, TOO.
NO WAY!
YES.
IT'S A BIG HIT.
YOU EVER PLAY CO-OP ...?
SURE. I'LL BRING MY COPY NEXT TIME.
WE SHOULD PLAY.
OH, THAT'D BE AWESOME. IT'S SO HARD SINGLE-PLAYER.
I'M ABOUT TO GIVE UP...
IT WAS DESIGNED WITH CO-OP IN MIND. ♡
I DIDN'T KNOW YOU PLAYED GAMES, HATO-KUN.
YES, AS MUCH AS THE AVERAGE PERSON.
BUT I HAVEN'T BOUGHT ANY OF THE NEW ONES SINCE SCHOOL STARTED.
WHY NOT?
MY MONEY GOES TO OTHER THINGS.
WHAT HUNTING GROUND IS THAT?
VALLEY OF DEFILEMENT II.
OH... LIKE YOUR CLOTHES AND BL STUFF?
THAT'S RIGHT ...

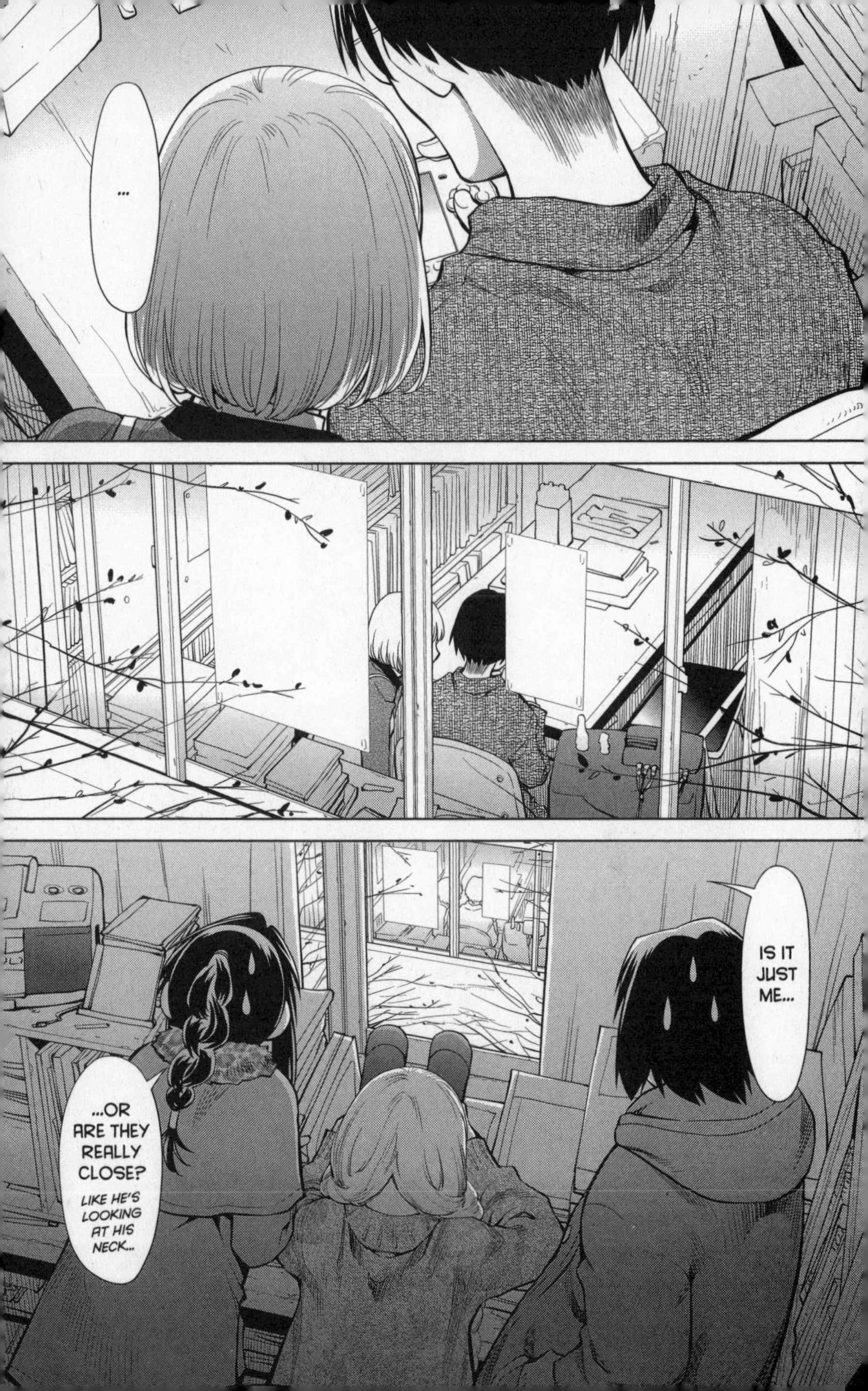
...
IS IT JUST ME...
...OR ARE THEY REALLY CLOSE?
LIKE HE'S LOOKING AT HIS NECK...

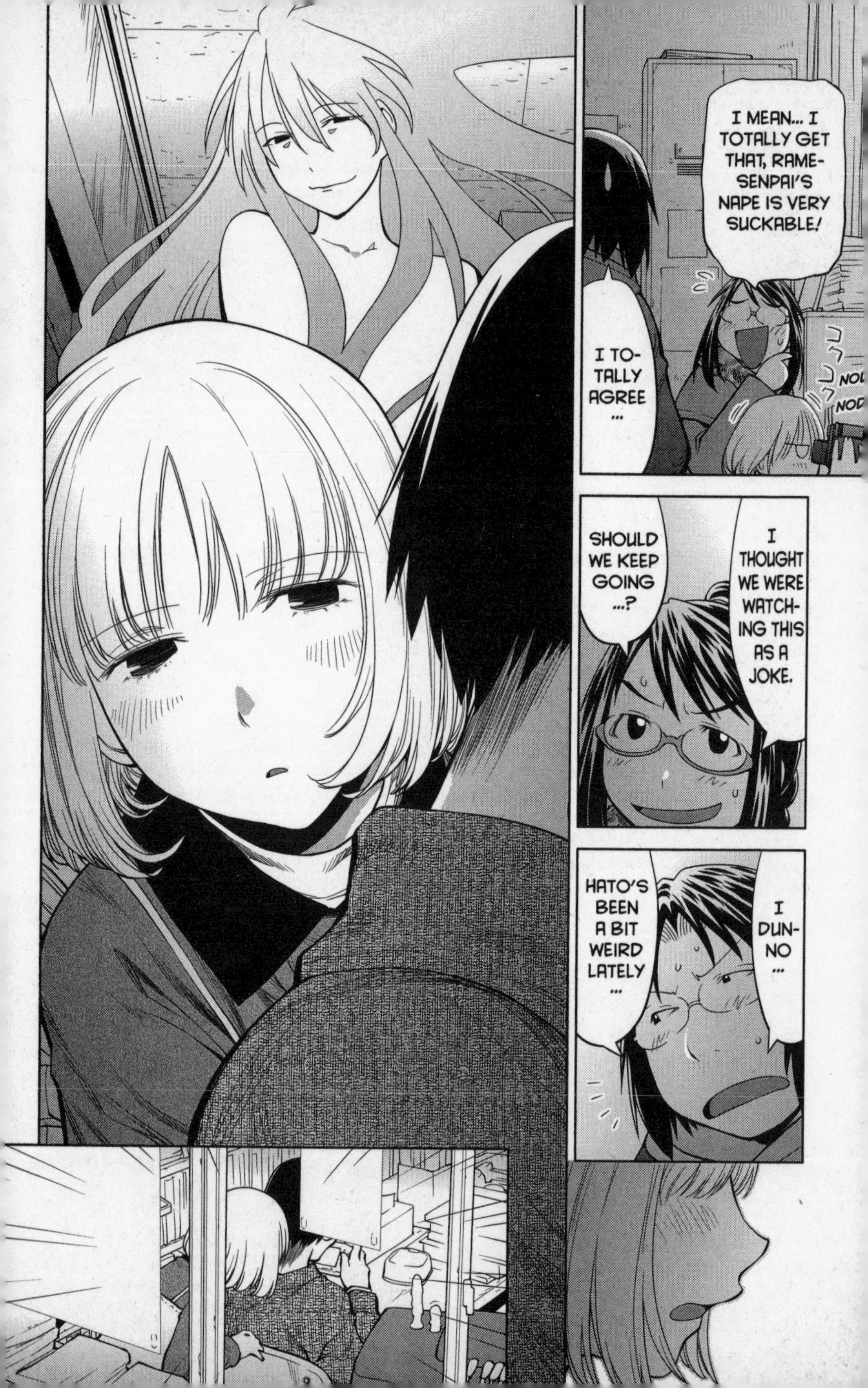
I MEAN... I TOTALLY GET THAT, RAME-SENPAI'S NAPE IS VERY SUCKABLE!
I TO-TALLY AGREE ...
NOD NOD
I THOUGHT WE WERE WATCHING THIS AS A JOKE.
SHOULD WE KEEP GOING ...?
I DUN-NO ...
HATO'S BEEN A BIT WEIRD LATELY ...

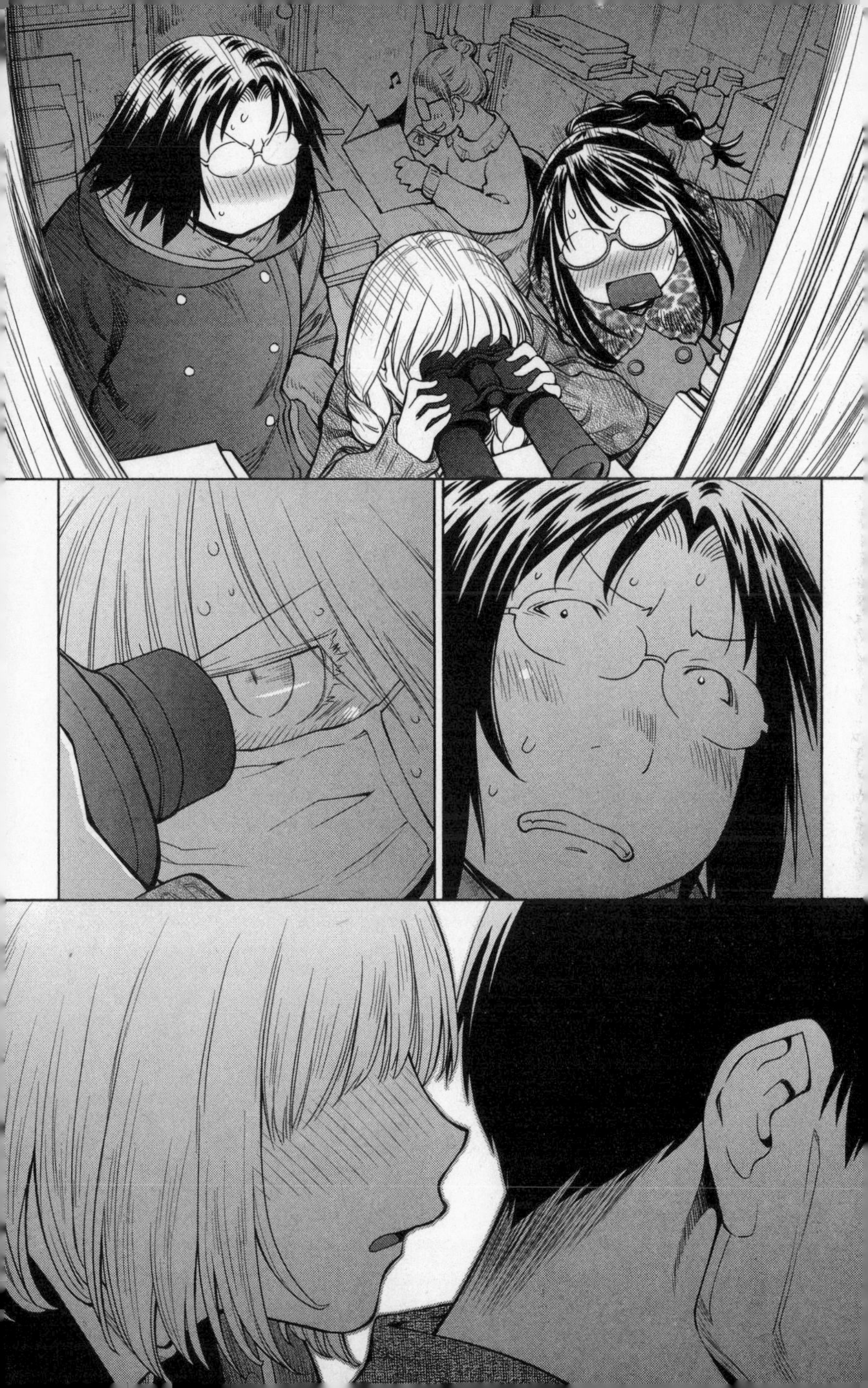

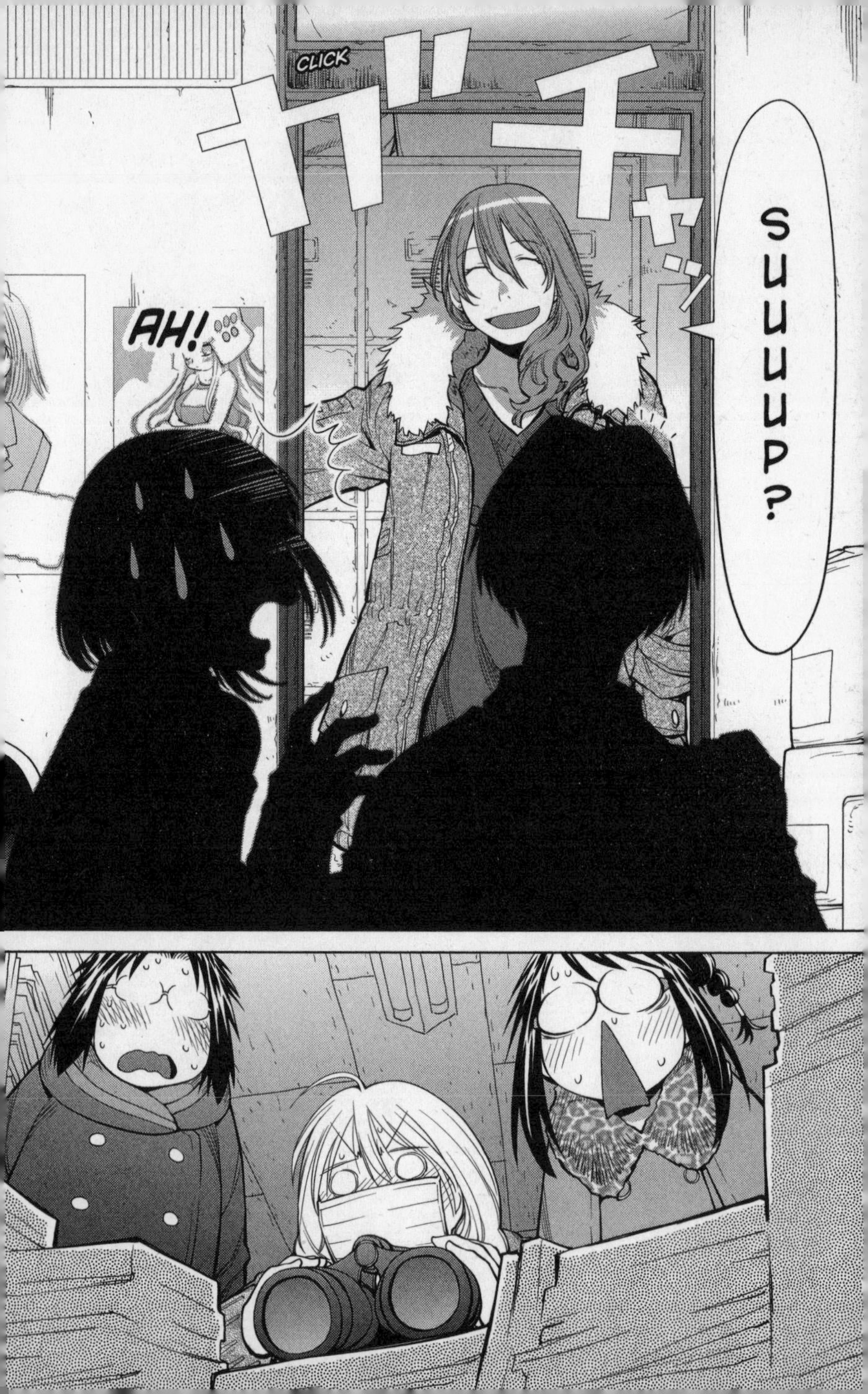
SUUUUUP?
CLICK
AH!

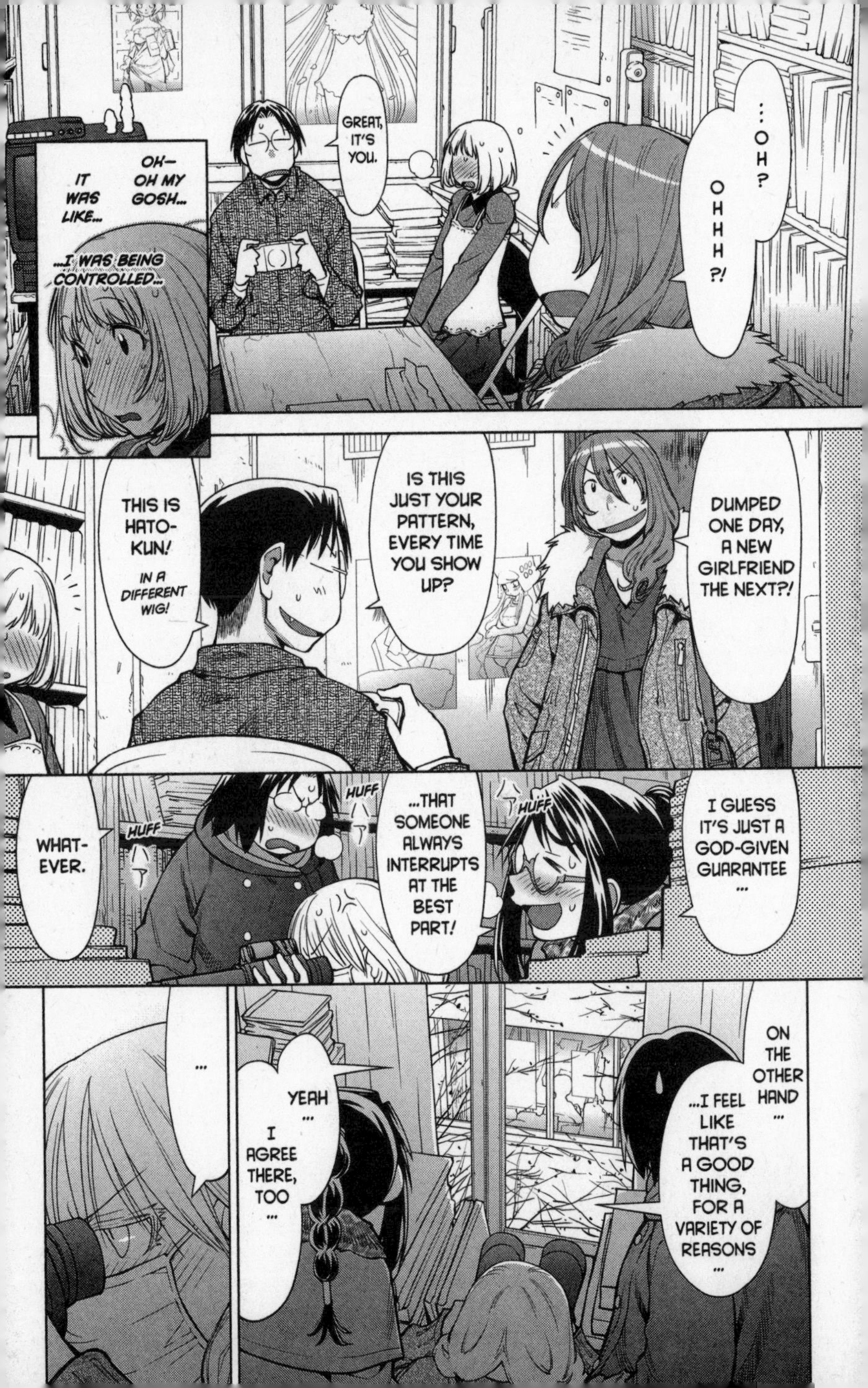
...OH? OHHH?!
GREAT, IT'S YOU.
OH— OH MY GOSH...
IT WAS LIKE...
...I WAS BEING CONTROLLED...
DUMPED ONE DAY, A NEW GIRLFRIEND THE NEXT?!
IS THIS JUST YOUR PATTERN, EVERY TIME YOU SHOW UP?
THIS IS HATO-KUN!
IN A DIFFERENT WIG!
I GUESS IT'S JUST A GOD-GIVEN GUARANTEE ...
HUFF
...THAT SOMEONE ALWAYS INTERRUPTS AT THE BEST PART!
HUFF
HUFF
WHAT-EVER.
ON THE OTHER HAND ...
...I FEEL LIKE THAT'S A GOOD THING, FOR A VARIETY OF REASONS ...
YEAH ... I AGREE THERE, TOO ...
...

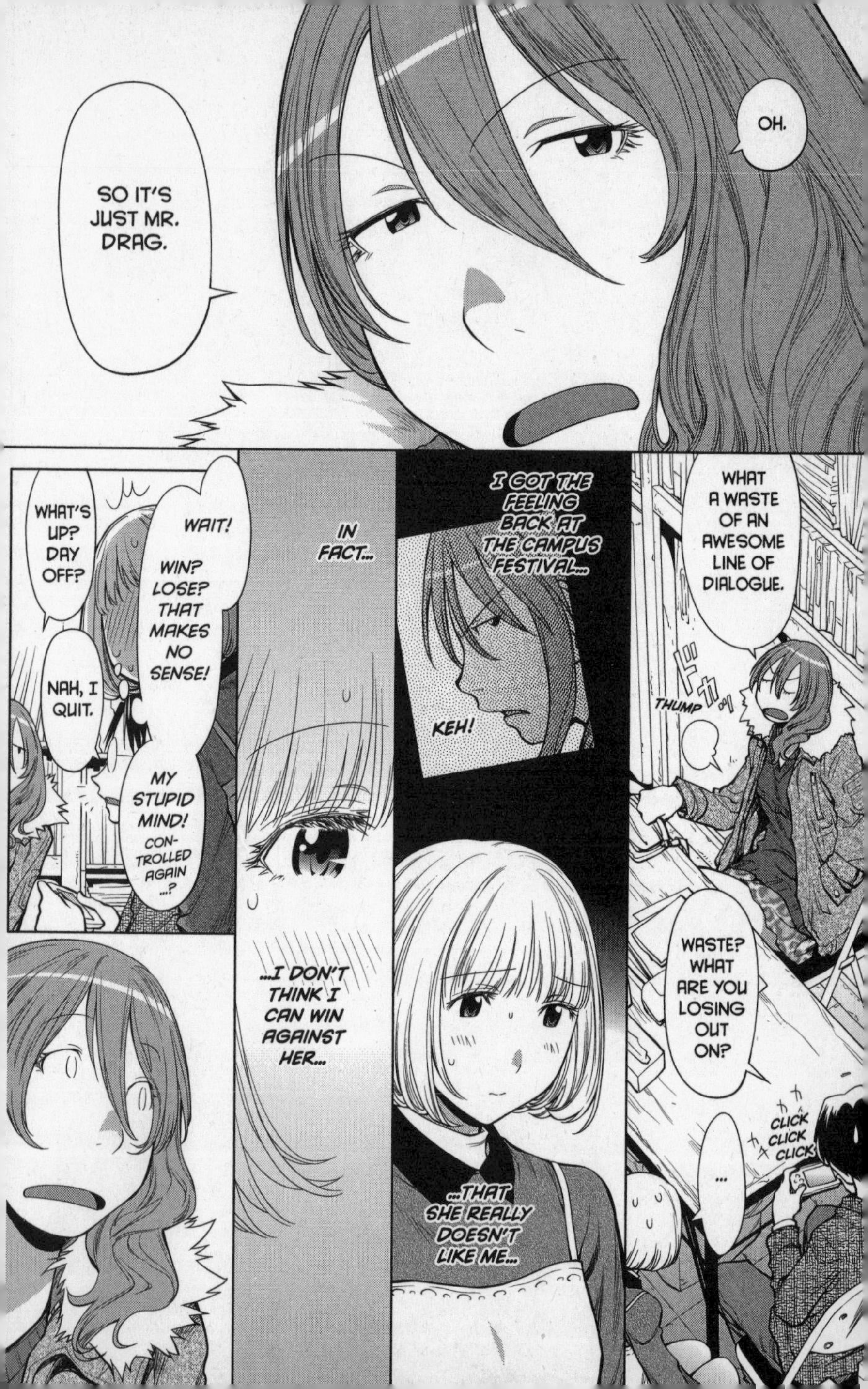
OH.
SO IT'S JUST MR. DRAG.
WHAT A WASTE OF AN AWESOME LINE OF DIALOGUE.
THUMP
WASTE? WHAT ARE YOU LOSING OUT ON?
CLICK CLICK CLICK
...
I GOT THE FEELING BACK AT THE CAMPUS FESTIVAL...
KEH!
...THAT SHE REALLY DOESN'T LIKE ME...
IN FACT...
...I DON'T THINK I CAN WIN AGAINST HER...
WAIT!
WIN? LOSE? THAT MAKES NO SENSE!
WHAT'S UP? DAY OFF?
NAH, I QUIT.
MY STUPID MIND! CON-TROLLED AGAIN ...?

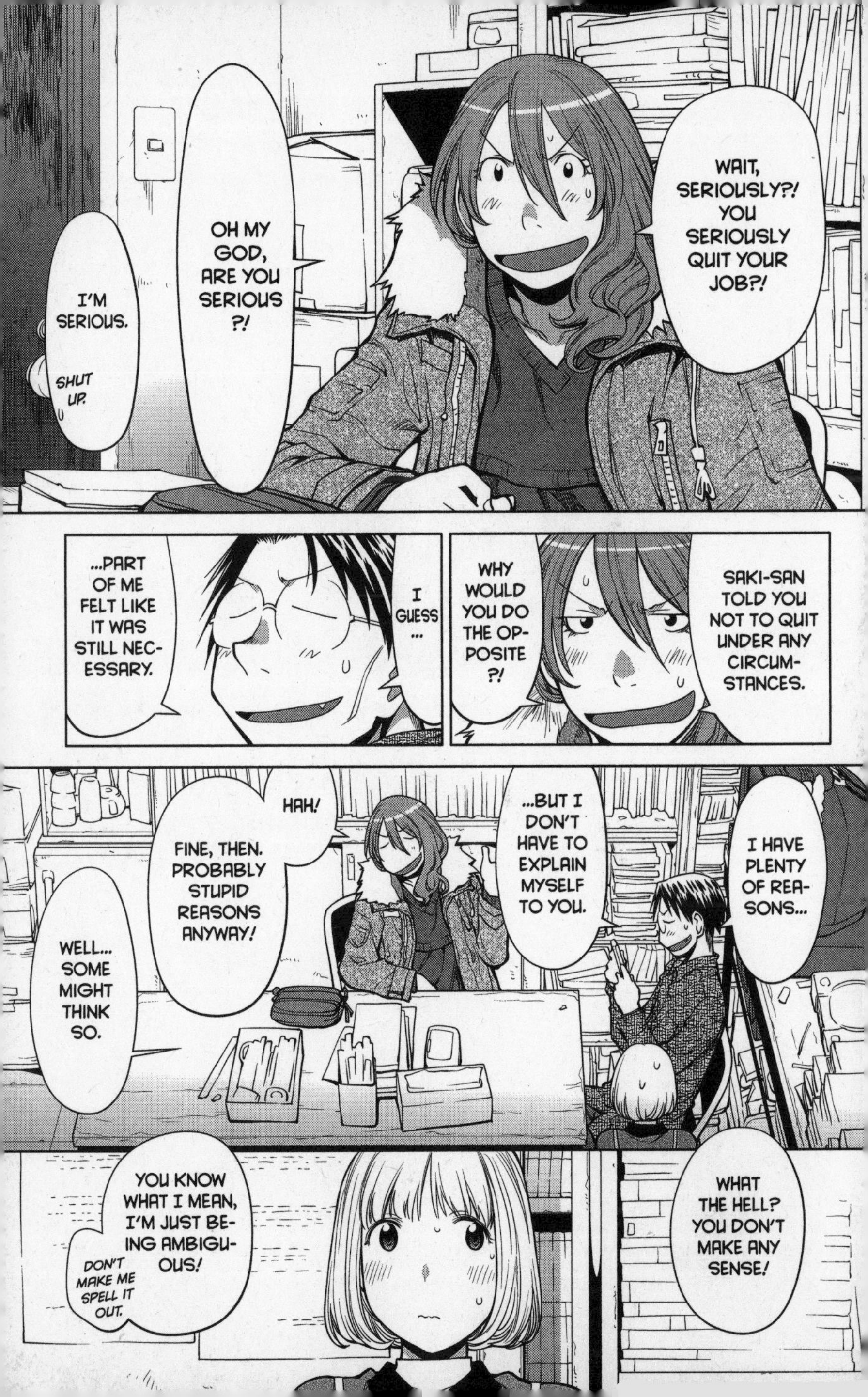
WAIT, SERIOUSLY?! YOU SERIOUSLY QUIT YOUR JOB?!
OH MY GOD, ARE YOU SERIOUS?!
I'M SERIOUS.
SHUT UP.
SAKI-SAN TOLD YOU NOT TO QUIT UNDER ANY CIRCUMSTANCES.
WHY WOULD YOU DO THE OPPOSITE?!
I GUESS...
...PART OF ME FELT LIKE IT WAS STILL NECESSARY.
I HAVE PLENTY OF REASONS...
...BUT I DON'T HAVE TO EXPLAIN MYSELF TO YOU.
HAH!
FINE, THEN. PROBABLY STUPID REASONS ANYWAY!
WELL... SOME MIGHT THINK SO.
WHAT THE HELL? YOU DON'T MAKE ANY SENSE!
YOU KNOW WHAT I MEAN, I'M JUST BEING AMBIGUOUS!
DON'T MAKE ME SPELL IT OUT.

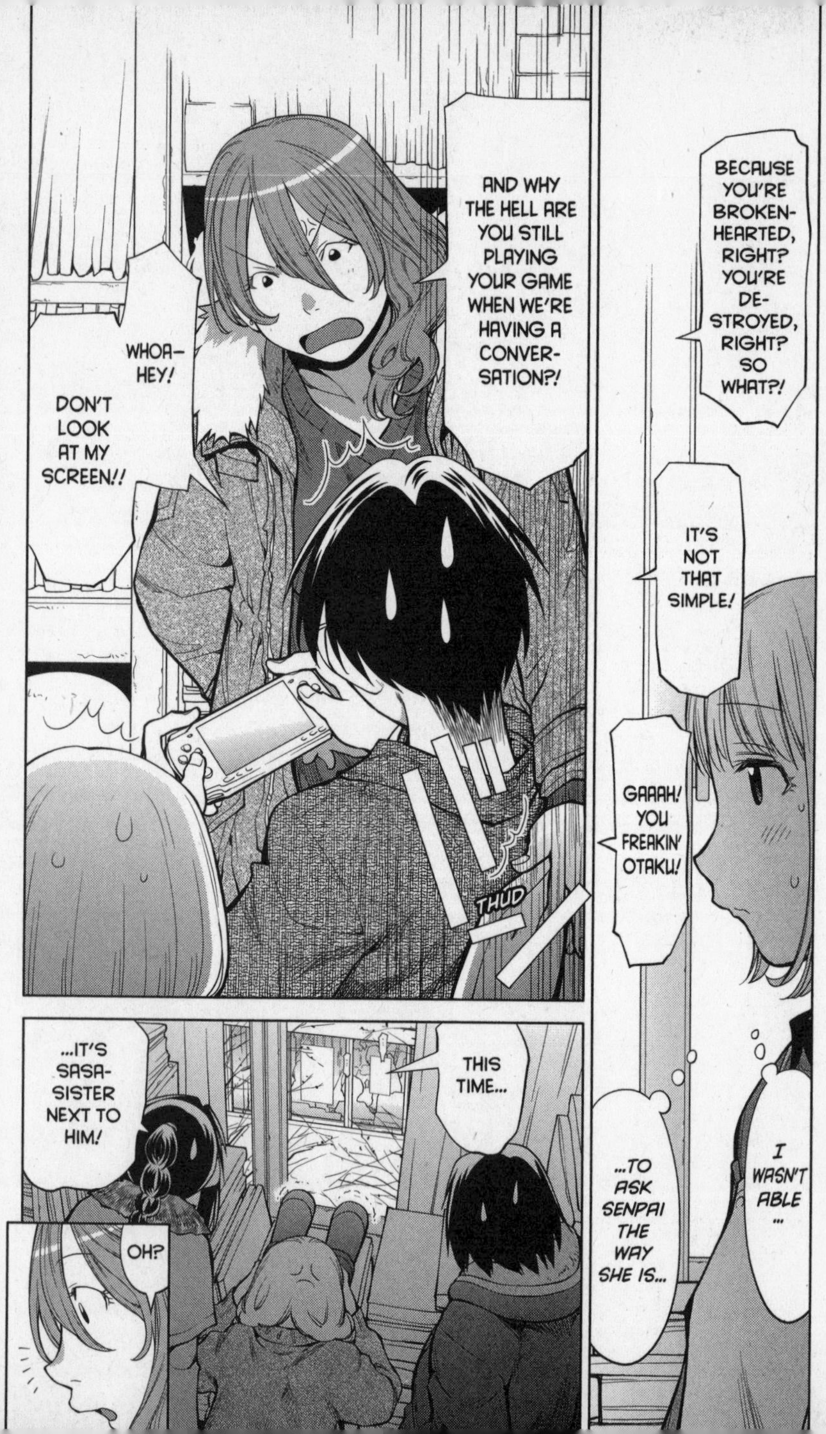
BECAUSE YOU'RE BROKEN-HEARTED, RIGHT? YOU'RE DE-STROYED, RIGHT? SO WHAT?!
IT'S NOT THAT SIMPLE!
GAAAH! YOU FREAKIN' OTAKU!
I WASN'T ABLE ...
...TO ASK SENPAI THE WAY SHE IS...
AND WHY THE HELL ARE YOU STILL PLAYING YOUR GAME WHEN WE'RE HAVING A CONVER-SATION?!
WHOA—HEY!
DON'T LOOK AT MY SCREEN!!
THUD
THIS TIME...
...IT'S SASA-SISTER NEXT TO HIM!
OH?

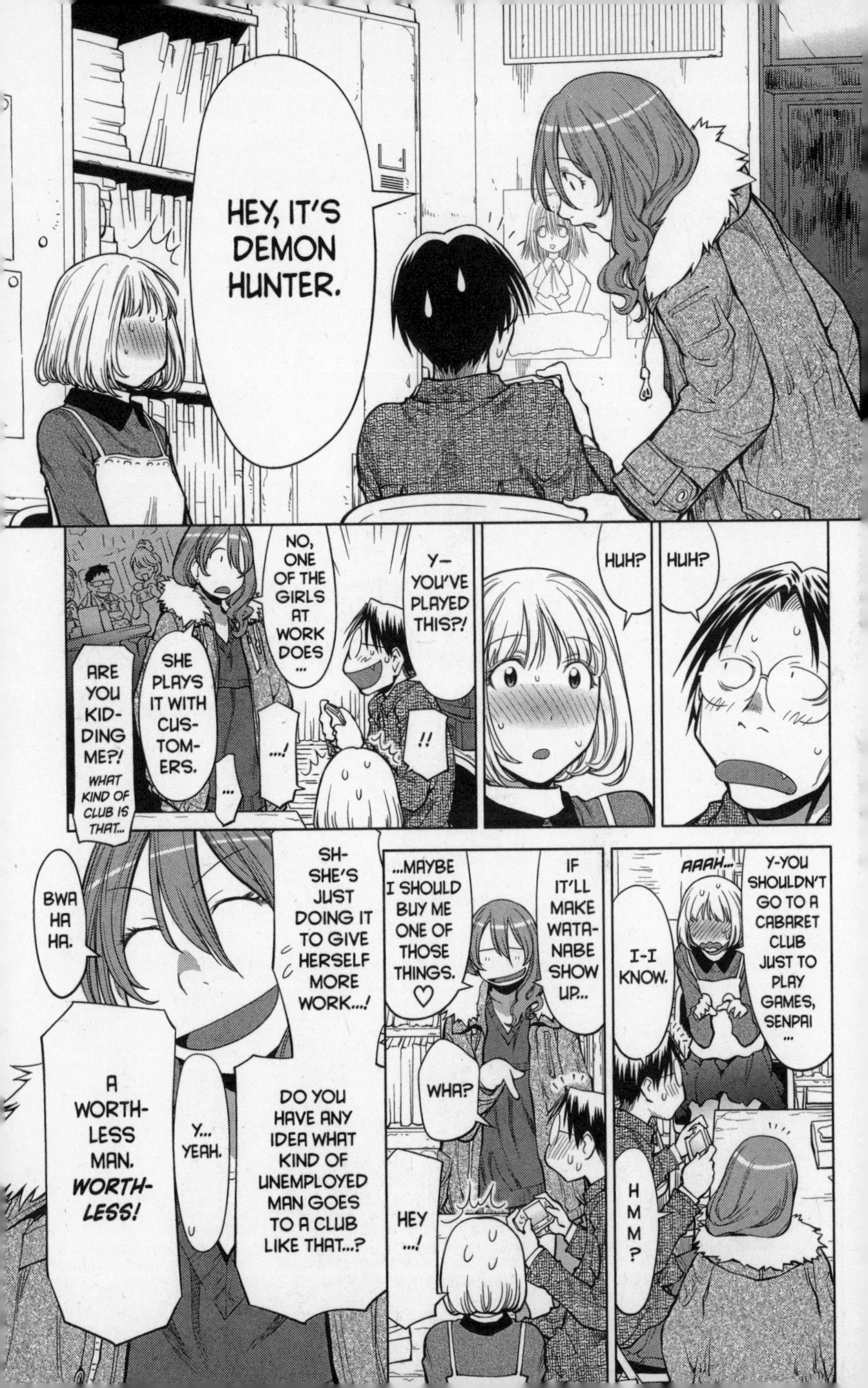
HEY, IT'S DEMON HUNTER.
HUH?
HUH?
Y— YOU'VE PLAYED THIS?!
!!
NO, ONE OF THE GIRLS AT WORK DOES...
...!
SHE PLAYS IT WITH CUSTOMERS.
...
ARE YOU KIDDING ME?!
WHAT KIND OF CLUB IS THAT...
AAAH...
Y-YOU SHOULDN'T GO TO A CABARET CLUB JUST TO PLAY GAMES, SENPAI...
I-I KNOW.
HMM?
IF IT'LL MAKE WATANABE SHOW UP...
...MAYBE I SHOULD BUY ME ONE OF THOSE THINGS. ♡
WHA?
HEY...!
SH-SHE'S JUST DOING IT TO GIVE HERSELF MORE WORK...!
BWA HA HA.
DO YOU HAVE ANY IDEA WHAT KIND OF UNEMPLOYED MAN GOES TO A CLUB LIKE THAT...?
Y... YEAH.
A WORTHLESS MAN. WORTHLESS!

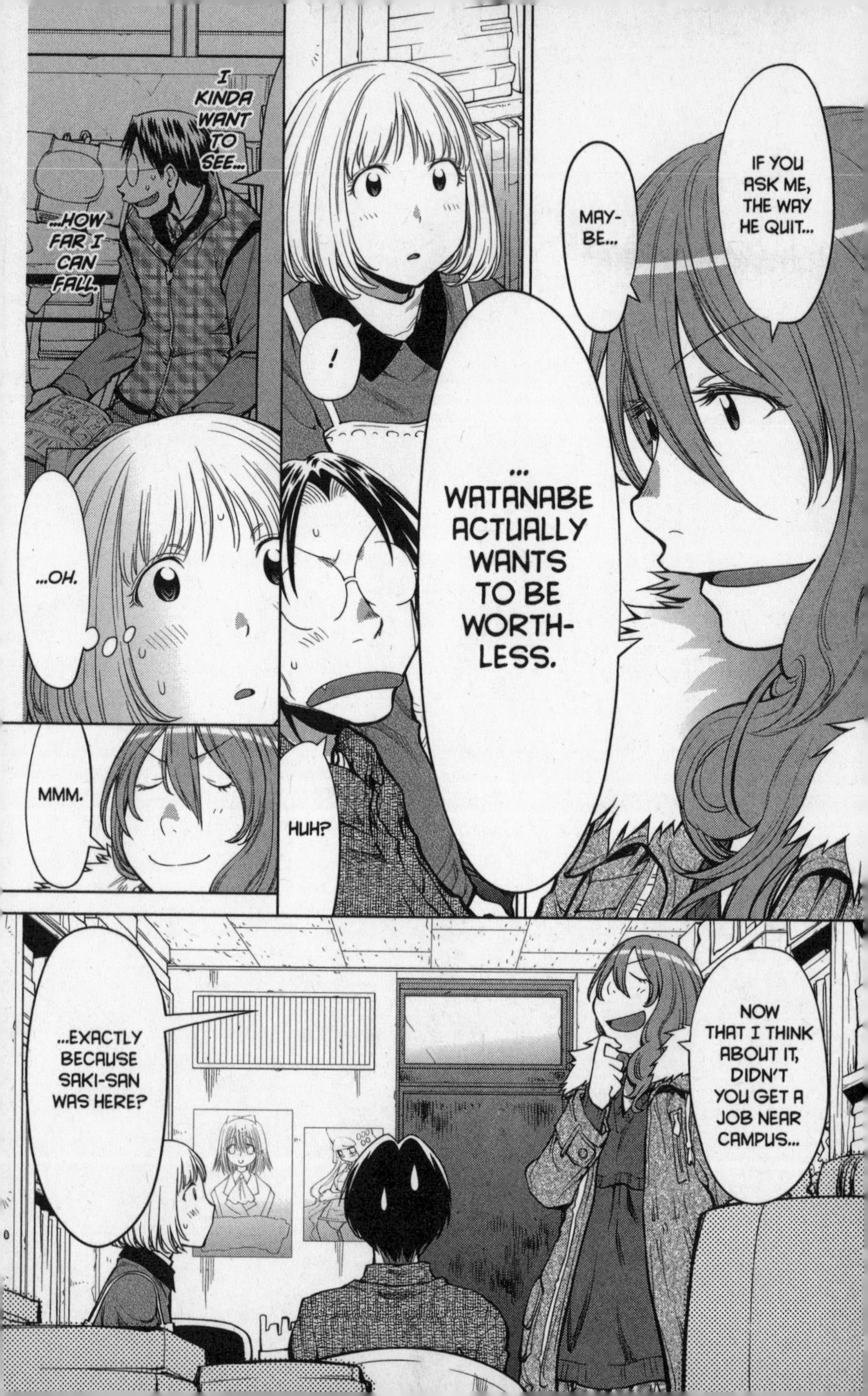
IF YOU ASK ME, THE WAY HE QUIT...
MAY-BE...
...WATANABE ACTUALLY WANTS TO BE WORTH-LESS.
!
HUH?
I KINDA WANT TO SEE...
...HOW FAR I CAN FALL.
...OH.
MMM.
NOW THAT I THINK ABOUT IT, DIDN'T YOU GET A JOB NEAR CAMPUS...
...EXACTLY BECAUSE SAKI-SAN WAS HERE?

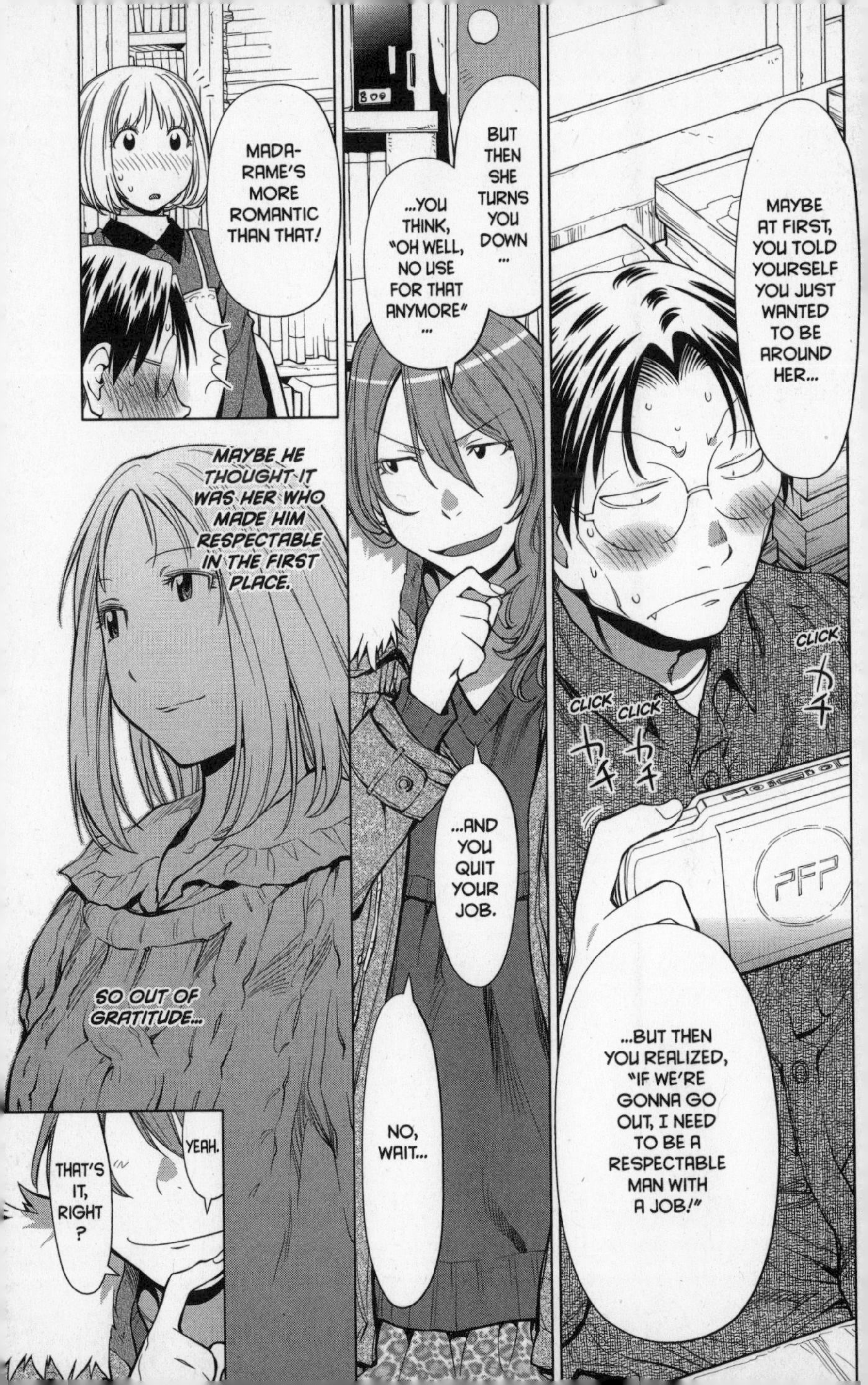
MAYBE AT FIRST, YOU TOLD YOURSELF YOU JUST WANTED TO BE AROUND HER...
CLICK
CLICK
CLICK
...BUT THEN YOU REALIZED, "IF WE'RE GONNA GO OUT, I NEED TO BE A RESPECTABLE MAN WITH A JOB!"
BUT THEN SHE TURNS YOU DOWN...
...YOU THINK, "OH WELL, NO USE FOR THAT ANYMORE"...
...AND YOU QUIT YOUR JOB.
NO, WAIT...
MADA-RAME'S MORE ROMANTIC THAN THAT!
MAYBE HE THOUGHT IT WAS HER WHO MADE HIM RESPECTABLE IN THE FIRST PLACE.
SO OUT OF GRATITUDE...
YEAH.
THAT'S IT, RIGHT?

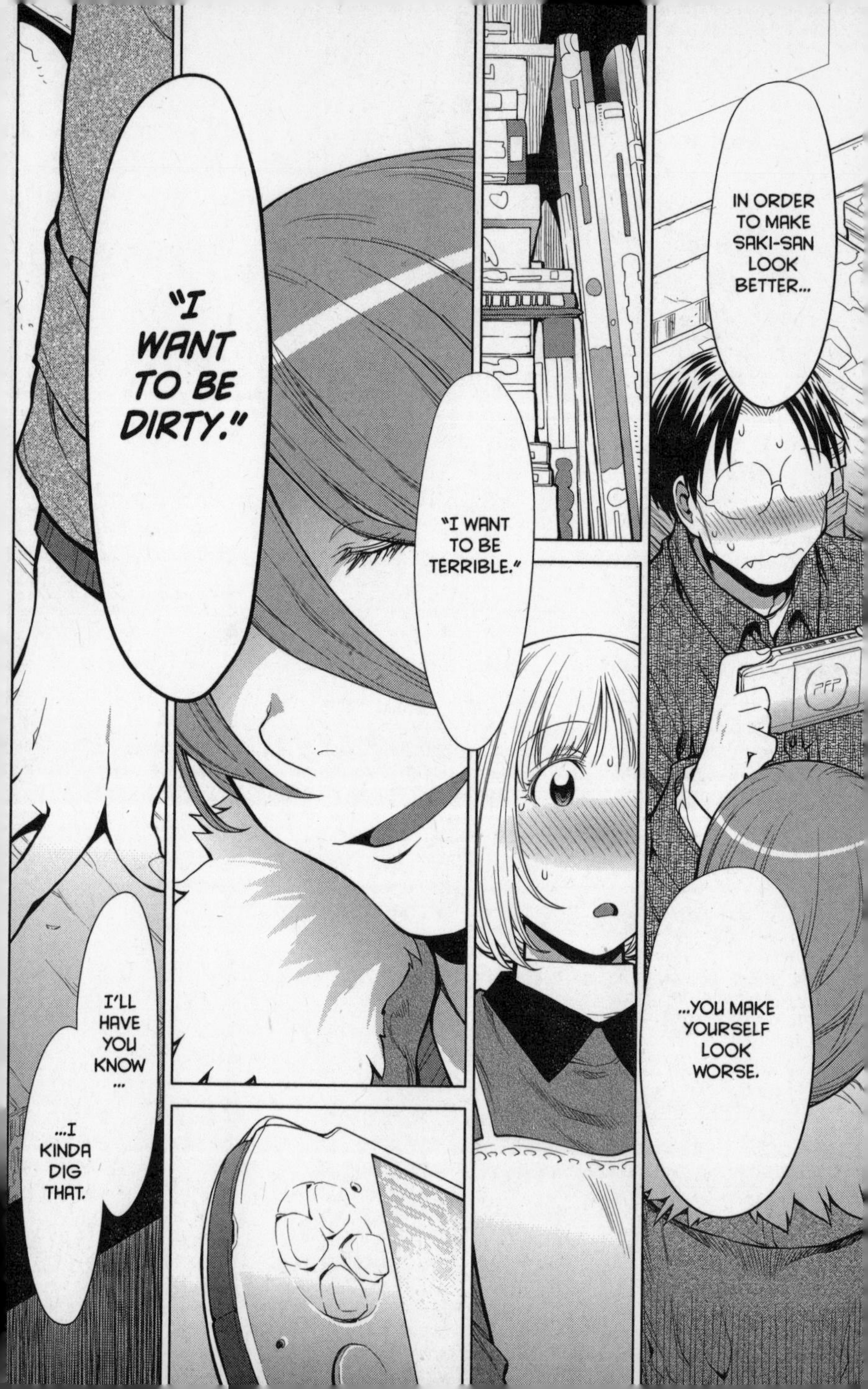
IN ORDER TO MAKE SAKI-SAN LOOK BETTER...
...YOU MAKE YOURSELF LOOK WORSE.
"I WANT TO BE TERRIBLE."
"I WANT TO BE DIRTY."
I'LL HAVE YOU KNOW ...
...I KINDA DIG THAT.

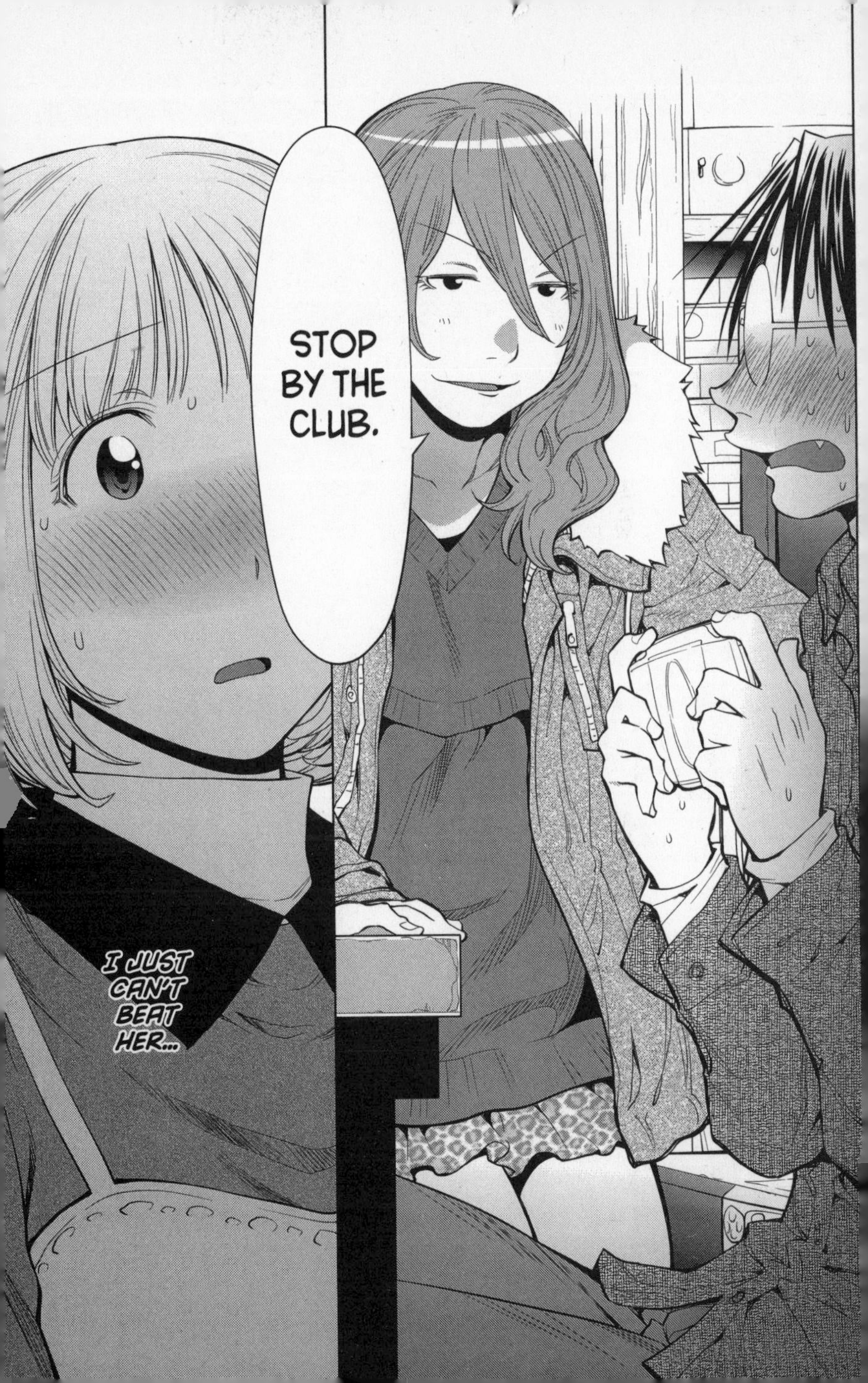
STOP BY THE CLUB.
I JUST CAN'T BEAT HER...

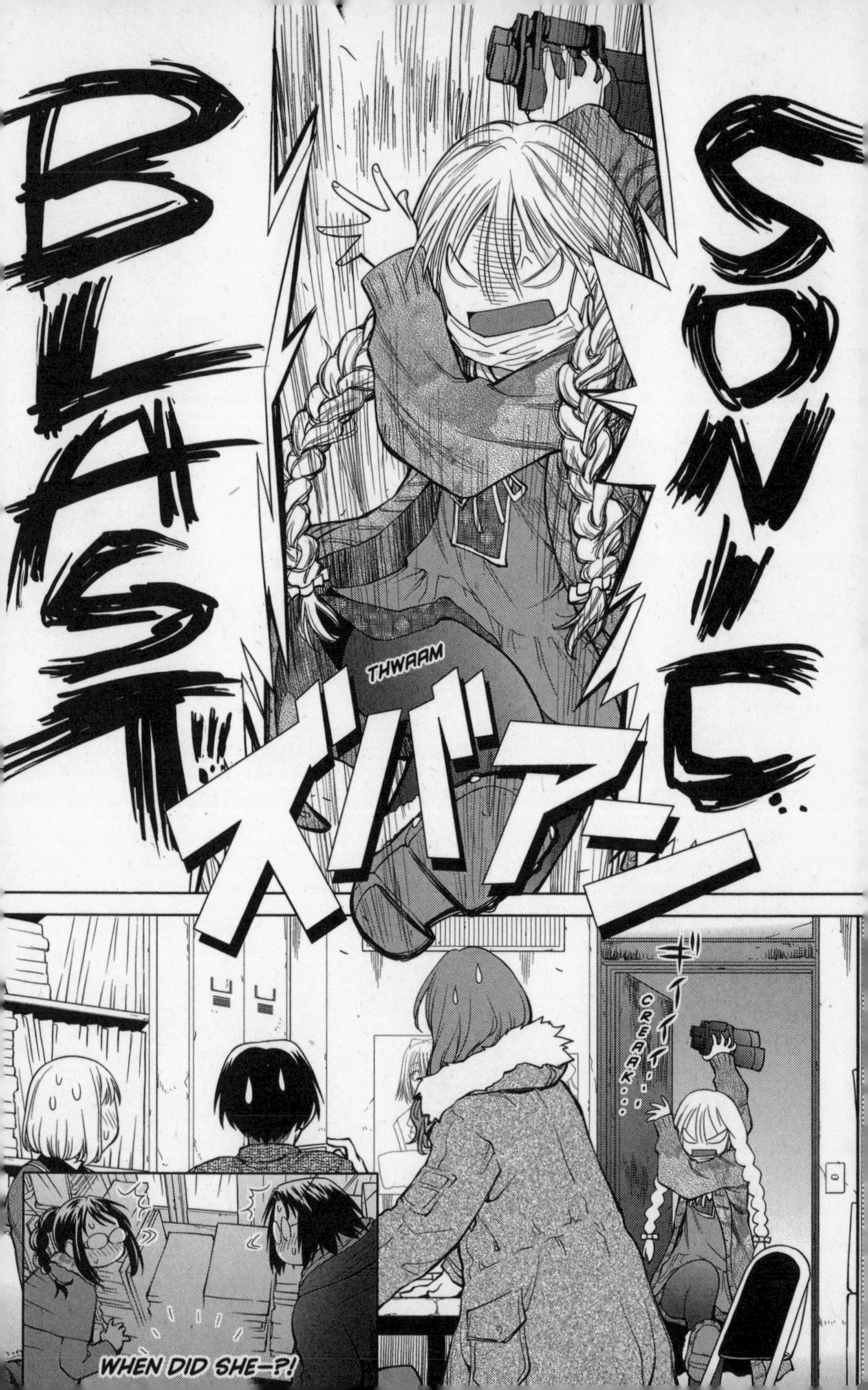
SONIC
BLAST!!
THWAAM
CREAAAK...
WHEN DID SHE—?!

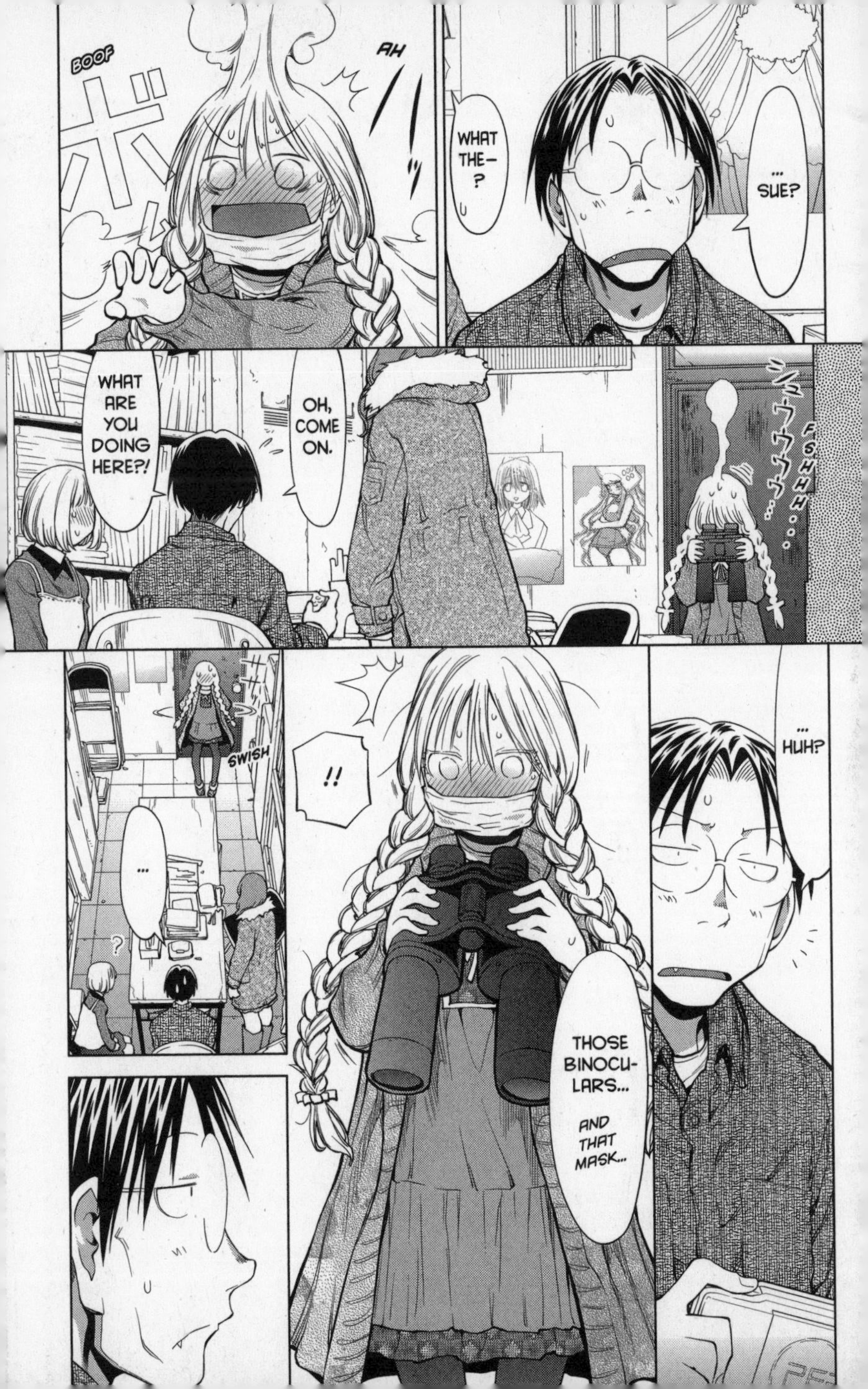
... SUE?
WHAT THE— ?
AH
BOOF
FSHHH...
OH, COME ON.
WHAT ARE YOU DOING HERE?!
... HUH?
THOSE BINOCU- LARS...
AND THAT MASK...
!!
SWISH
...
?

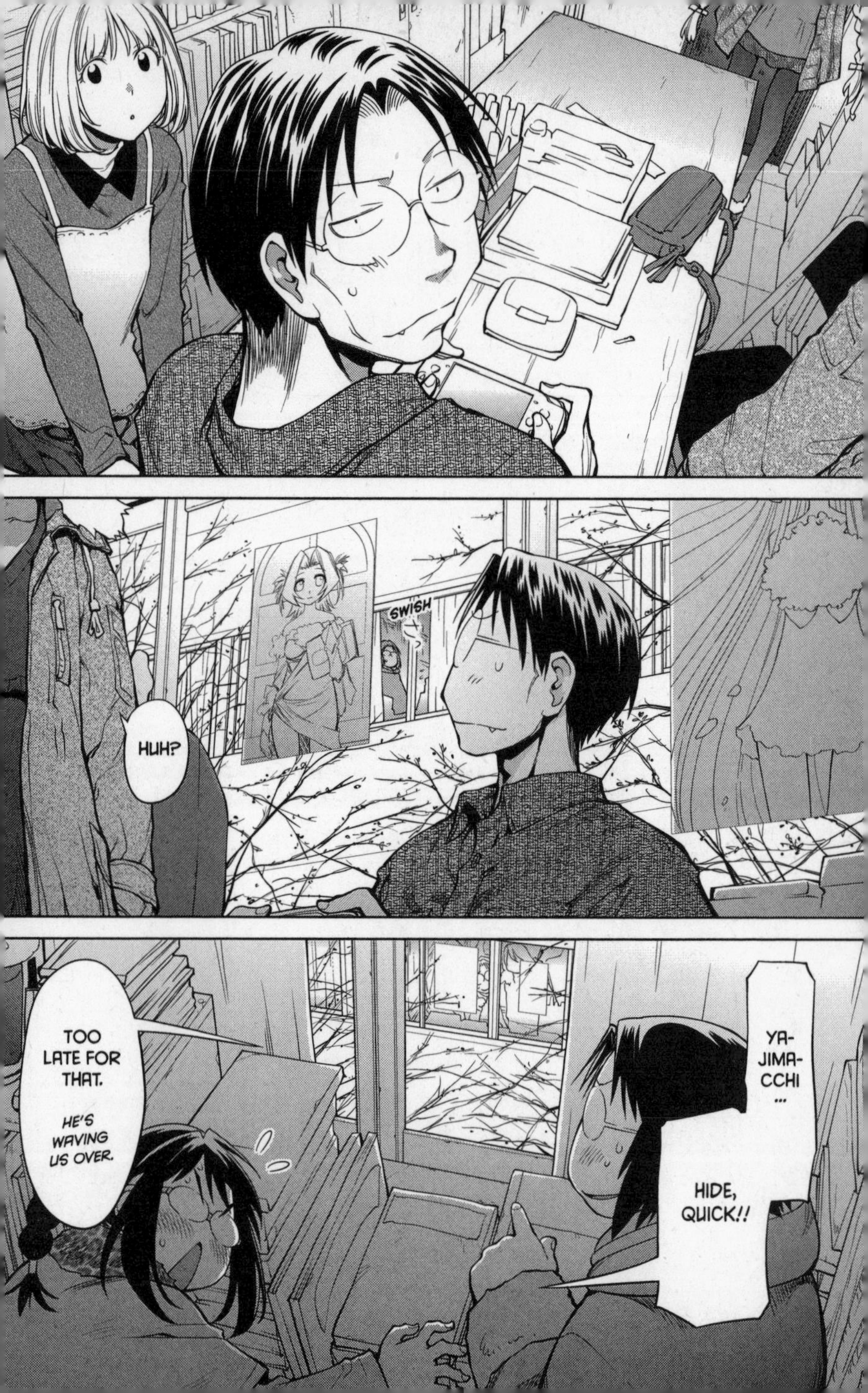
SWISH
HUH?
YA-JIMA-CCHI...
HIDE, QUICK!!
TOO LATE FOR THAT.
HE'S WAVING US OVER.

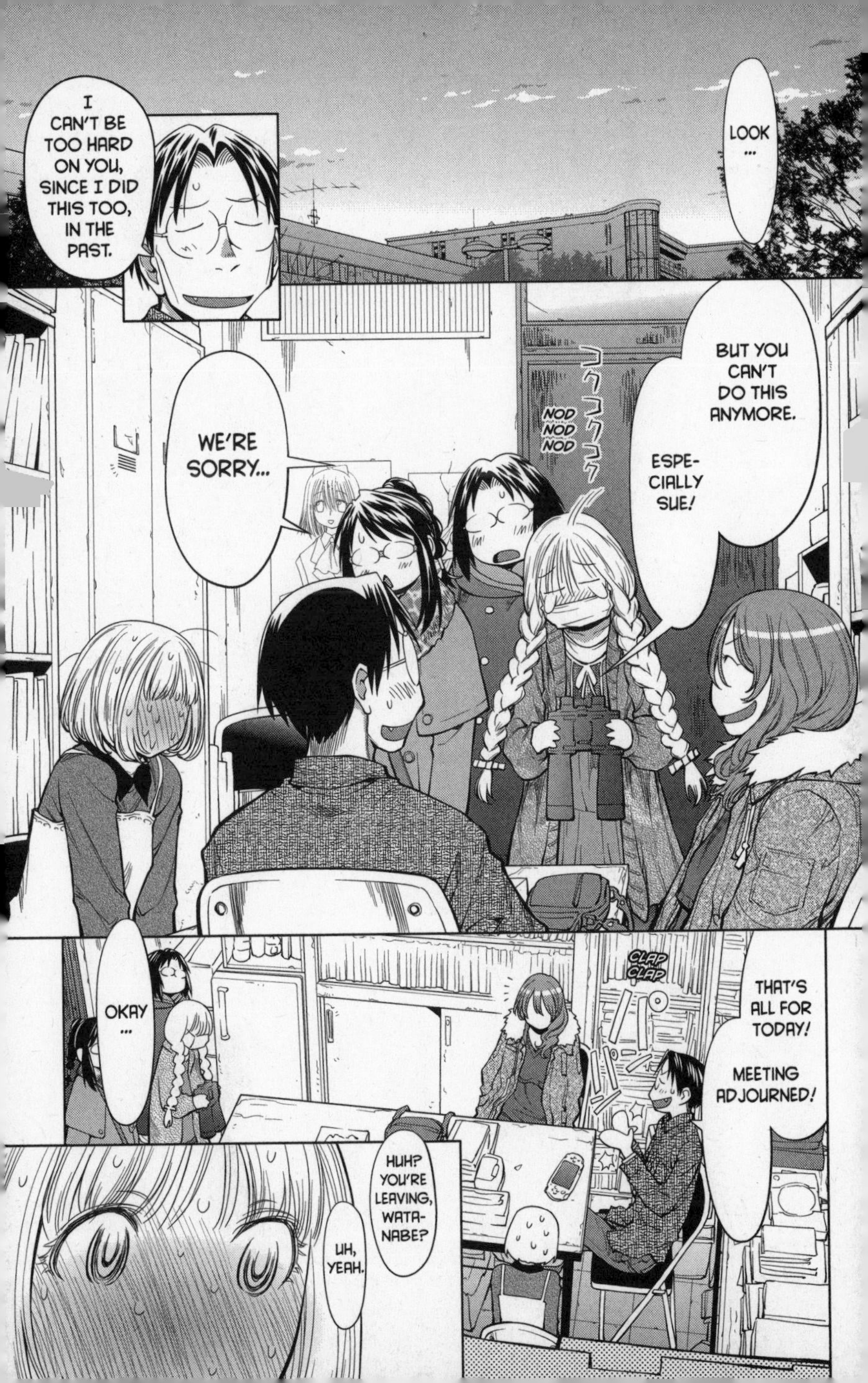

LOOK...
I CAN'T BE TOO HARD ON YOU, SINCE I DID THIS TOO, IN THE PAST.
BUT YOU CAN'T DO THIS ANYMORE.
ESPE-CIALLY SUE!
コクコクコク
NOD NOD NOD
WE'RE SORRY...
CLAP CLAP
THAT'S ALL FOR TODAY!
MEETING ADJOURNED!
HUH? YOU'RE LEAVING, WATA-NABE?
OKAY...
UH, YEAH.

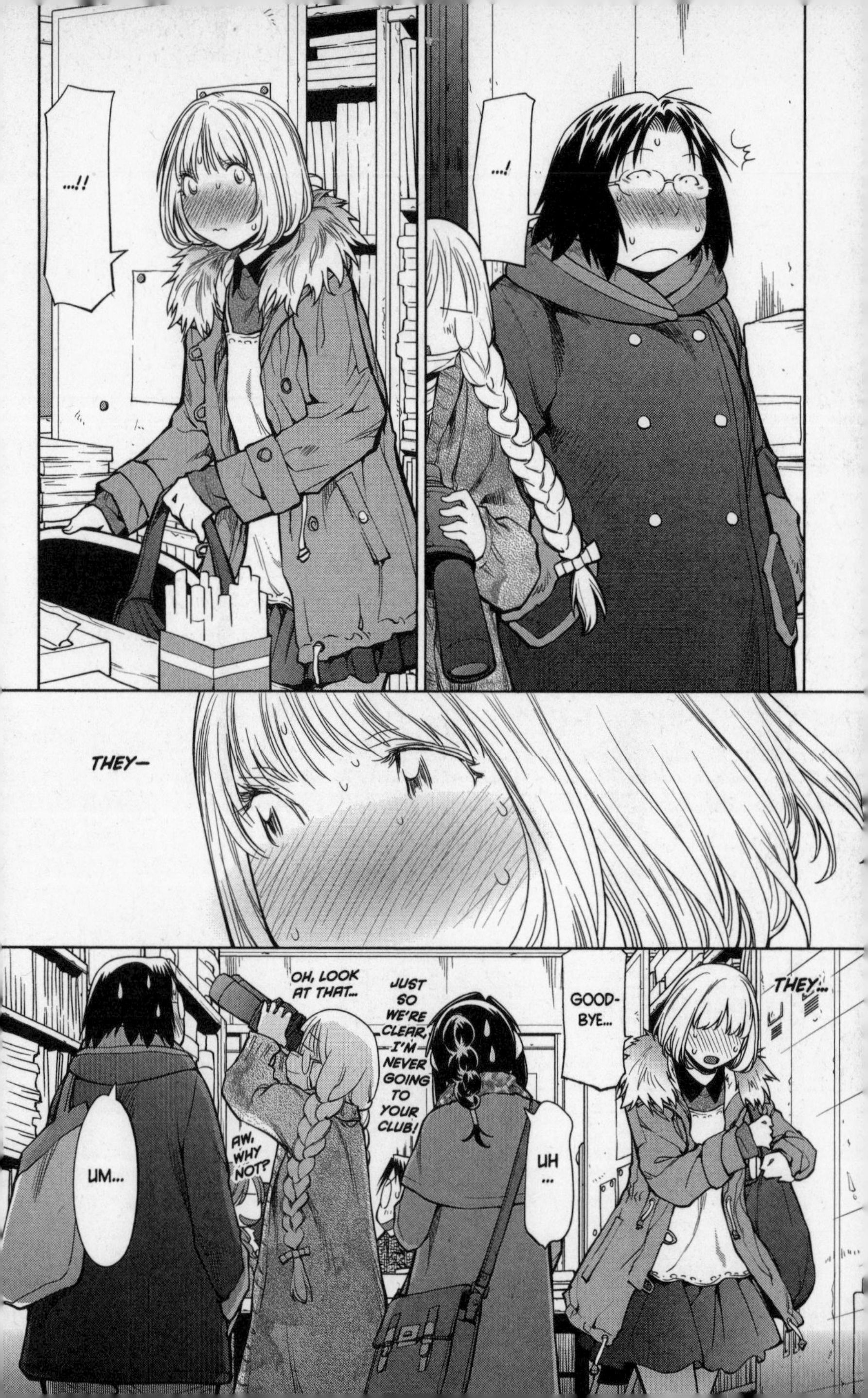
...!
...!!
THEY—
THEY...
GOOD-BYE...
JUST SO WE'RE CLEAR, I'M NEVER GOING TO YOUR CLUB!
OH, LOOK AT THAT...
UH ...
AW, WHY NOT?
UM...

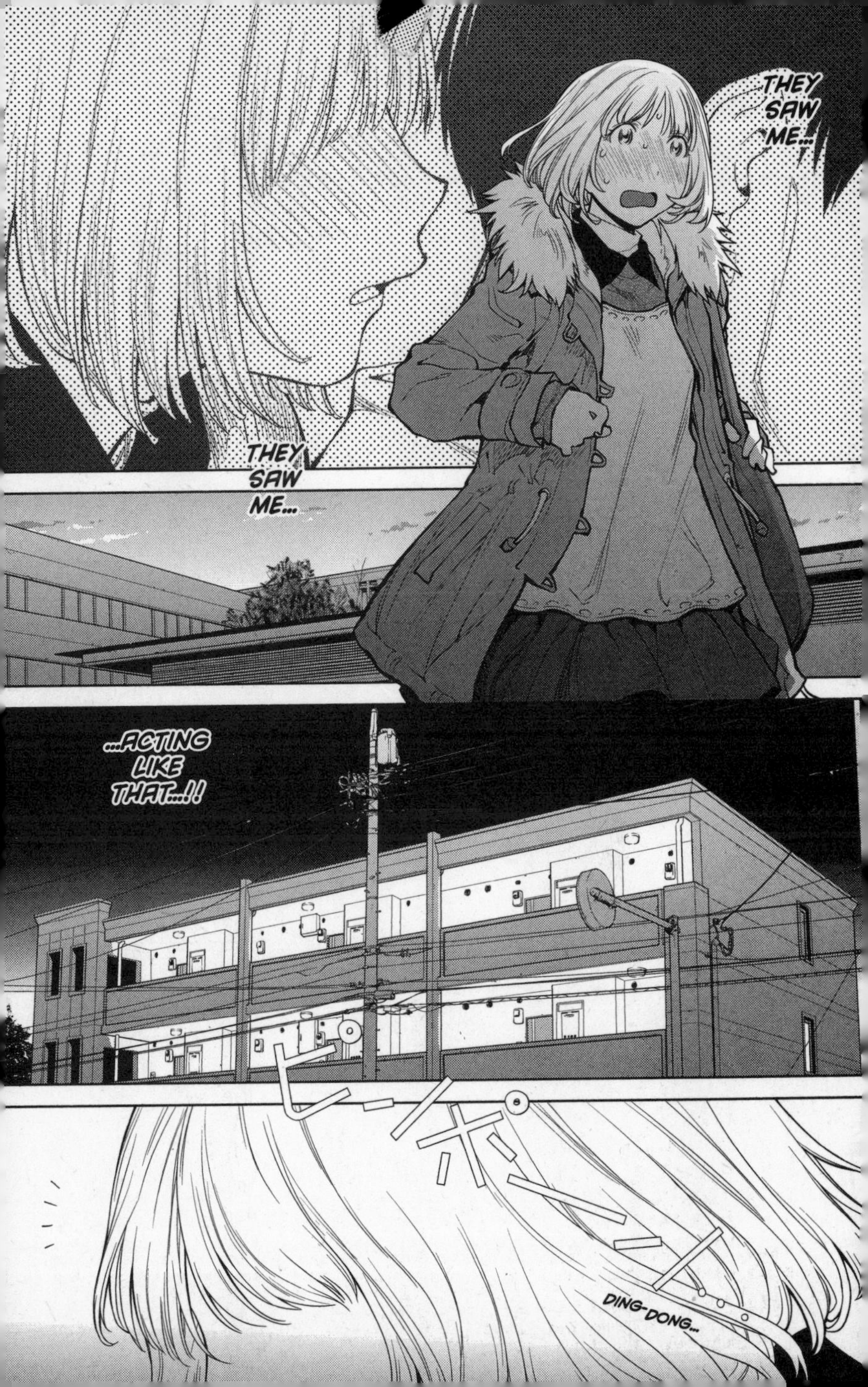
THEY SAW ME...
THEY SAW ME...
...ACTING LIKE THAT...!!
DING-DONG...

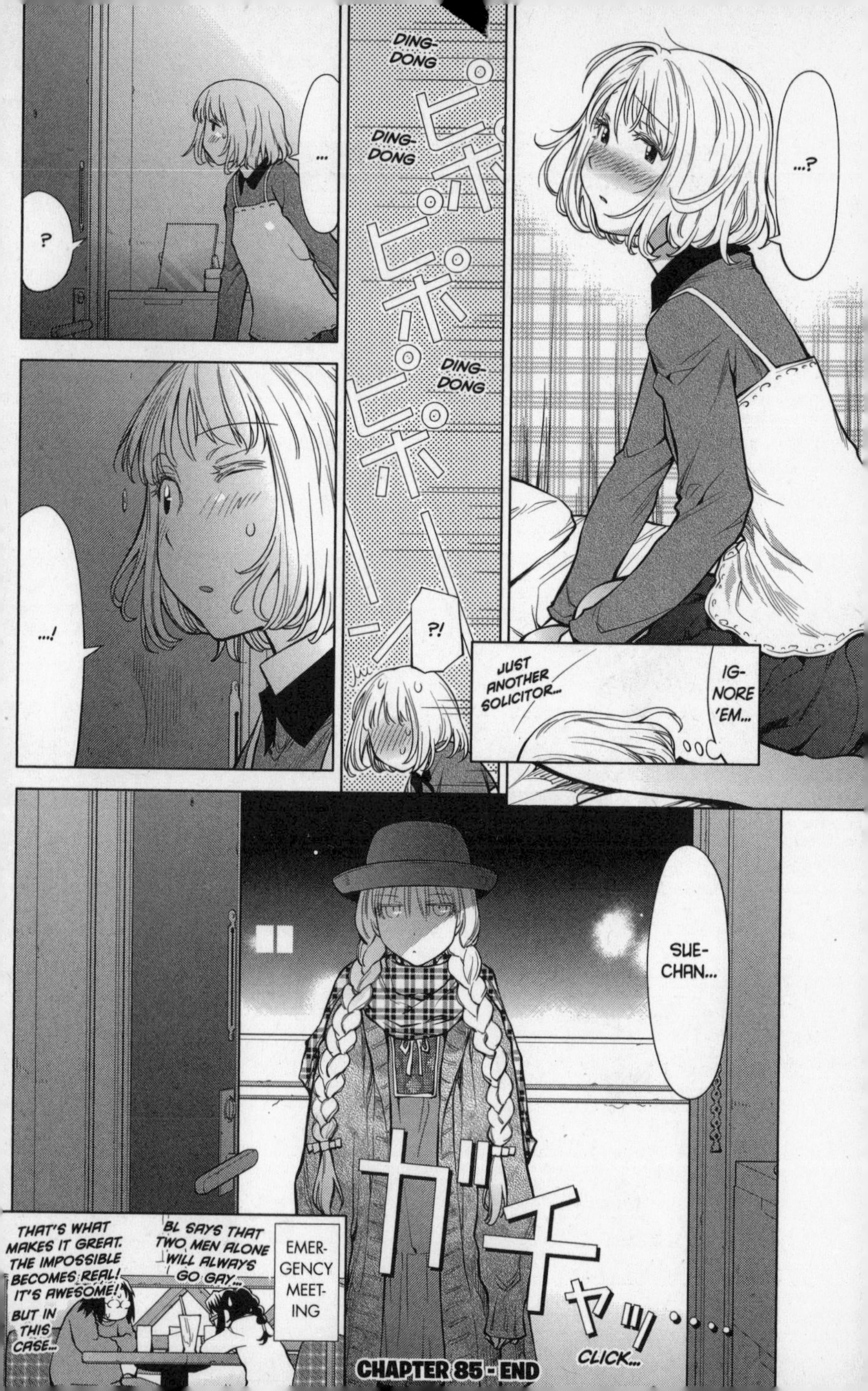
...?
IG-NORE 'EM...
JUST ANOTHER SOLICITOR...
DING-DONG
DING-DONG
DING-DONG
ピポピポピポーン
?!
...
?
...!
SUE-CHAN...
ガチャッ
CLICK...
EMER-GENCY MEET-ING
BL SAYS THAT TWO MEN ALONE WILL ALWAYS GO GAY...
THAT'S WHAT MAKES IT GREAT. THE IMPOSSIBLE BECOMES REAL! IT'S AWESOME! BUT IN THIS CASE...
CHAPTER 85 - END

I TOLD YOU, I DON'T BUY ERO-GAMES

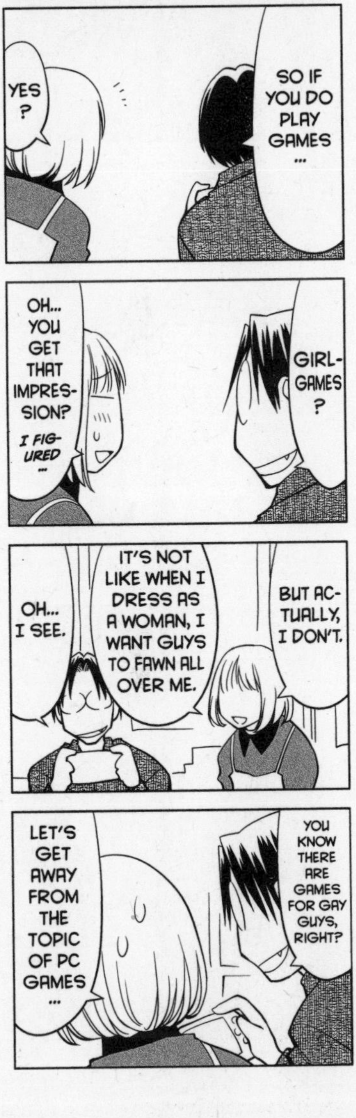
SO IF YOU DO PLAY GAMES ...
YES ?
GIRL-GAMES ?
OH... YOU GET THAT IMPRES-SION?
I FIGURED ...
BUT ACTUALLY, I DON'T.
IT'S NOT LIKE WHEN I DRESS AS A WOMAN, I WANT GUYS TO FAWN ALL OVER ME.
OH... I SEE.
YOU KNOW THERE ARE GAMES FOR GAY GUYS, RIGHT?
LET'S GET AWAY FROM THE TOPIC OF PC GAMES ...

THAT'S WHAT HIS PROFILE WAS LIKE

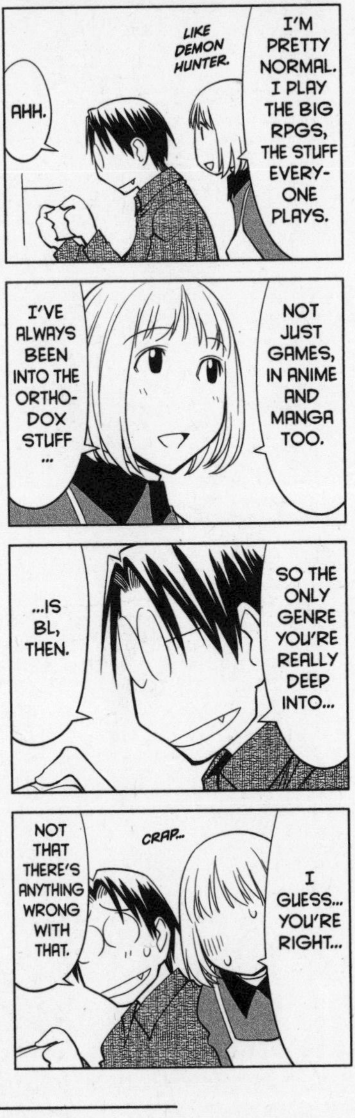
I'M PRETTY NORMAL. I PLAY THE BIG RPGS, THE STUFF EVERY-ONE PLAYS.
LIKE DEMON HUNTER.
AHH.
NOT JUST GAMES, IN ANIME AND MANGA TOO.
I'VE ALWAYS BEEN INTO THE ORTHO-DOX STUFF ...
SO THE ONLY GENRE YOU'RE REALLY DEEP INTO...
...IS BL, THEN.
I GUESS... YOU'RE RIGHT...
CRAP...
NOT THAT THERE'S ANYTHING WRONG WITH THAT.

OTAKU'S FAVORITE

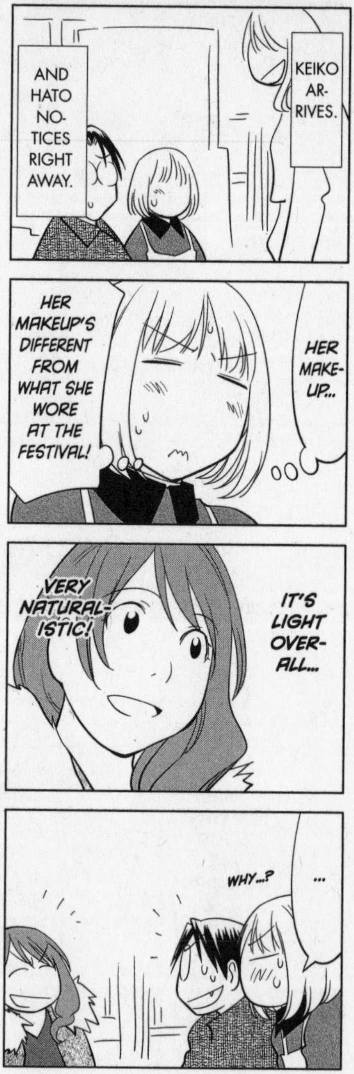
KEIKO ARRIVES.
AND HATO NOTICES RIGHT AWAY.
HER MAKEUP...
HER MAKEUP'S DIFFERENT FROM WHAT SHE WORE AT THE FESTIVAL!
IT'S LIGHT OVERALL...
VERY NATURALISTIC!
...
WHY...?

QUOTED

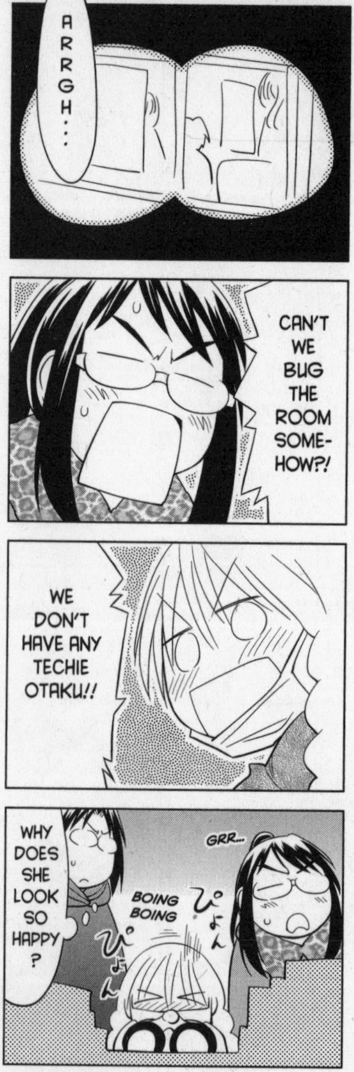
ARRGH...
CAN'T WE BUG THE ROOM SOMEHOW?!
WE DON'T HAVE ANY TECHIE OTAKU!!
GRR...
ぴょん
BOING BOING
ぴょん
WHY DOES SHE LOOK SO HAPPY?

SPECIAL BONUS MANGA

FESTIVAL AFTERPARTY IN MADARAME'S ROOM!

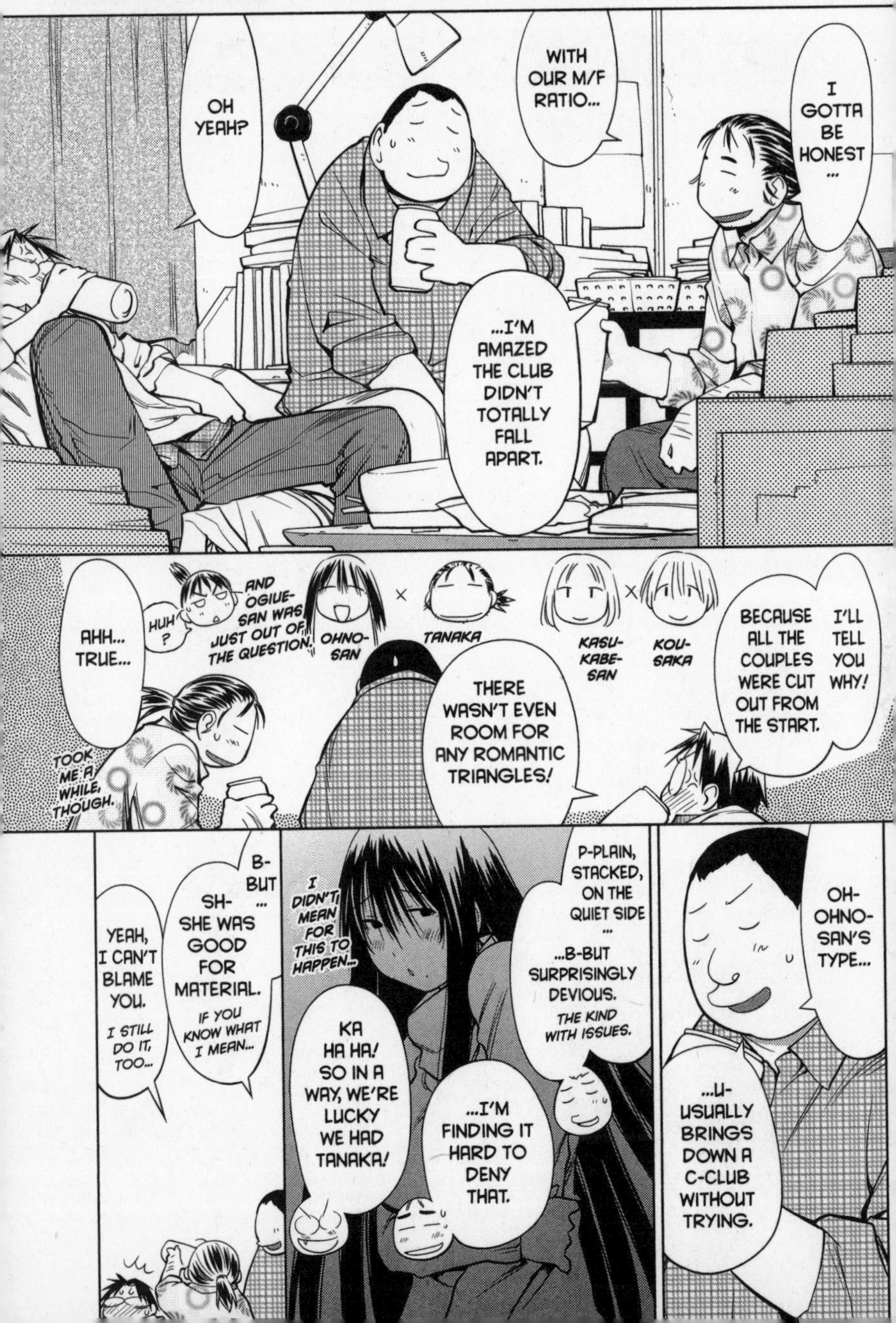
I GOTTA BE HONEST ...
WITH OUR M/F RATIO...
...I'M AMAZED THE CLUB DIDN'T TOTALLY FALL APART.
OH YEAH?
I'LL TELL YOU WHY!
BECAUSE ALL THE COUPLES WERE CUT OUT FROM THE START.
KOU-SAKA
KASU-KABE-SAN
TANAKA
OHNO-SAN
THERE WASN'T EVEN ROOM FOR ANY ROMANTIC TRIANGLES!
AND OGIUE-SAN WAS JUST OUT OF THE QUESTION.
HUH?
AHH... TRUE...
TOOK ME A WHILE, THOUGH.
OH-OHNO-SAN'S TYPE...
...U-USUALLY BRINGS DOWN A C-CLUB WITHOUT TRYING.
P-PLAIN, STACKED, ON THE QUIET SIDE ...
...B-BUT SURPRISINGLY DEVIOUS.
THE KIND WITH ISSUES.
I DIDN'T MEAN FOR THIS TO HAPPEN...
...I'M FINDING IT HARD TO DENY THAT.
KA HA HA! SO IN A WAY, WE'RE LUCKY WE HAD TANAKA!
B-BUT ...
SH-SHE WAS GOOD FOR MATERIAL.
IF YOU KNOW WHAT I MEAN...
YEAH, I CAN'T BLAME YOU.
I STILL DO IT, TOO...

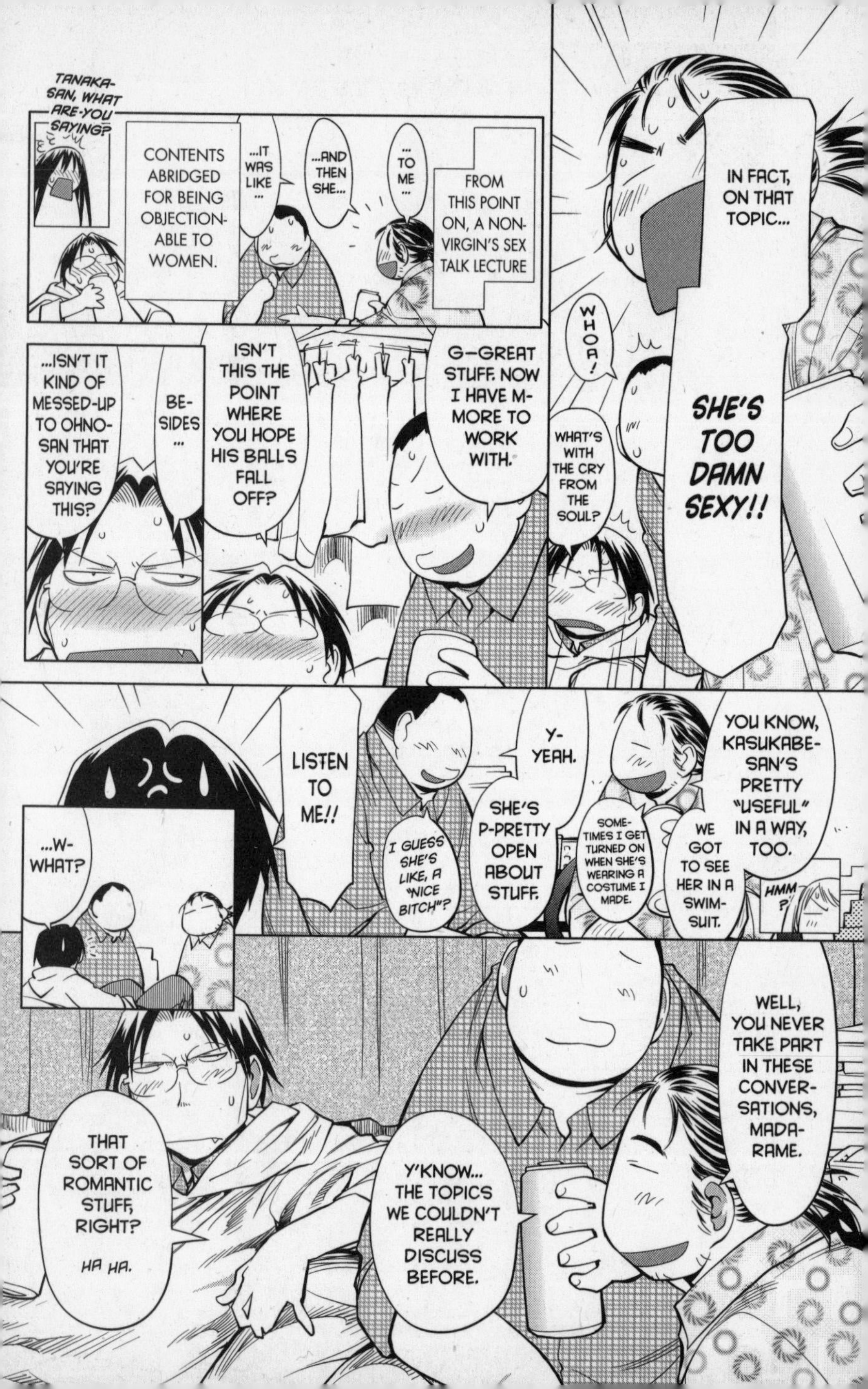
IN FACT, ON THAT TOPIC...
SHE'S TOO DAMN SEXY!!
WHOA!
WHAT'S WITH THE CRY FROM THE SOUL?
FROM THIS POINT ON, A NON-VIRGIN'S SEX TALK LECTURE
...TO ME...
...AND THEN SHE...
...IT WAS LIKE...
CONTENTS ABRIDGED FOR BEING OBJECTION-ABLE TO WOMEN.
TANAKA-SAN, WHAT ARE-YOU SAYING?
G-GREAT STUFF. NOW I HAVE M-MORE TO WORK WITH.
ISN'T THIS THE POINT WHERE YOU HOPE HIS BALLS FALL OFF?
BE-SIDES...
...ISN'T IT KIND OF MESSED-UP TO OHNO-SAN THAT YOU'RE SAYING THIS?
YOU KNOW, KASUKABE-SAN'S PRETTY "USEFUL" IN A WAY, TOO.
HMM?
WE GOT TO SEE HER IN A SWIM-SUIT.
SOME-TIMES I GET TURNED ON WHEN SHE'S WEARING A COSTUME I MADE.
Y-YEAH.
SHE'S P-PRETTY OPEN ABOUT STUFF.
I GUESS SHE'S LIKE, A "NICE BITCH"?
LISTEN TO ME!!
...W-WHAT?
WELL, YOU NEVER TAKE PART IN THESE CONVER-SATIONS, MADA-RAME.
Y'KNOW... THE TOPICS WE COULDN'T REALLY DISCUSS BEFORE.
THAT SORT OF ROMANTIC STUFF, RIGHT?
HA HA.

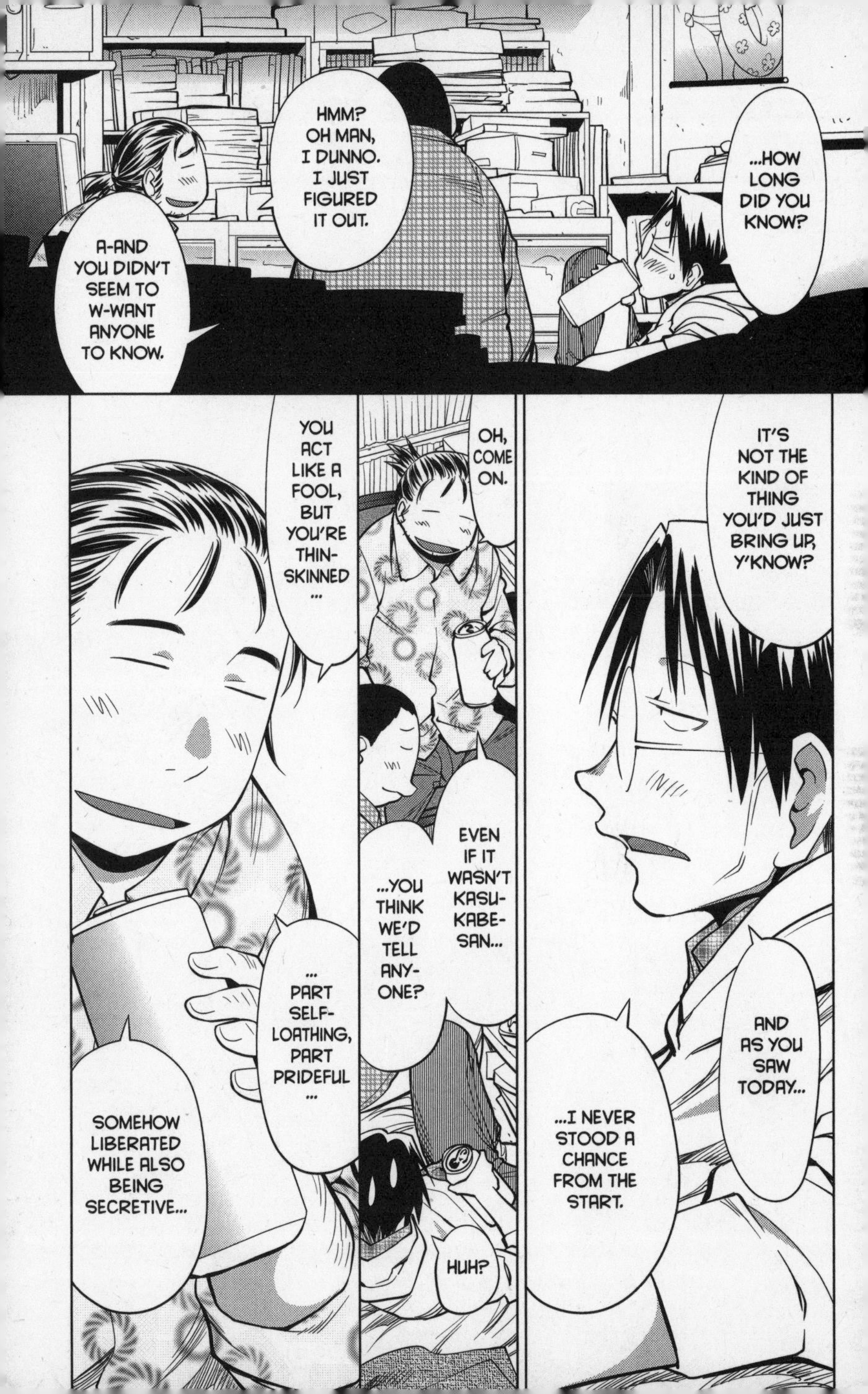
...HOW LONG DID YOU KNOW?
HMM? OH MAN, I DUNNO. I JUST FIGURED IT OUT.
A-AND YOU DIDN'T SEEM TO W-WANT ANYONE TO KNOW.
IT'S NOT THE KIND OF THING YOU'D JUST BRING UP, Y'KNOW?
AND AS YOU SAW TODAY...
...I NEVER STOOD A CHANCE FROM THE START.
OH, COME ON.
EVEN IF IT WASN'T KASU-KABE-SAN...
...YOU THINK WE'D TELL ANY-ONE?
HUH?
YOU ACT LIKE A FOOL, BUT YOU'RE THIN-SKINNED...
...PART SELF-LOATHING, PART PRIDEFUL...
SOMEHOW LIBERATED WHILE ALSO BEING SECRETIVE...

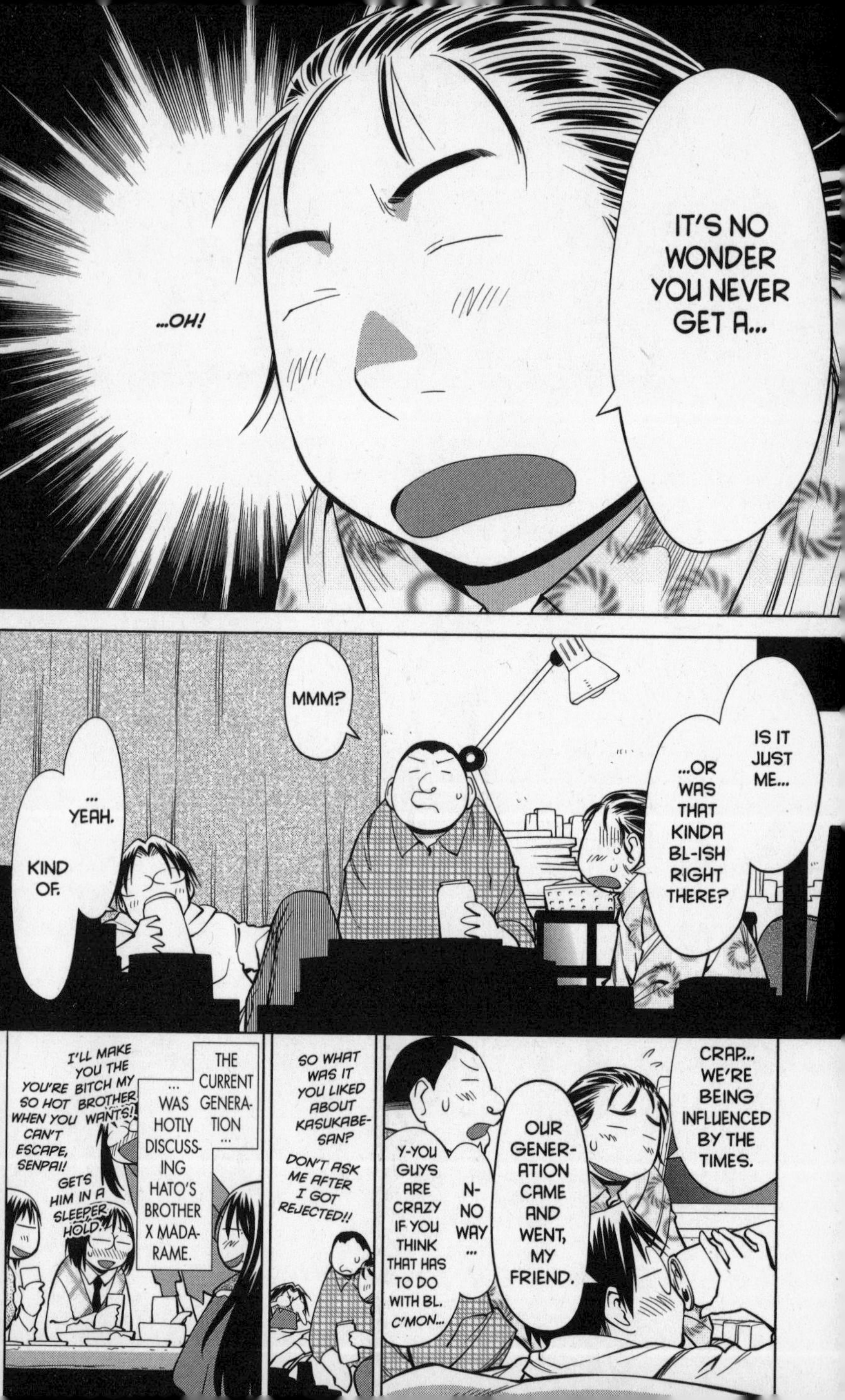
IT'S NO WONDER YOU NEVER GET A...
...OH!
IS IT JUST ME...
...OR WAS THAT KINDA BL-ISH RIGHT THERE?
MMM?
... YEAH.
KIND OF.
CRAP... WE'RE BEING INFLUENCED BY THE TIMES.
OUR GENERATION CAME AND WENT, MY FRIEND.
N-NO WAY ...
Y-YOU GUYS ARE CRAZY IF YOU THINK THAT HAS TO DO WITH BL. C'MON...
SO WHAT WAS IT YOU LIKED ABOUT KASUKABE-SAN?
DON'T ASK ME AFTER I GOT REJECTED!!
THE CURRENT GENERATION ...
... WAS HOTLY DISCUSSING HATO'S BROTHER X MADARAME.
I'LL MAKE YOU THE BITCH MY BROTHER WANTS!
YOU'RE SO HOT WHEN YOU CAN'T ESCAPE, SENPAI!
GETS HIM IN A SLEEPER HOLD.

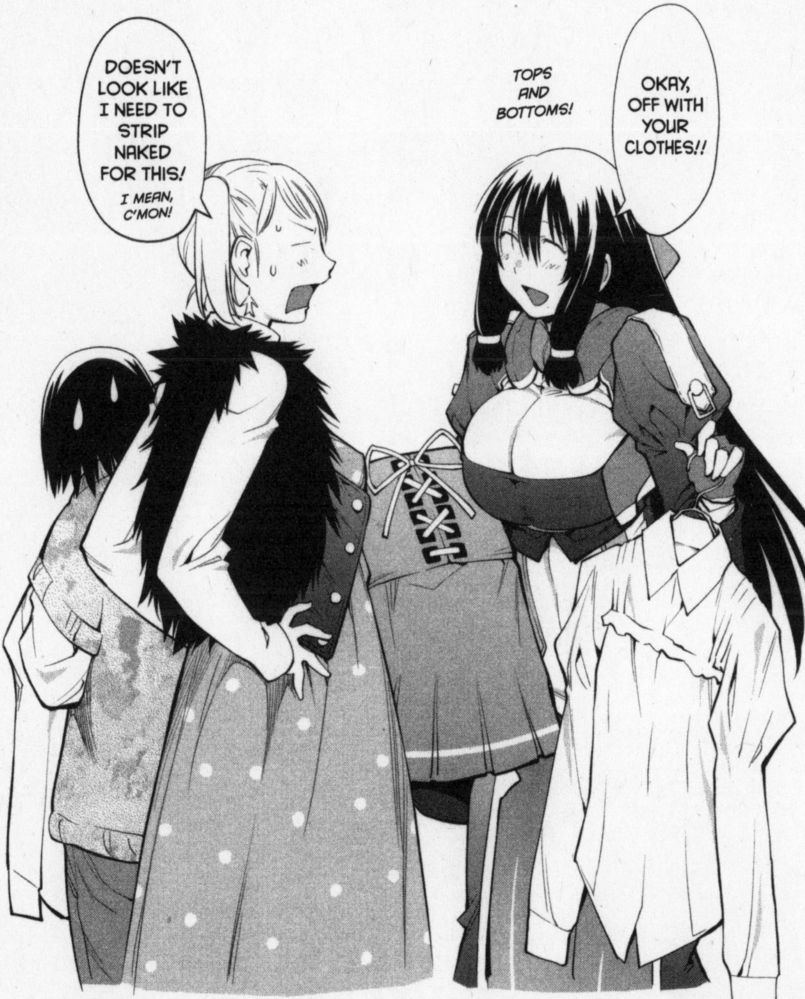
OKAY, OFF WITH YOUR CLOTHES!!
TOPS AND BOTTOMS!
DOESN'T LOOK LIKE I NEED TO STRIP NAKED FOR THIS!
I MEAN, C'MON!

Translation Notes

Japanese is a tricky language for most Westerners, and translation is often more art than science. For your edification and reading pleasure, here are notes on some of the places where we could have gone in a different direction with our translation of the work, or where a Japanese cultural reference is used.

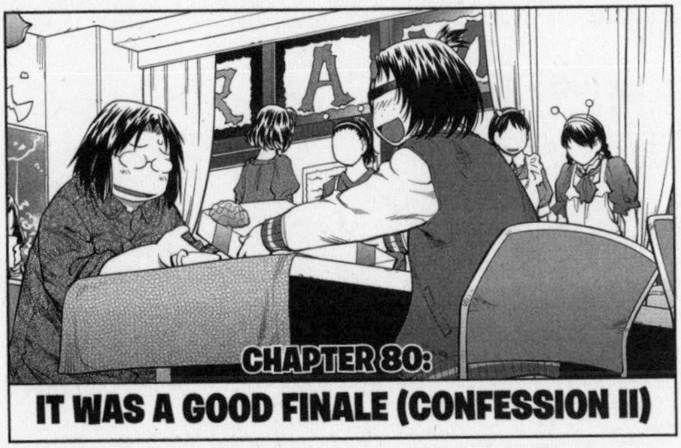
CHAPTER 80:
IT WAS A GOOD FINALE (CONFESSION II)

"It was a good finale," page 5

A common phrase used by otaku in Japan to describe any touching or satisfactory scene/episode, even when (especially when) it is not the final episode of the series.

Death during lovemaking, page 62

The opening line of Kenichi Sakemi's 1989 novel Palace Harem Story, a coming-of-age story about a teenage girl in the palace harem of a fictional Chinese kingdom, written in the style of historical fiction. It was later turned into an animated TV film titled Like the Clouds, Like the Wind by Studio Pierrot and Katsuya Kondo, longtime Ghibli character designer.

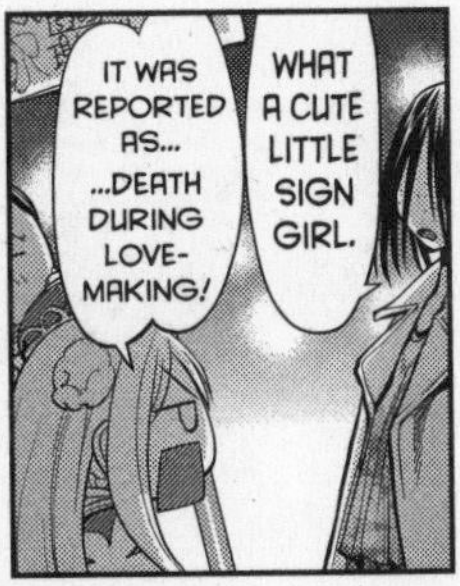
WHAT A CUTE LITTLE SIGN GIRL.
IT WAS REPORTED AS... ...DEATH DURING LOVE-MAKING!

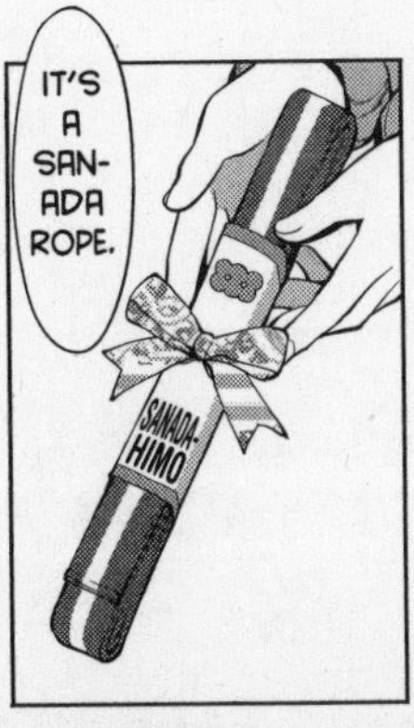
IT'S A SAN-ADA ROPE.
SANADA-HIMO

Sanada rope, page 76

A ceremonial woven cotton rope popularized by the Sanada clan, powerful rivals to the Tokugawa clan, in the 16th and 17th centuries. Some of the Sanadas wore them on their scabbards, which helped promote the association to the Sanada name in the minds of many, although the particular method of weaving had come to Japan from India several centuries before. Nowadays, they are largely used for ceremonial purposes.

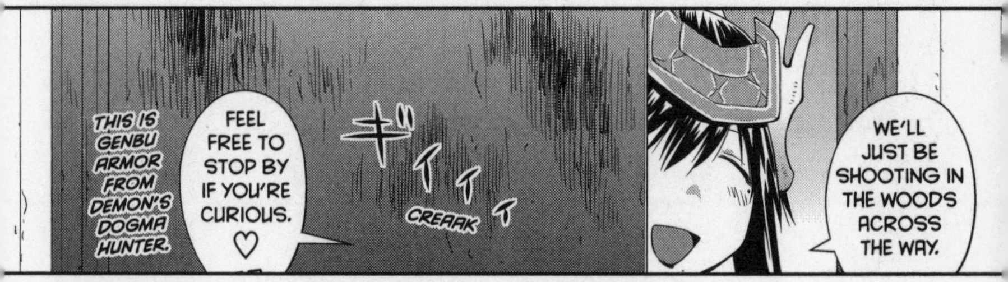
WE'LL JUST BE SHOOTING IN THE WOODS ACROSS THE WAY.
CREAAK
FEEL FREE TO STOP BY IF YOU'RE CURIOUS. ♡
THIS IS GENBU ARMOR FROM DEMON'S DOGMA HUNTER.

Demon's Dogma Hunter, page 89

A combination of the popular action games Demon's Souls, Dragon's Dogma and Monster Hunter. Aside from the similarity in their names, all three are known for their intense, difficult boss battles.

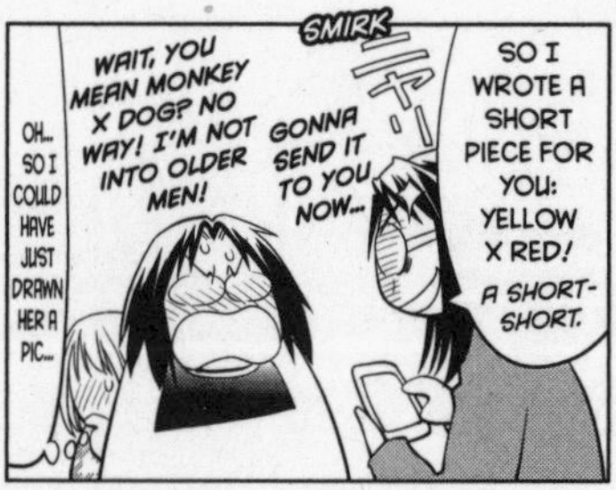
SO I WROTE A SHORT PIECE FOR YOU: YELLOW X RED!
A SHORT-SHORT.
SMIRK
GONNA SEND IT TO YOU NOW...
WAIT, YOU MEAN MONKEY X DOG? NO WAY! I'M NOT INTO OLDER MEN!
OH... SO I COULD HAVE JUST DRAWN HER A PIC...

Yellow Monkey & Red Dog, page 91

A reference to One Piece (parodied as "Ten Piece" in Genshiken) characters Kizaru and Akainu, whose names mean "Yellow Monkey" and "Red Dog," respectively. Both men are senior admirals in the Naval forces that bring pirates to justice, and their facial models are based on veteran film actors.

Life Instrumentality Project, page 94

A play on the Human Instrumentality Project from Neon Genesis Evangelion, the plot to bring about the forced evolution of humanity to a higher stage of life. The parody is easier in Japanese, where the words for "humanity" (jinrui) and "life" (jinsei) share the same first character.

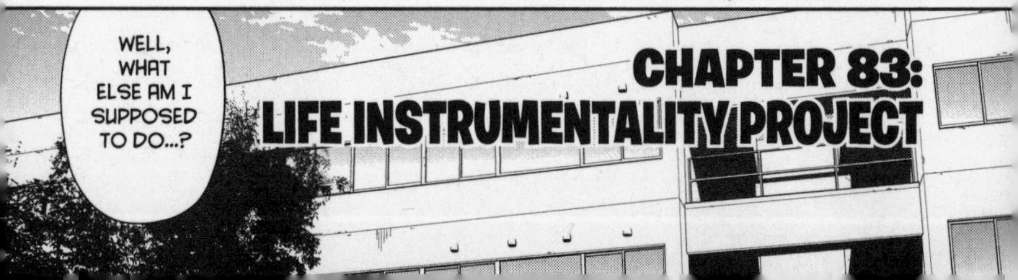
CHAPTER 83:
LIFE INSTRUMENTALITY PROJECT
WELL, WHAT ELSE AM I SUPPOSED TO DO...?

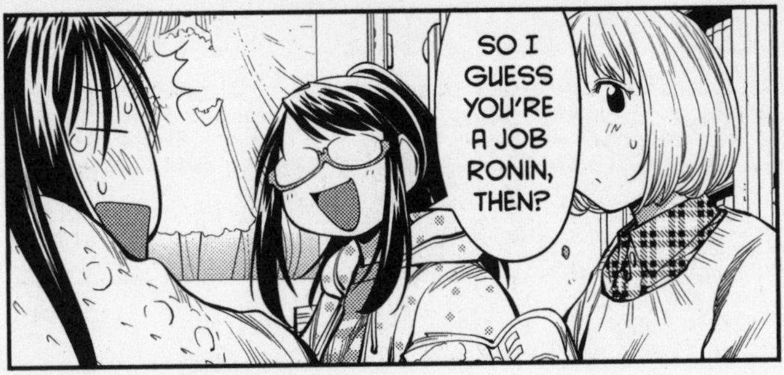
SO I GUESS YOU'RE A JOB RONIN, THEN?

Job ronin, page 95

A ronin was a masterless samurai forced to wander the countryside until he could find a lord who would accept him. In modern times, the term has come to apply to students who fail to pass the exams into their college of choice, and rather than utilize a backup plan, simply spend an extra year studying in the hope of passing next year. As many of the biggest and most stable companies in Japan make offers to potential employees while they are preparing to graduate college in the spring, a "job ronin" would be someone who stays in school for an extra year rather than emerge into the job market having missed the boat on the hiring season.

Sou-uke, page 124

In BL (boy's love) terminology, a sou-uke ("all-receiving") character is one whose passive and submissive nature means that no matter who he is paired with, he will be the uke, or "bottom" in the relationship.

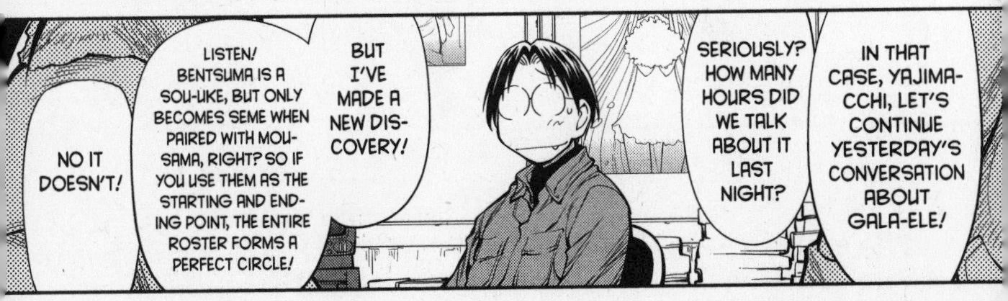
IN THAT CASE, YAJIMA-CCHI, LET'S CONTINUE YESTERDAY'S CONVERSATION ABOUT GALA-ELE!
SERIOUSLY? HOW MANY HOURS DID WE TALK ABOUT IT LAST NIGHT?
BUT I'VE MADE A NEW DIS-COVERY!
LISTEN! BENTSUMA IS A SOU-UKE, BUT ONLY BECOMES SEME WHEN PAIRED WITH MOU-SAMA, RIGHT? SO IF YOU USE THEM AS THE STARTING AND END-ING POINT, THE ENTIRE ROSTER FORMS A PERFECT CIRCLE!
NO IT DOESN'T!

Gala-Ele, page 124

A parody of the popular soccer video game series (and subsequent multimedia franchising), Inazuma Eleven. Unlike a pro-league simulation sports series, Inazuma features school kids in a story-heavy scenario, with the gameplay a mix of sports action and RPG mechanics. The shortened title above is most likely short for Galaxy (or Galactic) Eleven--the Inazuma series is known fondly as Ina-Ele in Japan.

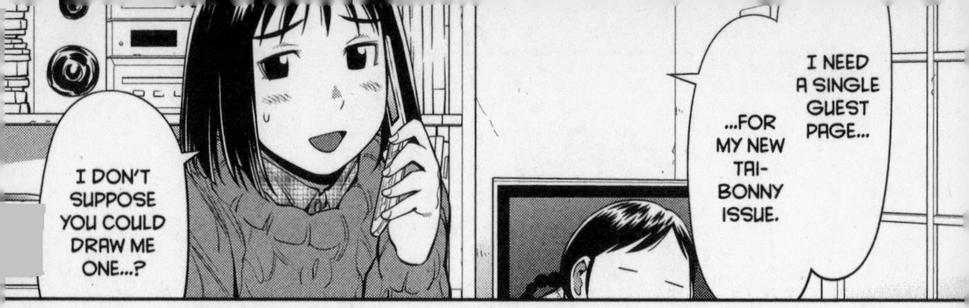
I NEED A SINGLE GUEST PAGE...
...FOR MY NEW TAI-BONNY ISSUE.
I DON'T SUPPOSE YOU COULD DRAW ME ONE...?

Tai-Bonny, page 129

A parody of recent anime series Tiger and Bunny, a superhero story about a veteran hero who is given a young sidekick to work with in a big city reminiscent of New York. Due to the dual male leads and the potential for fan-shipping, the series was especially huge with fujoshi.

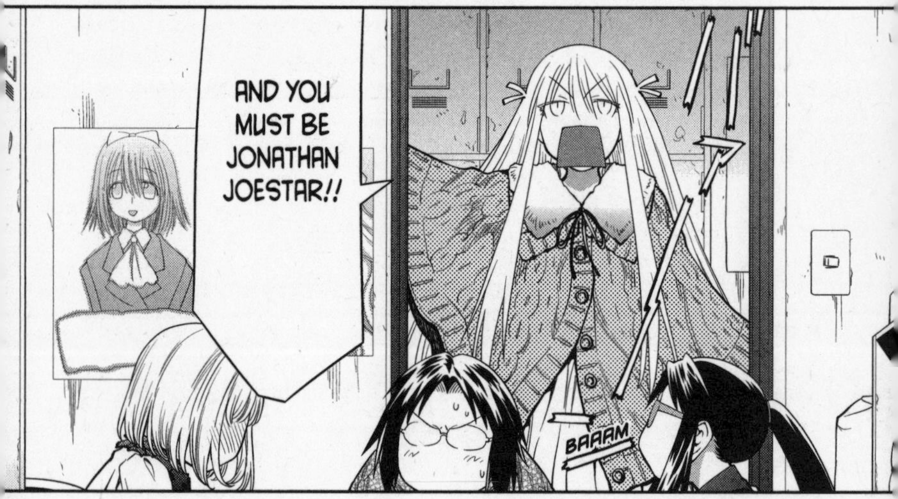
AND YOU MUST BE JONATHAN JOESTAR!!
BAAAM

Jonathan Joestar, page 140

The protagonist of the very first arc of the venerable Shonen Jump epic, Jojo's Bizarre Adventure. The scene Sue is referencing—in which villain Dio Brando kicks Jonathan's dog Danny—is infamous among Jojo fans in Japan for an error in the text of the volume. The highborn, proud-talking Jonathan exclaims, "Why'd you do that?" but the dialogue had to be redone for the printing of the volume. The resulting line was missing a single hiragana character that made the effect more like "Why you do that!" The dichotomy between the aristocratic character and his inadvertent country bumpkin speech was the source of many jokes among fans, but author Hirohiko Araki, who is very resistant to altering content between different printings of his books, did not have it corrected. It wasn't until 15 years and 66 printings later that the line was finally fixed, when the Jojo series was reprinted in the bunko format for collectors.

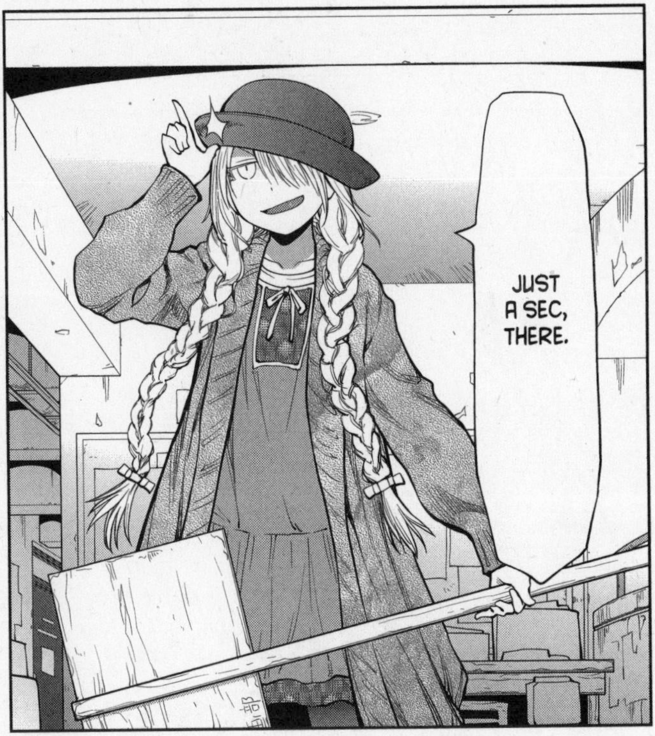
JUST A SEC, THERE.

"Just a sec, there," page 145

A reference from the 1980s series Kyukyoku Chojin R (Ultimate Superhuman R), a comedy about a teenage robot who attempts to live a normal life. The series was created by artist Masami Yuki, who went on to draw the manga version of mecha classic Mobile Police Patlabor. It must be a favorite of author Shimoku Kio, as it has been used for parody material several times in Genshiken.

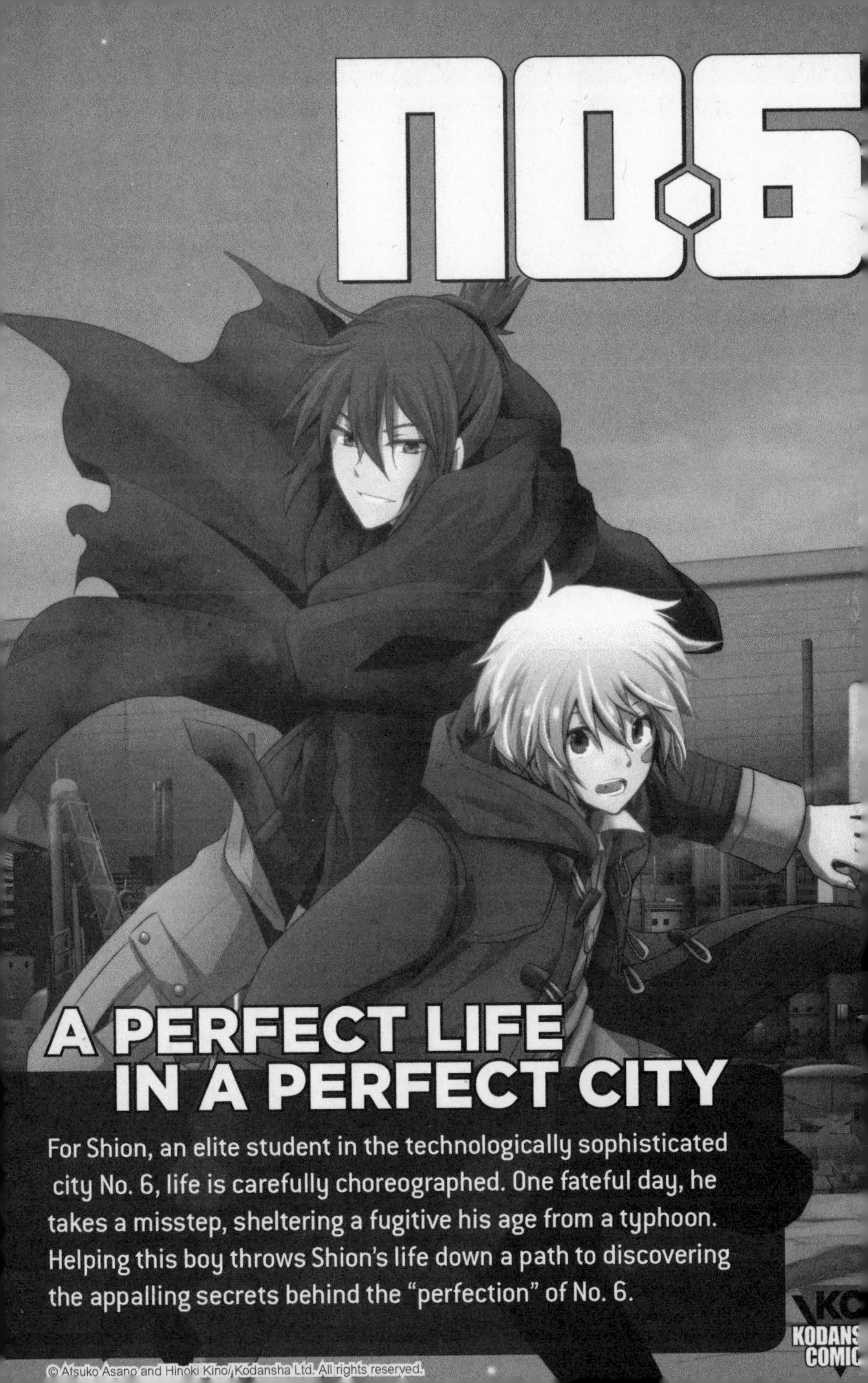
NO.6
A PERFECT LIFE IN A PERFECT CITY
For Shion, an elite student in the technologically sophisticated city No. 6, life is carefully choreographed. One fateful day, he takes a misstep, sheltering a fugitive his age from a typhoon. Helping this boy throws Shion's life down a path to discovering the appalling secrets behind the "perfection" of No. 6.
KC KODANSHA COMICS
© Atsuko Asano and Hinoki Kino/Kodansha Ltd. All rights reserved.

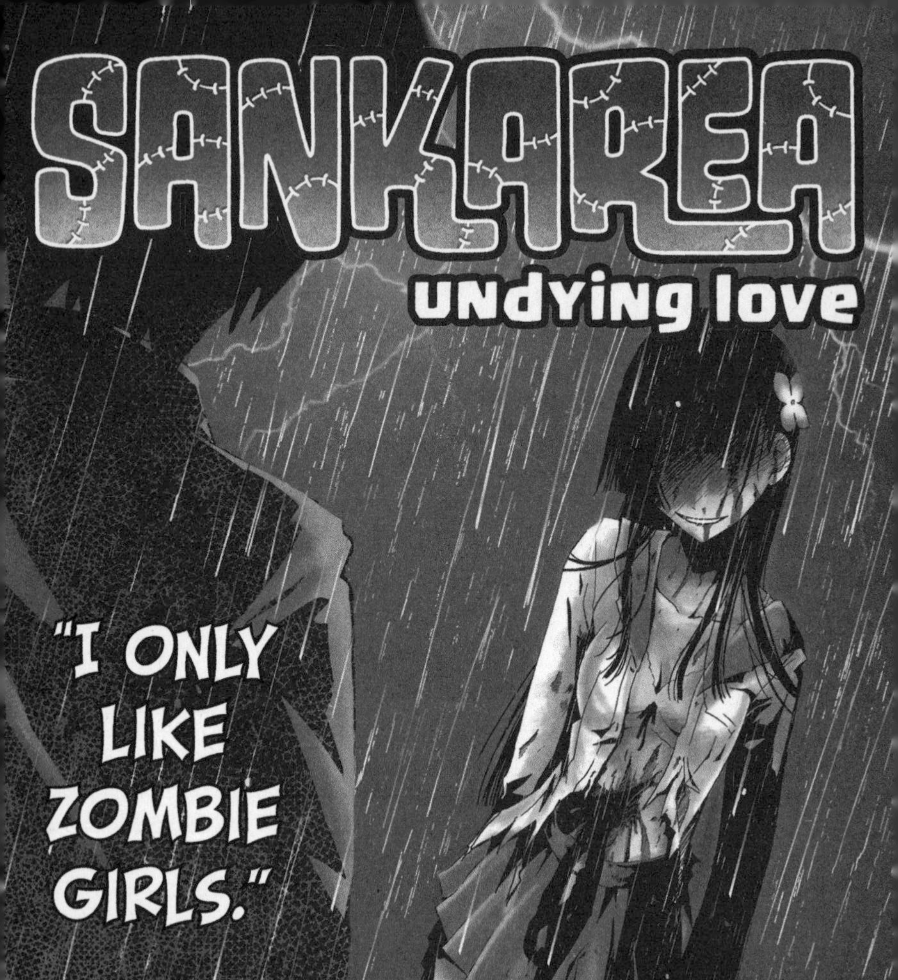

SANKAREA

undying love

"I ONLY LIKE ZOMBIE GIRLS."

Chihiro has an unusual connection to zombie movies. He doesn't feel bad for the survivors – he wants to comfort the undead girls they slaughter! When his pet passes away, he brews a resurrection potion. He's discovered by local heiress Sanka Rea, and she serves as his first test subject!

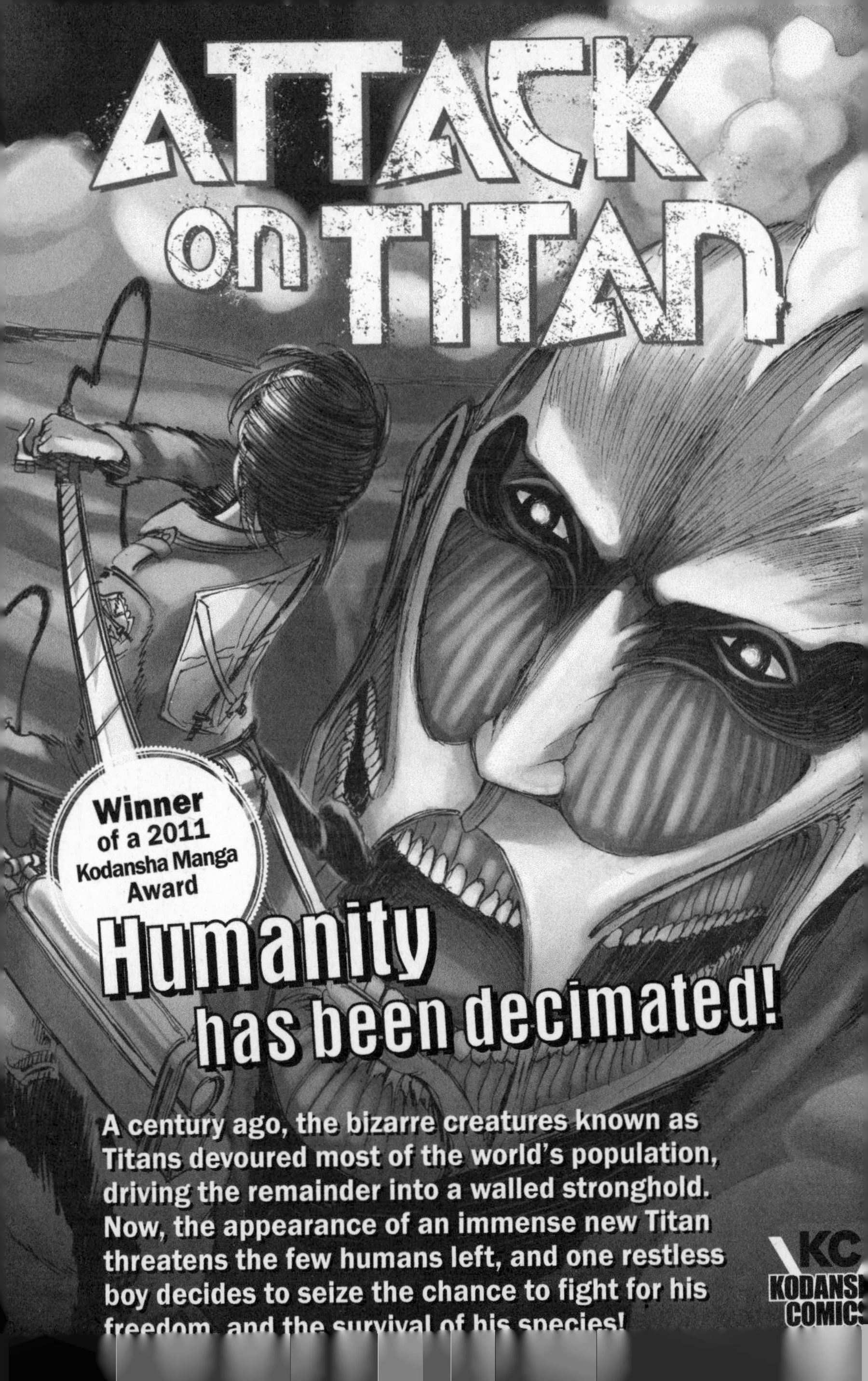

ATTACK on TITAN
Winner of a 2011 Kodansha Manga Award
Humanity has been decimated!
A century ago, the bizarre creatures known as Titans devoured most of the world's population, driving the remainder into a walled stronghold. Now, the appearance of an immense new Titan threatens the few humans left, and one restless boy decides to seize the chance to fight for his freedom, and the survival of his species!
KC
KODANSHA COMICS

Praise for the anime:

"The show provides a pleasant window on the highs and lows of young love with two young people who are first timers at the real thing."

-The Fandom Post

"Always it is smarter, more poetic, more touching, just plain better than you think it is going to be."

-Anime News Network

Say I Love You.

Mei Tachibana has no friends — and says she doesn't need them!
But everything changes when she accidentally roundhouse kicks the most popular boy in school! However, Yamato Kurosawa isn't angry in the slightest—in fact, he thinks his ordinary life could use an unusual girl like Mei. But winning Mei's trust will be a tough task. How long will she refuse to say, "I love you"?

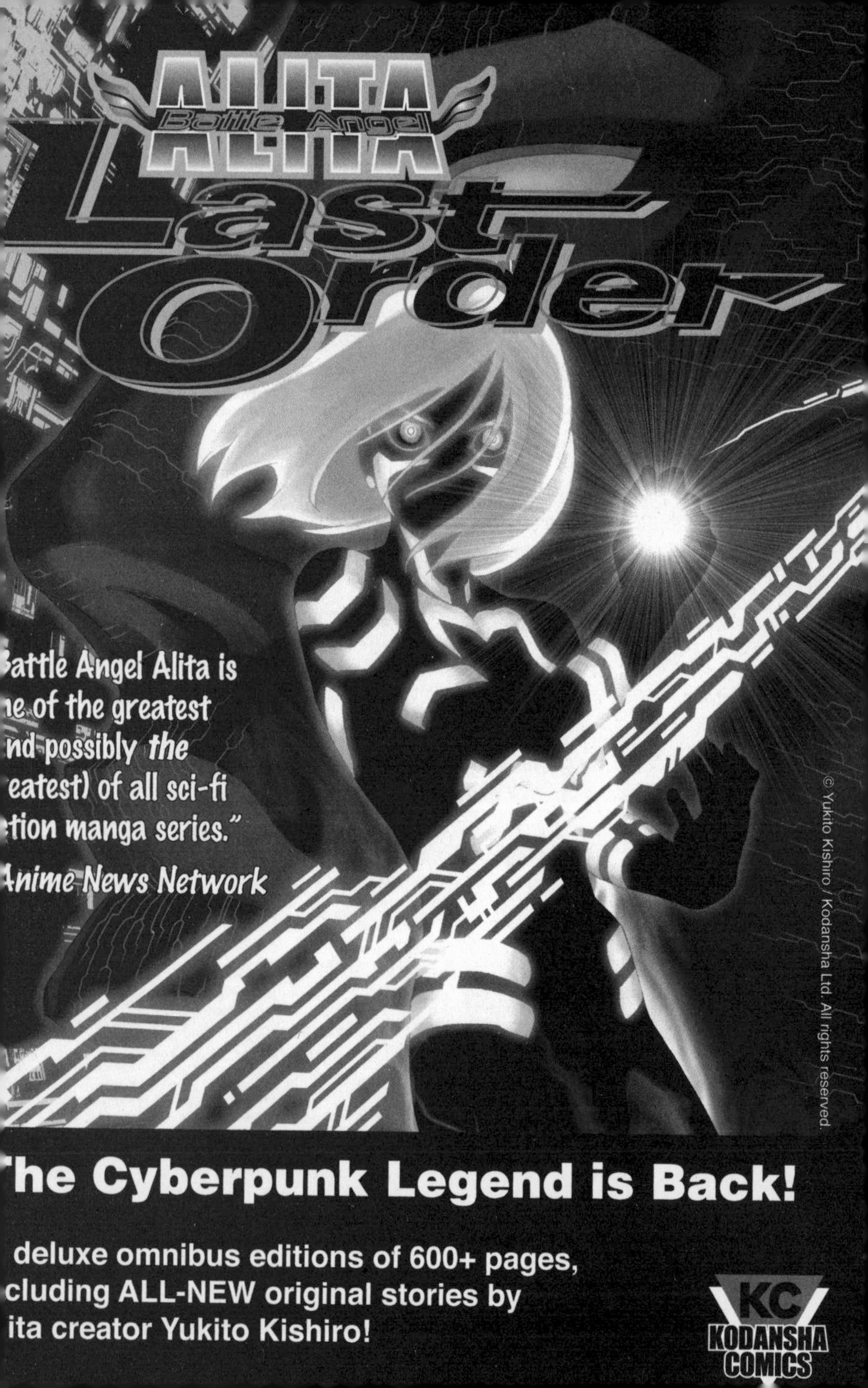
ALITA
Battle Angel
ALITA
Last Order
;attle Angel Alita is
ıe of the greatest
nd possibly *the*
eatest) of all sci-fi
tion manga series."
Anime News Network
© Yukito Kishiro / Kodansha Ltd. All rights reserved.

Genshiken: Second Season volume 5 is a work of fiction. Names, characters, places, and incidents are the products of the author's imagination or are used fictitiously. Any resemblance to actual events, locales, or persons, living or dead, is entirely coincidental.

A Kodansha Comics Trade Paperback Original.

Published in the United States by Kodansha Comics, an imprint of Kodansha USA Publishing, LLC, New York.

Publication rights for this English edition arranged through Kodansha Ltd., Tokyo.

First published in Japan in 2013 by Kodansha Ltd., Tokyo, as *Genshiken nidaime no go 14*.

ISBN 978-1-61262-576-8

Printed in the United States of America.

www.kodanshacomics.com

9 8 7 6 5 4 3 2 1

Translator: Stephen Paul
Lettering: Aaron Alexovich
Editing: Ben Applegate
Kodansha Comics edition cover design by Phil Balsman

TOMARE!
STOP

You're going the wrong way!

Manga is a completely different type of reading experience.

_____

To start at the beginning,
Go to the end!

_____

hat's right! Authentic manga is read the traditional Japanese way—
rom right to left, exactly the opposite of how American books are
ead. It's easy to follow: Just go to the other end of the book and read
:ach page—and each panel—from right side to left side, starting at
he top right. Now you're experiencing manga as it was meant to be!